The Middle East

The Middle East

Fourteen Islamic Centuries

Glenn E. Perry
Indiana State University

Prentice-Hall, Inc., Englewood Cliffs, New Jersey 07632

Library of Congress Cataloging in Publication Data

PERRY, GLENN.
  The Middle East.

  Bibliography
  Includes Index.
  1. Near East—History—1517–   2. Islamic
Empire—History.   I. Title.
DS62.P385 1983   956'.01   82-20514
ISBN 0-13-581603-3

Editorial/production supervision:
    Richard Kilmartin and Maureen Connelly
Cover design: Ray Lundgren
Cover art: Ottoman Tughra—Seal and signature
    of Abdul-Medjid ibn-Mahmud, Sultan
    of Turkey (1822–1861), From *Symbols,
    Signs & Signets* by Ernst Lehner.
    (New York: Dover Publications, Inc.)
Manufacturing buyer: Ron Chapman

Printed in the United States of America

10 9 8 7 6 5 4 3 2

ISBN 0-13-581603-3

Prentice-Hall International, Inc., *London*
Prentice-Hall of Australia Pty. Limited, *Sydney*
Editora Prentice-Hall do Brasil, Ltda., *Rio de Janiero*
Prentice-Hall Canada Inc., *Toronto*
Prentice-Hall of India Private Limited, *New Delhi*
Prentice-Hall of Japan, Inc., *Tokyo*
Prentice-Hall of Southeast Asia Pte. Ltd., *Singapore*
Whitehall Books Limited, *Wellington, New Zealand*

To my parents

Contents

Preface

This book was written in response to a widely expressed need for a fairly short introduction to Middle Eastern history, mainly for use as a textbook in undergraduate survey courses in this subject. It is largely a synthesis of other scholars' more specialized writings.

I had to remind myself repeatedly that such a survey could not be documented in the style of a monograph or journal article. Perhaps another volume would have been required just for the footnotes, for a single paragraph is often a composite account drawn from many works. I have given credit to certain writers in the text when referring to interpretations with which they are clearly associated. Otherwise, the bibliographical essay at the end of this volume must suffice in acknowledging my sources, as well as directing the reader to further resources. (Some popular and general works are included solely for the latter purpose). I regret the impossibility of listing the hundreds of articles and many other types of material that provided input for my work.

I have endeavored to provide several features that are not found in earlier surveys of this subject. The material is tied together, at least loosely, by a world historical perspective emphasizing the gradual emergence of an overall Middle Eastern civilization (culminating with the rise of Islam) and the region's interaction with—and ups and downs vis-à-vis—other parts of the world, particularly the West. However, no attempt has been made to fit the facts rigidly into one theme.

I have incorporated some social and economic history into my account but less than I would have liked had considerations of brevity and the anticipated needs of most teachers of survey courses not provided limitations. Some teachers will want to supplement this book with reading on social and economic matters. The chronological structure is partly unique, largely reflecting the world historical emphasis and, I believe, involving a minimum of arbitrariness; it should pose no problem for those who want to assign material in some other order. Most of all, I have strived for balance in the treatment of different parts of the area (although determining the appropriate amount of space devoted to, say, Egypt as opposed to Iran admittedly is not easy) and also in providing the reader a basis for understanding situations from different partisan perspectives.

I have followed a middle-of-the-road approach regarding transliteration, in keeping with the needs of students who do not know Middle Eastern languages but would like to have a rough approximation of the correct pronunciation of names and words. I have thus usually followed the vowel and consonantal structure of Arabic words (though offending the purist is some cases, as in "Mecca" rather than "Makkah") but have omitted diacritical marks, dots, and such. I have used apostrophes for medial *hamzahs* and *ayns,* without distinguishing between the two.

With numerous previously published ones providing indispensible guidance, all maps were prepared especially for this book. I tried, whenever possible, to include each place name mentioned in the text on at least one map. Locations may not always be precise and are intended only to serve a pedagogical purpose.

This account emphasizes the modern period. But while earlier times get a relatively telescoped treatment, this indeed is a history of "Fourteen Islamic Centuries," although of course not on a century-by-century basis (and, with beginning Western students in mind, dispensing with the *Hijri*—Islamic—dates). The nearly four millennia of pre-Islamic history are dealt with even more briefly in order to put the last fourteen centuries in perspective and to clarify certain factors that still survive in the area's linguistic, ethnic, and religious landscape.

This does not pretend to be a history of the whole Islamic world. Islamic areas like Pakistan or Soviet Central Asia are only occasionally referred to insofar as they exemplify broader trends. Even North Africa (aside from Egypt) is consigned to this sporadic treatment, althouth its exclusion from any definition of the notoriously ambiguous and even ethnocentric term *Middle East,* used for lack of a better alternative, cannot be easily justified except by the space limitations imposed by the short volume I was commissioned to write. Our focus is on a relatively restricted area that includes Egypt, Turkey, Iran, and the countries of the Fertile Crescent and the Arabian Peninsula.

I need to acknowledge the important help given to me by several people, starting with Steve Dalphin, history editor for Prentice-Hall, as well as his two immediate predecessors, John Busch and Brian Walker. In addition to Prentice-Hall's anonymous reviewers, several people read and offered valuable criticisms of some early chapter drafts. These included Daniel Sortwell, then of Forum Press; William Griswold of Colorado State University; Arthur Goldschmidt, Jr., of Pennsylvania

State University; Wadie Jwaideh of Indiana University; Abbas Hamdani of the University of Wisconsin (Milwaukee); and Linda Lau of the Library of Congress. Finally, my wife, Eleanor, provided the advantages of her keen editorial eye and her own specialization in Islamic history to help me iron out many wrinkles in the manuscript and even to help research and write some paragraphs in Chapter 3 and Chapter 4 dealing with art and architecture. She and Mildred Pendergast also helped with the preparation of the index.

Indiana State University provided important support. My departmental chairperson, Arthur Dowell, cooperated with me in many ways, particularly by making secretarial and duplicating facilities available. My thanks go to him and to other colleagues, notably John Crittenden and Robert Puckett, for the encouragement they provided. I also wish to thank the University Research Committee for the grant it awarded me.

Glenn E. Perry
Terre Haute, Indiana

The Middle East

I

Setting and Prelude

To A.D. 610

The term *Middle East* reveals a European-centered perspective of the world. The fact that Middle Easterners themselves now use this name for their own terrain is testimony to the extent to which the West[1] (i.e., Europe and regions such as North America that have been settled by Europeans) recently has been the center of world civilization and power.

Western preponderance, which goes back at least to the eighteenth century A.D., is the consequence of transformations in much of the West that often are labeled "modernization," of which the Industrial Revolution is the most salient aspect. Non-Western regions did not share in the early stages of modernization (except, some say, for experiencing a negative impact), and most of them have now discovered that there is a gap between their societies and the modernized West that cannot easily be bridged.

The present situation is atypical of the whole course of history. For a much longer period, as William McNeill shows in *The Rise of the West,* Europe, the Middle East, India, and the Far East were relatively equal centers of civilization. Europe and the Middle East alternately stood in each other's shadow from about 500 B.C. to

[1]While usage varies, the term *West* will be used to include the Greco-Roman world (minus its Middle Eastern conquests) and both its Orthodox Christian (Byzantine-Russian) and its Far Western offshoots. Toynbee, among others, reserves the word *Western* for the latter, but he recognizes the "affiliation" of the three, making the disagreement a semantic one. Needless to say, this bears no relationship to the so-called "East-West conflict" in the twentieth-century cold war sense.

1

about A.D. 1700, but their levels of technical development and long-range military capability were about the same. For even more millennia before 500 B.C., the Middle East clearly was ahead of the rest of humanity, as the advances initiated there slowly spread elsewhere.

THE PHYSICAL SETTING:
LOCATION, LAND, AND SEAS

The most lasting determinant of Middle Eastern society has been its physical setting. The region's central location, incorporating parts of Africa, Asia, and Europe,[2] has given it a crucial role in world history. It has alternated between being a leading center of cultural florescence and economic and military might—the world's hub—and a weak and "backward" area—merely a crossroads or bridge—that even then is a key object of contention among outside powers.

The unique intertwining of lands and seas in the Middle East has enhanced its position. Only a narrow isthmus, now traversed by the Suez Canal, historically interrupted water communications between the oceans. The great number of seas, gulfs, and straits (see the map on p. 3) provide a network of readymade highways.

The proximity of Europe to the Middle East via the Mediterranean has decreed a particularly intimate, if often adverse, relationship between these two regions. This has made for a similarity in their civilizations, even though their mutual distinctiveness is epitomized by the millennia-old appellations "East" and "West." The spread of Islam to the Indian subcontinent incorporated much of the latter into the sphere of Middle Eastern civilization, but India's distance from the main centers of Middle Eastern history produced a wider dichotomy between these two regions' civilizations in their formative stages. And yet, although modernization in recent centuries has set the West off from a residual "non-West," the civilizations of Europe, India, and the Middle East show a family resemblance that separates them from their more distant Far Eastern relative.

Geography has also dictated close relationships with the rest of Africa and with the central core of the Eurasian continent. Middle Eastern culture spread into both of these places, and movements of people and commerce have been recurrent in each direction. The ease with which horse-borne nomads could cross the arc of flat, arid grasslands (i.e., steppes) extending across central Eurasia from Manchuria to Hungary allowed them in premodern times again and again to overrun the Middle East and other civilized lands on Eurasia's periphery. The steppes also provided a link for slow cultural diffusion and trade between the Middle East and China.

---

[2]Asia is, of course, only a residual term for the Eurasian continent minus its European subcontinent. The terms *Asia* and *Europe* nevertheless make sense as geographical divisions from the perspective of the Mediterranean and Black Seas.

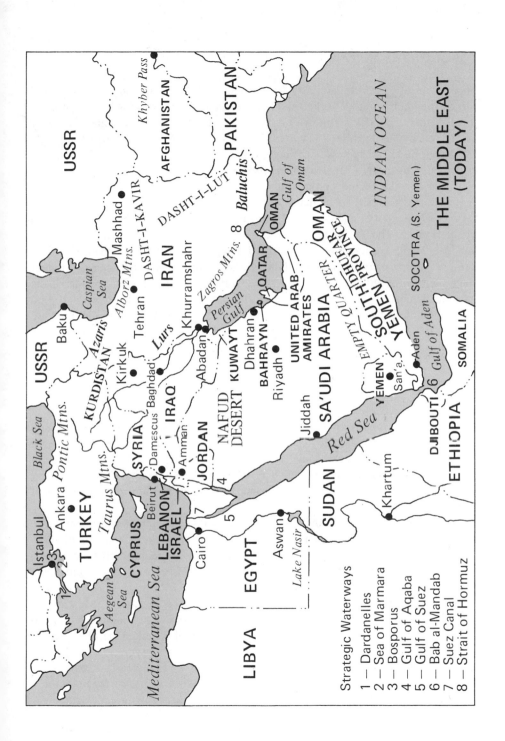

THE MIDDLE EAST
(TODAY)

Strategic Waterways

1 — Dardanelles
2 — Sea of Marmara
3 — Bosporus
4 — Gulf of Aqaba
5 — Gulf of Suez
6 — Bab al-Mandab
7 — Suez Canal
8 — Strait of Hormuz

TOPOGRAPHY

Topographically, the Middle East can be divided into northern and southern zones. The former, consisting of Turkey and Iran, tends to be a rugged, mountainous area. In Anatolia (i.e., today's Turkey in Asia) the Pontic and Taurus mountains roughly parallel each other from west to east. In Iran the Zagros Mountains cross the south, while the crescent-shaped Alburz range, reaching as high as 18,500 feet, lies south of the Caspian. Several smaller chains rise in the extreme east and northeast. High plateaus form the central portions of both Anatolia and Iran.

Though generally much flatter, the southern zone contains scattered mountain regions. Two parallel chains extend from north to south at the eastern end of the Mediterranean. These mountains taper off in Palestine but rise as high as 8,644 feet in Sinai. While western Egypt is known for its depressions rather than its mountains, a modest chain divides the Nile Valley from the Red Sea coast. Another chain, known by different names locally, stretches down the western side of the Arabian Peninsula. At the southern end, these mountains' height exceeds 10,000 feet in the interior of Yemen. The peninsula generally slopes from the south toward the low-lying region near the Persian Gulf, but the sudden, towering mountains of Oman provide a major exception to this picture.

CLIMATE

The Middle East is a region of hot summers. Daytime temperatures sometimes shoot up well past 120°F in some parts of the Middle East, such as southern Egypt and the Persian Gulf. Mountains and some coastal areas are cooler, and nighttime temperatures drop drastically in most places. The effects of heat are partly counteracted by dryness, although some areas, such as coastal Arabia, also suffer from high levels of humidity.

Differences of latitude and altitude make for diverse winter temperatures. The southern region is generally semitropical, although considerable amounts of snow occasionally fall as far south as Jerusalem. But much of the northern zone experiences severe winters, with blizzards raging at high elevations. Temperatures have dropped as low as −35°F in central Anatolia.

The area's most salient geographic characteristic is its aridity. Most of the region is uncultivable desert or is steppeland that receives only enough rainfall to support nomadic life. In most of the Middle East, rainfall is limited mainly to winter and is erratic from year to year. Rare cloudbursts in some deserts account for networks of dry riverbeds and for ground water that feeds wells and oases. Conversely, areas that normally receive the minimum of about seven inches of precipitation a year necessary for cultivation sometimes experience disastrously dry years.

Overall, the northern zone is less desertlike. This is particularly true for most of Anatolia and northwestern Iran. Some areas receive over a hundred inches of precipitation annually. The Persian word *jangal* (cognate of the English "jungle") is used to describe the dense vegetation of Iran's Gilan Province, at the southern end of the Caspian Sea. However, Iran's climate is mostly arid too, and a prominent feature of its agriculture is dependence on underground aqueducts (*qanats*) that bring ground water from high in the mountains. Large parts of Iran, such as the Dasht-i Lut and the Dasht-i Kavir of the east, are as barren as central Arabia, and much of central Anatolia is steppeland or even true desert.

The southern region includes large expanses of desert. The Nafud Desert and the greater Empty Quarter, an almost impenetrable sea of shifting sand dunes, occupy much of the interior of Arabia. Aside from some important oases fed by underground water and areas of the south and extreme east that get more rain, the peninsula is steppeland at best. Egypt, especially in the south, is virtually devoid of rainfall.

There are exceptions to the aridity of the southern area. The Yemeni highlands and some adjacent areas of southern Sa'udi Arabia, as well as a smaller region in Oman, lie on the edge of the monsoon zone, with its summer rains fed by winds from the Indian Ocean. Thus Yemen, with its sedentary agriculture, historically has accounted for perhaps a majority of the peninsula's population. Syria (or geographical Syria, since it includes Lebanon and Palestine) provides a better-known exception, as its littoral gets enough rain to turn it green for part of the year and to water nonirrigated crops.

Irrigated river valleys form a different kind of exception. The Tigris and Euphrates rivers rise from rain and melted snow in the Anatolian highlands to surge southeast toward the Persian Gulf. They merge to form the Shatt al-Arab in southern Iraq. These rivers historically have made Iraq (or Mesopotamia)[3] a major center of population and civilization. A much smaller river, the Karun, which rises in the Zagros Mountains of Iran, discharges into the Shatt al-Arab.

The Tigris-Euphrates Valley converges with geographic Syria to form a "Fertile Crescent." A steppe-desert region, the Syrian Desert, fits between the two horns of the Crescent and has offered an age-old starting point for nomadic infiltration into the settled lands.

The Nile offers Egypt unrivaled means for irrigation. This river forms in the Sudan from branches that rise in the Ethiopian highlands and in the tropical rain belt of central Africa. Until the Aswan High Dam tamed it in the 1960s, the annual inundation covered the Nile Valley and Delta during much of the year. Without the Nile, the narrow Valley of Upper (southern) Egypt, which averages about four miles in width, would be part of the empty desert, as is 95 percent of the country. Lower (northern) Egypt, the fan-shaped delta formed by the accumulation of silt, would be part of the Mediterranean Sea.

---

[3]The two names will be used interchangeably and refer roughly to the area within the boundaries of the twentieth century state of Iraq without regard to the distinction Arabs historically made between "al-Jazirah" and "al-Iraq."

NATURAL RESOURCES

Water is not the only natural resource that is scarce in the Middle East. There is also a limited amount of tillable soil, although areas such as the Nile Valley and Delta are extremely fertile. Forests always were restricted mainly to the highland regions, and even these tended to become casualties of civilization. Various minerals have been mined in many places, but supplies of most of these appear to be small. In general, the northern zone, particularly Anatolia, has greater quantities of materials such as copper, tin, lead, coal, and iron than does the rest of the Middle East.

There is one glaring exception to this. Almost 60 percent of the world's proven oil reserves—and also large reserves of natural gas—today are located in the countries bordering on the Persian Gulf. But this resource was largely irrelevant until the present century. Moreover, most of the Middle Eastern countries have only modest amounts of oil or none at all.

THE NEOLITHIC REVOLUTION

In past millennia, large parts of the Middle East possessed another rich resource in their unusual combination of wild flora and fauna, the ancestors of wheat and barley and of sheep, pigs, and cows, to mention a few examples. This provided the answer to the challenge of encroaching aridity 10,000 years ago, leading to the invention of agriculture. It is hard to deny that this was the greatest leap that the human race has ever made. Instead of continuing to depend on scouring the earth for the now less plentiful wild plants and on hunting game with crude stone weapons, people in geographic Syria, northern Mesopotamia, and parts of Iran and Anatolia began to domesticate plants and animals. Many present-day crops and farm animals emerged at this time.

A chain reaction of innovations ensued. Agriculture brought about settled village life, increased trade, and the invention of pottery, baskets, weaving, and spinning. Another development was the improved stone tools, like the hoe and the sickle, that gave the subsequent era the designation "Neolithic" (New Stone) Age. Despite occasional innovations in later periods (including a major cluster of innovations in Mesopotamia about five thousand years later), the basic nature of largely self-sufficient agricultural life endured to modern times. Well-developed Neolithic patterns could be found in places like Jericho in 8000 B.C. and extended from Palestine to western Iran during the next three millennia. It was not fully diffused to parts of western Europe and the Far East until the mid third millennium B.C.

NOMADISM

In addition to sedentary agriculture, the Neolithic Revolution also gave birth to the life style of the nomadic herdsman, pursued by perhaps 5 percent of the Middle Eastern population as late as the mid twentieth century A.D. People drove their sheep, goats, and donkeys (and later camels) in regular circuits that took them to water holes near the "sown" areas during the dry summers and to points farther into the desert or steppe when winter rains made vegetation shoot up there. In mountain regions tribes drove their flocks into the high areas during the summer and back into the valleys for winter. Governed by tribal councils and elective chiefs who were only first among equals and sharing property on a communal basis, the relatively democratic, classless character of nomadic life—within each kinship unit, but not on an intertribal level, as some tribes claimed greater "nobility" than others— contrasted with autocratic, exploitative, settled societies.

The feud between desert and sown dominated much of Middle Eastern history. The relationship was a symbiotic one, as nomads traded animals for grain and other village produce. But nomadic tribes, who knew no moral obligations transcending the tribe (sometimes even after nominally adhering to a universal religion) and were restrained only by the threat of retaliation, also raided each other and plundered, conquered, or exacted tribute from the less militaristic villagers.

Blood ties among nomads provided the unrivaled social solidarity within each tribal community that made desert life possible. The nomads' style of life made for mobility and discipline, and their tribal ethos emphasized military valor. All this made them a terror for villagers, and although the proud, freedom-loving nomads had contempt for those who tilled the soil, material rewards repeatedly lured them from the desert. As the fourteenth-century Arab historian ibn-Khaldun showed, such nomadic incursions periodically brought new dynasties to power and renewed the vitality of settled societies. New languages and corresponding ethnic identities also tended to rise with each conquest.

THE BIRTH OF CIVILIZATION

Long before the Neolithic Revolution caught on in most of Eurasia and Africa, the fourth millennium B.C. brought accelerated change with the emergence, again in the Middle East, of a style of life called "civilized." This went a step beyond the Neolithic transformations, with greater agricultural productivity relieving a portion of the population of the need to raise its own food. This nonagricultural population concentrated in cities, where occupations became specialized, and a ruling class took its toll of the peasants' produce to support luxuries, warfare, and works of art and architecture. A few people learned the art of writing, without which such a complicated society, with its need to keep records and transmit messages, would have hardly been viable.

The first breakthrough to this kind of society came with the Sumerians, a southern Mesopotamian people whose language seems to be unrelated to any others. Possibly originating in the Iranian highlands, the Sumerians were newcomers to Mesopotamia. It was the process of clearing the luxuriant growth from the land and constructing a complicated network of dikes and canals that evoked a remarkable series of innovations, including the wheeled cart, sailboats, plows, and awkward war chariots. A newly discovered technique of smelting allowed the Sumerians to use copper tools, and the process of alloying this metal with tin earned the period of early civilizations the name Bronze Age. Use of these metals plus gold and silver as media of exchange greatly enhanced trade, and soon merchants were borrowing and making loans for interest and even issuing letters of credit. Massive temples developed into the ziggurat, with its many floors built on top of each other in steplike fashion. A sexagesimal system of numbers was in use, whose only deficiency was the absence of the zero. Sumerians extracted square and cube roots, solved algebraic problems, and applied geometry. The cuneiform system of writing, which used wedge-shaped ideographs for concrete objects and for their abstract homophones, was employed by scribes and priests.

Egypt followed in the wake of Sumer and soon surpassed it. By 5000 B.C. Neolithic farmers had penetrated the Nile Valley and Delta. Perhaps gradual desiccation in northeast Africa and Libya forced the new settlement and the gradual development of a complicated irrigation network.

Linguistically, the ancient Egyptians belonged to what was traditionally called the Hamitic family of languages, which also includes the Berber tongues of North Africa and other languages extending today from Nigeria to Somalia. Modern scholars, however, consider these languages to constitute several distinct groups belonging to a larger Hamito-Semitic (or Afro-Asian) family that also includes the Semitic peoples, that is, those whose languages belong to the Semitic subfamily. Thus the Egyptians were linguistically related to the Semites, who then were limited to Southwest Asia (although the latter may have crossed from East Africa to Arabia during earlier millennia). Besides this original kinship, the Egyptian people and their language seem to have acquired some Semitic overlay as a result of an early influx of Semites from Arabia via Syria. If so, this provides one of the earliest examples of migration by Semitic tribes who periodically, at least according to a widely accepted theory, overflowed from the increasingly desiccated Arabian Peninsula into more fertile lands. But while the Fertile Crescent was almost fully Semiticized by the late Bronze Age, Egypt retained its Hamitic character until it adopted a Semitic language (Arabic) and identity (Arab) during Islamic times.

Egyptian civilization seems to have begun to develop independently, although the spread of ideas from Sumer largely spared it the process of reinvention. In any case, the two civilizations remained mutually distinctive. Not even a neophyte would confuse the massive, lifelike, naturalistic works of Egyptian art with the figures pictured in Mesopotamia. Even though Egyptian writing may have been inspired by the Sumerian example, the artistic hieroglyphics that look almost like a sequence of pictures on Egyptian tomb and temple walls, and even the more simplified hieratic (and later, demotic) script written on papyrus, were fundamentally different from the cuneiform on Mesopotamian clay tablets.

The early civilizations of Egypt and Mesopotamia experienced contrasting histories. Sumer's early period was one of separate city-states, such as Umma, Lagash, Uruk, and Ur, each with its priests ruling in the local deity's name, although the unity of the civilization was symbolized by a belief in an annual assem-

THE ANCIENT MIDDLE EAST
(DIFFERENT PERIODS)

—— Major Overland Trade Routes

9

bly of the gods. Peaceful coexistence eventually gave way to warfare and attempts to assert a particular city's hegemony, and the ruler of Umma established a short-lived empire in the twenty-fourth century B.C. that claimed to rule from the Mediterranean to the Persian Gulf. Then, in about 2385 B.C. the whole civilization was overrun by the Akkadians, Semitic people from further north, led by Sargon, ruler of the city of Akkad.

Under Sargon and his successors, the Akkadians began a process whereby Semites eventually absorbed the Sumerians but preserved their civilization. During about 180 years of Sargonid rule, Mesopotamia suffered increasing oppression, rebellion, and suppression, while other tribesmen pressed in. These included the Semitic Amorites from the southern desert and the Gutians in the Iranian highlands. The latter finally overran most of Mesopotamia, although the extreme south continued to resist. The ruler of Uruk liberated the country from the Gutians in about 2110 B.C., but another Sumerian city, Ur, then took control and ushered in the Indian summer of the Sumerian people, as the Akkadian language increasingly became the medium of everyday speech. Again, the state had gradually disintegrated by the end of the millennium, and it was left to the Amorite city of Babylon to reunite the valley in the late nineteenth century B.C. in an empire that survived over two centuries. Under Hammurabi, who came to the throne in 1792 B.C., the Babylonian empire repeated much of Ur's earlier glory, but the Amorites adopted the Akkadian language, and the age of the Sumerians now was finished.

Egyptian civilization also rose in separate centers, but political unity was achieved early as King Narmer combined Upper and Lower Egypt in about 3200 B.C. The natural unity of the country was matched by kings ruling from Memphis (near today's Cairo) who were worshipped as gods and claimed ownership of the whole land and its people. The Nile's gentle flow and predictable annual floods—in contrast to Mesopotamia's fragmentation and its rivers' capriciousness—enabled Egypt to maintain prosperity and stability for long periods. The ease of transportation on the Nile made the country relatively self-sufficient and long uninterested in foreign expansion, although Egyptian ships obtained Lebanese timber from the earliest civilized periods and began to ply the waters of the Red Sea to the land of Punt (modern Somalia) by the end of the third millennium. The extreme dichotomy between the densely populated Nile Valley and Delta and the desert hinterland that did not support even large numbers of nomads provided Egypt with a basis for defense that Mesopotamia never enjoyed. Although the upper Nile offered a route for commerce to the Egyptian frontier, the Cataracts (rapids) in the south had great defensive value. Only during periods of decay was Egypt susceptible to invasions, even from its relatively vulnerable northeastern frontier.

All these advantages allowed Egypt to surpass Sumer during the third millennium B.C. The beginning of the Third Dynasty in about 2700 B.C. ushered in a period of incredible splendor, the Old kingdom. Such pyramids as that of the Fourth Dynasty King Cheops at Giza, which covers over thirteen acres and reaches upward for more than 481 feet, remain awesome monuments to the age. But, by the twenty-third century B.C., the country was in decline, partly because building and maintaining the pyramids had exhausted the economy. There were peasant revolts, and Semitic nomads entered the country from the north and ruled much of the Delta.

A shorter period of brilliance, known as the Middle Kingdom, emerged in 2040 B.C. as the ruler of the Upper Egyptian city of Thebes reunited the country. Egyptian literature reached its zenith during the Middle Kingdom, and the southern frontier advanced into Nubia.

From Mesopotamia, civilization spread into adjacent areas. Excavations in northern Syria in 1974 revealed remains of the city of Ebla, which was the center of a flourishing civilization and empire in the mid third millennium B.C. The Eblaite langauge is the oldest known Semitic tongue. The third millennium B.C. also saw the rise of civilization in Elam, in southwestern Iran. Both Ebla and Elam borrowed Sumer's cuneiform script and became outlying areas of Mesopotamian civilization.

Although bronze tools and other products of advanced culture came into use over a wider area, civilization had not spread farther than the adjacent corners of Europe—Crete—and India—the Indus Valley—by 2000 B.C. Both of these civilizations seemingly developed under Middle Eastern inspiration.

END OF THE EARLY PERIOD OF CIVILIZATION

The early part of the second millennium B.C. witnessed a movement of peoples that profoundly influenced the course of history. Middle Eastern civilizations succumbed to "barbarian" conquerors, and lengthy interludes preceded revival. But when civilization sprang back, it spread farther out of the river valleys to encompass most of the region, and the old centers increasingly were thrown in contact with each other. More and more, this interaction gave the Middle East unity on both the political and the cultural levels. Instead of several Middle Eastern civilizations, it eventually became meaningful to speak of an overall civilization of the area that was distinct from those of regions like Europe and India.

Central Eurasia played a key role in this process, as Aryan (Indo-European) nomads from west of the Caspian Sea overran the continent's periphery. The Aryans' acquisition of bronze weapons from the Middle East helped to make them formidable, but they also made a basic breakthrough of their own in about 3000 B.C. by domesticating the horse. They now bred varieties of this animal strong enough to pull war chariots, but not yet strong enough for riding. The Aryans also invented a new kind of two-wheeled chariot by 1700 B.C. This, together with these people's nomadic habits and the ease of traversing vast distances of steppeland, put civilized lands, with their tempting riches, at the Aryans' mercy.

The ethnic pattern of the world was changing. By 2000 B.C., Aryan peoples were established in Anatolia. Farther east, the new ethnic-linguistic pattern emerging from the invasion earned a vast region the name "Land of the Aryans," or Iran. Europe and India were even more thoroughly transformed, as shown by the present prevalence of related Indo-European tongues in most parts of both subcontinents. The Aryans destroyed both Cretan and Indus Valley civilizations and made way for the emergence of their Hellenic and Hindu successors. Nomadic movements spread Middle Eastern ideas and artifacts across the steppes, and this resulted in a distinctive Chinese civilization by about 1500 B.C.

Farthest from the Aryan invaders, Egypt was the first civilized land to be overwhelmed by the resultant movement of peoples. With the end of the Twelfth Dynasty in 1786 B.C., weak rulers and civil war enabled mainly Semitic nomads from southwest Asia to infiltrate the Delta. The nomadic princes, known as the Hyksos, eventually overran most of the country, especially after their acquisition of horses gave them an extra advantage.

Horse-powered feudal kingdoms rose in the northern Middle East. One Aryan people, the Hittites, became a strong power in central Anatolia and developed a flourishing civilization that borrowed many features from Egypt and Mesopotamia. Some subjects of the Hittite kingdom made a major contribution to world civilization by learning to smelt iron soon after the middle of the second millennium B.C. Though inferior to bronze, this more plentiful material made metal implements available for the first time on a mass scale. But with production a Hittite state secret, the spread of the Iron Age was delayed.

Non-Aryan, non-Semitic tribesmen in the Anatolian and Iranian highlands threatened Mesopotamia. The Hurrians of the Kingdom of Mitanni, in the area later called Armenia, were led by an Aryan aristocracy whose members were recruited for their adeptness with horses and chariots. They eventually took control of northern Mesopotamia and northern Syria. A second such people, the Kassites of the Iranian highlands, occupied Babylon in 1595 B.C. but preserved the Akkadian language and eventually were absorbed into Sumero-Akkadian civilization.

RESURGENCE

Egypt led the way in the resurgence of the old civilized peoples. The princes of Thebes, in Upper Egypt, had never fallen under full Hyksos control and eventually learned to use horses and chariots against the occupiers. They reunited the country by 1567 B.C. and began the New Kingdom. The greatness of Egyptian civilization resumed, while the bitter experience with the Hyksos induced a feeling that Syria was vital to the country's security. The consequent policy of expansion led Egyptian armies to the Euphrates. A Mitanni-inspired Canaanite revolt brought King Thutmose III and his armies back into Palestine, where he defeated the Canaanite coalition at Megiddo (Armageddon), and on across the Euphrates to rout the Mitannians. Egypt also conquered Cyprus and Kush, reaching deep into present-day Sudan.

While tending to see southwest Asia as relevant only in terms of security, Egypt in many ways became a part of a wider Middle Eastern world. Egyptian kings married foreign princesses and exchanged letters and diplomatic missions with other rulers. Cuneiform became the international script, with Akkadian the diplomatic *lin-*

gua franca. Thus, in a sense, southwest Asia was gradually beginning to absorb the unique civilization of Egypt. On a spiritual level, the new cosmopolitanism inspired a short-lived vision of world unity during the mid fourteenth century B.C. as King Akhenaton proclaimed Aton, represented by the sun's disc, to be the "sole God."

While Akhenaton's reforms diverted attention from the empire, the Hittites went on the offensive and occupied much of northern Syria. The Egyptian empire fell apart as Canaanite cities asserted their independence or came under the rule of nomadic Habiru (Hebrew?) invaders. Under King Ramses II, the Egyptian army tried to reassert its control but failed to defeat the Hittites at the Battle of Kadesh in 1285 B.C. With Assyria emerging in northern Mesopotamia as a threat to both powers, they concluded a peace treaty in 1270 B.C. that provided for a mutual renunciation of force and for the partition of Syria.

An unexpected cataclysm ended the Egyptian-Hittite arrangement. "Peoples of the Sea," refugees from invasion or natural catastrophes in the Aegean basin, began to sail along the Anatolian coast or trudged overland in ox carts. The Hittites of Anatolia quickly succumbed and vanished as a people, although Hittite city-states survived in northern Syria until the eighth century B.C. With the fall of the Hittite Empire, the secret of forging iron was out, and iron weapons, combined with a ferocity created by desperation, helped to make the refugees invincible in the face of peoples still in the Bronze Age. Only Egypt succeeded in turning them back by the late twelfth century B.C., although many Berber tribesmen from Libya, who had joined with the Sea Peoples, settled in the western delta. The would-be invaders of Egypt, who were known as Philistines, settled on the coast of what thus subsequently came to be called Palestine and spread the use of iron and possibly Aegean cultural influences.

Defeat of the Sea Peoples exhausted Egypt and left it a "broken reed." For a while, the country split into two kingdoms and then, beginning in 975 B.C., fell under the control of Libyan mercenaries. It was left to the independent ruler of Kush, now culturally Egyptianized, to liberate the mother country and establish the Twenty-fifth Dynasty in 715 B.C.

THE DAY OF SMALL POWERS AND SYRIAN CREATIVITY

The end of Hittite and Egyptian power permitted a new wave of Semitic tribes to enter Syria. These groups joined some of their predecessors, particularly the Canaanites of Palestine and Lebanon, in making spectacular contributions to world civilization.

Mountains protected the northernmost Canaanites, the Phoenicians, from new Semitic invasions and allowed them to continue their earlier sea-borne commerce from city-states like Byblos, Sidon, and Tyre. Phoenician colonies (permanent settlements) dotted the Mediterranean as far west as Spain by the eleventh century B.C. Increasingly in contact with the Greeks, they brought further Hellenic-Oriental cross-pollination. The Phoenician-founded city of Carthage, near today's Tunis, eventually created its own empire.

The Phoenicians' greatest contribution was the invention, or at least the widespread dissemination, of the strictly phonetic alphabet. In common use in Phoenicia by the twelfth century B.C., the alphabet soon was adopted by other Syrian peoples, including the Hebrews and Aramaeans. It gradually replaced ideographic scripts and, with variations in the shape of the letters, later became the basis for the alphabet of all Old World civilizations except that of the Far East. Its simplicity allowed writing to spread to a vastly larger stratum of people than had been possible with earlier writing, whose difficulty had limited it to scribes and priests.

The new wave of Semites included Aramaeans in the north and Hebrews in the south. The Aramaeans established numerous small states, such as Damascus and Aleppo, and specialized in overland trade that extended throughout the Middle East. The Aramaic language later became the spoken tongue of the entire Fertile Crescent and replaced Akkadian as the *lingua franca* of the Middle East.

The main group of Hebrews was the Israelites, who conquered eastern Palestine and part of Transjordan. Organized in twelve tribes, the Israelites may have entered Palestine as early as the nineteenth century B.C. Then they (or some of them) migrated to Egypt, presumably as part of the Hyksos invasion. After the end of the Hyksos period, the Israelites lost favor and were led by Moses into Sinai and eventually invaded Palestine from the east. At first establishing several enclaves, they exterminated part of the Canaanite population but presumably assimilated others. They adopted a Canaanite dialect as the "Hebrew" language.

Although they were not yet monotheists, the Hebrews were already unique in their belief in one national god, Yahweh, who forbade worship of all others. Also unlike his rivals, Yahweh forbade his people to make "graven images." The other unique aspect of the Hebrew god was his transcendence over nature, for he did not represent any of its unexplainable aspects but rather existed outside his creation. Yet Yahweh's people repeatedly turned to idols, particularly the Canaanite storm and fertility god, Baal.

The Israelite invasion of Palestine came shortly after the Philistines had entered the land from the west. Defeat by the Philistines' iron weapons eventually induced the Israelite tribes to unite under a monarchy. At the beginning of the first millennium B.C., King David defeated the Philistines, whose city-states even then survived in much of the coastal region. He also eliminated the remaining Canaanite enclaves, such as Jerusalem, which became the Israelite capital. Ruling an area that included most of inland Syria, David and his son Solomon created a flourishing empire in a commercial and political alliance with Tyre, which funished the wood for Solomon's Temple in Jerusalem. A body of Israelite literature, later collected in the anthology known as the Bible, was beginning to emerge.

Tribal divisions ended the Israelite empire after the death of Solomon in 922 B.C. The northern tribes broke away but continued to be called the Kingdom of Israel, with Samaria as its capital city. Solomon's descendants retained control over a small region in the south, mainly their own tribe of Judah, and thus the southern kingdom, still centered at Jerusalem, was called Judah (Judea). Its people, as well as heterogeneous people who were later converted to their religion, eventually came to be known as Jews, while the northern Israelites took the name Samaritans.

BRUTALITY AND AMALGAMATION: THE ASSYRIANS

The day of small powers now made way for the rise of a new Assyrian empire that surpassed all its predecessors in size and brutality. Known by the name of their god of war, Assur, the Assyrians were perhaps the most militaristic people in ancient times. Assyrian aggressiveness was felt temporarily as early as 1100 B.C. and resumed in the late tenth century B.C. Further advances in horse breeding and the use of saddles, bridles, and bits in the Eurasian steppe spread to them by the eighth century B.C., enabling them to introduce cavalry forces into Middle Eastern warfare. After setbacks imposed by a Syrian coalition in the 850s B.C., the Assyrian tide reached new heights during the next century under Tiglath-Pilesar III. Aside from Babylon, most of Syria, including Israel, fell, although a few kingdoms like Tyre and Judah survived by paying tribute. In 671 B.C. another Assyrian king took Egypt; however, Egypt soon asserted its independence under the Twenty-sixth Dynasty. Elam came under Assyrian rule, as did parts of Arabia, which was increasingly brought into the view of history as a result of the large-scale domestication of the camel by the early part of the first millennium B.C.

Conquered peoples suffered a terrible fate under the Assyrians. Mass up rooting was common, especially of skilled craftsmen and potentially troublesome upper classes. The deported Israelites (Samaritans) are the best known example, while diverse peoples who settled in the former kingdom were absorbed by the remaining Samaritans.

Their cruelty notwithstanding, the Assyrians were a catalyst in the development of an overall Middle Eastern civilization. The political unity they provided made way for an even larger empire, and they built roads that encouraged economic unity. Even the dispersal of peoples enhanced cosmopolitanism.

Militarism exhausted the Assyrian people, and they increasingly depended on restive subjects as troops. A new wave of Semitic peoples, the Chaldeans, took control of Babylon in 626 B.C., while the Medes were a rising power in the Iranian highlands. In another wave of Aryan migration, the fierce Sythians now had a kingdom north of the Black Sea, from which they terrorized the Middle East. They pushed another Aryan Central Eurasian people, the Cimmerians, before them into western Anatolia, where they collided with the semi-Hellenized kingdom of Lydia. Now Medes, Sythians, Chaldeans, and others formed a great anti-Assyrian coalition. With the fall of the Assyrians' capital, Ninevah, in 612 B.C., King Necho of Egypt sent troops to prevent their complete defeat, but the anti-Assyrian allies prevailed.

UNIFICATION: THE PERSIANS

The fall of Assyria left southwest Asia divided mainly into two empires. The Medes ruled the area north of the Tigris and continued to expand into Anatolia. Farther south, the Neo-Babylonian (Chaldean) empire defeated Egypt at the Battle of Carchemish in 605 B.C. and established its hold on Syria. With the conquest of Judah, many Jews were carried away to Babylon. Babylonian power was matched by dazzling new monuments and the restoration of old ones, but a period of weak rulers again brought decline.

Now another people came to the fore in the empire of the Medes and gave it new vitality. The Persians, originally from a part of southern Iran called Parsa (now "Fars," or Persia),[4] spoke a language related to that of the Medes and other Iranian peoples. The Persian rulers, the Achaemenid house, were vassals of the Medes until Cyrus II ("the Great") gained control of the empire in 550 B.C. Within the following two decades he overran southwest Asia, including the Chaldean empire in 539 B.C. His successor, Cambyses, conquered Egypt in 526 B.C., while a third Achaemenid, Darius, extended his realm from the Indus Valley to the Danube. Despite instances of cruelty, the Persian Empire was relatively benevolent, and those peoples who had known Assyrian and Chaldean conquest welcomed the Achaemenids as liberators. Some exiled peoples, like the Jews, were permitted to return home, and they and others enjoyed autonomy and toleration. Still, an absolute "king of kings" (*shah an-shah*) kept the empire unified, ruling through his twenty satraps, a system of royal roads, and a postal service. The adoption of the Phoenician alphabet and the Aramaic language as the media of government facilitated administration. Political unity also enhanced commercial ties, as did the introduction of coined money.

SPIRITUAL RESPONSE: MONOTHEISM

Belief in one God climaxed the emergence of the increasingly cosmopolitan Middle Eastern world. Prophets, believed to be messengers of a god, long had existed among the Semitic peoples. Now Hebrew prophets in particular began to speak more clearly of Yahweh as the one God of the whole world, although the Israelites were still His chosen people. At about the same time, Iran provided the soil for growth of another monotheistic and transcendent religion, Zoroastrianism. Zoroaster, apparently one of the Iranian priests or Magi, attacked many older practices and emphasized that there was one God, Ahura Mazda ("the Knowing Lord"), whose Good Spirit was constantly opposed to the spirit of evil. Zoroastrianism was only one of many Iranian cults and did not predominate until much later.

This was a crucial era in Middle Eastern and world intellectual history. The philosopher Karl Jaspers calls the period from 800 to 200 B.C. the "Axial Age,"

---

[4]Westerners, including some leading scholars, conventionally use the name Persia for Iran as a whole.

while Toynbee singles out the sixth century B.C. as pivotal. Just as the Hebrew prophets and Zoroaster proclaimed their conceptions of one God and one humanity, people in other regions similarly looked beyond old myths that had explained everything in terms of personified natural forces. Early Greek philosophers such as Pythagoras began a rational, philosophical, scientific approach that continued to characterize Greek civilization and the much larger European civilization that eventually emerged from it. The idea of one transcendent God increasingly became a central part of the Middle Eastern tradition and later, in a process of persistent interaction between the two regions, became grafted onto the European tradition. Such men as the Buddha and Confucius took Indian and Far Eastern civilizations on quite different courses of thought, and the separate civilizations assumed forms that endured until the modern age.

THE WEST EMERGING

By the late sixth century B.C., the emerging classical civilization of Greece loomed on the Middle Eastern horizon. The Greeks had been reduced to illiteracy after invasion by new tribes in about 1200 B.C., but another Middle Eastern transfusion occurred as the Greeks belatedly adopted the Phoenician alphabet in about 750 B.C. Most of the foundations of Greek (Hellenic) civilization were borrowed from the Middle East, but it was one of the most creative civilizations that ever existed. It was distinctive in many ways, with its city-states (*poleis*; singular, *polis*) whose governments were based on citizen participation, with a worldliness unknown farther east, and with a spirit of inquiry that sought natural laws to explain all phenomena.

Hellenic civilization increasingly touched the Middle East. The favorable terms of trade commanded by Greek exports compared with, say, Egyptian grain were a basis for the prosperity of a wide segment of Hellenic society. Greek coins competed with those minted by the Persian king, even in his own domain, and Greek became a major commercial *lingua franca*. There were Greek commercial colonies at Naucritis, near the Egyptian coast, and also on the northern Syrian coast, as in other parts of the Mediterranean and Black Sea regions. The Twenty-sixth Egyptian Dynasty increasingly recruited Greek mercenaries, as did the Persian Empire. But even in 500 B.C. the East superficially seemed preponderant. A key part of the Greek world, the Ionian cities of western Anatolia, was subject to the king of kings, and the other Greek city-states seemed insignificant in comparison with the great Persian Empire.

THE EAST OVERRUN

A Greco-Persian conflict broke out as the sixth century B.C. began. A revolt of the Anatolian Greek cities in 499 B.C. brought Athenian help, but it succumbed to the shah's forces. In turn, King Darius vowed to punish Athens. His invasion of Greece was stopped at the Battle of Marathon in 490 B.C., but his successor, Xerxes, brought a larger army across the Dardanelles. To the Greeks, Xerxes' force was one of incomprehensible proportions, and they sometimes fancifully saw it as an Asian crusade against Europe. But a series of Greek land and naval victories ended the Persian threat.

From then on, the Achaemenid Empire went downhill. Intrafamily conflict, assassinations, and assertion of independence by satraps became commonplace. The erosion of toleration brought rebellion in Babylon and Sidon, and brutal suppression led to economic decline. With the help of Greek mercenaries, Egypt asserted its independence in 404 B.C., although the Persians restored their control briefly in 334 B.C.

The vitality of Hellenic civilization began to contrast with the stagnation prevailing in the lands to the east. There was no fundamental gap, certainly not of a technical nature, in development between the two regions comparable to that which emerged in the eighteenth century A.D. Yet a social gap was present, as the tightly governed Greek *polis,* with its citizen participation and its intense feeling of civic solidarity that had parallels elsewhere only on a tribal level, vied with the autocratic but less effective governmental pattern of the Achaemenid Empire. While the Persians had to depend on mercenaries and other soldiers who lacked sincere commitment to the state, the Greek armies were the product of close-knit communities in which military training was an integral part of the citizen's life.

Hellenic influence radiated eastward. Virtually independent satraps in Anatolia drew Greek artists and poets to their courts. Greek soldiers gained a reputation for invincibility and were now the bulwark of the Persian army. The kings of kings were able to buy time for themselves only by playing the Greek city-states off against each other. But it was becoming clear that, if the Greeks could unite and also preserve the *polis* as a vital local unit, they could easily slice through the Persian Empire.

The partially Hellenized kingdom of Macedon, north of Greece, finally provided this unity after King Philip II's forces defeated a coalition of Greek states in 338 B.C. The *polis* was rarely fully independent from now on, although participation in its institutions remained a hallmark of Hellenism that set it off from Eastern cultures in the Hellenistic age, as subsequent centuries came to be known. Philip was ready to inaugurate what was in effect the first age of Western colonialism, but his untimely death in 336 B.C. left the task for his nineteen-year-old son, Alexander II ("the Great").

Alexander routed Achaemenid forces in an easy march through Anatolia. In the Battle of Issus, near the present city of Alexandretta, Darius III fled in terror from the Macedonian's onslaught, and the Persian army fell apart. Alexander proceeded to conquer Syria and Egypt, where he consulted the oracle of Amon and seemed to begin a process of coming under the spell of the East. Leaving Egypt in 331 B.C., Alexander proceeded to northern Mesopotamia to meet an even larger Persian army at Gaugamela, near the ruins of Nineveh. Again the shah fled, this time even before the outcome of the battle was clear, and his troops fell back.

Continuing his escape, he was overthrown by one of his generals and left on the ground mortally wounded as the enemy approached. Completing the conquest of the Achaemenid Empire and much of India, Alexander returned to Babylon, which he planned to make his capital, but he died in 323 B.C. at the age of thirty two.

Alexander had transformed the Middle East, but it had also transformed him. He began to wear Eastern clothing, and at one point he demanded that his Macedonian officers prostrate themselves, like the subjects of a Persian king, in his presence. His role as the successor of the Achaemenids rather than as their conqueror began taking hold. He married two Eastern women, including the daughter of Darius III. On the return from India, a mass ceremony was held at which 10,000 of his soldiers took Iranian wives, and he began to incorporate Iranians into his army. It is unclear whether all this was mainly a pragmatic response to governing a vast empire or whether it represented an idealistic furtherance of the brotherhood of the human race. The incipient cooperation seemed to be limited to Hellenes and Iranians, but it is possible that Alexander, had he lived longer, would have led the West and East toward a new synthesis rather than to a subordination of the latter.

THE HELLENISTIC KINGDOMS
IN THE EAST

Alexander's death brought a struggle for power in the army that left separate kingdoms headed by Macedonian generals. These included Ptolemy in Egypt, whose dynasty at times also ruled other parts of the Eastern Mediterranean region, and Seleucus, who eventually took over most of Alexander's Asian empire. Despite political disunity, the Hellenistic world remained a cultural whole. Ideas and commerce flowed freely across frontiers, facilitated by a *lingua franca, koine* (common) Greek. The Hellenes, eventually including many Hellenized Easterners, were the ruling class throughout the Hellenistic world.

Ptolemaic Egypt was a flourishing center of Hellenistic civilization. Of all the Alexandrias founded by and named for the conqueror, the metropolis on the coast at the western end of the Nile Delta became the unrivaled city of the age. Despite a large Egyptian population that inhabited its own quarters, Alexandria was a Hellenic city and was officially described as "by [not in] Egypt." It is paradoxical that this cultural capital of the Hellenistic world was no real *polis* but was governed autocratically by the king, although particular sections of the city, known as *politeumata* (singular, *politeuma*), did have their own local self-government. It is also noteworthy that the country with the largest Hellenic city was otherwise the least Hellenized in the region. Although the Ptolemies ruled Egypt through a Greek bureaucracy as a private estate and exploited it mercilessly, they became increasingly Egyptianized in some ways. The kingdom was decaying rapidly by 100 B.C., and only Roman intervention preserved it for a while longer.

Seleucus was the Macedonian general who came closest to inheriting Alexander's mantle. A long line of the Seleucid kings, mostly named Seleucus or Antiochus, ruled from Antioch-on-the-Orontes, in northern Syria. They lost India to its own empire-builder, Chandragupta Maurya, and later Iran and most of Anatolia asserted their independence. They took southern Syria from the Ptolemies during the second century B.C., but their rule eventually was limited to northern Syria.

The Seleucids' rule was like that of the Ptolemies in some ways. They became absolute monarchs and assumed titles such as *Theos Epiphanes* ("God Made Manifest"), although the geography of their territories made their rule less rigid. Some temple-states remained under the autonomous rule of priests, while vassals or satraps gained de facto independence. There were also many *poleis*, with local autonomy under their own charters and institutions that represented the citizenry. Although these cities were settled by Greek immigrants, Hellenized Easterners also gained citizenship. Even those people in the *polis* who were not fully Hellenized controlled their own affairs within their own *politeuma*. In many cases, Eastern cities were given the privilege of organizing themselves as *poleis*, with a Hellenized minority forming the citizenry. The *polis* was the primary vehicle for Hellenization in the East, and its citizen army provided the king with vital military support. In addition to the *polis*, the Seleucids established numerous military settlements called *katoikiai* (singular, *katoikia*), often adjacent to Eastern cities, and soldiers were given land.

Several states emerged in Anatolia and further illustrate the interaction of East and West. Kings of countries like Armenia, Cappadocia, and Pontus fashionably adopted Greek royal titles and often spoke Greek, but their Hellenism was extremely shallow. The western Anatolian kingdom of Pergamum, founded in the third century B.C., supported Hellenic learning, and its library was second only to that of Alexandria.

The East-West encounter continued in Iran and areas further east. Two eastern satrapies of the Seleucids, Bactria (in today's Afghanistan) and Parthia (eastern Iran) established their independence in about 250 B.C. The new Bactrian kingdom became one of the most dynamic seats of Hellenistic civilization. It conquered part of India and renewed Hellenic influence there. Parthia soon was overrun by Central Asian Sythian nomads, who established a new dynasty that lasted for more than four centuries and, at its height, ruled all of Iran and Mesopotamia. The Parthian rulers represented an Iranian revival to a slight extent, although they perpetuated a gradually weakening Hellenism. A new Iranian language, Pahlavi (or Middle Persian), emerged alongside Aramaic and Greek. The still-evolving Zoroastrianism was only one of several important religions.

Central Eurasia continuously provided new nomadic Aryan invaders. In a movement of peoples that started with the expansion of the Han Empire in China, a group known as the Kushans took control of Bactria, and later of northern India. The Kushan Empire, with its amalgam of nomadic, Indian, Middle Eastern, Chinese, and Hellenic influences, became an important link in a chain of states that included the Parthian and Roman empires to the west and the Han Empire to the east. Central Eurasians now also bred horses that were strong enough to allow them and their riders to wear coats of mail, and this form of heavy cavalry was adopted by the civilized states. The Parthians began a long-term worldwide trend toward feudalism by establishing large fiefs devoted to raising horses and producing armor.

THE JEWS AND HELLENISM

The somewhat unique interaction of the Jews with Hellenism became a special part of the heritage of later ages. After the Achaemenid-sponsored return of some Jews from Babylon to Judea, the Jews embraced a staunch monotheism that contrasted with their ancestors' proneness to turn to other gods. They also committed themselves to a fierce sense of separateness from other peoples.

By Hellenistic times most Jews had migrated beyond Judea to establish the Diaspora ("dispersion"), and they formed an important minority in many cities. Alexandria became the home of the largest Jewish community in the world. The Jews in the Diaspora underwent Hellenization in some ways, and even the Bible was translated into Greek. But their religion prevented full Hellenization, which involved participation in a *polis,* particularly the worship of the *polis'* gods. Although few Jews opted for such citizenship, they were free to worship and to follow the Mosaic law. Like other groups, they controlled their own *politeuma*.

Judea had a different experience. As a temple-state under its high priest, it seemed content under Ptolemaic and then Seleucid domination, although Hellenic influence seeped in from nearby Greek cities in other parts of Palestine and Transjordan. But a big shock hit the country when members of a Hellenizing party obtained the appointment of one of their fellows, Jason, as high priest. In 175 B.C., Jason achieved what, from a Hellenic perspective, was a great privilege for Jerusalem: The city became a *polis,* renamed Antioch. This evoked rebellion, followed by the high priest's replacement by a more extreme Hellenizer, Menelaus, who turned the temple treasury over to the Seleucid king, Antiochus IV ("Epiphanes"). The king ruthlessly suppressed the rebellion in 169 B.C. and forced Jerusalem to become a *katoikia,* with non-Jewish troops brought in to occupy a citadel adjacent to the Temple. For the first time, the Seleucids engaged in religious intolerance, abolishing the Mosaic Law and forbidding Jewish worship. Jewish scriptures were burned, and the Temple was turned over to the worship of Zeus and the sacrifice of pigs.

A humble priestly family, the Hasmonaeans, emerged as the leaders of national resistance. Turning to guerrilla warfare, the Hasmonaeans, led by Judas Maccabaeus, eventually took control of Jerusalem and assumed the high priesthood. They began to raid territories outside Judea and even sent troops to help their Seleucid overlord put down other rebellious peoples. A later Hasmonaean, Simon Maccabaeas, obtained full recognition for his state, which grew into a small empire. The coastal cities of Palestine, which had never been Jewish (although there was now a Jewish minority there, as elsewhere outside Judea), fell to Hasmonaean armies. Samaria also succumbed, and the Samaritans' temple to Yahweh was destroyed. Sometimes large-scale slaughter followed invasion, and such peoples as the

Ituraeans of Galilee and the Idumaeans, south of the Dead Sea, were forcibly Judaized.

The Hasmonaeans illustrated the seeming futility of trying to keep the Hellenic tide from seeping into Eastern seas. The rulers adopted the superficial earmarks of Hellenism, such as Greek names and Greek inscriptions on coins, and even decorated the Temple in a Greek manner. They proclaimed themselves "philhellenes." Among other examples of disrespect for their own heritage, they forbade observance of the Sabbath at one point and even tried to abolish the Judaic Law. Pious Jews began to form anti-Hasmonaean rebel movements.

ROME IN THE EAST

With less opposition than in the East, Hellenistic civilization also spread westward into the barbarian lands of Europe. Despite its substitution of Latin for Greek, the city of Rome was an emerging power that represented an extension of Hellenism. After expanding in the western Mediterranean, Rome was able to throw its weight onto the scales to prevent any Hellenistic monarch from gaining preeminence. From about 200 B.C. on, states such as Pergamum and Ptolemaic Egypt owed their continued independence to Roman support against the Seleucids. Beginning in 133 B.C., when King Attalus of Pergamum left his kingdom as a legacy to the Romans, the western giant began to acquire Middle Eastern territory. There were challengers, particularly King Mithradites VI of Pontus, who drove Roman troops out of Anatolia in 88 B.C. and, reminiscent of Xerxes, temporarily invaded Greece. But the Roman general, Pompey, took over the rump Seleucid kingdom and then occupied the Jewish state in 63 B.C. Finally, Octavian (later called Augustus when the Roman Republic formally turned into an empire, with him as the head) defeated the last Ptolemaic queen, Cleopatra, and her Roman husband, Mark Antony in 31 B.C. and created the Roman province of Egypt.

The incorporation of the Middle East (excluding Iran and Arabia and usually Mesopotamia and Armenia) into the Roman Empire sometimes is considered the end of the Hellenistic period. In reality, the Roman is an extension of the Hellenistic age, which lasted until the Arab Muslims displaced Roman rule in Egypt and Syria in the seventh century A.D. (and longer in the case of Anatolia). Just as Hellenic civilization continued to predominate in the East, the *lingua franca* there continued to be Greek. This resulted in a new bifurcation of the Hellenic world into a Latin West and a Greek "East" (both Greece and the East proper) that later was perpetuated by a division of the Empire into eastern and western halves and eventually by a schism of the main body of the Christian Church along Latin (Roman Catholic) and Greek (Orthodox) lines. Yet this overlooks the basic cultural unity of Greece and Rome that makes them both "Western" in the broad sense, in contrast to the Middle East.

Some earlier patterns of rule survived. The *poleis* continued to be the mark of Hellenism. Many new *poleis* came into existence, such as the city of Berytus (Beirut), whose law school made it one of the greatest centers of intellectual life. Ironically, it was not until A.D. 197, under Roman rule, that Alexandria got a truly Hellenic form of *polis* government. Provinces were organized under the control of proconsuls. Tax-farmers (*publicani*, "publicans") extorted all they could from the public, keeping everything over a fixed amount for themselves. Client kingdoms were another feature of Roman rule, although there was a tendency for these to be transformed into provinces.

Egypt continued to be ruled along the Ptolemaic pattern. The country was still essentially a large plantation, with its grain flowing to Rome to provide a major part of the food supply. Forced labor and the requisitioning of property made life hard for the peasants, who periodically went on strike or fled the land when the yoke became too great. Peasant revolts were endemic to Egypt, but the geography of the country made suppression easy. Among other changes, the Romans introduced some private ownership of land, which produced absentee landlords.

If Egypt was the most exploited province, Judea was the most troublesome area for the Romans. At first the new conquerors made it a client state (taking away some of the territories outside Judea proper) under King Herod, the son of an Idumaean soldier. Ruling for thirty three years, Herod acted like a Jewish king by building a new, enlarged Temple in Jerusalem, but his real face was turned westward as he built Hellenic theaters and hippodromes and sponsored Roman-style games. His new city of Caesarea, on the Mediterranean, was graced by Roman gods and goddesses. For Toynbee, Herod became the prototype of the ruler who chooses to emulate a dominant, intrusive civilization, though (unlike some later "Herodians," who intended to learn from intruders in order to resist them) this king of Judea was a willing collaborator with the occupiers. His cruelty made him so detested that, after his death in 4 B.C., some of his former subjects asked for full incorporation into the Roman Empire rather than have another ruler from this family, and indeed Judea became a part of the province of Syria in A.D. 6.

A new, uncompromising Jewish faction, the Zealots, emerged. Their approach was to devote themselves increasingly to the traditions that their foreign rulers and native collaborators violated. For Toynbee, the Zealots became the prototype of a more general "Zealot" approach that rejects the influence of an intruding civilization. Although some Zealots in the Toynbeean sense have been politically docile, the original ones were not; with an unparalleled nationalistic fanaticism they suicidally hurled themselves against the occupiers. Judea and the newly Jewish Galilee were scenes of revolt with little letup from the time the Romans first arrived.

The Jewish revolt reached its zenith in A.D. 66–70. After a long siege by Roman forces, Zealot-held Jerusalem finally succumbed. Many thousands of Jews died or were sold into slavery, and Herod's Temple was destroyed. Zealots in the mountain fortress of Masada held out for three more years and chose to commit mass suicide rather then to surrender.

A Zealot named Simon Bar Kokhba, hailed as the Messiah, led another revolt in 132–135. Suppression ended with the exile of the remaining Jews from Judea, although some Jews remained in parts of Palestine lying outside their homeland. Galilee in particular retained a substantial Jewish minority for a while and became the home of an important rabbinical school and the seat of the patriarch, who was the official leader of the Jewish community in the empire until the fifth century. With periodic conversion adding to the widespread Jewish community, whose membership came generally to be defined in religious terms, the national connection of the Jews with their ancient coreligionists became a moot point, but they continued to identify themselves as the "People of Israel," whom a future Messiah would restore to the "Land of Israel."

TIES WITH THE WORLD AT LARGE

Despite political divisions, the Middle East increasingly was tied together and connected with the rest of the world. From the time of Alexander, Hellenism was a force that united the dominant rungs of society in Mediterranean Europe, the Middle East, India, and parts of Central Asia. Even when Hellenism weakened in its easternmost reaches, new commerical routes supplemented the old ones to bring a wider world into contact. Increased prosperity among a small segment of society brought greater traffic in luxuries, which further created lucrative rewards for traders and for the cities along the trade routes.

Trade with India, which exported spices and a variety of other products, was a long-established part of life in the Mediterranean region. The goods came overland through the Hindu-Kush along a route that passed through Bactria and Iran or else came by sea to Mesopotamia. Other Indian spices came to southern Arabia to be loaded on north-bound caravans. There was a network of ancient caravan routes connecting different parts of the Middle East. Goods moved farther west from ports such as Berytus and Alexandria or else along the land route through Anatolia. Ptolemaic domination of the Red Sea provided an alternative to land routes from southern Arabia, and the Romans (or possibly the last Ptolemies) began direct shipping to India, no longer staying near the coast. During the early period of Roman rule, ships from Egypt also reached China.

China's contact with the Middle East had been indirect up to this time. But by about 100 B.C., the expanding Han Empire overlapped the territory in Central Asia that Alexander had once conquered. A Chinese ambassador appeared in the Kushan Empire soon after its establishment, and Chinese silk started moving along a regular caravan route—the Silk Road—to the Kushan Empire, continuing across the Parthian Empire and on through northern Mesopotamia and Syria to the Mediterranean. Chinese silk became an important luxury item throughout the Mediterranean world, but sixth-century Christian missionaries smuggled silkworms into the Roman lands of the Middle East, which developed their own silk industry.

TWO TIERS OF INTELLECTUAL TRADITION

The Middle East was the scene of remarkable intellectual activity during the Hellenistic-Roman era. Alexandria, with its museum and 700,000-volume library (finally burned by a Christian, antipagan mob in the late fourth century) was probably the greatest intellectual center of the time. Yet the flowering was among Hellenes, who were alien to the indigenous culture of the region. Although some of these were Hellenized Easterners rather than the Greek colonists, the vast majority of the Easterners were at most little affected by the dominant Greek civilization. Only in parts of western Anatolia were native languages displaced by everyday Greek speech.

The indigenous traditions retained their creativity in some places. Babylonian astronomers made some important discoveries during the third century B.C., and Akkadian writing in cuneiform appeared as late as the first century A.D. Aside from the Apocrypha, several books of the Old Testament were written during the post-Alexander period.

By A.D. 200, the greatest creativity was to be found neither in Europe nor in the Middle East, but in India under the Gupta dynasty. Indian religious and philosophical concepts penetrated many schools of thought in the Mediterranean world. The Indian game of chess and several Indian agricultural innovations spread to the Middle East. Most of all, the Indians' development of the zero completed the number system that came to be called "Arabic."

While the Middle East remained submerged politically and intellectually, its religions spread westward. From Syria came the cult of the Invincible Sun, while Roman emperors built temples to Isis in the capital. Anatolia contributed the cult of Cybele, and the worship of Mithra came from Iran, as did the doctrine of Manichaeism, whose name derived from its founder, Mani, believed to be the "seal of the prophets." The Manichaean dualism that stressed the polarity of Ahura Mazda and the evil Ahriman was an outgrowth of Zoroastrianism, but in combination with Christian, Buddhist, and other influences. Judaism also proved attractive, and some Jews engaged in widespread proselytism. While full conversion was limited by the reluctance of most people to assume the obligations of an alien legal system, a large semi-Judaized group, called the Reverent Ones, was found in cities throughout the Mediterranean region.

Christianity was the most successful Oriental religion. It started as a Jewish sect but soon outgrew the parent religion as missionaries turned to the conversion of the world. The small group of Christians who insisted on remaining a sect of Judaism, observing the Mosaic Law, soon withered away. Following a long period of rivalry by other Oriental religions and periodic outbreaks of anti-Christian persecution, the Emperor Constantine gave Christianity recognition in 313, and he later was baptized. This religion now was clearly displacing paganism, especially in the Roman Middle East and somewhat more slowly in the West. Thus, paradoxically, from the period of Hellenic dominance came a strong Oriental strain that transformed Hellenism and became a fundamental part of subsequent European civilizations.

The East-West interaction was nevertheless a reciprocal one. In becoming the religion of a Hellenic-dominated world, Christianity was put in Hellenic dress. To make their religion meaningful to those with Greek education, the Christians explained that Christ was the "Word [*Logos*] of God." The *Logos*, a polestar of Greek thought, described the concept of a rational ordering of the universe. Thus the divine nature of Christ was identical with the impersonal God of the philosophers. On this point, the Jewish Philo of Alexandria, a contemporary of Jesus, had prepared the way by identifying the *Logos* as the Word (and, figuratively, the Son) of God. The gospel was spread by a New Testament written, not in Aramaic or Hebrew, but in Greek, and thinkers continued to reconcile their Hellenic and Christian heritages.

RULE FROM BYZANTIUM

In 330 Constantine moved the capital of the Roman Empire to a "New Rome"—Constantinople—on the site of the old Greek town of Byzantium. With the practice of appointing a coemperor for the largely peripheral western provinces, which eventually were overrun by barbarian Germanic tribes, the unity of the empire came to be a legal fiction. What west Europeans called the "Byzantine" Empire was thus the continuation of the state of the first Caesars, although in many ways it was increasingly transformed. The state long had ceased to be one in which one city ruled over the rest, as all the free population possessed citizenship by the early third century. There were even emperors of Oriental origin, including Philip the Arab in the mid-third century.

The basic Hellenic character of the empire remained intact. The capital had only moved closer to the original home of Hellenism. Although the sixth-century Emperor Justinian temporarily restored imperial control over most of the western Mediterranean littoral, the empire that continued to subordinate the Orient was increasingly a Greek rather than a Latin one.

Christianity permeated the civilization of the empire. This was an age of building great churches, with massive round domes set atop square structures. The Church of the Holy Sepulchre in Jerusalem, which embraces the reputed site of Christ's crucifixion and burial, and the Church of the Nativity in Bethlehem, both constructed by Constantine, have remained landmarks of the Christian faith. The magnificent Hagia Sophia, built by Justinian in Constantinople, represents the height of Byzantine ecclesiastical architecture. Icons and church paintings of the Good Shepherd and the Holy Virgin also demonstrate the dominant trends of the period.

Oriental influences increasingly infiltrated the empire's Hellenic character. The government absorbed forms such as prostration before the ruler from Eastern monarchies even before the capital was moved to the Bosporus. The autonomy of the *poleis* gradually faded away. The Christian art and architecture of the period shows heavy Eastern, particularly Iranian and Armenian, influences. Literary and artistic activity largely took place in the non-European parts of the empire, and indigenous forces were bound to show through.

A HELLENIC-ORIENTAL RELIGIOUS SPLIT

Religious schisms within Christianity provided an outlet for the assertion of Eastern distinctiveness. The great issue of the age was the nature of Christ, that is, whether He was divine or human and, if both, how they could belong to the same person. In what seems to have been largely an ideological disguise for nationalistic and cultural dissatisfaction, doctrines eventually determined to be heretical by a Hellenic-dominated church invariably gained overwhelming support in Egypt, Syria, and the less Hellenized parts of Anatolia. Even the third-century heresy known as Arianism, the doctrine that Christ was created and was thus a lesser being than God, had widespread support in the East, although other heterodoxics soon took its place.

Fourth-century Antioch produced the doctrine that Christ has the two completely separate natures of God and human. Nestorianism, as this belief is known, was rejected by the Third Ecumenical Council in 431. Now persecuted by the Roman government, many Nestorians fled to the Sasanian (Persian) Empire and organized their own church hierarchy, with Syriac (a form of Aramaic) as its liturgical language. This became the predominant form of Christianity in the Persian Empire, with many adherents particularly in the Mesopotamian region.

Then another movement, Monophysitism, appeared. According to this doctrine, Christ has only one nature, the divine, which has completely displaced the human aspect. This swept through the Eastern part of the Roman Empire and continued to prevail there even after the Fourth Ecumenical Council rejected it in 451 in favor of a declaration that Christ has two inseparable natures. While some emperors sought Eastern support by espousing either Monophysitism or a compromise doctrine, the Monophysites knew only persecution after Justinian's death in 565 and were ready to greet a foreign deliverer.

Separate Monophysite churches came into being. The Egyptian (Coptic) Church was the largest and eventually predominated in Ethiopia too. The ancient Egyptian language, Coptic (now using the Greek alphabet), was adopted for liturgical purposes. In Syria, the Monophysites, sometimes known as the Jacobites, established the Syriac Church, although a few Syrians followed Constantinople's lead. The church in Armenia, which had become the world's first Christian land in the early fourth century, mistakenly often has been labeled "Monophysite," although it took an intermediate position in the dispute.

Religious divisions were not the only sign of weakness. Wars exhausted the economy, and the government's consequent fiscal problems led to heavier taxes and more suffering. An outbreak of the plague in the 540s depopulated whole cities. Corruption and anarchy ate at the heart of the empire.

SASANIAN IRAN

The third century saw a resurgence of Iran under a new dynasty, the Sasanians. Ruling from Mesopotamia to northern India, they posed as restorers of the empire of the Achaemenids. And in many ways this was an assertion of Iranian traditions vis-à-vis Hellenism, although there was no attempt to uproot the influence of the latter. As late as the sixth century, the Sasanians gave refuge to Greek philosophers, whose school in Athens was closed, and Greek as well as Sanskrit works were translated into Pahlavi. A new Pahlavi literature also emerged.

Zoroastrianism became the Sasanian state religion. What was in effect a Zoroastrian Church came into existence for the first time, with the priests who maintained the sacred fire organized along hierarchical lines. Adherents to other religions sometimes met severe persecution. These included Christians, Jews, and Buddhists, although such groups continued to exist and even were allowed autonomy under their own religious leaders, who collected a special tax for the state. Native Iranian heresies, including Manichaeism and the sixth-century communist doctrine of Mazdakeanism, faced much harsher measures and were forced underground.

By the sixth century, signs of decay were evident. The last great Sasanian king, Khusraw Nushirwan, whose reign (531–578) superficially appears as the high point of the four-century period, was unable to stem the tide of collapse. He undermined the power of the great lords in an attempt to consolidate central control, but instead his successors found the petty nobles (*dihqans*) entrenched even more securely in their feudal domains. The many wars sapped the empire's strength, and increasingly high taxes bore down on the poor. Society had become rigid, with a caste system of priests, soldiers, scribes, and commoners that undermined the loyalty of the masses to the state. Mazdakeanism was one reaction to social injustice. The rich agricultural land of southern Mesopotamia, long the economic mainstay, became less productive, and the cultivation of silkworms in the Roman Empire reduced Sasanian revenues from the formerly lucrative Silk Road. Rigid rules of behavior and a backward-looking attitude epitomized the period's stagnation. Rivals fought for the throne of an empire that now hardly offered viable hope for an Eastern upsurge.

Rome and Iran, the two greatest empires west of China, faced each other in perennial combat. The two armies sometimes seesawed from Syria to western Iran. The Christianization of the Roman Empire gave the conflict a religious dimension, with Christians sometimes seen as a Roman fifth column. But with the Christian schism, Nestorians became free of suspicion in the Sasanian state and even became an instrument to subvert the Western enemy.

In 602 Shah Khusraw Parvis started the last Sasanian offensive against the Romans. For a time it seemed that the enemy would be completely overrun. But as the two giants exhausted themselves, their common nemesis soon was to come from an unsuspected direction.

TURKS ON THE HORIZON

Central Eurasia might have seemed to be a potential source of a reorganized Middle East. Instead of the Aryan tribes that had predominated since 2000 B.C., a new ethnic, linguistic element appeared from farther east. These different peoples spoke languages that modern scholars call Altaic or Uralic-Altaic, from their location between the Ural and Altai mountains. First were the Turkish-speaking Huns, in the fourth century, who overran the old Kushan territories. Other Turks dominated the steppe by the sixth century and began to penetrate the area just north of the Oxus River. They eventually were to transform the Middle East, just as tribesmen from both Central Eurasia and the Arabian Peninusla had done so often before. But the turn of the latter region came first, and it is to there that one must look for an alternative to the two dying empires.

ARABIA: CRADLE OF EASTERN RESURGENCE

Because of its size and desert climate, the Arabian Peninsula had been the area least affected by Middle Eastern civilization or by Hellenism. Tribes of Arabian origin had established empires, but Arabia itself never had been the seat of a major empire. Neither had outsiders controlled large parts of the peninsula for long. Still, an image of ancient Arabia as a civilizational vacuum inhabited only by nomads would be highly inaccurate, as recent archaeological findings make ever more clear. The Persian Gulf coast in particular was the site of sophisticated commercial centers on the route to the Indus Valley in the period of the Sumerians.

Southern Arabia was the the home of an elaborate civilization from at least the eighth century B.C. Of the various southern Arabian kingdoms, Saba (Sheba) was the largest and tended to dominate the others. Dams and terraced mountains supported an agricultural society. The Sabaeans also provided an important link in world commerce by bringing Indian spices by sea to Southern Arabia and exporting them, together with Arabian frankincense and myrrh, along caravan routes to the Mediterranean world.

Southern Arabia was in decline as a new dynasty, the Himyarites, dominated the country from the second century B.C. to the sixth century A.D. While legend attributes this to the breaking of the vital Ma'rib Dam, the more complex set of reasons for decline included Roman commercial competition, recurrent Ethiopian invasions, the rise of feudal challenges to royal power, and nomadic encroachments from the north. Many South Arabians turned nomadic and formed a diaspora throughout the peninsula.

The rest of Arabia was the home of nomadism *par excellence*. The tribes in the north were classified, often without much factual basis, as northern (Adnani) and southern (Qahtani) Arabs—that is, those indigenous to the area and those who had migrated from the south. These bedouin, literally desert people, were essentially like the earlier, non-Arab Semitic nomads that appeared in the Fertile Crescent. Although Arabic was the last Semitic language committed to writing, it may in some ways be older than the others. It spread south by the seventh century to supplant the ancient South Arabian language.[5] Thus if language is the criterion, the South Arabians were only belatedly Arabized, although legend reverses the distinction between northern and southern tribes. The latter, supposedly descended from Qahtan, a great-great-great-grandson of Noah, were known as "Arab Arabs," while the former, who traced their lineage to Adnan and his father, Ishmael (Isma'il), the son of Abraham (Ibrahim), were called "Arabized [i.e., assimilated as] Arabs."

Several Arab kingdoms emerged in the steppelands adjacent to the Fertile Crescent. Arab tribes known as the Nabataeans established the Kingdom of Petra, in southern Transjordan, in the sixth century B.C. Astride the north-south trade route, Petra became a flourishing center of commerce and civilization. At their zenith, the Nabataeans ruled much of the Syrian interior, including Damascus, and resisted attacks by several Hellenistic rulers. But they eventually became a client state of Rome, providing a convenient way for Rome to maintain order on its desert frontier. Vassal status gave way to complete absorption into the Roman Empire as Provincia Arabia in 195 A.D.

Another Arab client state of Rome was based in Palmyra, an oasis in the Syrian Desert. The Palmyrans controlled a trade route that connected Mesopotamia with the Mediterranean, and protection for the caravans provided a lucrative source of income. In the third century, King Udaynath became vice-emperor of the Roman Empire, but the excessive ambitions of his widow, Queen Zenobia, who later temporarily drove the Roman legions out of most of the Middle East, ended with the downfall of Palmyra in 272.

At least three other Arab kingdoms should be mentioned. The Byzantines relied on a buffer state, the Ghassanids, allegedly of South Arabian origin, in the Syrian interior to guard the Arabian frontiers until the early seventh century. The Ghassanids became Christians, as did another "Southern" group, the Lakhmids, who performed a similar buffer role on the Sasanian frontier. In Central Arabia, other South Arabian tribes formed the Kingdom of Kindah for a while during the fifth century as allies of the decaying Himyarites.

Three cities—Mecca, Ta'if, and Yathrib (later called Madina)—emerged in the Hijaz, the coastal region[6] north of Yemen. The largest of these, Mecca, was located at the intersection of the Yemen-to-Syria route and a less important east-

---

[5]The South Arabian language has been preserved in some local vernaculars, particularly on the South Yemeni island of Socotra.

[6]Strictly speaking, the Hijaz does not refer to the immediate coastal region but only to the nearby mountain "barrier."

west route. After centuries of decline, the north-south route gained a renewed role in the sixth century, as Roman commerce on the Red Sea dwindled and as the northern routes were interrupted by Roman-Sasanian warfare. Mecca's brackish well of Zamzam made the city a convenient stop for parched caravans. The clans of the tribe of Quraysh, which settled there during the sixth century, became the predominant element of the population. Qurayshi merchants avidly engaged in commerce and came to control a major part of the caravan traffic, especially on the Mecca-to-Syria link. A council of clan chiefs governed the city.

Mecca was also a religious center. A cube-shaped building, the Ka'bah, housed a black stone venerated by pilgrims from all over Arabia, and idols of various tribes were placed there. According to tradition, Adam first built this sanctuary, and Abraham and Ishmael restored it. The Arabs' lunar year included the Month of the Pilgrimage, during which worshippers performed prescribed rites (the Greater Pilgrimage) that included a procession to the nearby Plain of Arafat and the sacrifice of sheep. A distinct ritual, the Lesser Pilgrimage, included the circumambulation of the Ka'bah and kissing the black stone. Both pilgrimages later became part of the religion of Islam, while the ceremonies at the Ka'bah also were combined with the Greater Pilgrimage.

Animistic religious concepts still predominated in most of Arabia. Invisible humanlike, and usually evil, spirits, called *jinn* were believed to share the world with people and sometimes to possess their bodies.

Other religions gradually gained favor. Christianity percolated into Arabia from the Ghassanids and the Lakhmids, as well as from Ethiopia. Judaism also had footholds at Khaybar Oasis, in the north, and at Mecca's rival city, Yathrib. The latter was founded by Jewish tribes, although pagan tribes, mainly the Aws and the Khazraj (both known as southern Arabs), later settled there. Unlike Mecca, Yathrib was a cluster of separate agricultural communities sharing a large oasis, without much unity. Yemen also underwent partial Judaization, and the last Himyarite kings converted to this religion.

The concept of one God was familiar to many Arabs. Mecca's main deity was known simply as The God (to translate literally the Arabic word *Allah,* which is used by all Arabic-speaking monotheists). According to Arab tradition, the Ka'bah originally had been devoted to the worship of God alone. While there were people called *Hanifs* who preached a local form of monotheism, the idea of God was normally combined with the concept of many lesser gods that included his daughters, Allat ("the goddess"), Manat, and Uzzah.

Later Arabs called the pre-Islamic period, particularly the sixth and the early seventh centuries in Arabia, the *Jahiliyyah,* literally "the Age of Ignorance." With the decline of South Arabia, the peninsula had relatively little civilization, but while literacy was somewhat rare, a city like Mecca can hardly be called barbarian. Still, from a Muslim point of view, this was an age of ignorance of "true religion." Certain pre-Islamic customs also seem barbaric to Muslims, a case in point being the practice of burying unwanted baby girls alive, a survival of the infanticide that was common elsewhere in ancient times.

Poetry experienced a remarkable development, and the verses of this Heroic Age—"the Days of the Arabs"—never have ceased to reverberate from Arab tongues. This poetry presented vivid, if romanticized, images of Arabia at the time and of the bedouin culture and its values. Courage, eloquence, unquestioning loyalty to the tribe, undying revenge against enemies, help for the weak, idealization of the hard life, extremes of hospitality, pride in noble ancestry and the virtues of one's people, and glorification of romantic love and sexual prowess are recurring themes.

Poetry was no avocation of the cultured few. Poets were great popular heroes, believed to possess magic gained from the *jinn* that inhabited their bodies. And indeed the words, repeated by professional reciters, seemed to work magic on the listeners. The verses not only related tales of intertribal vendettas but were seen as veritable weapons in these conflicts, as satires and lampoons were thought to wound the enemy against which they were written. Poetry contests highlighted the annual twenty-day fair at Ukaz, near Mecca, with fighting forbidden as representatives of all tribes came together in a fantastic expression of Arab cultural unity.

Poetry achieved its zenith in the form of the highly stylized *Qasidah,* or Ode. The *Qasidahs* of seven poets have come down to us as the Suspended Poems, or the Golden Odes, since they are said to have won the annual prize and, inscribed in gold letters, to have hung on the door of the Ka'bah.

Arabia increasingly was involved in world politics. Cities like Mecca played the Romans and the Sasanians off against each other. From the fourth century on, international rivalry took on a religious coloring, with Jews and Nestorians favoring the Persians. Despite the Monophysites' persecution in the Roman Empire, Constantinople supported them elsewhere against Nestorians and non-Christians. By the early sixth century, religious intolerance appeared on all sides. While the Christian town of Najran persecuted those who would not adopt its faith, the Jewish King Dhu al-Nuwas of the Himyarites persecuted the Christians, allegedly incinerating some of them alive. Ethiopia invaded Yemen to help its coreligionists as well as to gain control of the trade routes, and Ethiopian rule there lasted for half a century.

In a row started because of rivalry between his new church and the Ka'bah as religious centers, an Ethiopian governor named Abraha sent elephant-borne troops to attack Mecca in about 570, but they were unsuccessful. In the same year a future prophet, Muhammad, of the Hashimite clan of the Quraysh tribe, was born there. But Ethiopian control soon gave way to a Sasanian invasion of Yemen, which became a loosely governed satrapy of the shah.

CONCLUSIONS

Beginning with the Neolithic Revolution, which started about ten thousand years ago, the Middle East was continuously in the forefront of human progress. After the Middle East went on to invent civilized life about five thousand years ago, it was the central stage of world history for the next two and a half millennia. During this time, separate Middle Eastern societies gradually merged on both the political and the civilizational levels, while non-Middle Eastern civilizations caught up.

Certain aspects of Hellenic civilization enabled it to dominate the Middle East for about a millennium, beginning in the fourth century B.C. Hellenism became the elite culture of the area and left an indelible imprint. Still, this was only a veneer over the largely dormant cultures of the East, which had in the meantime left their own permanent marks on the West.

The Middle East increasingly was part of a wider world. A common experience with Hellenization reinforced the ties of Europe, the Middle East, and India, and none was immune from the cultural influences emanating from the others. Also, for the first time the Far East came into direct contact with the other civilizations.

At the beginning of the seventh century, the Middle East had still not regained the role it had held in the ancient world. A limited Eastern reaction against Hellenism had taken place in Iran under the Sasanians, but internal decay eventually set in. Sectarian divisions within Christianity provided outlets for Syrian and Egyptian distinctiveness vis-à-vis the West, but these countries offered neither the military means nor the cultural creativity necessary to lead an overall Eastern upsurge. Instead, a lasting revival of Middle Eastern civilization and power was destined to come from outside the old centers of civilization from among tribes possessing intense solidarity and a fresh approach. The Turkish tribes of Central Eurasia already loomed on the horizon. Of more immediate importance was the Arabian Peninsula, with its Arab tribes, who now showed an exceptional cultural effervescence. With leadership and inspiration the Arabs could climax the ancient process of invasion and renewal by Semitic tribes.

2
The East Reborn
610-750

Sasanian armies were pushing fast into Roman (Byzantine) territories in A.D. 610. The Roman military governor of northwestern Africa, Heraclius, had already taken upon himself the task of stemming the empire's decline and launched a revolt that Roman forces in other provinces soon joined. But as Heraclius occupied Constantinople and began a new imperial dynasty, the Sasanian advance accelerated. Wracked by Monophysite dissatisfaction with Orthodox doctrines that reflected the age-old dichotomy between East and West, Syria and Egypt rapidly succumbed to the invading army. Persian forces in Jerusalem destroyed the Church of the Holy Sepulchre and carried the "True Cross" to Ctesiphon, the Sasanian winter capital. Another Sasanian army fought its way across Anatolia and encamped across the Bosporus from Constantinople in 614.

In a brilliant offensive, Heraclius's forces sailed to the eastern end of the Black Sea in 622. They invaded Sasanian domains via the Caucasus and reached the outskirts of Ctesiphon in 628. After Shah Khushru Parviz was murdered by his own men, a succession of short-lived rulers sat on the shaky Persian throne. Later legends of visions and signs portending disaster carry a ring of poetic truth. A peace settlement of 630 restored the conquered provinces to Constantinople and the "True Cross" to Jerusalem.

The two great empires were left exhausted by this veritable fast-motion replay of earlier encounters between the Eastern and Hellenic worlds. And Heraclius was

THE MIDDLE EAST, ABOUT A.D. 600

—— Approximate Boundaries of the
Roman and Sasanian Empires

not destined to repeat the feats of Alexander, for seemingly unimportant events in a heretofore remote Arabia combined with the weakened condition of the two empires to make way for a new Middle Eastern order that would destroy the Sasanian Empire and leave the Roman Empire truncated almost beyond recognition. Arab client states that had stabilized the desert frontier were vanishing as the Sasanians abolished the Lakhmid kingdom in 602 and the Romans could no longer afford to restore their subsidies to the Ghassanids following the repulsion of the Persians. As early as 611, greater events to come were presaged when Arab tribesmen defeated a Sasanian force in southern Iraq. But few would have guessed that Arabia was to provide a new synthesis for Middle Eastern culture and lead the region in a reassertion of its pre-Hellenistic primacy.

MUHAMMAD'S MESSAGE

A renewed Middle East began to form in 610 as a voice[1], afterward identified as that of the Angel Gabriel, commanded a forty-year-old Meccan, Muhammad, to "Recite!" The scene of this event, which in the long run would dwarf the significance of the change of dynasty in Constantinople the same year, was a mountain outside Mecca where Muhammad had sometimes sought quiet and privacy in order to contemplate about matters that troubled him. His familiarity with Christians and Jews (subsequently known by Muslims as "Peoples of the Book"), together with his serious, reflective nature, had perhaps brought Muhammad to see the need of the still largely animistic Arabs for a holy book of their own, in the Arabic language. Himself an orphan reared by his grandfather and later by his uncle, Abu Talib, Muhammad was sensitive to the plight of the unfortunate and was sickened by the money-grubbing practices of the large merchants, whose prosperity caused them to forget their former egalitarian tribal values.

Although active in commerce, Muhammad's Hashimite clan was one of the relatively poor and uninfluential divisions of the Quraysh tribe that dominated the city. Muhammad is said to have accompanied his uncle's caravan to Syria at the age of twelve, and of the many legends about his early life, one of the most quoted is that of the Syrian Christian monk who noticed that a cloud moved with the boy to protect him from the sun and who found the signs of a prophet on his back. Muhammad's profound intelligence and admirable character, which earned him the nickname Amin ("Trustworthy") eventually brought him success in the business world, leading caravans to and from Syria. One employer, a forty-year-old widow named Khadijah, was so impressed with Muhammad, who was fifteen years her junior, that she asked him to marry her. Not only did the marriage give Muhammad the economic security that permitted him to devote his mind to religious matters, but as a woman of elevated character, Khadijah was subsequently one of her husband's

---

[1]It is not for the historian to say whether such a statement is literally true. The non-Muslim, in particular, may choose a rational explanation, but no fair-minded person believes that Muhammad was insincere.

greatest sources of strength. Muhammad was deeply devoted to Khadijah and took no other wife as long as she lived.

At first Muhammad was confused by the voice. Fearing that he was mad, thoughts of suicide kept passing through his mind. One of Khadijah's cousins, who probably was a *Hanif,* advised her that the revelations were like those of the biblical prophets, and she reassured her husband. Indeed, she became his first convert, followed by his ten-year-old cousin, Ali, who lived in Muhammad's house and ever remained one of his most devout followers. Others who heeded Muhammad's warnings included persons who lacked the protection that only kinship ties could provide in this tribal society as well as members of weak clans and even some less influential members of the leading units. Uthman ibn Affan, of the dominant Umayyad clan, is an example of the latter. The mild-mannered Abu Bakr, a successful merchant, was another of Muhammad's early followers.

Muhammad's prophetic experiences continued at irregular intervals. Sometimes he heard a voice, accompanied by a "ringing of bells"; at other times he had visions or even felt intense pain and fell to the ground in a trance. Following these occurrences, he conveyed passages of rhymed prose to his followers, who committed them to memory. Sometimes these passages (the Qur'an, "recitation," as they are collectively known) were written down on whatever material was at hand, and only after the Prophet's death were they collected in one book. The non-Muslim reader may find translations of the Qur'an dull and sometimes incomprehensible. The later arbitrary arrangement of 114 *suras,* or chapters (except for the short "Opening" one) in order of length, with some *suras* consisting of separate, unrelated revelations, makes a cover-to-cover reading as unrewarding as, say, reading a Christian hymnal in the same fashion. And, in fact, the Qur'an is a book of separate devotional readings. Perhaps more than any other literary work, the Qur'an loses its impact in translation, and most Muslims reject the very possibility of translating it. Even if non-Arabic speaking Muslims sometimes use another language version to explain the meaning of the passages that they "read" (pronounce) in the original, the translation is not, in their view, really the Qur'an. Muslim doctrine holds that the chapters of the Arabic Qur'an are taken letter-for-letter from a book in Heaven.

In the original Arabic the Qur'an's effect is almost hypnotic. It was the only "miracle" that Muhammad produced as proof of his prophethood. It was said that all "men and jinn" together could not compose such a work, and indeed no person since has succeeded in producing a piece of literature with the same impact or one that is read and recited so much. For Muslims, who today number about one fifth of the inhabitants of the Earth, a final proof that the book came by way of revelation is the alleged fact, which skeptics question in view of his business activity, that Muhammad did not even know how to read and write.

The essentials of a new monotheistic faith were taking shape. It was in the tradition of Judaism and Christianity, and Muslims ("those who submit") do not see their religion, Islam ("Submission" to God), as starting with Muhammad, who is rather the "seal" ("last") of a series of prophets or messengers and, of course, only a man. (Muslims often resent uninformed references to them as "Muhammadans," which may incorrectly imply that they worship Muhammad the way Christians worship Christ.) Submission included prayer, although the requirement of five daily prayers at specified times, was not fixed at the beginning. Earlier prophets such as Adam, Abraham, Moses, and Jesus, and those who submitted to the messages conveyed by God through them are also considered to have been Muslims. Just as the nonbeliever may conclude that many passages in the Qur'an are garbled versions of Biblical stories, the devout Muslim believes that the Christian and Jewish scriptures were revealed to earlier prophets but have been tampered with since their revelation. To a great extent, Christian and Muslim doctrines are similar. Thus, Muslims believe that Jesus was not only a prophet but also the Messiah, born of a virgin, ascended to Heaven without dying (the doctrine of the crucifixion is regarded as demeaning to such a great prophet), and will come again. But the idea that Jesus was the Son of God is adamantly rejected, and Muslims, who stress the oneness of God, view the Christian doctrine of the Trinity as smacking of polytheism.

Muhammad's early messages were particularly reminiscent of biblical concepts. The Last Judgment, he warned, was near, with human beings to be resurrected and rewarded in Paradise or punished in the flames of Hell. God is all-powerful and righteous, to be feared, but "beneficent and merciful." In return for God's goodness people are expected to be generous with the needy and, seemingly with the rich in mind, the Prophet warned against pride and ungratefulness. People are to worship God, and the ritual of prayer—involving a repeated sequence of kneeling and prostration until the forehead touches the ground—was evolving.[2]

From the beginning, Islam incorporated indigenous Arabian features. Not unlike other local monotheists, the Muslims performed the pilgramage to the Ka'bah. Belief in *jinn*—some of whom are said to have also converted to Islam at one point—joined with Judeo-Zoroastrian-Christian concepts of angels, Satan (the leader of the evil *jinn* or *shaytans*), and the like. Although numerous social reforms were later pushed, Muhammad took for granted many of the practices of his people.

Most Meccans, particularly the leaders of the influential merchant families, rejected Muhammad's message and became increasingly hostile. They disliked attacks on their selfish behavior. They also resented claims of prophethood made by a person of modest social status and even feared that acceptance of his message would give him a position of political leadership. Some Meccans were offended by attacks on their ancestral practices. Muhammad's frank admission, after being put on the spot by a clever opponent, that his own grandfather would be punished in Hell, was used against him. But perhaps economic motives were more important in creating opposition, as many feared that the pagan shrines, a major factor in Mecca's prosperity, would lose their attraction if the new doctrine gained acceptance. For a brief

[2]The "Five Pillars" sum up the basic duties of a Muslim. The first is a profession that "There is no god but God, and Muhammad is His Prophet." Although this alone is sufficient to make one a Muslim, there are the other pillars of prayer; giving alms (*zakat*, sometimes collected by Islamic governments); fasting during the month of Ramadan (total abstinence from food, drink, and sexual intercourse except at night); and for those who can afford it, making at least one pilgrimage (*hajj*) to Mecca, which involves circumambulating the Ka'bah and kissing the black stone, a trip to the Plain of Arafat, sacrificing a sheep, and other specified rituals on an annual occasion set aside for this purpose.

time Muhammad temporized. A new revelation proclaimed "God's three daughters"—deities central to the profitable pilgramage—to be intermediaries between God and humans. But Muhammad soon announced that he had been deceived by "Satanic verses" and henceforth stuck to his original strict monotheism.

Muhammad's increasing attacks on polytheism met still greater opposition. Islamic doctrines, like that of the resurrection, were ridiculed. Muslims were harassed and sometimes even murdered, especially if they lacked blood ties or were disowned by their own kin and were unable to find a clan to guarantee their protection. Meccan society still was stateless, and law and order rested on the threat of retaliation by a clan if one of its members or someone else given its protection was wronged. Possibly with the aim of starting a new commercial center to rival Mecca, one group of Muslim families migrated to Ethiopia. Muhammad was fortunate in having the Hashimite clan's protection as long as Abu Talib headed it, and for two years this clan even weathered an economic boycott by the others. New converts kept entering the fold, the most notable being Umar ibn al-Khattab, a tall, austere man of commanding mien who had once beaten his own sister for accepting Islam but afterwards became one of the most devoted Muslims. Among Muhammad's experiences in his last years in Mecca was his ascent in a dream to the "Seventh Heaven," transported on a winged horse via the site of Solomon's Temple in Jerusalem. This would lead future Muslims to consider Jerusalem's Temple Mount one of the holiest places. But in 619 Abu Talib died and his successor as head of the clan was bitterly opposed to the new religious movement. The death of Khadijah in the same year was another personal blow to Muhammad. He traveled to Ta'if in the hope of being given refuge there, only to have stones hurled at him as he left.

MUHAMMAD IN POWER

A turning point for the Muslims came in 620, when six men from Yathrib came to Mecca for the pilgrimage. These Yathribis were impressed with Muhammad's message, and they apparently hoped that he could provide leadership for their anarchy-ridden city, in which no one had authority over the separate tribes. Two years later (622), a larger group of Yathribis pledged to obey Muhammad and to fight with him. Thus, about the time of the Roman offensive against the Persians, the way was made clear for the Prophet to move his activities to Yathrib, and from that point on it was called Madina (*Madinat al-Nabi,* "the City of the Prophet").

The Emigration (*hijrah*) of the Muslims—literally a breaking of kinship ties and the establishment of new bonds—took place gradually and at first gained little notice. By September of the same year, only Muhammad and his close associates, Ali and Abu Bakr, remained behind. Now the Meccan leaders realized that something was happening and plotted to kill Muhammad, who, with Abu Bakr, slipped out at night and hid in a cave for three days before proceeding nine more days by camel to Madina. With the Prophet himself aiding in the work, the Emigrants (as those who left Mecca were termed) and the Helpers (as those Madinan Muslims came to be known) constructed Muhammad's modest brick house, whose courtyard became the center of congregational prayers, that is, the first mosque (*masjid,* "place of prayer").

With the *hijrah,* the Muslims were transformed from a persecuted minority into an autonomous religiopolitical community (*ummah*). The importance assigned to this development—epitomized by the fact that the year of the *hijrah* soon was designated as the Year One of the Islamic calendar—points to an important difference between Islam and Christianity. From the start, the concept of a division between religious and political authority ("God and Caesar") would have been foreign to Muhammad's thinking. According to the Muslim concept, all believers form a separate community (*ummah*) whose ties with each other are more basic than are any tribal, ethnic, or racial divisions. This *ummah* must have its own government, whose purpose is to enforce God's law (the *shari'ah,* literally, "the way"), to pursue God's purposes, and to help the members to find salvation.

The *ummah* was analogous to a new tribe, based on religion rather than kinship ties. Headed by Muhammad, the Emigrants were in effect one clan of the tribe. The so-called Constitution of Madina may not have existed in full at the beginning, but it shows some of the principles that are accepted as the basis of the *ummah*. The Constitution clearly enunciated the primacy of the whole community by providing that—unlike the old kinship system, in which each clan protected its members against outsiders—an offender against a member of another clan would be turned over for punishment.

This does not mean that a centralized government under Muhammad's rule was established at first. His chief political function for the whole *ummah* was that of arbitrating interclan disputes. Muhammad ruled his own "clan," although more as a democratic tribal *shaykh* than as a despot of a more advanced state. The Helpers accepted his authority when it was in the form of Qur'anic revelation. Most of the non-Jewish Madinan clans at least nominally embraced the new faith. But certain individuals called the "Hypocrites" remained hostile to Islam and the influence of the newcomers.

The Jewish clans were in an anomalous position in Madina. The Constitution made them part of the *ummah* and forbade any molestation of those who sided with the Muslims. Since they were already worshippers of one God, it probably did not occur to Muhammad to ask them to convert to Islam. Instead, he assumed that they would welcome him as a carrier of their common monotheistic message to the Arabs. His teachings underwent so much Jewish influence for a while that, in retrospect, one can imagine that Islam might have evolved into the status of a Jewish sect. The Muslims adopted the Jewish feast of Yom Kippur, as well as the Jewish practice of facing Jerusalem in prayer.

Instead of confirming Muhammad's message, the Madinan Jews recognized discrepancies between it and their own scriptures. By ridiculing his doctrines, they appeared as a threat to the new religion, and thus Muhammad emphasized the idea of Islam as a primordial religion of Abraham that preceded Judaism. Some Jewish elements in Islam were dropped, although Muslim scholars deny that this resulted from the break with the Jews. In any case, instead of Yom Kippur, the Muslims adopted the month of Ramadan (when Muhammad's first revelation occurred) as a period of fasting and turned to pray toward Mecca rather than Jerusalem. Although Islam does not require a weekly day of rest, Friday became the day of congregational noon prayer.

The Jewish clans became increasingly hostile to Muhammad and began to collaborate with his enemies. In turn, they received harsh treatment that contrasts with Islam's overall toleration of Jews and Christians. Those small clans of Jews who were not perceived as a threat continued to live in Madina, while two main clans were expelled and their land was taken over by the Emigrants. Men of another clan were executed and their women and children enslaved.

Muhammad continued to receive revelations in Madina. Those *suras* are generally distinguishable from the earlier, Meccan ones by being longer, often dealing with practical matters of the moment, and lacking an apocalyptic character. Reflecting Muhammad's responsibility as head of a political community, some of the Madinan *suras* are of a legislative type. While no changes were made in most customary rules, a number of changes were decreed in family law and other matters improving the status of women.

Some of the Qur'anic reforms were radical for the time, although their realistic compromises with tradition make the same rules objectionable to many today. Thus, while daughters previously had been excluded from inheritance, the Qur'an provided that they would receive half as much as sons. Although a variety of marriage customs had coexisted in pre-Islamic Arabia, there had often been no limit to the number of wives a man could have at one time. But now the Qur'an set four as a maximum. Even that was on the condition, labeled an impossibility, of completely equal treatment that some modernists now reread as a veiled prohibition. A man was permitted an unlimited number of sexual relationships with his own unmarried, willing slave girls, who gained a special status and eventual freedom after the birth of a child. Actually, Muhammad received a revelation excepting himself from the four-wife limitation and married several women after Khadijah's death, but most of these unions can be explained either as a charitable way of looking after the widows of Muslims killed in battle or else in terms of political connections with leading personalties and families. While Uthman married two of Muhammad's daughters and Ali married another, Fatimah, the Prophet wedded Abu Bakr's daughter, A'ishah, who at first was so young that she still played with dolls but later became his favorite wife.

Soon after the *hijrah,* Muhammad and the Emigrants began to make war on their native city. After all, raiding was an old tribal practice. More than that, the Emigrants had reason for revenge. In addition, they needed a new source of livelihood; they were attracted by the prospect not only of acquiring booty but possibly of taking control of the trade route. And they surely realized that their movement could not be a true success without incorporating Mecca and places beyond into the realm of Islam.

Before two years had passed, Muslim raiders met their first success. Members of a small party, having opened sealed instructions from the Prophet after their departure from Madina, attacked a Meccan caravan. This was during the annual truce, violation of which caused uneasiness in the *ummah* at first. But for Muhammad the old pagan customs were no longer binding, and this symbolized his break with the past. Besides, newly revealed verses approved the raid on the grounds that it was against those who persecuted the Muslims.

Soon afterward, a bigger victory ensued at Badr, south of Madina. A three hundred-man Muslim force, including Helpers, intercepted a large Meccan caravan led by the Umayyad chief, Abu Sufyan. Another Meccan, Abu Jahl, brought an army out of his city to join in the caravan's defense, and the Muslims were grossly outnumbered. But Muhammad planned the battle astutely, posting his forces at wells where the caravan would have to replenish its water supply. According to Muslim tradition, Muhammad's force was not outnumbered at all, as legions of angels fought by his side. The Meccans were routed, leaving the Muslims vast amounts of booty and, more important, evidence that God's help had made them invincible.

Muslim confidence was shaken in 625 by a Meccan force that sought revenge for Badr. Enticed out of Madina by the Meccans' pasturing their horses and camels in vital fields of unharvested grain, the Muslims again stood outnumbered—ten to one, it is said, in addition to a virtual lack of horses and armor—at the foot of the hill of Uhud. Although the Muslims prevailed at first, a tough, bloodthirsty Meccan cavalryman named Khalid ibn al-Walid took advantage of temporary confusion in one section of their army. Khalid broke through to attack the Muslims in the rear and inflicted severe casualties. Yet the Meccans, seemingly satisfied by avenging their earlier losses, departed from the field without pressing their victory. They knew that the complete defeat of the Muslim forces, now positioned on the hill, was beyond their capability, and the Muslim challenge to Mecca was left unbroken.

Then, at the Battle of the Trench (627), the Muslims frustrated a final attempt of Meccan-led tribes. A huge army, said to have numbered 10,000 men, headed for the Prophet's city. To hold back such a force, a defense tactic previously unknown in Arabia was proposed by a former Persian slave: to dig a deep ditch around the part of Madina that was not already protected by hills. The proposal was tried and it worked. The Meccan mainstay, the cavalry, could not cross, and after two weeks the entire army, now tired and running low on provisions, returned home.

The Meccan challenge was broken, and Meccan caravans no longer dared move to Syria. More and more tribes moved over to Muhammad's side, and his position in Madina was increasingly like that of a monarch. Even some Meccans wondered whether they should come to terms with their challenger, especially when they saw that Islam would not be a threat to the city's religious importance. Meanwhile Muhammad apparently realized that the administrative and commercial assets of his enemies would be valuable to the *ummah*. When Muhammad led a large group of Muslims toward Mecca in March 628 to celebrate the Lesser Pilgrimage, another battle appeared imminent, but envoys met the pilgrims just outside the city. A compromise was worked out whereby the Muslims would go back to Madina this time but would be allowed to make the pilgrimage a year later.

A ten-year truce was agreed upon, but Muslim power became increasingly irresistible. Expeditions to northwest Arabia imposed the Muslims' will on various tribes. A treaty with the Jews at Khaybar Oasis providing for tribute to Madina in return for protection became a precedent for subsequent toleration of Peoples of the Book. Opportunistic Meccans like Khalid and the crafty Amr ibn al-As came over to the Muslim side and were soon to be in command of Muslim armies. Even Abu Sufyan softened (the marriage of his daughter, an early Muslim, to Muhammad may have been helpful) and came to Madina to work out terms of surrender. When Muhammed led a large force into Mecca in 630 (the year Heraclius retook Jerusalem), he met scarcely any resistance and proceeded to grant amnesty to his former foes, who at least nominally accepted Islam, and to destroy all the idols in the Ka'bah.

The submission of Mecca accelerated the momentum of Muslim success. Ta'if soon surrendered too, and a confederation of tribes east of Mecca was broken by a large Muslim force. A "Year of Delegations" followed, as representatives of tribes or factions of tribes as far away as the Persian Gulf offered their fealty to Muhammad, but his effective rule never extended much further than western Arabia, and most of the tribes did not truly become Muslim. Even the Persian governor of Yemen submitted, although a revolt soon broke out there. Other challenges to Islam arose, notably the emergence of rival claimants to prophethood.

The seeds of bigger things to come could be seen. As the tribes joined together in one *ummah*, their tradition of internecine raids was to be turned outward into an ever wider circle of conquests. In late 630, Muhammad mustered a force of 30,000 fighters for a campaign in northwestern Arabia. A smaller force had already gone farther north for an unsuccessful encounter with Roman forces on the border of Syria, and the Prophet was preparing for a return engagement. While the story that Muhammad sent messages to Constantinople and Ctesiphon demanding submission may be apocryphal, such was the emerging challenge to the old empires in 632 when the Prophet suddenly became ill with a fever. He spent his last days in the apartment of A'ishah, where his breath stopped as his head lay on her lap.

ABU BAKR, THE CALIPHATE, AND CONSOLIDATION

Some Muslims could hardly believe that the Prophet was dead. But, as Abu Bakr reminded them that God was the object of their worship and that He was still alive, the community held to its faith, and before the irreplaceable Prophet was buried (at the spot of his death), the question of leadership arose. All the old divisions came to the surface. The leaders of the Helpers, who resented the newcomers' position in Madina, met and proposed one of themselves as the new leader, but the Aws and Khazraj were also jealous of each other. When a group of Emigrants joined the meeting, someone even suggested that the Emigrants and Helpers have their own separate leaders. Then, when Umar nominated Abu Bakr, the others went along.

During Muhammad's illness, he had authorized Abu Bakr to lead prayers, an act symbolic of leadership in a religiopolitical community, although it is doubtful how much weight this fact carried at the time. The seeds of a permanent sectarian division in Islam appeared, as some Muslims, possibly at this time but mainly later, believed that the youthful Ali, as Muhammad's son-in-law (he had no surviving son) was the rightful successor. Actually, the concept of hereditary monarchy was unfamiliar to most Arabs at that time, but Ali's supporters later maintained that he had been designated by Muhammad for the succession.

The sixty-year-old Abu Bakr became the first "successor [*Khalifah;* "caliph"] to the Prophet of God." He was the successor in all capacities except that of prophethood; that is, he assumed political leadership of the *ummah*. In the orthodox concept that eventually emerged, each caliph was to be chosen by the *ummah*, though in an informal kind of election. Each man theoretically was able to withhold the *bay'ah,* a touch on the hand that signified allegiance. The caliph was also known as the *imam* ("leader")[3] and, after Abu Bakr, as commander of the faithful.

When Abu Bakr took office, the greatest challenge came from nomadic tribes throughout the peninsula. Conventionally termed "Apostates," the tribes renounced their loyalty to Madina, which they considered to be terminated with the Prophet's death. They stopped sending their *zakat* (alms payable to the state and one of the requirements of Islam) and sometimes expelled the envoys that had been sent. Claimants to prophethood proliferated. Only Mecca and Ta'if, together with a few neighboring tribes, remained loyal, and the "Apostates" seemed to pose a mortal danger to the capital itself.

Then after a two-month delay caused by Abu Bakr's decision to go ahead with the plans for an expedition to Syria, the campaign to subdue the tribes began. These "Wars of Apostasy," the label subsequently given to the struggle against tribes that had mainly never been Muslim in the first place, were conducted by eleven separate armies, and more than a year elapsed before every corner of the peninsula was under the caliph's rule. The most notable commanding role was played by Khalid, in northern and eastern Arabia, and with a degree of inhumanity that shocked such men as Umar. Characteristically, Khalid barely waited for some of his victims to die before marrying their widows and consummating the marriages on the blood-soaked battlefields. Yet this "Sword of Islam," a title bestowed by a sometimes disapproving Muhammad, was such an effective general that the scandalized Abu Bakr could not afford to do more than reprimand him.

Even before Arabia was fully subdued, the conquests began to overflow into Sasanian and Roman lands that already were weakened by internecine conflict. Armed with swords, lances, and bows and with siege engines that hurled stones or fire, Arab cavalry and infantry moved on. Khalid joined with the powerful Bakr tribe, in the region of Arabia next to Iraq, and defeated the wobbly Sasanians in several engagements during 634. Hira, the old Lakhmid capital, submitted to the Muslim forces and agreed to pay tribute. Other columns sent from Madina entered Syria, and, as Heraclius sent in massive reinforcements, Abu Bakr conveyed orders to Khalid to join the fight there. In a legendary, seemingly incredible feat, Khalid

---

[3] The word *imam* is used in several contexts, particularly for the leader of prayers in the mosque.

crossed the Syrian Desert with about five hundred men in eighteen days, allegedly sustained by water from the stomachs of slain camels, to begin a series of victories on the Romans' eastern frontier. This was the state of affairs when death ended the two-year rule of the first caliph, who had already nominated Umar as his successor.

UMAR AND THE CONQUESTS

During the ten-year reign of Umar as caliph, the Arab tribes swept in all directions to create a vast empire. Before his death (he was assassinated by a Persian slave) in 644, Umar selected a five-man council to choose his successor. The electors finally settled on Uthman as the third caliph, and the conquests continued until they were halted temporarily by growing conflict within the *ummah*.

After Khalid and his warriors reached the Syrian front, the Arab forces there quickly crushed larger Roman armies. The Romans depended on mercenaries, including Syrian Arab tribesmen, some of whom quickly changed allegiance. So poor was the morale of many Roman fighters—the same was true of the Sasanians—that at times they were chained together in battle to prevent desertion. The local population often faced the change of overlords with indifference and even saw the Arabs as deliverers from the high taxes and the religious intolerance of the Romans. Heraclius had attempted to impose a Monothelite compromise doctrine— that Christ has two natures but only one will—to bridge the gap between the Orthodox, Hellenic population and the Monophysite Orient, but with little success, although the Maronites of Lebanon (who later embraced orthodoxy) may have accepted the new position. Also, the Jewish minority, whose forcible conversion to Christianity had been decreed by Heraclius in 634, foresaw a new kind of toleration and collaborated with their Arab cousins against Christian Roman rule. The conquest, in effect the final rollback of a millennium of Hellenic domination from the East, was seen as a disaster mainly by the Greek-speaking upper crust, many of whom fled with the Roman armies to Anatolia.

With all of the solidarity of the Arab tribes channeled outward, armies of their enemies stood no chance. Religion was a contributing factor; at least some of the Arabs saw themselves fighting a holy war, *jihad,* and were willing to die in battle with the assurance that they would pass directly into Paradise if killed. Yet too much may be made of this. Many were Muslims in name only, and for that matter Christian Arab tribes joined in this greatest of all onslaughts of the desert against "the sown." The invaders were mostly inspired by a mundane consideration, the prospect of booty. The Arabs, after all, had started out by merely raiding and had turned to outright conquest as an afterthought. Once the outflow started it gained its own momentum, and no central authority could have changed its course.

Syria was soon in Arab hands. The Arabs' defeat of a large Roman army in Palestine soon after Khalid's arrival and their acceptance of him as the overall commander in the area (until Umar dismissed him) left much of the area open to them. Damascus soon surrendered, although the Arabs later withdrew to the Yarmuk River (an eastern tributary of the Jordan) as a large Roman offensive was launched

EXPANSION OF THE EARLY
ISLAMIC STATE TO A.D. 750

During Muhammad's lifetime (to A.D. 632)

During the Rule of the First Four Caliphs (to A.D. 661)

During the Umayyad Period (to A.D. 750)

by Heraclius's brother. The Roman army, allegedly numbering 140,000, was almost decimated by 36,000 Arab horsemen in the Battle of the Yarmuk in 636. Umar came up from Madina to help organize the new territories. Typical of his magnanimity toward the conquered was his refusal to enter the Church of the Holy Sepulchre lest other Muslims follow him and eventually turn it into a mosque.

Syria provided a staging point for further expansion. One force moved eastward across the Euphrates and soon invaded Armenia. Also, despite Umar's misgivings, Amr led 3,500 men, later reinforced, on to Egypt, where the Coptic population was embittered by Roman rule, and a series of easy victories followed. The Roman fort of "Babylon" (inside what later became Cairo) fell, and the Bishop of Egypt soon surrendered Alexandria. Although the Roman navy later retook the city, the Arabs' setback was temporary, and soon they advanced westward into North Africa, to take Barqah (Cyrenaica) and temporarily to occupy part of Tunisia by 647.

Control of Alexandria and the Syrian coast brought ships and experienced sailors into Arab hands, and Arab naval domination ensued in much of the Mediterranean. As governor of Syria, Uthman's cousin and Abu Sufyan's son, Mu'awiyyah, assumed the leadership in this field. Raiding as far west as Sicily, the new fleet seized several islands, including Cyprus in 649, and in a decisive encounter wrought havoc on the Roman navy off the southern coast of Anatolia in 655.

By this time, the Arabs had occupied almost all of the Sasanian Empire. The Persians at first laughed at the Arabs' small spears, and stories abound depicting the tribesmen's simplicity amidst the splendors of the lands they overran. Terrorized by the Sasanians' war elephants, the invaders met a setback in the "Battle of the Bridge," on the Euphrates, in 634 but then, under the command of Sa'd ibn Abi-Waqqas, an early convert to Islam and one of the Emigrants, proceeded from victory to victory. Defeating a Persian force at Qadisiyyah in 637, they quickly took control of Ctesiphon, as the new shah, Yazdagird III, took flight. With the rich yet declining agricultural land of Iraq taken, the Iranian highlands did not suffice to support the empire, although the rough terrain and a certain amount of popular resistance slowed the Arab advance. But a Sasanian defeat in 642 at Nihawand in western Iran, the Arabs' "Victory of Victories" brought the end near. As the local *dihqans* came to terms with the conquerors, the shah fell at the hands of one of his own satraps at the northeastern corner of his domain.

Umar confronted the problem of administering the vast empire. Each province had a governor, appointed by and responsible to the caliph. Except at the top levels, the government of the provinces remained largely as it had been before the conquest. Greek and Pahlavi long continued as the languages of the administration, with the same officials in charge. Each conquered religious community had its own law and courts. Little thought was given to converting non-Arabs to Islam.

The newcomers remained aloof from the conquered populations. Except for some Syrian cities, where they took over the property of the departed Hellenic upper class, the Arabs were confined to their own garrison towns (*amsar*), such as Kufah and Basrah in Iraq and Fustat in Egypt. Each was located on the margins of the familiar desert, where the conquerors could retreat if necessary. According to a decision made by Umar, Arabs did not become landowners in the new domains. While the former state lands and unclaimed land became the collective property (*fay*) of the *ummah,* tilled by the same peasants as before, other land retained its original ownership. The non-Muslim landowners paid a land tax (*kharaj*), in addition to a poll tax (*jizyah*) that was levied on those male adults who were able to pay, although the clear distinction between the two taxes only emerged gradually. Special terms for towns that submitted without resistance led to a lack of uniformity in such matters at first. Muslim landowners in Arabia paid a smaller tax, the *ushr* (tithe) in addition to the *zakat.*

Rules emerged to govern the distribution of the new wealth. Movable property at the time of conquest was treated as booty (*ghanimah*), to be divided on the spot after one-fifth was sent to the caliph. Similarly, a fifth of the tax revenue went to the caliph. In both cases, the fifth was intended to be used for general matters, especially for distribution among the poor, not solely for the ruler's private purposes. From the remainder of the tax revenue were deducted local administrative and military expenses. What was left belonged to the Faithful as a body. Umar organized a *diwan* (register) of the Muslims, providing annual stipends whose sizes depended on each person's rank in the community. Thus each of the Prophet's widows, at the head of the list, received 12,000 dinars; most Helpers and Emigrants got 3,000; and those Meccans who had held out until Muhammad's conquest of their city got 2,000.

THE FIRST CIVIL WAR

Under Uthman, the *ummah* underwent increasing strains that culminated in Islam's First Civil War (*fitnah,* literally "trial"). Most accounts have attributed much of the problem to Uthman's weak leadership, although in some ways the opposite is true, for this third caliph attempted to tighten up the loose, sometimes almost negligible, control of Madina over the *amsar.* Weakness in leadership seemed apparent in his reliance on members of his Umayyad clan to fill top positions. It was not that nepotism per se was so objectionable. Rather it was the fact that these were the very people who had persecuted the Prophet for such a long time that was galling to the Madinans. Governors who tried to counter the centrifugal forces made many enemies for the caliph in the *amsar.* Terminated officials, particularly Amr, the dismissed governor in Egypt, became embittered. On the other hand, the loyalty that Mu'awiyyah gained among the Arab tribes in Syria made that province a bastion of the Umayyad clan. There was also much criticism of Uthman's alleged arbitrariness when he established a standard version of the Qur'an and ordered those copies with minor variations burned. Although Uthman has sometimes been portrayed as too busy reading the Qur'an to govern, there was also opposition to his government because it seemed to have strayed from Muhammad's example. Ali, in particular, was emerging as a focus of pious dissatisfaction.

The underlying problem had little to do with Uthman's qualities. The quantity of booty, even with continuing expansion, could not equal the riches that had so quickly fallen into Arab hands during the first conquests. In addition, ever growing numbers of tribesmen, including former Apostates, were settling in the *amsar* and decreasing the slice of the pie for those who won these territories and considered them rightfully their own.

With Madina already wracked by disturbances, five hundred men from Fustat came to the capital to present their grievances. Taking Uthman at his word, the petitioners believed that he had given in to them. But on their return to Egypt, they discovered that they had been betrayed and that punishment awaited them. Returning to Madina, a small group broke into the unprotected home of the caliph and thrust a dagger into his back as he was praying. For the first time, internecine bloodshed threatened to tear the *ummah* apart.

Although accused of complicity in Uthman's murder, Ali succeeded to the caliphate. But he met violent opposition, including, for personal reasons, that of some of Muhammad's closest companions and Uthman's most avid opponents. Two Emigrants, Talhah and Zubayr, returned to Mecca to establish an opposition movement. There they joined forces with A'ishah, who was possessed by a violent hatred for her stepson-in-law, perhaps dating back to an earlier time when he was receptive to an accusation that she had been unfaithful to her husband. From Mecca, the three proceeded to Basrah with a small party, while Ali, in what turned out to be the end of Madina as the capital of Islam, moved to Kufah. Ali's forces met the rebels outside Basrah in 656 and crushed them in the Battle of the Camel, so-called from A'ishah's presence inside a curtained litter on the back of a camel at the center of the fight. Talhah and Zubayr, as well as many of their followers, were slain in this clash, while A'ishah received Ali's forgiveness.

Ali's greatest threat came from Syria, where Mu'awiyyah remained in control and demanded punishment for his uncle's murder. Ali led troops toward Syria, and the two armies met on the Euphrates at Siffin. After months of facing each other, the two sides began to battle, and Ali's forces seemed to be prevailing. But on the clever suggestion of Amr, who had now become one of the leading Umayyad supporters, Mu'awiyyah saved the day by having his men march toward the enemy with pages from the Qur'an attached to their lances. In effect, Ali was being asked to allow the question of leadership to be arbitrated on the basis of the principles of the Qur'an. Ali had misgivings, as he had nothing to gain and would only undermine his own authority by putting himself on par with a rebel. But some of the caliph's pious supporters fell for the scheme. With each side choosing a member of the arbitral tribunal, Ali went along with the spirit of the agreement and chose an impartial man. Mu'awiyyah stacked the cards in his own favor by picking his friend Amr. Although there are varied accounts of the details of the arbitration, that which comes through clearly as Amr's success in duping his colleague into agreeing that both Ali and Mu'awiyyah were unfit for the caliphate. But after they announced that Ali was deposed, Amr reneged on the part of the agreement relating to Mu'awiyyah.

Seeing what had happened, Ali rejected the decision. But the balance of opinion was clearly shifting into his opponent's favor. Ali had lost the support both of those who opposed arbitration and of those who thought that he was obligated to accept the decision. Mu'awiyyah immediately extended his territorial base, as Amr reconquered Egypt for him.

Ali's acceptance of arbitration had been bitterly rejected by one group of his supporters. These tribesmen, who came to be known as Kharijites ("seceders"), withdrew from his camp and proclaimed themselves the only true Muslims. Ali sent a force to defeat them, but these fiercely egalitarian Muslim purists would be heard again and again as they proclaimed the necessity of making war on the alleged pseudo-Muslims. A Kharijite assassinated Ali in 661, a year after a conclave of Mu'awiyyah's troops had proclaimed their leader to be the new caliph. Now Mu'awiyyah proceeded to gain control of the Islamic domains. Ali's son, Hasan, was accepted by the Kufans as the new caliph, but he was interested in his own personal pleasure far more than in politics and gladly accepted Mu'awiyyah's offer of a handsome pension in return for withdrawing his claim.

Although the First Civil War was over, its imprint never faded. Aside from the Kharijites, the Islamic world continues even today to be divided into two main sects, the Sunnites[4] (as the majority of Muslims later became known) and diverse groups of Shi'ites or followers of the party (Shi'ah) of Ali. Differences later took on other dimensions, but although there is no longer a caliph and there is little thought of restoring the office, the issue of succession is the main theoretical problem dividing them. The Sunnites came to accept the principle of a caliph "elected" from the Quraysh tribe, whereas the Shi'ites believe in a succession of hereditary leaders starting with Ali. The Kharijites say that no caliph is necessary but that if one is to be chosen, lineage is irrelevant.

MU'AWIYYAH AND THE UMAYYAD DYNASTY

From a later perspective, the accession of Mu'awiyyah to the caliphate marked a sharp turn in the life of the *ummah*. No longer was the person in command one of Muhammad's close associates, as the first four (so-called "Rightly-Guided") caliphs had been. In their place were Muhammad's longstanding enemies, the sincerity of whose conversion was suspect. Instead of the simplicity of Madina, the seat of government was now located in a sophisticated ancient center of civilization, Damascus. The Rightly-Guided caliphs had been the epitome of unpretentiousness; Abu Bakr, for example, continued for several months to go to the marketplace. But now this simplicity gave way to pomp and splendor befitting successors of emperors and shahs. Instead of personal ties of freedom-loving tribesmen to the chief of their "supertribe," who was only the first among equals, an elaborate bureaucracy emerged. The mainstay of the regime was now the Arab tribes of Syria, including those whose residence there had predated Islam. Other provinces became virtual subjects of Syria and, especially in the case of Iraq, were ruled largely through

---

[4] The full name is "People of Custom (*Sunnah*) and Community."

force. Some of the Syrian Arabs were still Christians, and these and other Christians often enjoyed high positions in the government. For pious Muslims, the godly order seemed to be giving way to a secular state, or as the accusation went, there was no longer a caliphate but merely a "kingdom."

Mu'awiyyah started an Umayyad dynasty whose rule would last nine decades. Admittedly, the hereditary theory was never accepted, and for a while the scions of the Umayyad house had rivals for succession. Only with the coming of another branch of the Umayyad house, the Marwanids in the 680s, did the fact of a dynasty became clear. The theory of "election" by the leaders of the *ummah* continued to persist in orthodox Islam, but Mu'awiyyah made this a legal fiction when long before his death he cajoled the notables to accept his son Yazid as his successor. This precedent would be followed again and again.

During his nineteen-year reign, Mu'awiyyah kept the *ummah* on a steady course. The manner in which he induced Hasan to give up his claims is characteristic of the caliph's pragmatic dealing with all former or potential opponents. Known for his adeptness at using persuasion whenever possible and coercion only as a last resort, Mu'awiyyah was a master of the art of government. A corps of skillful and loyal provincial governors included Amr in Egypt and Ziyad ibn Abi Sufyan for Kufah and Basrah (and the eastern half of the empire generally). The latter, because of his illegitimate birth, had been known simply as "Ziyad, the Son of His Father" but was glad to trade his support for recognition as the caliph's half brother. With a large measure of harshness, Ziyad prevented the resurgence of opposition in Iraq and kept his half of the empire stable.

Under Mu'awiyyah, Muslim armies moved on to still more conquests. From Egypt, Amr sent forces deep into North Africa. A base at Qayrawan (in Tunisia) was established, and Arab forces reached the Atlantic Ocean in 682, although a subsequent Berber revolt temporarily pushed them back. While the Civil War had brought the temporary loss of eastern Iran, Ziyad sent forces east as far as the Oxus. Each summer, an expedition was launched against Anatolia, but no long-term conquests were made in the high Anatolian country (the "Land of Rome," as it came to be known). On the sea the Arab fleet temporarily occupied Crete and Rhodes, as well as bases in the Straits near Constantinople. Two campaigns sent against the Roman capital nearly succeeded, first from a base established just across the Bosporus in 668–669 and again in the form of annual expeditions during 674—680 from a point on the Sea of Marmara. On the latter occasion, Greek fire, a newly invented form of petroleum that burned on water, held back the would-be conquerors.

THE SECOND CIVIL WAR AND THE MARWANIDS

Mu'awiyyah's death in 680 brought new disorder, the Second Civil War of Islam. Ali's second son, Husayn, rushed from the Hijaz to Kufah to lead his father's old supporters. But deserted by the fear-ridden Kufans, the Alid claimant and his small band of followers were overwhelmed outside the city at a place called Karbala.

Husayn's severed head was sent triumphantly to Damascus. But instead of being the end of the Shi'ite movement, the martyrdom of Husayn was the real beginning. It became an event that evoked continuous calls for revenge, rallying the downtrodden against those in power. To this day, Husayn's grave at Karbala remains a holy spot for Shi'ites, who mourn the martyrdom with passion plays and ceremonies of self-flagellation.

In the short run, a bigger challenge to the Umayyads emerged in the Hijaz, led by Abdullah, the son of Zubayr. Mecca, where Abdullah set up his headquarters, was besieged by Umayyad forces, but the death of Caliph Yazid in 682 (and then of his teen-age son), brought a crisis of succession that gave Abdullah's challenge a new lease on life. The army was ready to recognize him as a caliph, but only if he would move his capital to Damascus, which he was unwilling to do. Although later tradition labeled him the ''anti-Caliph,'' he was at one point acclaimed everywhere except in Syria.

Then a new Umayyad candidate came to the fore. This was Marwan, from another branch of the clan. The Marwanids were able to provide an uninterrupted succession of rulers until 750. The first challenge met by Marwan was in Syria, where the tribes that once had united in support of the Umayyads now formed two rival groups, the Qays and the Kalb, labeled respectively as ''northern'' and ''southern'' Arabian in origin. The Qays, backers of Abdullah, met defeat by the pro-Marwanid Kalb in 684. Once established in Syria, the new caliph soon also gained control over Egypt, but his death left the task of conquering the rest of the empire to his successor, Abd al-Malik. To complicate the picture, a man named Mukhtar emerged in Kufah as the leader of a new Shi'ite movement, proclaiming his revolt in the name of Muhammad ibn al-Hanafiyyah, a son of Ali (but by another wife, not Fatimah, and thus not the Prophet's grandson).

With Ali's son acclaimed as the Mahdi—that is, the ''rightly-guided one'' who would establish justice—the movement took on messianic tones and drew support from new, non-Arab converts who sought equality in an Arab-dominated *ummah*. Some Shi'ites, called *Ghulat* (''exaggerators'') by their opponents, accepted the concept of a succession of rightful *imams* possessing divine qualities. Although Abdullah's supporters in Basrah suppressed Mukhtar's revolt in 687, it nevertheless became another important part of Shi'ite tradition. For a while, claimants to the caliphate had to deal with Kharijites and other rebels, but then Abd al-Malik sent an army headed by a former schoolteacher, the brutal Hajjaj, to the Hijaz. After a seven-month siege during which the city of Mecca was bombarded with catapults and the Ka'bah was destroyed, Hajjaj captured the city and killed Abdullah in 792.

Abd al-Malik, who ruled for twenty years (until 705), eventually restored order to the Islamic lands. A newly established postal service enabled the ruler's will to emanate quickly to the empire's four corners. A unified, Arabicized bureaucracy emerged, and what the late Professor Marshall Hodgson has called the ''High Caliphate'' replaced the more primitive earlier government. Abd al-Malik's success was a consequence of his reliance on Hajjaj, whom he named governor of rebellion-wracked Iraq after his success in the Hijaz. Appearing in the Kufah mosque incognito, the new governor removed his mask and issued blood-curdling threats against anyone who might think of opposing him. Indeed, 120,000 people were executed at his command. He established his headquarters at a place he called Wasit (literally, "Middle"), halfway between Kufah and Basrah, in order to be close enough to both places to suppress any rebellion. Ruling with an iron hand throughout the east, he snuffed out rebellions of Kharijites and others, and all who opposed him succumbed to his reign of terror. At the same time, Hajjaj directed his military leaders eastward, while in Iraq he devoted attention to restoring agricultural productivity. Never forgetting his teaching days, he still had time to make some permanent improvements in the Arabic alphabet.

The reigns of the early Marwanids (including Abd al-Malik and four of his sons) brought the borders of the Arab Kingdom to its farthest limits. Except for the survival of Roman Anatolia and the failure of another Arab attempt to take Constantinople in 716-717, the conquerors swept up everything before them. One of Hajjaj's generals, Qutaybah ibn Muslim, penetrated deep into Central Asia to Turkish lands that had adopted Buddhism and had come under the suzerainty of an expanding Chinese empire ruled by the T'ang dynasty. The realm of Islam reached the Jaxartes, and Arab armies came into contact with the Chinese. Many wars were fought with the Turkish tribes of Central Asia and their relatives west of the Caspian, the eventually Judaized Khazars.[5] Another Arab force occupied Sind, the Indus region of the Indian subcontinent.

From Qayrawan a general named Musa ibn Nusayr reached the Atlantic again. Now the pagan Berbers, whose tribal organization and culture made them reminiscent of the pre-Islamic Arabs, rapidly accepted the religion of their conquerors and gave Islamic expansionism in the far west a new lease on life. In 711 one of Musa's subordinates, a freedman named Tariq, crossed to what has since been known as Jabal ("the mountain of") Tariq, corrupted in European languages to "Gibraltar," and the Visigothic-dominated Iberian Peninsula (which the Arabs called al-Andalus, "the land of the Vandals") was quickly brought under the caliph's rule. Before long, the Arabs had crossed the Pyrenees to occupy parts of France for a few years. The minor defeat (not the great decisive battle so often imagined) by the Frankish Charles Martel in 732 near Tours, not far from Paris, marks the farthest extent of raids by the Islamic East into Europe's western flank, after which the tide slowly receded.

RIVAL VISIONS OF THE NEW EAST

Among the several issues that began to tear the *ummah* apart, the greatest one was, in effect, whether this was to be an Arab or an Islamic state. Should the Arabs as an ethnic group be the dominant caste, or should all Muslims, Arab and non-Arab

---

[5] There has been much speculation, especially by twentieth-century opponents of Zionism, that the European Jews today are primarily of Khazar origin. It is unlikely that this can ever be proved or disproved.

alike, fill this role? The equality of Believers is a prime postulate of Islam, and yet it was originally taken for granted that the faith was revealed especially for the Arabs. Although pagan Arab tribes had been forcibly converted, the Peoples of the Book, a term that was eventually stretched to include most religions, were allowed to keep their faiths. When non-Arabs embraced Islam, it was necessary for them to attach themselves to Arab tribes as Clients (*mawali;* singular, *mawlah*), just as individuals, particularly freedmen, had been brought under the protection of a tribe in pre-Islamic times.

During the Umayyad period, the Clients were generally not given equal status with the Arab Muslims. This is part of the reason for the charge that the Umayyad Caliphate was merely an "Arab kingdom." On the other hand, ethnic discrimination was far from complete, for while some Arabs failed to attain elite status, the Persian aristocracy, headed by the *dihqans,* quickly and opportunistically converted to Islam and joined the new ruling class. And although the Arab conquerors tried to stay in the *amsar,* apart from the conquered population, the line of separation began to blur as some Arabs acquired large estates (even though officially leased from the state) and as Clients began to settle in the *amsar* and to outnumber the Arabs.

Also new converts could gain the same exemptions from the land tax that Arabs enjoyed, a situation that began to deprive the state of important revenue. It was the Caliph Abd al-Malik and his viceroy, Hajjaj, who took action to stem this development by forcing the Clients back from the *amsar* to the land and by requiring continuous payment of the land tax after conversion, although the Clients remained exempt from the *jizyah.* In effect, conversion was officially discouraged. Only with the accession of Umar II (717–720), whose piety sets him apart from the other members of his dynasty, was an attempt made to remedy this situation. Umar II again exempted the Clients from payment of the land tax, but with the provision that no land could be transferred to a nontaxable status after the Islamic year 100 (A.D. 719). He also entered the names of Client soldiers in the *diwan* to allow them to draw pensions. The corollary to this policy was the application of previously neglected restrictions on the *dhimmis* in such matters as clothing, banning the construction of new houses of worship, and forbidding *dhimmis* to ride horses (rules that were rarely enforced during Islamic history). But while the forces of assimilation were irresistable in the long run, little of Umar II's policy of nondiscrimination against Clients outlasted his short reign.

Most of the later Marwanids gained a reputation for a moral degeneration that put pious Muslims to shame. One caliph is said to have swum in a pool of wine, but the obvious exaggeration that he drank enough to lower noticeably the level of the pool so strains credibility that one is warned not to take all the polemical accounts of later anti-Umayyad historians too seriously. In any case devout people doubted whether their rulers were Muslims at all.

Conflict between rival Arab tribes helped to tear the state apart. Described in terms of particular tribes and clans, like the Qays and the Kalb in Syria, belonging to the northern (Adnani) and southern (Qahtani or Yemeni) groupings respectively, the rivalry has conventionally been understood simply in terms of mutual prejudice.

But some modern scholars believe that profound ideological issues were at stake, with the alliances actually cutting across the southern-northern division. A recent writer, M. A. Shaban, maintains that the so-called southern tribes were those who were established in the conquered territories, who developed roots in these lands, who resented the continuing wars of expansion that disrupted their lives, and who wanted to merge with the non-Arab Muslim population and allow the Islamic identity to predominate. The northern Arabs, as this theory goes, were simply newcomers who supported expansion and who wanted to keep themselves apart from the natives. Whichever the case, successive Marwanid caliphs were unable to stay above the fray and aligned themselves with one group or the other, with the northern tribes favored at the end.

The Alid party became a focus for pious opposition to the Umayyads. Clients increasingly rallied to Alid banners, and partly as a result of resentment against Syrian domination, Iraq remained a Shi'ite stronghold. Separate Alid movements initiated sporadic revolts as various descendants of Ali or other relatives of the Prophet claimed to be the "designated" one. Thus one of Husayn's grandsons, Zayd, rose in 740 in Kufah, and his short-lived revolt began a subsect of the Shi'ah, the one nearest to the Sunnite position, that lives on today in Yemen. The majority of later Shi'ites accepted a line of *imams* that included Muhammad al-Bakr (brother of Zayd) and his son Ja'far al-Sadiq. Of more immediate importance was the so-called Hashimite movement of Abu Hashim, son and successor to Muhammad ibn al-Hanafiyyah. And by stretching the legitimist concept a little, members of the Abbasid house (descendants of Muhammad's uncle, Abbas) also began to claim the right to lead the *ummah*. One Abbasid reported that Abu Hashim had willed his rights to him, and so this family, which could also invoke the prestige of membership in the Hashimite clan, now took up the leadership against the Umayyads. A secret organization came into being in Kufah (ca. 718) and sent missionaries to spread the party's propaganda in all directions. Propagandists stationed at strategic points on caravan routes were able to reach large audiences. The greatest success came in Khurasan.

When the twenty-year reign of Caliph Hisham ended in 743, the Islamic world found itself in a Third Civil War. Rebellion was rampant, with peoples like Berbers and Copts rising at different times. Conflict within the Syrian army and palace coups within the Marwanid house undermined the foundations of the regime. A Shi'ite revolt flared in Iraq and western Iran. As ever, Kharijites were a thorn in the side of the established order.

When the Abbasids sent a former Persian slave, the awe-inspiring, austere Abu Muslim, as their representative to Khurasan in 746, the condition of the Islamic world was rapidly coming to a head. A man of mysterious origin, Abu Muslim was uniquely qualified to unite different Arab tribes and Iranian Clients. A capable, ruthless general, he was able to lead them to victory over the disintegrating regime that even the relatively able Marwan II, who took the helm in 744, could not save. Before an assembly of his supporters in 747 near Marv, Abu Muslim unrolled the black flag that became the symbol of the Abbasid movement. Having started as the

Prophet's standard, the black banner had been used by various rebel movements. It now conveyed an eschatological sort of symbolism. The Ummayads yielded to the ever-increasing numbers rallying behind Abu Muslim throughout the east. Kufah fell to the advancing force in 749, and the latest scion of the Abbasid house, Abu al-Abbas (who was nicknamed al-Saffah, "the Bloodletter"), was proclaimed caliph in the Great Mosque there. A battle fought on the Great Zab, a river in northern Iraq, left the way to Syria open to the new claimant, and in the spring of 750, the end came to the Umayyads as Damascus fell and as the members of the family fled, with nearly invariable futility, from the exterminating hands of the new regime. The last Umayyad caliph to sit in Damascus was caught and killed in Egypt, while the graves of his predecessors, Umar II's being a notable exception, were desecrated.

BIRTH OF A CIVILIZATION

The Arabs unification of the Middle East and lands beyond left many facets of life largely unaffected. The peasant majority might at times hardly have known that their rulers had changed, although the taxes generally were less oppressive. The people in conquered territories were governed by their bishops or, as in Iran, by *dihqans,* with only the top echelons of the old empires replaced by the Arabs. The man that Heraclius had appointed as governor of Damascus still held the post under Mu'awiyyah and although remaining a Christian, became the head of financial matters for the empire. The bureaucracy long continued to be non-Arab, and it was not until the reign of Abd al-Malik that Arabic became the administrative language. Roman and Sasanian coins were not replaced by an Islamic currency until Abd al-Malik did so. There were as yet mere beginnings of a two-pronged process of Islamization and Arabicization. Only gradually did a new civilization emerge, a synthesis of ancient Middle Eastern and Hellenistic heritages, with Islam—itself a synthesis of Jewish, Christian, and Arabian traditions—providing the unifying element. However important in providing building blocks, the older Aramaic, Coptic, and even Pahlavi incarnations of Eastern civilization—above the folk level of culture—were far too weakened as a whole to rival the newly rising structure.

Starting from the architectural barrenness of pre-Islamic Arabia, the new faith developed its own styles, which emulated and rivaled Hellenistic and Persian patterns. The mosque became a vehicle of Islamic architectural distinctiveness. The courtyard of Muhammad's house in Madina, where the faithful lined up to perform their rituals of kneeling and prostration before God, became a model for numerous crude mosques in the *amsar;* these were soon replaced by monumental buildings. Besides being places of worship, mosques also served as schools where children began their training by reading and memorizing the Qur'an.

By Marwanid times there was the dazzling splendor of such structures as the Umayyad Mosque (formerly the Cathedral of St. John the Baptist and even earlier a pagan temple) in Damascus and the Dome of the Rock, built over the stone on which an angel is expected to stand while blowing the last trumpet at the Resurrection and from which Muhammad ascended into Heaven. Both this and al-Aqsa

Mosque are located in the former Temple Mount that forms the Islamic Sacred Precinct (Haram al-Sharif) in Jerusalem. In each, the *qiblah* (direction of prayer) was marked by a semicircular niche in the wall, the *mihrab,* while other characteristic features included the high *minbar* ("pulpit"), whose steps a preacher ascended to deliver the Friday noon sermon, and the high tower (*minarah,* "minaret") above the mosque, from which a *mu'azzin* announced the time of prayer five times each day. Thus were established some of the permanent features of mosque architecture.

There were already other splendid architectural achievements. Examples included the Umayyad Palace in Damascus and the many "hunting lodges" scattered over the desert. Fine frescoes decorated the walls of secular buildings, but although such prohibitions do not seem to have become fixed in Islamic doctrine at first, the likenesses of human and animal figures were avoided in mosques.

Busy with conquests and inhibited by restraints against continuing pagan tradition, the Arabs were slow to make new literary contributions. One poet, Labid, was so overwhelmed by the power of the Qur'an that he decided to give up his vocation and indeed lived thirty years longer without composing another verse. Although poetry was suspect in Islamic eyes, some poets devoted their talents to the Prophet's cause even during his lifetime. Recitations of poetry sometimes rallied the Arab conquerors before battles. During the Umayyad period, several schools of poetry flourished. Some followed the *jahiliyyah* tradition, while others modified these forms. Poets like the Christian bedouin, al-Akhtal, Abd al-Malik's poet laureate, who is said to have appeared in his patron's presence wearing a large gold cross and with wine dripping from his beard, exemplify the secular, irreverent trends, as do many writers of verses glorifying drink and free love. At least one poet dared to compare paradise unfavorably with earthly pleasure. Love lyrics began to abound in Mecca, whose reputation for wine and dancing girls exasperated pious Muslims. Love ballads flourished, and those of Qays ibn al-Mulawwah (Majnun, "the Demented"), who described his insanity as coming from unrequited love for a girl named Layla, would be repeated in the literature of many Islamic languages.

Rudimentary beginnings of Arabic prose literature appeared. Early writings on the life of the Prophet, commentaries on the Qur'an, and histories of the conquests have disappeared except insofar as they were quoted by later authors. A special body of literature was developing in the form of stories (*hadiths,* literally "news reports") about the life and sayings of the Prophet. Each story included a chain (*isnad*) or oral transmitters (telling who heard it from whom, etc.).

As Islamic concepts of a legal system inseparable from religion later matured, *hadiths* were to be accepted as the basis of "the *sunnah*" (practice; literally, "trodden path") of the Prophet, a body of rules second in authority only to the Qur'an. Indeed, pious Muslims already looked to *hadiths* as guides to ideal behavior, and there was a faction, the People of Hadith (Traditionalists), that demanded their systematic use. But modern scholarship demonstrates that Islamic law (the *shari'ah,* "the Way") was then still rudimentary. Judges (*qadis*) appointed by the Umayyads' provincial governors enforced some distinctively Islamic rules, such as the few found in the Qur'an. Otherwise, they relied on caliphal decrees, personal judgment (*ra'y,* "opinion"), local or tribal custom, and rules borrowed from Sasanian, Roman, Jewish, or Christian law. Such judicial practice contributed to the content of Islamic law in its later form. By the late Umayyad period, groups of pious scholars in cities like Madina and Kufah—the "ancient schools of law"—were developing their own concepts of law, but this had little to do with judicial practice, although the tendency for religious specialists to be appointed as judges already had some beginnings. The ancient schools called their extra-Qur'anic body of rules "the *sunnah* of the Prophet," but theirs was a "living tradition" without any real attempt to base it on *hadiths.*

Partly resulting from the staying power of Hellenism, the beginnings of theological debate were visible. Contact with such Christian leaders as St. John of Damascus, an influential person in the Umayyad court, was commonplace. And avid, seemingly friendly religious disputes with these Christians led Muslims to think about new questions. Apparently influenced by the Hellenic concept of "*Logos,*" Muslims always referred to the Qur'an as the "Word" of God.

An early debate among Muslims centered around whether a person who commits a major sin can be considered a Muslim at all. In response to the Kharijites' "no," a more moderate theological school, the Murji'ites, said that only God could make such a judgment. This was a question of great political relevance, since a decision that the Umayyads, who were so obviously sinful, were not Muslims would mean that their rule was illegitimate.

A third theological position, first associated with a devout preacher and judge, Hasan al-Basri, and then with a group known as the Mu'tazilites, held that sinners who professed Islam occupied an intermediate position between true believers and complete unbelievers. Another Mu'tazilite doctrine borrowed from Hasan was that of free will, a rejection of other Muslims' belief that all human acts are directed by God. This and other Mu'tazilite doctrines would later take on great significance during an age of more intense Hellenic impact.

CONCLUSIONS

As the Roman and Sasanian empires fought each other to exhaustion, events in little-noticed Mecca made way for a new religious, political, and cultural order for the Middle East and much of the world. With their new faith enabling them to make a long-lasting transformation, Semitic tribesmen from Arabia again overran and renewed the civilization of the area. The conquerers did not immediately create a new civilization, but they provided a thread that would tie together diverse elements of ancient Middle Eastern civilizations and some aspects of the Hellenism whose encroachment they repelled.

The new Muslim Empire's conquest of the Sasanian Empire and its expulsion of the Romans from all Eastern lands except Anatolia allowed it to resume the career of the Achaemenids that decay and Hellenic conquest had interrupted for more than a millennium. Now again, the reincarnated East was on the offensive against the remaining Roman lands and had extended, via North Africa, as far as France and eastward to occupy part of India and to border on China. The Arabic language assumed more successfully the ancient role of Aramaic as the *lingua franca,* and Islam began to displace Christianity and Zoroastrianism, providing the region with its first overall religious unity. The dichotomy between East and West would thereafter coincide at least roughly with a Muslim-Christian confrontation.

Even as it spread, the Islamic community underwent a series of internal crises that threatened its existence. The Abbasid Revolution now promised to resolve the problems. Whether or not it would succeed, the new civilization was on the threshold of maturity. Admittedly, as William McNeill points out, the absolute primacy that the Middle East had enjoyed before 500 B.C. was not destined to reappear. Possibly more than Islam, T'ang China inherited the mantle of creativity that had been held successively by Hellenism and by Gupta India. But for a while the reborn Middle East would have no other real rival in either the politicomilitary or the cultural sphere.

3

The East Florescent

750-1260

The Abbasid Revolution inaugurated a new era for the Islamic world. The classical period of Islam emerged in full splendor at a time when Christian Europe was in its "Dark Age." Paradoxically, the only real center of European, if somewhat oriental-ized, civilization was largely in the Middle East in a Roman (Byzantine) Empire that was reduced mainly to Balkan and Anatolian territories, and the only civiliza-tion of consequence in western Europe was a Middle Eastern one in Spain. For cen-turies, the civilization of the Middle East dazzled the world, particularly Europe.

Even though the unity of the Islamic world would give way to political frag-mentation, the florescence of Islam was to increase. Geographic expansion— mili-tary, religious, and cultural—gained periodic momentum on several fronts. But the century following 750, when the sons of Abbas—caliphs like al-Saffah (749–754), Mansur (754–775),Mahdi (775–785), Hadi (785–786), Harun al-Rashid (786–809), Amin (809–813), Ma'mun (813–833), Mu'tasim (833–842), Wathiq (842–847), and Mutawakkil (847–861)—still effectively ruled much of the Atlantic-to-China region, was always to be regarded as a Golden Age.

THE ABBASID REGIME

Completing the process that was already apparent under the Marwanids, the Islamic state was no longer the simple, unpretentious, and in some ways democratic regime of the early caliphate. It had now assimilated the autocratic patterns of earlier civilized Middle Eastern empires. A burgeoning bureaucracy of clerks (*katibs*), organized in separate bureaus (*diwans*) and supervised by the vizir (*wazir,* "prime minister"), carried out the ruler's will. Exalted caliphs bore titles like "the shadow of God on Earth" and "caliph of God," rather than, as before, merely "caliph of the Prophet of God."

Posing as the executor of God's eternal law, and seeking the support of the religious scholars (*ulama*) and the pious in general, the new rulers in effect claimed divine right. The Abbasids were not more devout than their predecessors, for they had their share of drunkards and worse, but their hypocrisy quotient was higher, as was their reliance on brute force, exemplified by the executioner, when their claim to religious authority was insufficient.

SHIFT TO THE EAST

The Abbasid Revolution has often been represented as the displacement of Arab by Persian dominance, but this is at best a half truth. The Abbasid family based its privileged status on its place in the Arab Hashimite clan alongside the Prophet. Often mothered by non-Arab slaves, the Abbasid caliphs might have less and less Arab "blood" in their veins, but in a patrilineal society that did not matter much.

The Abbasids brought the Iranians and other non-Arabs fully into the Islamic fold. The core of the army became the Khurasanian guard, which consisted of both Persians and Arabs who had settled in Khurasan. Persians filled high posts in the government. One Central Asian Persian family in particular, the aristocratic Barmakids, was at the center of the power structure in the early Abbasid period, beginning with Khalid ibn al-Barmak, al-Saffah's secretary, and continuing with a series of Barmakid vizirs. This family finally lost favor during the reign of Harun, and the then-prominent scion of the house, Ja'far, was catapulted from the vizirate into the hands of the executioner. Such a demise was only to be expected for anyone whose power potentially threatened the position of an autocrat. Although the Barmakids never regained influence, other Persians continued to be important.

Persian ways began to predominate at the court. In fields ranging from wines to high cone-shaped hats, the Arabs emulated the sophistication of an older civilization. A literary movement known as the Shu'ubiyyah ("of the peoples") that flourished especially among the Persians, but also among other non-Arabs, flaunted these peoples' allegedly superior heritage. Also, during the late eighth century some important Persian officials who technically were Muslims held Manichaean doctrines and attacked Islam. But, while Zoroastrians were treated as one of the Peoples of the Book, those accused of being *zindiqs* (Manichaeans) were severely persecuted. The term came to indicate heretics in general.

The Abbasid Revolution ended Syria's role as the center of the Islamic empire. The capital was henceforth in Iraq, first at Kufah or nearby. Then, during Mansur's reign, it was moved to the newly established "City of Peace," always better known as Baghdad. Located where the Tigris and the Euphrates come close together and in the vicinity of Ctesiphon (and the even earlier Babylon), the new capital was made defensible by the two rivers and a network of canals, which also provided an intersection for water-borne commerce that extended eastward to China and for the overland traffic that connected the Mediterranean with regions further east. With the move of the capital, the Islamic empire's orientation was to be away from the old Roman lands, and it appeared more as a new incarnation of its Sasanian and Achaemenid predecessors.

Baghdad was perhaps the greatest city of its age. Its population may have exceeded a million. Enclosed by a double round wall, the city was centered around the caliph's palace; other royal residences were built outside the walls. On four sides, gates opened to the highways over which the caliph's postal system connected the empire to the capital.

Military expansionism decreased, although war with the Byzantines sputtered on from time to time. Dramatic success for an Islamic offensive occurred under Harun's generalship during the reign of Mahdi, but that proved to be temporary. Harun's army got to the Bosporus but withdrew in return for payment of tribute. An offensive during Harun's reign brought Muslim troops deep into Anatolia, but it ended in the same way. Sometimes the Romans invaded parts of Syria, and sometimes the Muslims temporarily penetrated Anatolia. With their string of fortifications, a frontier society of ghazis ("warriors for the faith") and their Christian counterparts on the other side alternated between friendly contact and warfare for centuries, but no more major shifts in the border occurred until the late 1000s.

THE ECONOMIC FOUNDATION

A flourishing economy provided the basis for the imposing civilization of early Abbasid times. Trade was not limited to the usual luxury items. There was a wide variety of industries—like Egyptian linens, Syrian and Iraqi silk, and paper from Samarqand; these and agricultural products, such as Egyptian grain and Iraqi dates, found their way to many parts of the Islamic world and beyond. A merchant class gained importance; a banking system evolved, with the use of checks (significantly, a word of Arabic origin) and letters of credit. Urbanization was on the upsurge. Political unity facilitated trade, and it continued after the gradual breakup of caliphal power. The flow of gold from Nubia and the western Sudan (which includes such present-day states as Mali and Niger) gave a boost to the Middle Eastern economy, but also brought a rise in prices.

Trade with other areas was of major importance. The simultaneous flowering of T'ang China allowed the two regions to reinforce each other's prosperity. Chinese ships sailed to Baghdad, and there were Middle Eastern merchant settlements in eastern China. Besides sea traffic, caravans carried goods along the ancient Silk Road, and major Middle Eastern–Indian trade also followed both land and sea routes. Trade with sub-Saharan Africa was especially vigorous, with gold and slaves exchanged for a variety of Middle Eastern goods.

Despite sporadic warfare, there was much trade with Byzantium. Christian western Europe, however, long remained a dark, unknown region. Still, there was some overland traffic across Russia as far as the Baltic region, partly through Jewish intermediaries, with Europeans exporting Slavic slaves to the Middle East.

SOCIAL DIVISIONS

Like in other civilizations, social classes developed in the Islamic world. Various medieval writers offered their own classifications. Sometimes society was divided into men of the pen, men of the sword, men of negotiation (including merchants and artisans), and men of husbandry, but these divisions are largely of a vertical nature rather than representing purely horizontal strata. Another medieval writer speaks of four categories, ranging from the ruler to the cultured middle class and dismisses all the rest as "mere scum." Others speak of the ruling elite and the masses, with the latter term including everyone from vagabonds to rich merchants. Some writers specify that a function of government is to keep the classes in their places.

Using modern terminology, we might warily divide medieval society into upper, middle, and lower classes. Starting with the latter, the bulk of the population of course tilled the soil, as in all premodern societies except in nomadic areas. In early Abbasid times, the peasants tended to own their own land, but landlordism later became more common, with the person furnishing just his own labor typically getting a fifth of the produce. It should be noted that Islamic law and practice allow for several types of land ownership, including state or crown lands (by far the most widespread in later periods so far as agriculture was concerned), land owned collectively by a tribe or a village but with the shares periodically redistributed, endowments administered for charitable or other purposes (i.e., *waqfs*), and private land (*mulk*). However, even when title to the land was vested in the state, the cultivator possessed a hereditary, salable right to the land (usufruct) that in some ways was analogous to ownership.

Nomads, even those belonging to "noble" tribes, would have to be grouped generally with peasants in the lower classes, as would most crafts workers, who were often organized in guilds, at least during the latter part of this period. In an altogether different category were the beggars, persons performing disrespectable jobs (e.g., usurers), criminals, and others at the bottom of urban society.

On the opposite extreme was the small upper class, which might be defined to include the ruling families, high officials in the government, and leading establishment-oriented ulama, as well as wealthy merchants and large landholders. Power, wealth, family antecedents, religious learning, and other matters were marks of upper-class status from the perspective of those possessing each one. But social scientists who have defined the premodern upper strata in terms of power (which also led to wealth) are basically correct.

Besides the central ruling class, there were always the "notables," including ulama, merchants, and heads of traditionally prominent families on a local level. Such people not only had their mass followings but also acted as intermediaries—

"patrons" obtaining favors for their "clients" and in turn making it possible for the rulers to rule—between the masses and the central elite. But, when the central government was weak, the notables tended to become independent rulers.

There was a wide gulf between the luxurious life of a few and the meager existence of the many. However, relative to other preindustrial societies, a commercial middle class was fairly large in early Abbasid times, and the term "middle classes" might also describe the bulk of government officials and ulama. Aside from their low ranking by medieval writers with a ruling-class bias, some artisans and shopkeepers would seem to fit properly in the middle classes, and even medieval classifications deemed them "respectable."

In contrast with the caste systems of other areas and sometimes of the pre-Islamic Middle East, there was in theory no barrier to social mobility. Perhaps this was one concrete result of Islam's emphasis on the equality of believers, distinguished only by degrees of piety. And indeed this theory converged with the reality of political instability to bring many individuals from the bottom to the top of society, while others lost their privileged positions. Aside from the prestige of descendants of the Prophet, called *sayyids* or *sharifs,* no hereditary aristocracy emerged.

Slavery was widespread, and although slaves were inherently at the bottom of society, it has already become apparent that slavery was often a road to ruling-class status. Aside from those purchased for training as soldiers, slaves were used mainly as domestic servants and were treated as subordinate members of the family. They sometimes were able to purchase their freedom. Despite notable exceptions, slaves were rarely used in agriculture or other labor on a large scale.

There were slaves of all races, but one important source was sub-Saharan Africa. Prejudice against both Nordic and Negroid racial features was always discernable, but Islamic society has possibly been the least race-conscious of any in history. No kind of racial segregation ever existed in the Islamic world, and blacks have tended to melt into the general population rather than being singled out as a distinct ethnic group.

Religious divisions overshadowed the racial ones. The Islamic pattern of autonomy for *dhimmis* has already been described. Living under their own law, their position contrasted with the widespread persecution of religious minorities in the Christian world even in the few instances in which Islamic governments made an effort to apply the most overt discriminatory rules that existed in theory. *Dhimmis* had their own law and courts and could worship freely, although they were second-class citizens in some ways; for example, in case of conflict between a *dhimmi* and a Muslim, the law of the latter prevailed. Christians and Jews, however, often held high positions in the society and government.

A pattern of male supremacy is one of the best known aspects of the Middle East. Even here, a comparison with other nonmodern societies—with such practices as Hindu suttee (the death of a widow on her husband's funeral pyre) and Chinese foot binding—may put the matter in a different perspective. Some aspects of Islamic practice were drawn from Sasanian and Byzantine customs. Feminists would applaud some of the rights given to women in Islamic society; for example, women keep their maiden names after marriage, and Islamic law gives them the right to own property and to keep control of it. But polygamy (although necessarily the exception in practice), the seclusion of women in the harem (private, literally "forbidden" quarters of the house), and the largely urban practice of veiling (i.e., covering the face) have been important aspects of Islamic culture. Even when the veil has not been deemed obligatory, Islamic principles have required women to cover their heads, exposing only hands and faces in public. Men's almost exclusively one-sided right to divorce their wives at will is another characteristic of Islamic law, although the practice whereby part of the dowry payable to the bride is delayed until divorce takes place can be an important inhibition. While it is true that Islam guarantees many rights to a woman, such as inheriting half as much as her brother's share (a radical reform when first instituted), the Islamic heritage is such that calls for sexual equality have been a key part of modern reform movements.

THE SHI'ITE OPPOSITION

The Shi'ites who helped bring the Abbasids to power soon experienced intense disillusionment. The Shi'ites had expected a descendant of Ali to be put on the throne and were not impressed with the Abbasids' claim to rule. Understandably, the divergent intentions of the anti-Umayyad coalition now came into the open. Abu Salama, a leader of the Abbasid revolution who insisted on an Alid caliph, was soon executed, and Abu Muslim's turn was not long in coming. Early Abbasid caliphs often saw the Alids as a threat and sometimes harshly suppressed them. The Alid proclivities of Kufah were a main reason for building the new capital at Baghdad. Ma'mun was an exception; he designated one of the recognized Shi'ite *imams,* who was descended from Ali, as his successor. But the non-Shi'ite majority was horrified, and so he eventually gave up the idea.

Shi'ite doctrines crystallized during the early Abbasid period. The earlier vague concept of succession belonging to Ali's descendants (or even his relatives' descendants) gave way to a recognized line of *imams.* (Shi'ites have tended to emphasize this title but also use the term caliph.) Thus all Shi'ites came to agree on a common list of five successors to the Prophet, starting with Ali, Hasan, and Husayn.

But the name of the rightful sixth *imam* is a matter of contention. A few, known as Zaydis and eventually concentrating in Yemen, recognized Zayd and a subsequent line of *imams* who are theoretically elected from among the descendants of the Prophet. Among Shi'ites, the Zaydis' doctrines of the imamate come closest to Sunnism.

Most Shi'ites recognized Ja'far al-Sadiq as the sixth *imam.* From here on, another division occurred, as Ja'far outlived his designated successor, wine-imbibing Isma'il. One group, which came to be known as Isma'ilis (or Seveners), insisted that Isma'il and his son belonged next in line (as sixth and seventh respectively, since Ali in this case is given an even more exalted title and not considered one of the *imams*). The other group accepted another son of Ja'far and a line that ends with the twelfth *imam*. This subsect, which is now dominant in Iran and southern Iraq, is known as the Twelvers, Ja'faris, or Imamis.

Acceptance of these men as *imams* does not mean that they actually ruled or even necessarily aspired to do so. Some of them were politically inactive, but from a Shi'ite point of view, they were the rightful rulers. The moderate Zaydis apart, Shi'ites attribute a far more exalted role to the right *imam*, who is deemed infallible, than do Sunni Muslims to their caliph.

Shi'ites (again excepting Zaydis) share an emphasis on messianism. Twelvers believe that the Twelfth Imam went into hiding in 874 but ultimately will return as the Mahdi, who will restore justice to the world. Isma'ilis hold that their seventh *imam* became invisible to all but a few of his purest followers and that he or, in the doctrine of most factions, one of his descendants will emerge (or already has emerged) as the Mahdi. Both Isma'ilis and Twelvers agree that the universe could not exist without an *imam*. They also accept the principle of *taqiyyah* ("dissimulation"), that is, that it is permissible to deny one's real beliefs if necessary.

The Isma'ilis adopted other distinctive ideas. There was a hierarchy of missionaries (*da'is*) engaged in propagating an elaborate view of history, with the Mahdi to provide the climax. In addition to the apparent meaning of the Qur'an, Isma'ilis developed the doctrine that a hidden, allegorical meaning awaited discovery by the few. Some extreme Isma'ilis place the *imam* higher than the Prophet or deify Ali, but these are not typical.

DEVELOPMENT OF ISLAMIC LAW

The Islamic system of jurisprudence (*fiqh*) took shape during the early Abbasid period. As it eventually developed, this body of law, called the *shari'ah* ("the way"), is considered to be God's eternal set of rules, and governs all aspects of a pious Muslim's life. Rules forbid or require certain acts; other kinds of behavior are merely recommended or are declared reprehensible but still permitted (divorce is an example), and the law even expresses its indifference in some matters. The *shari'ah* includes everything from criminal law to rules of worship, and some rules are not even theoretically enforcible by governments. The degree to which the *shari'ah* was observed in practice varied from field to field. The constitutional rules (qualifications for the caliphate, etc.) rarely limited powerful rulers; however, the law of personal status (marriage, divorce, inheritance, and charitable endowments or *waqfs*) has generally been a relatively sacrosanct area. Even in matters of personal status, local custom (*adah*) sometimes prevails over the *shari'ah*. But from an Islamic point of view, the *shari'ah* is always the ideal, true law.

Islamic jurisprudence generally came to recognize four main sources of law. The Qur'an is the most authoritative, but it provides only a handful of legal rules. Second comes the *sunnah* (tradition), based on the *hadiths* (reports) of the Prophet, whose words and actions are believed to have provided an ideal human model. Other conclusions may be derived by analogical reasoning (*qiyas*) from other rules (e.g., The Qur'an forbids wine because it intoxicates; since liquor also intoxicates, it is forbidden by analogy). Finally, whatever the Islamic community—in practice, the *ulama*—agrees on must be right; this is the principle of *ijma* (consensus of juristic opinion). There has never been anything comparable to a church council in Islam, for Islam has no church (no formal organization distinct from the state, no sacraments that require priests, and in fact no priests, for such religious tasks as leading prayer can be performed by any Muslim). *Ijma* could only emerge informally (somewhat like, say, modern scientific opinion), and its failure to attain universality within the Islamic community on important points accounts for sectarianism. A final possible source of law, personal judgment (*ra'y*), which was so important for early Islamic judges, came to be rejected by Sunnis or else restricted to a minor role under other names.

At least two factors in the early Abbasid period brought this concept of law into the form just described. First, the Abbasid posture as a truly religious state required the appointment of specialists in religious law as judges, which enabled a theoretical body of law to take on the character, at least to a large extent, of positive law almost for the first time. But as shown in the previous chapter, the concepts of the ancient schools of law during the Umayyad period were quite unsystematic. The second factor in the development of the law was the contribution of a jurist, Muhammad ibn-Idris al-Shafi'i, who died in 820. Al-Shafi'i's stress on the necessity of basing the entire *sunnah* strictly on *hadiths* meticulously documented by uninterrupted chains (*isnads*) of authorities going back to the Prophet eventually won out over less rigorous practices.

To a large extent, this meant finding *hadiths* to support a body of rules that had already evolved in the "ancient schools." There was no shortage of *hadiths*, as anyone wanting to push his own views on any matter could invent a story and a spurious *isnad*. This required the development of a whole science of *hadiths*, with scholars separating the weak from the sound. Since the character of the people in the *isnad* was the key factor in evaluation, great emphasis was put on collecting biographical information. Collections of *hadiths* came into existence; of six main ones accepted by the Sunni Muslims, those compiled by two ninth-century scholars, Bukhari and Muslim, are of special significance. Often described as canonical, they (not the Qur'an, the "Word of God") are the rough equivalent of the Christian Gospels.

Sunni Islam came to be divided into so-called schools (*madhhabs*) of law. This reflects the fact that consensus did not develop on some minor points except in the sense that everyone agreed, in effect, that the disagreements were unimportant and accepted each other as orthodox. There are even some disagreements within each school, and it would be inaccurate to describe the separate schools as subsects. One of the schools—the Shafi'ite—was founded by al-Shafi'i and predominates today in Lower Egypt, much of the Red Sea region, and Southeast Asia. The Hanafite school, which is dominant in the Indian subcontinent, all Sunni Turkish areas, and parts of the Fertile Crescent, is not only the most widespread but also the most liberal one in its use of the roots of law, even giving a limited role to personal judgment. Both the Hanafites and the Malikites, the group found in most Islamic parts of the African continent (including Upper Egypt), grew out of earlier legal schools after taking over al-Shafi'i's emphasis on *hadiths*. The most strictly *hadith*-minded school is that of the Hanbalites, founded in the ninth century by the zealous Ahmad ibn-Hanbal. It rejected the validity of *ijma* except for that of the Prophet's generation (later extended to the first three centuries) and at first disfavored the principle of *qiyas*. The Hanbalites' strict opposition to theological speculation made them much more than just another school of jurisprudence. Lacking official backing, the Hanbalite school later almost disappeared, but sponsorship by the Sa'udi family gave it a new lease on life in Central Arabia during the eighteenth century.

Much the same is true of the Shi'ites. The *sunnahs* of the various Shi'ite subsects differ from the Sunni *sunnah* in only a few details. For example, sanction for temporary marriage—from one day to ninety-nine years—is perhaps the most unusual feature of Twelver Shi'ite law. A distinctive feature of the Shi'ite theory of law is that no *hadith* is valid unless one of the recognized *imams* is included in the *isnad*. Since the *imam* is infallible as a source of law, the principle of *ijma* became relevant only after his disappearance and was never emphasized as much as by Sunnites. Also, most Shi'ites (the Zaydis are an exception) reject *qiyas* in favor of an at least theoretically less restrictive principle, the use of "intellect" (*aql*).

Originally a flexible body of law, the *shari'ah* gradually took on a rigid character. Until the tenth century, religious scholars claimed the right to exercise *ijtihad* (literally, "striving" for the truth), which meant a continuous rethinking of the rules. A learned Muslim might choose to reinterpret a *hadith* or a passage in the Qur'an or to apply analogy in a different way, and a new *ijma* could conceivably evolve as issues were seen in the light of new circumstances. But gradually the idea took hold that the "door of *ijtihad*" was closed, cracked open only for a "relative *ijtihad*" on minor points. Now the principle of *taqlid* ("imitation") prevailed; that is, whatever issues early Muslim scholars agreed on could not be reopened.

Perhaps this was a necessary means for the *ulama* to resist future pressure from tyrants to exercise *ijtihad* arbitrarily, but a law that could not evolve with the times later came to be blamed by Islamic modernists for inhibiting progress. This may be a case of backward looking that points to the waning creativity and ultimate decline of Islamic civilization. Admittedly, Shi'ite legal theory continued to recognize a few *mujtahids* ("ones practicing *ijtihad*"), and Hanbalites like the fourteenth- century Damascene scholar Ibn Taymiyyah, being less restricted by existing *ijma*, asserted the same right. But this did not make much difference in practice.

There continued to be some development in the *shari'ah* on points where no previous consensus existed, as legal authorities known as *muftis* responded to individual inquiries in the form of *fatwas*. Sometimes attached to courts, *muftis* provided decisions on points of law, which judges applied to the cases in question.

Also, sometimes tricks (*hiyal,* literally "devices") were used to enable the letter of the law to be followed while effectively evading its spirit in matters like the rule against usury.

DECLINE OF CALIPHAL POWER: THE MAMLUKS

Long before Islamic legal institutions fully evolved, the actual power of the caliphs began to wane. The empire split apart as local dynasties sprang up in province after province. At the same time, army commanders became the real rulers in the capital itself.

To begin with the latter phenomenon, important changes emerged in the composition of the army. Of unexcelled military proclivity, Turkish tribesmen from the Eurasian steppes appeared as an alternative to Khurasani troops. For the next thousand years one of the most important phenomena in Islamic history would be Turks as soldiers—and as rulers. Later on, they came in as tribes, but the predominance of Turks in the Islamic army got started in another equally enduring form.

Such soldiers, particularly Turks during the Abbasid period but also including members of other ethnic groups, were known as *mamluks.* Literally, this means "those who are owned," that is, slaves. Boys were bought in the slave markets of the steppes, given military training and simultaneously Islamized, and then manumitted. Having lost their ties with their own kin, such children developed intense familial loyalty to those who became first their masters and then their patrons. The recruitment of slaves as troops was not unusual in itself; what was unique in the Islamic world was that, over the centuries, *mamluks* became generals, usurped power, and continued to recruit more *mamluks,* some of whom would also rise to the top and perpetuate the process. A military oligarchy of slave origin thus recurrently took hold of the Islamic world.

While we hear of Turkish troops early in the Abbasid caliphate, the beginning of *mamluk* predominance came during the reign of Mu'tasim. His newly established 60,000-man *mamluk* force, loyal to him alone, provided an unsurpassed means of control over the empire. But to the populace of the capital, the *mamluks* were crude and overbearing, so much so that in 836 Mu'tasim moved the seat of government sixty miles northward to the newly established Samarra. While Baghdad remained the cultural center, the caliphs and their *mamluks* remained at a distance for over half a century.

Even during the Samarra period, the *mamluks,* sometimes in league with a caliph's slave mother, began to take control. Throughout the late ninth and early tenth centuries, caliph after caliph was assassinated or deposed by the Turkish troops. Attempts to balance the Turks with *mamluks* of other ethnic backgrounds and to play them off against each other failed to restore caliphal authority. The real rulers continued to give largely figurehead caliphs recognition by having their names mentioned in the Friday prayer and struck on coins. Even this honor was shared with the *mamluk* general who held the title of commander of commanders from 936 on. Anarchy prevailed as the various *mamluk* commanders struggled for supremacy.

THE BREAKUP OF ISLAMIC POLITICAL UNITY

By the mid-tenth century, the central government's power did not extend far from the capital. Taking advantage of the difficulty of controlling such a vast empire, opportunistic commanders set themselves up as de facto rulers, usually acknowledging the formal authority of and being officially accredited by the caliph, and began their own dynasties.

The breakup of Islamic political unity dates back to the Abbasid Revolution, for Spain never came under the sway of the new regime. A young Umayyad prince, Abd al-Rahman, fled from the Abbasids. After a harrowing five-year trek, he reached Spain and rapidly gained the support of Syrian Arab troops there. This was the beginning of an independent Umayyad amirate that rejected even the titular authority of Baghdad. Beginning in 929, these Umayyad rulers assumed the title of caliph. One of the most dynamic regions of Islamic civilization, Muslim Spain later split into numerous small states and sometimes came under the control of North African dynasties. Although the last Muslim kingdom in Spain finally succumbed in 1492, with the Muslim population eventually expelled or forcibly Christianized, indelible Arab imprints have remained on the Spanish and Portuguese languages and cultures.

In the face of Berber, sometimes Kharijite-inspired, separatism, Abbasid control over the Maghrib was tenuous and short-lived. A local dynasty, the Rustamids, asserted its independence in 761 in part of Algeria. Fleeing after the failure of his rebellion in Madina, Idris ibn-Abdullah set up a Shi'ite dynasty in Morocco in 789 that would survive for two centuries. The region between Morocco and Egypt—then known simply as Ifriqiyyah ("Africa") and centering on Qayrawan—gained de facto independence under the Aghlabid dynasty, starting with the governor sent by Harun in 800. The Aghlabids, who lasted until 909, dominated the western Mediterranean and even extended the realm of Islam by conquering Sicily and other islands.

BREAKUP IN THE EAST

Closer to Baghdad, numerous rebellions threatened the new Abbasid order from the beginning. Several extreme Shi'ite movements, sometimes with Iranian national overtones, were suppressed. Kharijites, in one of their numerous revolts, established themselves during the late 700s in Oman, where they remain today.

Violent conflict sometimes raged within the Abbasid house. The most notable

BREAKUP OF THE ISLAMIC WORLD AFTER A.D. 750

ILIQ KHANS
KHWARAZM
Bukhara

SAMANIDS
TAHIRIDS

GHURIDS

GHAZNAVIDS
SAFFARIDS

• Nishapur

Caspian Sea

• Alamut

Manzikert •
Samarra •
Baghdad •

BUYIDS

IBADIS

INDIAN OCEAN

HAMDANIDS
ATABEGS

ZANGIDS

ZANJ

AYYUBIDS

ZAYDIS

QARMATIANS

Black Sea

Red Sea

BYZANTINES

Ayn
Jalut •

Mediterranean Sea

Cairo •

TULUNIDS
IKHSHIDIDS
AYYUBIDS

Adriatic Sea

AGHLABIDS

FATIMIDS

Mahdiyyah •

RUSTAMIDS

IDRISIDS

UMAYYADS

ATLANTIC
OCEAN

CRUSADER STATES
ABOUT A.D. 1131

1. Kingdom of Jerusalem
2. County of Tripoli
3. Principality of Antioch
4. County of Edessa

Edessa •

ZANGIDS

Damascus •
Hattin •

4

2

3

1

Jerusalem •

FATIMIDS

case of this was a Fourth Islamic Civil War, between two of Harun's sons. Harun left the caliphate to the degenerate, weak Amin, with the able half-Persian Ma'mun in Khurasan in charge of the eastern part of the empire and designated as his brother's ultimate successor. Amin broke the agreement in 810 and named his own son as his successor. But Ma'mun's forces, commanded by the Persian General Tahir, pushed back all the armies that Amin could send. After a year-long siege in which Amin's loyal followers endured severe hardships and the city suffered greatly from catapults and Greek fire, Baghdad finally succumbed to Tahir's army, and Ma'mun was installed as the new caliph. Again, during Ma'mun's pro-Shi'ite period, a rival Abbasid claimant was proclaimed caliph in Baghdad, and two years passed before Ma'mun's forces restored control in 819.

With Ma'mun belatedly moving his residence from Khurasan back to Baghdad, the east began to assert its independence. Appointed governor of Khurasan in 821, Tahir began a separate dynasty that did not always bother to give the caliph formal recognition. In the late ninth century, the Tahirids were replaced by another Persian dynasty, the Saffarids, founded by a popular brigand, Ya'qub ibn al-Saffar ("the Coppersmith"). Then Iranian particularism reached a high point under the Samanid dynasty, named for an ancestor of Nasr I, who established his rule over all of Transoxania in the late ninth century. The Samanids ruled from Bukhara as amirs under the titular authority of the Abbasid caliph. Relying heavily on Turkish *mamluk* troops whose source was close at hand, the Samanids united most of eastern Iran under their control by the mid-tenth century to form one of the Islamic world's most powerful and culturally brilliant states.

REVOLUTIONARY MOVEMENTS
IN THE EAST

Heterodox parties challenged Baghdad's power in Iraq and Arabia during the late ninth and early tenth centuries. A fierce revolt that espoused Kharijite doctrines and brought the deaths of perhaps a half million people occurred in southern Iraq and spread to adjacent parts of Iran from 870 to 883. This movement found its main following among the largely East African (Zanj) slaves, who had suffered harsh treatment in the salt mines of that region, but it also drew some Arab support. Its leader was an Iranian, Ali ibn-Muhammad, supposedly a descendant of Ali. Protection by almost impenetrable marshes made the Zanj rebels seem nearly invincible. At one point they captured and looted Basrah and came close to Baghdad. They committed merciless massacres and received similar treatment at the hands of Abbasid forces that finally overcame them.

Soon it was the turn of a new Isma'ili movement called the Qarmatians ("Carmathians") after its founder, the Iraqi Hamdan Qarmat. As was the case with other Isma'ili movements, a network of missionaries carried their message far and wide. Drawing support from bedouin tribes and idealistic young men from the cities who aspired to end injustice, the Qarmatians were initiated into an exclusive society and an early kind of welfare state that enabled their enemies and later historians to portray them inaccurately as communists who shared all property and (even more ludicrous) wives. Organized in the Syrian desert at the end of the ninth century, the Qarmatians raided the Fertile Crescent lands for several years before being suppressed. Another Qarmatian movement appeared on the Persian Gulf coast of the Arabian Peninsula where a "republic" was established in the region then called Bahrayn, now al-Hasa. They invaded or raided much of Arabia, snatching the Black Stone away from Mecca at one point, and were not fully uprooted until the eleventh century.

Among other heterodox regimes, a Zaydi state emerged in Yemen in 897. Another dynasty that eventually adopted Shi'ism was the Hamdanids, of bedouin origin, who established themselves in northern Iraq in 890 and later conquered northern Syria. Ruling from Aleppo after 944, the Hamdanids vigorously resisted Roman offensives that sometimes penetrated far into Syria and they also provided a flourishing center of civilization.

Claiming Sasanian descent, the Persian Twelver Shi'ite Buyids established their rule in the early tenth century in the rugged region south of the Caspian. After expanding into other parts of western Iran, they took Baghdad in 945, thus ending whatever power the *mamluk*-surrounded caliphs could sporadically exercise. Ruling from Shiraz, the Buyids pragmatically chose not to abolish the figurehead Abbasid caliphs. They preferred instead to be the real power as "commander of commanders" and eventually adopted the old Persian title "king of kings." The Buyids split into several branches ruling different areas well before the end of the century. They also increasingly relied on and then were dominated by *mamluk* troops.

EGYPT AND THE FATIMIDS

A series of separatist dynasties gained control of Egypt. The process began when the caliph sent a Turkish *mamluk* general, Ahmad ibn-Tulun, to Fustat in 868. Ibn-Tulun soon quit sending tax revenues to Samarra and thereafter hardly paid more than the usual formal allegiance to the Abbasids. Soon adding Syria to their patrimony, ibn-Tulun and his descendants ruled a prosperous, powerful, and culturally florescent amirate with an army of African and Turkish *mamluks* until 905, when Baghdad restored its control.

Another Turkish *mamluk* general, Muhammad ibn-Tughj, repeated ibn-Tulun's defiance of the caliphate in 935. This was the beginning of a short-lived regime known as the Ikhshidids, so-called from the Persian title awarded by the caliph. In reality, a Black African general named Abu al-Misk Kafur, first as regent and finally assuming the formal title, ruled the Ikhshidi domain (including Syria and the Hijaz most of the time) from Muhammad ibn-Tughj's death in 946 until Egypt fell to the armies of a rising North African power, the Fatimids, in 969.

Established in Tunisia as a new caliphate rivaling the Abbasids, the Fatimids had deep roots in the Isma'ili movement. The dynasty began with one who later took the name al-Mahdi, a claimant to descent from the seventh Isma'ili *imam,* and the dynasty itself was given the name Fatimid after his ancestress, Fatima, wife of Ali and daughter of the Prophet. After extensive propaganda activity in various parts of the Islamic world, his chief missionary went to North Africa and rapidly gained support among Berbers. After this preparation, al-Mahdi left his headquarters in Syria and made a perilous trek to North Africa. By 909, he had taken over the Aghlabid territories and established his capital near Qayrawan. The Qarmatians seemingly accepted the Fatimids' nominal authority at first, and sporadically thereafter, despite the latter's moderate, pragmatic policies.

The Fatimids soon became the dominant power throughout North Africa. Their great military leader, the Sicilian ex-Christian *mamluk* Jawhar, overran Egypt in 969 and ended Ikhshidi rule. The Fatimid capital moved to the newly acquired land and to a new city named al-Qahirah ("the Victorious," corrupted to "Cairo" in Western languages).

Cairo became the greatest Islamic city and the center of possibly the most powerful state in the Islamic world. Egyptian agricultural wealth was combined with an upsurge of commerce that now extended to western Europe, with Egyptian fabrics and other exports gaining prominence and with the Egyptian route between the oceans achieving renewed prominence. Cairo was now the center of a great ideological movement, with the chief missionary one of the top officials in the government and with the newly established al-Azhar mosque-university training a missionary army. Paradoxically, the regime normally was also highly tolerant of other religions and apparently never made any serious dent in the overwhelmingly Sunni character of the population.

An old process repeated itself as the Fatimid state began to decline by the eleventh century. Weak rulers lost control to the heterogeneous *mamluk* forces, whose various ethnic elements, particularly blacks, Turks, and Berbers, vied for supremacy.

The Fatimid Caliph al-Hakim (996–1021) proved to be one of the most unusual monarchs of any dynasty. His capriciousness extended to banning honey and grapes. He alternately put *dhimmis* in high positions and then, in violation of Islamic law, persecuted them. He even ordered the destruction of the Church of the Holy Sepulchre but later rebuilt it. He remained an ally of Constantinople all the while. No one ever found out what happened after he suddenly rode a mule into the desert, although one man later proudly claimed to have killed him. Contrary to conventional accounts, al-Hakim may not actually have proclaimed himself an incarnation of God (a highly un-Islamic concept). But the Druzes, a small sect that emerged in Syria, accept his alleged divine status even today.

TURKISH DYNASTIES
AND THE SUNNI UPSURGE

Contact with the Samanids had brought about the conversion of Central Asian Turks to Sunni Islam. By the eleventh century, Turkish dynasties began to champion the Sunni cause and to reverse the previous Shi'ite tide.

The first Turkish dynasty, the Ghaznavids (from their capital, Ghaznah, in Afghanistan) was founded by a *mamluk* named Alptigin in the service of the Samanids. The Ghaznavids displaced the Samanids in most of their territories except in Transoxania, where another Turkish dynasty, the Iliq Khans, took over. The third member of the Ghaznavid dynasty, Mahmud of Ghaznah (998–1030), conquered large parts of northern India, much of which thus was permanently Islamized, and he raided and plundered even further. The caliph awarded Mahmud such titles as "ghazi" and "sultan" ("he with power"), henceforth a common designation for independent rulers who paid formal obeisance to a caliph.

It fell to another group of Turkish tribesmen, the Saljuqs, to unite most of southwest Asia in the name of Sunnism and the Abbasid caliph. Known from the name of one of their ancestors, Saljuq, the new dynasty displaced the Iliq Khans and moved south in 1040 to vanquish the armies of the Ghaznavids, whose rule was afterward limited to Afghanistan and India. In 1055 the Saljuq Tughril Beg entered Baghdad and liberated the caliph from the Buyids. Recognized as "sultan" and "king of East and West," Tughril restored control after a Buyid army returned to establish the short-lived nominal authority of the Fatimids in Baghdad. On an intellectual level, the Saljuq championship of Sunnism soon involved the establishment of institutions of higher education, called *madrasahs,* in cities like Baghdad and Nishapur. While this was the beginning of a widespread kind of university, these in particular were known as *Nizamiyyahs* after the name of Sultan Alp Arslan's and Sultan Malikshah's brilliant Persian vizir, Nizam al-Mulk, who was mainly responsible for them.

In 1071, Alp Arslan achieved a success that matched that of the Ghaznavids in India by defeating the Byzantines at the Battle of Manzikert in eastern Anatolia. Already, during the previous thirty years, the Saljuqs had directed the aggressiveness of unruly Turkoman tribes into Anatolia, and parts of the peninsula had come under their control. But only after Manzikert did large-scale Turkish settlement begin, although the subsequent Turkification of what is now the Republic of Turkey (and parts of Iran, including Azarbayjan) probably owes more to assimilation than to immigration. The local population mostly was not displaced, and non-Chalcedonian Christians like the Armenians were delighted to have the tolerant Turks replace their former Orthodox master. Indeed, the process of Islamization remained incomplete until the twentieth-century exodus of Greeks and Armenians, while the Muslim, Indo-European Kurds still prevail in southeast Anatolia. This westernmost peninsula of geographic Asia that had been largely Hellenized for a millennium and thus culturally a part of Europe, was being incorporated into the Middle East.

Reaching its height under Sultan Malikshah, the Saljuq empire was divided among rival members of the house after his death in 1092. Of these, the Sultanate of Rum ("Rome"), whose effective independence in Anatolia had already emerged soon after Manzikert, was to play an important role as a link between the Saljuq empire and the later Ottomans. A second branch, centered in Hamadhan, in western Iran, long dominated the caliph. Another Saljuq, Sultan Sanjar, prevailed in all the eastern territories.

For a while, Sanjar was able to keep a restive Turkish dynasty, the shahs of Khwarazm, south of the Aral Sea, under control. He also bore the brunt of other Turkish tribes moving westward along the Central Asian steppes. Sanjar was captured by rebellious Turkish tribes in 1154, after which the eastern Saljuqs were so weakened that the Khwarazm-shah now took over their territories and became the main power in that region.

In the southwest Saljuq territories, local dynasties proliferated. In most cases nominally headed by Saljuq princes, the real powers in each were usually Turkish freedmen officers known as *atabegs* (literally, "father-lords"). One *atabeg* dynasty that provided the seed for greater things in the future was founded in Mosul by Imad al-Din Zangi in 1127 and soon expanded into northern Syria.

During the late twelfth century, especially after 1194, when the Hamadhan-centered Saljuqs succumbed to the Khwarazm-shahs, the Abbasid caliphs were able to assert some real power again. Caliph Nasir (1180–1225) astutely entered into the interdynastic rivalries of the region by playing off various rulers against the Khwarazm-shahs. He also found an effective base of political support in Baghdad in the chivalrous Futuwwah brotherhood, an organization that was widespread in Middle Eastern cities during this period. Aside from his importance as the formal head of Sunni Islam, his political control extended over most of Iraq and some small parts of southwestern Iran. However, in 1216 the Khwarazm-shah Muhammad was preparing to occupy Baghdad and set up a descendant of Ali as caliph. Nasir saved the Abbasid dynasty for a short time but invited its ultimate destruction, which may have been inevitable anyway, by appealing for help from the rising power of Chingiz Khan, whose loud rumbles could already be heard across the great distance separating Baghdad from Mongolia.

A NEW ISMA'ILI MOVEMENT: THE "ASSASSINS"

In reaction to the firm Sunni order of the Saljuqs, a new Isma'ili movement gained importance at the end of the eleventh century. Led by its chief missionary, the Persian Hasan ibn al-Sabbah, these revolutionaries took control of the impregnable mountain citadel of Alamut, in northwest Iran. From this main base other scattered fortresses in Iran, and soon also in Syria, came under their control. A corps of missionaries spread the doctrine, while trained *fida'iyin* ("self-sacrificers") took the lives of political leaders, beginning with Nizam al-Mulk, who posed a threat to the movement.

Hasan's followers broke with the Fatimids over a question of succession. They are properly called the Nizari Isma'ilis because they accepted Nizar as the rightful Fatimid caliph-*imam* after the death of his father in 1094. But they are better known as *Hashshashin* ("takers of hashish," corrupted in English to "Assassin") as a result of a set of seemingly apocryphal stories about the *fida'iyin's* being given the drug before their missions.

The Nizari strongholds lasted until the late 1200s. Though eventually losing its original revolutionary character, this branch of Isma'ilism survived as a small minority. Headed by their *imam*, the Agha Khan, most of the members now live in the Indian subcontinent.

WESTERN OFFENSIVE: THE CRUSADES

By the eleventh century, still largely semibarbaric western Europe was flexing its muscles. Venice and other Italian city-states that had grown up in the light of Byzantine civilization were taking over the Muslims' former naval dominance in the Mediterranean. Towns, crafts, and trade were growing in other parts of Europe. Norman adventurers wrested Sicily from Muslim control in 1071. Christians had already retaken about half of the Iberian peninsula and were slowly pushing the Muslims southward. With Christians responding to calls by their Spanish coreligionists for help, the Latin Christian version of holy war later known as the Crusades took form.

Although the rapid breakup of Saljuq unity left the Islamic world vulnerable, Constantinople was too weak to take advantage of the situation. One tactic of the Byzantine emperor was to ask for help from the Latin West. Byzantium and the Far West had little affection for each other, and the break between the Christendom of the remaining imperial territories (the Greek Orthodox) and that led by the Pope in the Far West (the Roman Catholic) had been finalized in 1054. Still, the emperor hoped that some knights would enter his service as mercenaries, but the surprising response was so immense that it frightened him.

The west Europeans had their own reasons for marching to Palestine. There had been stories of mistreatment of pilgrims by Turkish rulers. As always, the facts are complicated. Large bands of pilgrims, sometimes heavily armed, had often aroused popular resentment. The Saljuqs had facilitated pilgrimages, but with the breakup of the empire, the visitors often endured a degree of anarchy or else resented paying taxes to every petty prince whose domains they entered. Hakim's destruction of the Church of the Holy Sepulchre was also fresh in some Christian minds, while the fact that this was an aberration and was repudiated by Muslims, even by Hakim, may have been less well understood.

This was a spiritual age, in which a call to fight for one's faith was compelling. Still, materialistic motives may have been more important, as noblemen hoped to find principalities for themselves and as the bored, poverty-ridden masses sought excitement and plunder. Cities like Venice had an eye on commercial gains in territories conquered by Christendom. The Papacy may have hoped to reunify the Church under its authority. In any case, when Pope Urban II called for a crusade in 1095, cries that "It is the will of God" rang out in the enclave and echoed from the British Isles to Italy.

The "First Crusade" reached Constantinople in 1097. It joined imperial forces in recovering much of Anatolia for Byzantium, although the Sultanate of Rum survived in the interior. As city after city in Syria fell to the Crusaders and as the Venetian and Genoese fleets took coastal towns for them, Muslims and Jews were massacred, although the people in the countryside, among whom Christians were still quite numerous, survived and remained a majority in Crusader territory. The blood of the Muslim dead in Jerusalem is said to have been ankle deep as the Crusaders took control from the Fatimids in 1099, while the small Jewish community was burned alive in the Chief Synagogue.

Crusader leaders established kingdoms for themselves. Technically owing fealty to Constantinople, a king of Jerusalem ruled a state that included about all of Palestine and part of Transjordan all the way to the Gulf of Aqaba. A County of Tripoli, a County of Edessa, and a Principality of Antioch owed nominal allegiance to Jerusalem.

The uncultured Franks disgusted both Byzantines and Muslims with their cruelties and their manners. One Arab writer compared them to animals, but they gradually absorbed the refinement of the area, even Middle Eastern food and clothing. Those who returned to Europe may have helped to introduce more cultivated ways there. With Muslim rulers reacting pragmatically from the start, the Latin states also began to enter into alliances with them as their interests dictated and thus tended gradually to become part of the interstate politics of the area.

Despite their quick victories, the Crusaders—or "Franks," as the Muslims indiscriminately called them—scarcely extended their sway beyond the Mediterranean littoral. They were never more than a pinprick for the Islamic world as a whole. They could survive only as long as naval domination by the Italian states, who indeed became important middlemen for the Middle East and Europe, allowed the flow of reinforcements to continue and as long as Saljuq disintegration was not followed by the rise of another strong Muslim power.

THE EAST RECOVERING:
ZANGIDS AND AYYUBIDS

By the mid-twelfth century, the Muslim East began to repel the Western intrusion. With his army of Turkish *mamluks* and Kurdish tribesmen, the *atabeg* Zangi had created the first Muslim state able to confront the Franks. He dealt them a serious blow in 1144 by taking Edessa, and some Franks, but not Eastern Christians, were massacred. In response, a Second Crusade was organized, but it ended with the unsuccessful siege of Damascus. By this time, Zangi was dead, and his capable son, Nur al-Din, who ruled from Damascus, beleaguered the Crusaders. He finished off the County of Edessa and won some victories against the remaining Latin states.

Under the tottering Fatimid dynasty, Egypt provided the vigorous Zangids with a field from which the countercrusade would gain force. The last Egyptian-held enclave on the Palestinian coast was lost to the Franks in 1153, and they raided the

Nile Delta and exacted tribute. Shawar, a former Fatimid vizir who lost to a rival, took refuge in Syria and sought aid from Nur al-Din.

The Zangid ruler's right-hand man, a Kurdish general named Shirkuh, took an army to Egypt and restored Shawar to power. But the ungrateful Egyptian refused to pay the compensation that he had promised and called on the king of Jerusalem to help get rid of the Syrian army, whose only alternative was to return empty-handed. A return campaign by Shawar to Egypt was also foiled by the Crusader-Fatimid alliance. But Shawar implored Nur al-Din to send help again, as the Crusaders, who on one occasion carried out an indiscriminate massacre of both Muslims and Copts, again tried to take control of Egypt. This time (in 1169), Shirkuh's strong army assured his success, and the Crusaders withdrew from the country. With Shawar beheaded before he could carry out another plot, Shirkuh became the new vizir, but he died two months later. The vizirate passed on to his nephew, Salah al-Din Yusuf ibn-Ayyub (corrupted by Westerners to "Saladin"), a studious, intensely religious young man who had participated ably, if at first reluctantly, in his uncle's three expeditions.

Salah al-Din's leadership of the Islamic world's upsurge was to make his father and the Zangids a mere prelude. For eighteen years he worked to consolidate his position before pursuing the drive against the Crusaders. Soon after he became vizir, a joint Frankish-Byzantine expedition descended on Egypt by land and sea, but a shortage of provisions, and finally a storm, put an end to the invasion. Salah al-Din battled occasionally with the Crusaders, and a Norman Sicilian naval invasion of Alexandria was foiled in 1186, but he gave more attention to other matters for several years.

Symbolizing the Sunni restoration, Salah al-Din dropped the name of the figurehead Fatimid caliph from the Friday sermon in 1171 in favor of his Abbasid rival. Aside from *jihad* against the Franks, Salah al-Din's passion was Sunnism, and he strove to let the *shari'ah* guide his government. Following the Saljuq example he supported the establishment of Sunni *madrasahs* that temporarily replaced al-Azhar, itself later to be transformed into the greatest training ground for Sunni Islam.

The abolition of the Fatimid caliphate was an anticlimatic end for the previous Isma'ili political upsurge. Isma'ilis became a small minority even among Shi'ites. The few who still accepted the leadership of the last Fatimid caliphs soon vanished. Aside from the Nizaris, the main group of Isma'ilis was to be the Tayyibis, who recognized a different branch of the Fatimid family from 1130 on and survive mainly in Yemen and in India as a commercially oriented Bohora ("trader") community.

Salah al-Din was in an anomalous relationship with the Zangids. Egypt was naturally the main base of Muslim power in the eastern Mediterranean region, but he continued to submit to some control from Damascus. The relationship was already tense when Nur al-Din died in 1174, after which several weak members of the Zangid family set up virtually independent states. Salah al-Din had extended his control to the Hijaz, Barqah, and Yemen, while a number of internal threats, ranging from plots to restore the Fatimids to a mutiny of black African troops, were suppressed. From Nur al-Din's death until 1186, Salah al-Din was busy with a series of military campaigns in Syria and northern Iraq that essentially brought the former Zangid territories under his control. Syrian-Egyptian unity created a ring around the Crusaders, who were now wracked with internecine conflict as well.

Salah al-Din put diplomacy to work in preparation for the coming battle. Commercial relations with the Italian states enhanced Egyptian prosperity and decreased the Crusaders' usefulness to them. A Cairo-Constantinople treaty of 1181 encouraged the growing Byzantine-Frankish breach. Then the Crusaders attacked a Muslim caravan in 1187, in violation of a peace treaty concluded two years earlier.

Salah al-Din had been waiting for just such provocation. The war resumed with an immediate blow to the Crusader movement. In the Battle of Hattin, in northern Palestine, the Franks suffered severe losses, and the 20,000 who survived, including the king of Jerusalem, fell into captivity. Within the next six months, the Muslims took city after city, including Jerusalem. The Crusaders were left only a few enclaves on the coast north of Palestine. While not all of his commanders rose above the cruelty expected in this age, Salah al-Din earned a reputation in East and West for magnanimity by freeing thousands of Frankish captives who could not pay the customary ransom. While Frankish settlers fled, indigenous Christians were respected and sometimes appeared to welcome the change of regime, and the Muslims allowed Jews to settle in Jerusalem again.

Latin Europe responded with a "Third Crusade," led by its greatest monarchs. Following a two-year siege, the Frankish forces took Acre, followed by the massacre of 2,700 Muslim prisoners. Then, after this modest achievement, the Crusaders were willing to accept a peace settlement in 1192 that limited them to a narrow strip from Jaffa to Acre but gave their unarmed pilgrims the right to visit Jerusalem.

From his death in 1193 until the mid-thirteenth century, Salah al-Din was followed by a series of sultans from his family, the Ayyubids. The Syrian part of the empire tended to break up as various Ayyubids established their own principalities. While Egypt was able to maintain a tenuous hegemony for a while, it later lost control.

The Franks even regained some of their earlier position. Although those domiciled in the East seemed to lose their crusading zeal and devoted their energies to internal squabbling, reinforcements renewed the old spirit. In 1219 and 1249 the Fifth and Sixth Crusades struck at the Egyptian Delta with some initial success but got bogged down each time in the floods and networks of canals. In the Sixth Crusade, the army of the saintly King Louis IX of France suffered disaster, and the king was captured.

Ayyubids sometimes demonstrated pragmatic policies in these matters. Sultan Kamil disgusted the Islamic world in 1229 when he let his alliance with a Holy Roman emperor who agreed not to organize a new crusade induce him to cede Jerusalem and a corridor connecting with Acre to the Franks. But the Franks were hardly a force to contend with a newly unified Egypt and Syria.

EMERGENCE OF THE MAMLUK SULTANATE

The seed of such a revived power—and for the end of the Ayyubids—was planted by Sultan Malik al-Salih (1240 –1249). Instead of the former Ayyubids' heavy reliance on Kurdish troops, al-Salih turned to the more traditional basis of an Islamic army, Turkish *mamluks*. The largest group of al-Salih's *mamluks* was stationed on the island of Rawdah in the River (*Bahr*) Nile; with their successors, who provided a series of sultans, they were consequently known as the Bahri *mamluks*. It was these soldiers, foremost of whose commanders was Baybars, who defeated King Louis IX in 1250.

Already, a remarkable series of events was bringing the *mamluks* to power. When Malik al-Salih died in 1249, his widow, Shajar al-Dur (a former slave) strove to prevent a struggle for power in the army by keeping the death a secret until the return of his son, Turah Shah, from a military campaign. In the meantime, she managed to rule in the late sultan's name. When the son returned, he soon antagonized the Bahri *mamluks* by showing partiality for other troops. Conniving with Shajar al-Dur, the Bahris murdered Turan Shah and made her "sultan." Taunted by a letter from the caliph offering to send a man to rule if none was available in Egypt, the *mamluks* got Shajar to marry one of their commanders, Aybak, who now assumed the sultanate jointly with a six-year-old Ayyubid puppet. But Shajar continued to be in effective charge of the government.

Set afire with jealousy when Aybak decided to take another wife, Shajar had him murdered in his bath in 1257. In turn, she was beaten to death, and another *mamluk* commander, Qutuz, soon became the new ruler.

The so-called Mamluk[1] dynasty thus emerged. In fact, it was not a dynasty, as succession was not mainly hereditary (and sons of *mamluks* were mostly barred from the elite corps) but often emerged from struggles among the army commanders. Following the general pattern begun under the Abbasids, the *mamluk* oligarchy in Cairo was perpetuated over the centuries through the continuous purchase of slaves.

MUSLIM RECOVERY IN ANATOLIA

The Saljuq sultans of Rum eventually recovered from the blow of the First Crusade and paralleled the Ayyubids' success against Christendom. For a while the sultans were dominated by another Anatolian dynasty, the Danishmendids, but Sultan Mas'ud asserted his primacy in the remaining Turkish territories of Anatolia by the mid-twelfth century and began to expand at Byzantine expense. When the Second

---

[1]The word "Mamluk" is capitalized here when it refers to this specific state or regime, but not when it refers to members of the freedman military and ruling class in this and other regimes.

Crusade tried to cross Anatolia in 1147, Turkish forces defeated it. Those who could not afford to continue their journey to Palestine by ship became the recipients of Turkish charity, and some converted to Islam. The last Byzantine attempt to restore control in Anatolia ended in utter failure in 1176.

With subsequent expansion extending its rule over most of Anatolia, the Sultanate of Rum reached its height in the 1220s and 1230s. Its armies defeated Crusaders, Khwarazmis, and Ayyubids at different times. The Kingdom of Lesser Armenia, which had emerged in southern Anatolia, came under the sultan's hegemony. However, the incompetent sultans who followed, in addition to a revolt led by the Turkish chieftain and "prophet" Baba Ishaq, who was suppressed with great effort in 1240, left the state weakened in the face of an emerging threat from Mongolia. But now it is time for us to turn from politics and war to cultural developments.

ISLAMIC CIVILIZATION

The period from the eighth to the thirteenth century was one of cultural florescence. During the early Abbasid period a prosperous empire poured vast amounts of wealth into the capital, and the government lavished it on patronizing artists, writers, and scholars. Then, rather than dimming as the empire fell apart, the light of Islamic civilization glowed brightly from new centers and in sundry colors as rival dynasties vied with each other culturally as well as politically.

The early Abbasid period saw a convergence of the world's heritages that enriched a civilization whose core was Islamic and Arab. To take one example, a clash of Islamic and Chinese armies in 751 resulted in the capture of Chinese paper makers and the consequent use of paper in the Middle East and the West. Sanskrit mathematical texts were translated into Arabic. Other works were translated from Pahlavi, perhaps the best known being the Persian government official ibn-Muqaffa's version of the book of animal fables called *Kalilah and Dimnah,* which was originally written in Sanskrit. The popular stories that were evolving into *The Thousand and One Nights* also exemplify the diversity of sources, particularly Indian. But no other alien culture had an impact on Islamic civilization comparable to the Hellenic.

The usual division of fields of intellectual endeavor into "Arab" and "foreign" (basically Greek, secondarily Indian) sciences epitomizes the two strains in medieval Islam. The "Arab sciences" were those connected with Islam and the Arabic language, of which we have already seen the study of jurisprudence and *hadith.* Aside from theology, which was largely in response to Hellenism, other fields of literature connected with Islam were the commentaries on the Qur'an, including that of the ninth- to tenth-century al-Tabari, or the biographies of the Prophet like that of ibn-Hisham. Al-Tabari was perhaps the most important medieval Islamic historian. He is reputed to have written forty pages a day for forty years. The *History of al-Tabari,* which survives only in a condensed version now published in ten large volumes, provides the typical chronological account, mainly of Islamic history, but it also presents divergent versions of the same stories and the author's source for each. Unlike the usual annalists was the tenth-century al-Mas'udi, whose descriptions of different countries like those in the one surviving fragment called *Meadows of Gold* has earned him comparisons with Herodotus. Conquests, pilgrimages, trade, and the postal service also inspired many writers to produce important geographical works.

Since the study of religion involved an Arabic Qur'an, a body of literature emerged in the related fields of grammar and lexicography. While Arabs were more likely to take their own language for granted, the conversion of Persians gave a special fillip to these studies.

The rules of literary (classical) Arabic were permanently established. The models were the Qur'an and pre-Islamic poetry. Arabic has evolved into many "colloquial" dialects that vary from country to country about as much as Italian does from Spanish, both of which developed in a similar way from Latin. But the literary language that educated Arabs read and write or use in formal lectures (and which even non-Arab Muslims use as a religious language) is the same everywhere and has not basically changed since early Islamic times.

BELLES-LETTRES

Literature came to be associated with a kind of sophisticated, well-mannered society, particularly that of the high bureaucracy. A refined person (*adib*) was expected to possess broad knowledge, especially about the Arab heritage and Arabic literature, and to be able to quote from it extensively. The ornate, artistic essays on subjects ranging from animals to the alleged superiority of the black race written by the ninth-century Amr al-Jahiz, whose grandfather was a black African slave, set the standard for a kind of literary polish for the *adib* to match. *Adab*, an Arabic word that might originally have been translated as "urbanity" came to mean "literature" or *belles-lettres*.

The Arabic language's endemic genius for poetry reached its zenith at the Abbasid and Hamdanid courts. Freeing themselves from long-lasting rigid conventions developed by what one writer now contemptuously called "bedouin vagabonds," countless poets nevertheless continued their predecessors' tradition of irreverence. There was the part-Persian Abu Nuwas, patronized and befriended but sometimes imprisoned by Harun al-Rashid. One of Abu Nuwas' hedonistic wine poems proclaimed his unhappiness with ever having to be sober and advocated enjoying as many sins as possible in the belief that God would be forgiving. And there was one nicknamed "al-Mutanabbi" ("the Pretender to be a Prophet," once imprisoned for this light-hearted sacrilege), whose eulogies at the court of the tenth-century Hamdanid ruler, Sayf al-Dawlah, led him subsequently to be deemed by many Arabs as their greatest poet.

The blind Abu al-Ala al-Ma'ari also received Sayf al-Dawlah's favors for a while, but spent most of his life as a recluse and a vegetarian in his small Syrian hometown. Abu al-Ala cynically described the evils of a world into which he resented having been born. He denounced all conventional religion, Islam included, as superstition and sought refuge in a rationalistic concept of God and an ethic of love and compassion. When he failed in an attempt to prove that a mere human could imitate the Qur'an, he insisted that this must be because so many readers had edited it to perfection for centuries.

Rhymed prose became another important Arabic literary medium. In particular, the pens of the Persian Badi al-Zaman ("the Wonder of the Age") Hamadhani and the Basran Abu Muhammad al-Hariri developed a genre known as *maqamat* ("assemblies," so-called because the storyteller usually performed before the assembly of men after Friday prayers) in the tenth and eleventh centuries. In a highly ornate style that tends to make use of linguistic gymnastics, the *maqamat* relate stories of the narrator and a clever, eloquent trickster that he continuously meets during his travels and vividly portray the life of the age. Some aspects of the *maqamat* exerted a strong influence on Italian and Spanish literature, as shown in works like *Don Quixote*.

THE HELLENIC IMPACT

The impact of Hellenic civilization on the Islamic world accelerated after 750. Moving the center of the empire away from the Mediterranean littoral did not make Hellenic influence more distant, for it had continued to live in places far removed from the original source. Nestorian and Monophysite Christians, as well as the pagan "Sabians" in northern Iraq, had absorbed much of Hellenic civilization, and many Greek writings had been translated into Syriac and Pahlavi. Jundi-Shapur, in western Iran, had been a major center of Greek learning, with emphasis on medicine, since Shah Khusraw Nushirwan welcomed the arrival of Nestorian Christian scholars in the sixth century. For that matter, both Indians and Central Asian Buddhists, who had never completely shaken off Alexander's cultural legacy, provided sources of indirect Hellenic influences. This time Greek civilization came, not like before as a blow to moribund ancient Middle Eastern civilizations, but as welcome food for a vigorous, self-confident one. And just as the ancient East provided the West's spiritual element, the still-glowing coals of the ancient "West" strengthened the Islamic East's rational, scientific side. Like ancient Jews and Christians, Muslims also struggled with the problem of integrating the two parts.

The first stage, which gained full speed soon after 750, was the translation into Arabic of Greek philosophy, a term used broadly to include fields like medicine and mathematics. Manuscripts were eagerly sought out, and the "House of Wisdom" in Baghdad stored them and served as a translation center, as well as offering instruction. A corps of translators turned Plato, Aristotle, Plotinus, Galen, Claudius Ptolemy, Euclid, and a host of others into Arabic, sometimes directly but mostly from Syriac versions. While indeed Constantinople and the lands it controlled also preserved ancient Greek civilization, much would have been lost except for the Muslims, and it is paradoxical that the dose of Hellenism that later inspired the western European Renaissance came largely by way of the Islamic world, particularly through Spain.

ISLAMIC SCIENCE AND PHILOSOPHY: CARRYING THE HELLENIC TORCH

Islamic scholars proceeded from translations to original contributions in the Hellenic and Hindu traditions. A few examples of Islamic science will show that this was a high point of creativity, perhaps overshadowed only by the burst of discovery that occurred much later in Europe. Medieval cities like Baghdad and Cairo had pharmacies and hospitals, and medical researchers, whose religion forbade the dissection of human bodies, sought apes as the best substitute. Among the many medical treatises, those of the eighth- to ninth-century Persian physician al-Razi were standard texts in western Europe until the sixteenth century. Advances occurred in many fields of mathematics, and the word "algebra" is a corruption of part of the title of a book by the ninth-century Iranian mathematician, Muhammad al-Khwarazmi, whose receptivity to the Hindu-invented zero initiated the use of "Arabic" numerals in the West. As early as the reign of Ma'mun an observatory existed in Baghdad. Islamic astronomers knew that the earth is round, and another eleventh-century Khwarazmi, al-Biruni, was familiar with the still-disfavored idea that it rotates on its axis. Patronized successfully by the Samanids and by Mahmud of Ghaznah, al-Biruni also wrote penetrating treatises on many subjects, including Sanskrit philosophy and Indian society.

This was also an age of philosophical writing in a more specialized sense. Such names as the ninth-century Arab al-Kindi, the tenth-century al-Farabi (of Turkish origin, patronized by the Hamdanids), and the eleventh-century Persian ibn-Sina (who served the Buyids as vizir) are prominent in any truly worldwide history of philosophy. Absorbing the writings of Plato and Aristotle and drawing heavily on neo-Platonic writers like Plotinus, Islamic philosophers strove to combine and reconcile Hellenic concepts with Islam. To cite some typical ideas, the concept of God came to be identified with the philosophical notion of "First Cause," taken from Hellenic cosmological doctrines, with the universe "emanating" from it via such phenomena as "absolute reason" and "active intellect." A prophet—equated with Plato's Philosopher King—was one who used "imaginative faculties" to provide the same truths obtainable through reason, but in a symbolic form understandable by the masses. Such philosophical activity was anathema to people with conventional religious ideas and generally withered after the twelfth century, although new kinds of "philosophical theology" flourished long afterward.

DEVELOPMENT OF THEOLOGY

Islamic theology emerged largely in response to the philosophical movement. One group of scholars began to turn Hellenic methods to the defense of Islam and developed the theological school of Mu'tazilism, which was infused with rationalism. Sometimes misunderstood as being "free-thinkers," the Mu'tazilites nevertheless were ardent Muslims whose monotheism was carried to great lengths.

One Mu'tazilite doctrine related to God's not determining human acts. To the horror of many Muslims, who stressed God's absolute power (and thus the inapplicability of human concepts of justice to Him), the Mu'tazilites conceived of a God of justice, who would not arbitrarily punish people for acts that He had forced on them. Thus they insisted on the doctrine of free will.

Other Mu'tazilite concepts are related to a stress on the oneness of God. The Mu'tazilites objected to the anthropomorphic idea that God literally has hands and other parts mentioned in the Qur'an and insisted that to treat the ninety-nine Qur'anic names of God ("the Beneficient," "the Victorious," etc.) as "attributes" was contrary to the fact of his unity. Of special importance in this regard, the Mu'-tazilites rejected the idea that the Qur'an is uncreated (i.e., that it has always existed) as meaning that God has a partner. Instead, they argued that the Qur'an was created when it was revealed to Muhammad. The more literalist Muslims, known as "people of *hadith*," or Traditionalists, whose most ardent exponents were the Hanbalites, bitterly rejected such speculation, as did later schools of theology.

For a while, beginning with the era of Ma'mun, Mu'tazilism was in official favor. A *mihnah* ("inquisition"), the only example of such an institution in Islamic history, was set up to test the doctrines of teachers, judges, and such. The acid test was to ask whether the Qur'an was created. Ahmad ibn-Hanbal's resolute refusal to accept the Mu'tazilite doctrine, despite imprisonment, beatings, and threats of execution, earned him the admiration of later ages of Muslims. But soon afterward, the state turned away from Mu'tazilism, which, without official support and in the face of new theological formulas, eventually died out among the Sunnis. However, Shi'ites have preserved some of its doctrines.

It was in reaction to Mu'tazilism that orthodox Sunni theology was formulated. Among the conservative theologians who turned this kind of disputation against the Mu'tazilites was Abu al-Hasan al-Ash'ari, an early tenth-century Basran who once embraced the doctrine himself but turned away from it after the Prophet Muhammad appeared to him, so it is said, in a series of dreams. For al-Ash'ari, the Qur'an is uncreated, and anthropomorphic passages, though inexplicable, cannot be treated as merely metaphorical. Free will was rejected too; God alone determines our acts, because a person's "free will" itself is predetermined. It is the choice put in the mind by God, although He somehow allows us to "acquire" the responsibility. In the Ash'arite conception, described as "atomistic," God recreates every phenomenon in the universe separately every instant, and no one has control over his future. Other theologians, notably the more liberal al-Maturidi, a Central Asian contemporary of al-Ash'ari, were to have less influence on the Islamic mainstream.

Of course, the Hanbalites, with their total rejection of Hellenic rationalism, also survived, and not just as a school of jurisprudence.

Although this is susceptible to oversimplification, it is sometimes suggested that the Muslim's resignation to God's will, following al-Ash'ari's theory, has held back progress. Ash'arite theology does seem to typify a rejection of innovation and generally of Hellenic and other influences that contributed to the Islamic world's early flowering. But it is doubtful that such a doctrine has affected people's efforts in any area of life. In any case, great achievement by Muslims did not end with Ash'arism.[2]

SUFISM

Another strain of thought that began early in Islam has so far escaped mention. Known as Sufism, apparently from the plain wool (*suf*) clothing that its originators wore, the movement provided an alternative to an intellectualism that few understood and to the legalistic rules of the *ulama* and their concept of a stern, remote God. Stressing the mercy and love of God and their love for Him, Sufis renounced the world in favor of voluntary poverty. And, citing a Qur'anic verse that declared God to be as close to each person as his own jugular vein, the dervishes ("*darvish*," "poor," in Persian; "*faqir*" in Arabic) turned to mystical communion with the Divine. From there they sometimes turned to the goal of drowning their own independent existence in union with him. Ceremonies developed in which constant repetition of words and body movements put devotees in trances.

Sufism produced many examples of sainthood. The woman Sufi Rabi'ah, who died in 901, epitomized the spirit of the movement by declaring her love of God to be so overwhelming that she had no time even for hating the devil and by asking God to send her to Hell if she worshipped him only for the sake of Paradise. She refused all offers of marriage on the ground that she did not exist apart from God. When another Sufi, al-Hallaj, told of his attainment of union with the Deity by saying "I am the Truth" (one of the Qur'anic names of God), the authorities took this as blasphemy and crucified him in 927. Following the example of Jesus, a figure especially revered by many Sufis, Hallaj asked God to forgive his executioners, whose actions he described as natural for people who had not been favored by what had been revealed to him.

A vast Sufi theological literature emerged that included some of Islam's most lofty poetry. The *Epistles* of the eleventh-century al-Qushairi outlined forty-five stations (stages) on the Sufi way that ended with incessant desire to be with God. Other writers identified as many as a hundred stations. The concept of a hierarchy of saints emerged. The voluminous esoteric writings of the tenth-century Spanish-born ibn-al-Arabi, who apparently claimed to be the "Seal of the Saints," were of particular

---

[2]Also, the later transition to modernity was unique to parts of the West (and paradoxically sometimes attributed to Calvinist predestinationism). It is not the failure of the Middle East, along with most of the world, to undergo such abnormal developments that requires explanation.

importance. Another example of Sufi writing was that of the great Persian poet Jalal al-Din al-Rumi, who lived in the Sultanate of Rum during the thirteenth century.

Begun in individual practice, Sufism soon developed into monastic orders (*tariqahs,* "ways") with networks of meeting places or monasteries. Groups like the Mevlevya (or Mawlawa), which claimed Rumi as its founder and was famous for its "whirling dervishes," had leaders (*shaykhs,* Persian "*pirs*") who were accorded the status of saints after their death. Practices varied widely from order to order, with celibacy practiced by a few. Large numbers of lay members were attached to each lodge and participated in its ceremonies.

This became a popular form of religion that seemed to be increasingly at variance with official Islam. Not only did such Sufi corruptions as snake-handling, taking drugs, and saint worship pose dilemmas for all who understood Islam, but even moderate Sufism seemed alien to most of the *ulama* and perhaps threatened to displace orthodox observances. While several men tried to reconcile the two divergent approaches, the success of such an attempt awaited the writings of Abu al-Hamid al-Ghazali, who died in 1111.

AL-GHAZALI: "RENEWER OF THE FAITH"

In the tradition that Islam has a renewer every hundred years, al-Ghazali is reputed to be the one who rose at the beginning of the sixth Muslim century. Already one of the most highly recognized scholars of his time, the thirty-seven-year-old professor of Shafi'i law and the head of the Nizamiyyah Madrasah in Baghdad, was overtaken by a spiritual crisis in 1095. He had already written several important books, including the *Incoherence of the Philosophers* (later answered by the leading Spanish Muslim philosopher ibn-Rushd's book, the *Incoherence of Incoherence*), which struck a blow at the recent wave of Greek-inspired writing while using much Greek philosophy in the process. But now he was dissatisfied with striving for wealth and recognition in the academic world and became so obsessed with the danger of hell that he developed a speech defect and could not teach.

Al-Ghazali told how he had already turned to philosophy, Isma'ilism, and theology but found each inadequate. For a while he lost all faith. Now, in 1095, he left his family and position behind to make pilgrimages to Jerusalem and Mecca and finally to take up a life of mysticism in his native town in Khurasan. It was ten years before he was persuaded to take a professorship in the Nishapur Madrasah. In works such as *The Revival of Religious Sciences* he demonstrated convincingly to Islamic scholars that orthodoxy and Sufism, at least if not carried to extremes, need not be opposed, how indeed rituals like prayer were the foundation but that a deeper meaning can be provided by mysticism. It is to al-Ghazali that much of the credit is due for the continued, if sometimes uneasy, coexistence, of the two approaches to Islam.

THE RISE OF THE NEW PERSIAN

The emergence of independent dynasties in Iran brought a linguistic and literary revival that perpetuated the Persian national identity and put the Persian tongue alongside Arabic as a supranational Islamic language. The older Pahlavi (Middle Persian) survived only as a language read by Zoroastrian priests, whose religion was reduced to a small minority by the tenth century. (About 20,000 Zoroastrians still live in Iran today, but there are more in India, where they are known as Parsis.)

Persians had long written a disproportionate share of Arabic literature, and even the Shu'ubiyyah movement had used Arabic as its medium. Arabic was to remain an important language for Persians in the religious field, but, aside mainly from the southwestern province of Khuzistan, the language of Arabia would never displace the local forms of speech, which include several minor regional languages such as Kurdish and Baluchi.

Beginning with the Tahirids and the Saffarids, a body of literature developed that transformed a post-Pahlavi patois into the Iranian national language, New Persian. The Samanids, who nevertheless still used Arabic as the official language, accelerated this trend through their generous patronage of Persian poetry. The linguistic legacy of the Arab conquest remained in the form of the Arabic alphabet, which, with minor adjustments, became the vehicle for New Persian writing. Also, much like the Latin contribution to English, the vocabularies of New Persian and other languages of Islamic peoples have borrowed many Arabic words, particularly in matters relating to religion and government.

The rise of Turkish dynasties brought new momentum to Persian culture, as Turkish rulers eagerly sought Persian sophistication in their courts. The Turks who entered the Middle East did not produce any written literature in their own language during this period, but a host of writers gained Persian poetry, and, to a lesser extent, prose, an unexcelled place in world literature.

It was the pen of Firdawsi who brought the rhymed couplet and Persian poetry generally to a climax with his monumental *Book of Kings (Shah Namah)*. Writing for Mahmud of Ghaznah, Firdawsi set the standard for the Persian language and, with his immortal portrayal of ancient Persian heroes, kept the country's pre-Islamic past alive in the memory of all Iranians.

The Islamic conquest brought a break with the Iranian heritage in the sense that Pahlavi literature was subsequently known only in the form of translations into New Persian. Paradoxically, conversion to Islam was eventually nearly universal in Iran, whereas large Christian groups continued to exist in Syria and Egypt. But the survival of Iranian ethnic and linguistic distinctiveness—and thus of a separate national identity—would be in contrast to the Fertile Crescent's and Egypt's nearly total Arabicization.

Under the Saljuqs the geographic realm of Persian literature was extended into most Islamic regions north and east of the Fertile Crescent. Nizam al-Mulk's *Book of Government* is a prime example of the "mirror for princes" genre, dealing with the art of government. Its keen insight deserves an important place in political thought. Strangely, it is the great mathematician, astronomer, and masterful amateur poet Omar Khayyam, whose quatrains (*Ruba'iyat*) are best known in the English-speaking world. The mystical writings of Rumi and his contemporary, Sa'di, represent a poetry that continued to flourish for centuries.

ART AND ARCHITECTURE

With the Abbasids' shift of the capital to Iraq, the Eastern features of art and architecture became more evident, as Sasanian influence emerged in mosques and palaces. While few of the spectacular examples have survived, the Great Mosque of Samarra, with its spiraling minaret, even reflects the historically remote example of the Sumerian ziggurat. The Mosque of ibn-Tulun in Egypt also shows some remarkable similarities to this. Indeed, the Samarran style of enormous fortified palaces and mosques using ornamental stucco over burnt brick became widespread. A great deal of carved stucco and carved wood ornamented the doors and walls, typically in rosette and vine leaf designs. The Samanids, in the tomb of Isma'il at Bukhara, built in 907, contributed the overhanging niche (stalactite) which fills in the space wherever a circular dome rests on a square frame. This is an exclusively Islamic development and was used throughout this period.

Despite its short life Samarra produced artistic results that served as models for the entire Islamic realm. Not only was its stucco famous, but Islamic pottery styles were first found here. Especially noticeable during this period is the impact of T'ang Chinese porcelains on Muslim ceramics. The Samarrans imitated the Chinese techniques, and from this emerged the exclusively Middle Eastern polychrome lusterware pots and vases. Most of the figures on these were Central Asian, with even the Bactrian (two-humped) camel rather than its Middle Eastern one-humped relative depicted.

Indicative of the great diversity of styles are the many varieties of minarets. Spain showed a preference for square shapes, while Central Asia opted for cylinders. Conical ones existed in Iran, and something resembling a candle extinguisher appeared at the top of some in Anatolia. Of course, climate had a great deal to do with the shape and materials of buildings. Tops of Anatolian structures had to be built to shed the rain, and it was more practical to work with brick than stucco. The Saljuqs used bricks in their mausoleums, mosques, and *madrasahs*. Covering an entire wall with glazed tile is considered one of their innovations.

Islamic strictures against human or animal figures diverted art to the prolific use of foliated inscriptions, begun in Kufah and perfected by artists in Fatimid Egypt. Fancy calligraphy was used in an artistic, geometric Kufic script, with final letters ending in elaborate shapes of palms or flowers. Within the paintings were often hidden different animals, and a sharp eye could sometimes pick out a human form. The combination of people and animals cleverly formed a message, often verses of the Qur'an. European Christian cathedrals sometimes copied this work without realizing that it contained Qur'anic inscriptions.

While diverse dynasties built their mosques, palaces, mausoleums, and *madrasahs,* artisans throughout the Islamic world showed their creativity in working with metals, pottery, and even cloth. Damascus and Mosul became famous centers for intricate inlaid metal work. Weapons, trays, and vases were much sought after. Along with this, the art of inlaid wood carving developed, using mother-of-pearl and ivory. Mosaic techniques taken from the Byzantines emerged in Islamic tiles. Aside from their use of glazed tiles, the Saljuqs brought carpet making into the Middle East. Originating in Central Asia, this art, like other forms, turned up in Iran and Egypt. The pattern in the carpet was usually geometric, with Kufic around the borders. Most of the printed textiles produced in Fatimid Egypt utilized this same kind of pattern.

ECONOMIC DECLINE

While the expensive monuments to this civilization took form, economic deterioration made way for a long-range decline of the Middle East. Agriculture in particular became less productive, as irrigation brought salinization in some places and as governments became increasingly lax in maintaining complicated irrigation systems. There may even have been geological changes that caused the Tigris, Euphrates, and their tributaries to flow faster, aggravating the problem. The decline of Iraq is notable after the early Abbasid period and helps to account for the shift of the centers of power and civilization to Egypt and other sites in the Islamic world. Nomadic incursions sometimes devastated agricultural land, although the primary example of such a phenomenon occurred with the Hilali tribes' invasion of North Africa in the eleventh century. In any case, well before the thirteenth century the decline of agriculture was widespread, both absolutely and relative to developments in Europe such as the use of new kinds of harnesses or the windmill (the latter ironically invented and formerly used in Iran). Some villages were deserted, and government revenues fell dramatically.

Administrative patterns gave impetus to decline. With revenues harder to come by, governments turned collection over to tax-farmers, who, being allowed to keep all above a fixed sum for themselves, gouged the peasantry. Corruption became increasingly commonplace. The use of property sometimes became immobilized as perpetual trusts (*waqfs*) were set up either for the support of mosques, schools, and the like or simply for members of the family as a way of avoiding confiscation. From Buyid times on, and increasingly under the Saljuqs, Ayyubids, and Mamluks, a kind of feudalism emerged, but it was unlike the European version in many ways. In the Middle East, holders of fiefs (*iqta*) lived in the cities, not on self-sufficient manors, and holdings were rarely hereditary and were often rotated. This gave fief holders little identification with the land and little incentive to make improvements; instead, it gave them every reason to squeeze all they could from it. Thus while European feudalism may have provided a transition for recovery from the Germanic onslaught, the Middle Eastern variant portended stagnation and decay. But now it is time to return to our political narrative and to the final blow that was to fall on the classical age.

THE MONGOL INVASION

As the Christian tide receded in Syria and Anatolia, a more serious threat rose in the northeast. At the beginning of the thirteenth century the tribes of Mongolia were welded together by a chieftain subsequently known as Chingiz Khan. Within a half century he and his successors led their armies, which included both Mongols and Turks along with Chinese engineers and artillery, as far west as central Europe and as far east as the Sea of Japan. When they came to the Islamic Middle East, they demonstrated a ferocity that was apparently based on both calculated terror and sheer sadism. In Middle Eastern eyes, they appeared as monsters who threatened all civilization and human life.

Some Christians had a different reaction. They wishfully hoped that Chingiz, whose people included a few Nestorians, would prove to be the legendary Far Eastern Christian "Prester John," or at least would convert to their faith and join Europe in a pincers movement against Islam. Although Christian Europe was not spared the Mongol scourge, Christian kingdoms like Armenia and Georgia collaborated with the new power, and the Christian population of conquered territories in the Middle East was sometimes favored.

Chingiz at first overestimated Khwarazmi power and sought an alliance rather than conquest. But Shah Muhammad was angered by a letter addressing him as his "son," and the Mongol emissaries were killed. What Mongol expansionism made inevitable in the long run thus came quickly as the angry Chingiz led his horsemen westward in 1219 and overran Khwarazm. Cities like Bukhara, Samarqand, Marv, and Nishapur were destroyed and never fully recovered. The Mongols strove to wipe out the conquered population, although some whose skills as artisans could be used were taken to Mongolia. Mounds of human skulls were left, and estimates of the number killed run as high as 15 million. Hordes of refugees loosely designated as Khwarazmis poured westward. Some were welcomed as mercenary troops in various places and even helped the Ayyubids recover Jerusalem in 1243, but more often they excited fear in the lands where they sought refuge.

A respite for the Middle East followed as Chingiz returned home weighted down with booty. His successor was busy with the conquest of China, but Anatolia felt the storm in 1242 as the Mongols defeated the Saljuqs and then penetrated deep into the peninsula. Although facing increasing Mongol domination, the Saljuqs of Rum avoided extermination by agreeing to pay tribute.

In 1253 Great Khan Mengu sent an army commanded by Hulagu, grandson of

Chingiz, to finish the conquests in the Middle East. After a three-year siege, Alamut fell, and the power of the "Assassins" was uprooted. When Baghdad's turn came in 1258, it was sacked, and a large proportion of its population was massacred. The caliph and other members of the Abbasid house were killed, and for a while Sunni Islam lacked a head. While Arabia was spared, Hulagu, named *il khan* ("viceroy") for the Middle Eastern territories with loyalty to a great khan soon to be seated in Beijing, swept through Syria.

Egypt proved to be the only power west of Japan capable of stopping the Mongol tide. After Sultan Qutuz executed the emissaries sent to ask for his submission, Baybars defeated an advance unit at Gaza and proceeded to northern Palestine, where the Mongol army was encamped at a place called Ayn Jalut ("Goliath's Spring"). By this time, Hulagu had left for the Far East to involve himself in a struggle for power after Mengu's death. The troops Hulagu had left behind in Palestine were greatly outnumbered by the *mamluks,* who were themselves ferocious sons of the Eurasian steppe. On the other hand, the Mongols had never in memory lost a major battle. But, pursuing the first Egyptian attackers in the decisive Battle of Ayn Jalut in September 1260, the Mongols were then decimated by the *mamluk* horsemen and quickly withdrew from Syria.

CONCLUSIONS

The five centuries following the Abbasid Revolution saw one of the world's golden ages. As the Middle East again played a leading role in world history, its rich, mutifaceted civilization reached maturity. Its own creativity was matched by an early receptivity to outside ideas. While the contemporary West had little to offer, the ghost of ancient Hellenic civilization provided the renewed Orient its greatest cross-fertilization. A new ethnic group, the Turks, entered the area and gave Islamic expansion a new lease on life from separate centers, while New Persian provided another important literary medium.

Several signs of decline were visible long before the thirteenth century. While Islam provided for a system of universal government in principle, centrifugal forces made this largely theoretical. Sometimes rival concepts of legitimacy, posed in religious terms, were at stake. More often, the unworkability of the ideal left the field open to a sheer struggle for power among alien troops that had no ties with the society.

The receptivity to new ideas had yielded to certain kinds of rigidity. A divine law was no longer susceptible to new interpretation, and "innovation" became a term of reproach. The Hellenic impact had largely given way to a theology that feared reason and even denied human beings' control of their own actions in the face of an all-determining God. At the same time, long-term economic forces and a type of feudalism undermined Middle Eastern greatness, while a Western Europe that had seemed to be destined for perpetual backwardness began to catch up.

A Western military thrust into Central Islamic lands proved temporarily successful but was gradually being repulsed. The Crusaders reassured the East of its superority and perhaps in the long run contributed to dangerous complacency. Finally, the Mongols dealt the Middle East a harsh blow. While the Egyptian-based Mamluk army stopped the invaders, the survival of Islamic civilization may have seemed in doubt.

4

Recovery, New Zenith, and Decline

1260-1774

The aftermath of the battle of Ayn Jalut in 1260 saw the Middle East divided into Mamluk and Mongol realms. For a quarter of a millennium, a series of Mamluk sultans ruled in Cairo. Besides Egypt and Syria, they soon controlled the Hijaz, parts of the Sudan and Cyrenaica, and sometimes Cyprus and parts of southeast Anatolia.

At first technically only as *il-khans* (''viceroys'') of the great khan in Beijing, Hulagu and his line predominated east of the Euphrates. This was basically Iraq and Iran, although some parts of the region were only under loose Il-Khanid overlord-ship most of the time. The Saljuq sultan of Anatolia was also under Il-Khanid suze-rainty for a while.

Middle Eastern civilization survived the ravages of the Mongols. The con-querors soon were absorbed by the region and patronized some of its greatest cul-tural achievements. Furthermore, this period made way for larger empires that re-newed the momentum of Islamic power. Despite Europe's overseas expansion and renewed cultural vigor, it was still often in the shadow of the Middle East, and this relationship between the two regions was not fundamentally to be reversed until the eighteenth century.

THE MIDDLE EAST AFTER
THE MONGOL CONQUEST
— Boundaries in About 1300

WHITE HORDE (Mongols)

CHAGHATAY
MONGOLS

Samarqand
TIMURIDS

Aral
Sea

KARTS

SULTANATE OF
DELHI

INDIAN OCEAN

Caspian Sea

MUZAFFARIDS

IL-KHANID (MONGOL)
EMPIRE

JALAYIRIDS

BLACK
SHEEP

AZARBAYJAN

Persian Gulf

TREBIZOND
(Greek)

WHITE
SHEEP

ARABIA

GOLDEN HORDE (Mongols)

Black Sea

Constantinople

TURKISH
PRINCIPALITIES
KARAMAN

Red Sea

BYZANTINES

Cairo

Kossova

MAMLUK
EMPIRE

Mediterranean Sea

HAFSIDS

THE MAMLUK SULTANATE

On their return to Egypt after defeating the Mongols, a group of *mamluks* assassinated Sultan Qutuz. Baybars, whose treacherous kiss provided the signal for the attack, became the new ruler. He proved to be as capable in charge of an empire as he had been in battle and may be considered a founder of the Mamluk state. The hereditary principle sometimes was followed, as Qalawun, a commander who rose to power after Baybars' death, started a line of real or nominal sultans that lasted off and on until the late fourteenth century. But the *mamluk* army was the real arbiter, periodically bringing new freedmen commanders to power. The sons of mamluks were allowed to serve only in secondary military units, while the continuing purchase of Turkish boys by both the sultan and fief-holders continuously renewed the warrior class.

The Mamluks were an alien ruling group. Except for the *ulama* who held offices of an educational or legal nature, the indigenous people were excluded from public positions. Tribal rebellion against such an order was recurrent, particularly in Syria and Upper Egypt, and there were other popular revolts. Still, recent studies show that the Mamluks did not rule through force alone but through a pattern of patronage extending to the *ulama* (who tended to represent local interests) and other notables, and even to potential opposition groups in the general population.

A member of the Abbasid family escaped from the Mongols and found refuge in Cairo to perpetuate the ghost of the caliphate. As had often happened in Baghdad, figurehead caliphs provided some religious legitimacy to the Mamluk sultans, although most of the Islamic world ignored this claim.

The Mamluks tightened their grip on the Crusaders. Baybars and Qalawun took several of their remaining strongholds and also finished off the Syrian Nizaris ("Assassins"), who had joined forces with them. The Mamluks' siege engines brought the capitulation of Acre, the last Frankish coastal enclave, in 1293. Thus ended western Europe's premature thrust into the Middle East.

The early Mamluk period was one of prosperity. Egypt was a burgeoning emporium of East-West commerce, and the government was enriched by customs duties on Indian goods, including spices sold to Italian merchants. An attempt by the Pope to get a Christian boycott of the Muslims fell on its face. Gold from present-day Mali and silver from Europe flowed into the Mamluk treasury to pay for canals, bridges, hospitals, and impressive mausoleum-mosques. This prosperity and relative stability, plus an influx of refugees from Mongol-occupied lands, brought an upsurge in the size of the population.

Only with the appearance of a new enemy, the plague, in the mid 1300s did this prosperity end. Even the Mongols' human devastation had been small in comparison. According to some estimates, as much as a third of the population of Egypt and Syria died during this one epidemic. Although some groups, such as the surviving skilled laborers, made economic gains as a result of the deaths of so many of their associates, the overall impact was disastrous, and agriculture and trade were disrupted.

New ethnic elements began to predominate among the *mamluk*s. As a counterweight to the Turkish Bahris, Sultan Qalawun began the practice of keeping another group of *mamluk*s in the Citadel (*burj*). These were ethnically diverse but mainly Circassians, a people in the Caucasus region known for their military qualities. Beginning with Sultan Barquq in 1382, the second phase of Mamluk rule, that of the Burjis, was ushered in. Most of the remaining sultans were Circassians, although two were Greeks. The hereditary principle was henceforth almost completely disregarded and made way for a rapid succession of unrestrained power struggles and of sultans who sometimes maintained only a precarious hegemony over their fellow commanders.

THE IL-KHANS

As for the Mamluks' enemies, Chingiz Khan's descendants split his patrimony into virtually independent realms. The great khan, in China, retained only nominal control over his viceroy, Hulagu, in southwest Asia. These two Mongols maintained a close mutual alliance against their cousin of the Golden Horde, who ruled in Russia, and another cousin in Transoxania. The Il-Khans fought many wars with their northern neighbors, especially with the Golden Horde over the Caucasus region.

Inter-Mongol conflict meshed with a broader pattern of rivalries. For the Crusader states, the Il-Khans were allies against the Mamluks. The Il-Khans established friendly diplomatic contact with the Pope and various western European capitals, but offers to join in a concerted drive against the Islamic world never materialized. The Mamluks, on the other hand, found allies in the Golden Horde, not only because the Il-Khans were their common enemy but also because of a traffic in slaves that was as lucrative for the Mongol exporters as it was essential for the Mamluks to perpetuate their army and regime. The Golden Horde's early conversion to Islam facilitated the alliance with the Mamluks, whose sultan they even formally recognized as overlord. The Saljuqs looked to Baybars for support in overthrowing Il-Khanid hegemony, and he entered central Anatolia in 1277 to occupy the Saljuq throne but soon withdrew as the enemy prepared for another offensive.

The Il-Khans continued to press on Syria. They took Damascus in 1300 but withdrew to deal with threats on other frontiers. The last of many unsuccessful Il-Khanid crossings of the Euphrates came in 1313, and a peace treaty with the Mamluks soon followed.

The early Il-Khans repressed the Sunni Muslim majority in favor of religious minorities, including Christians and Shi'ites. A few Mongols were Nestorian Christians even before the conquest, while others were Buddhists, which was also the faith of some of Hulagu's successors.

The early Il-Khanid period was one of economic decline. Unprecedented slaughter left the region severely underpopulated. Nomadic incursions and exactions by tax-farmers that forced many peasants to flee the villages were severe blows to agriculture. Seemingly unlike anything in earlier Islamic periods, a pattern of binding peasants to the soil emerged. Some formerly great cities shrank almost to the status of villages, and many artisans who were not killed or carried away were reduced to slavery. On top of all this, in 1294 one Il-Khan blindly introduced a radical innovation from China, paper money, and decreed death for anyone refusing to accept it. The result was that for a while merchants stopped selling altogether, and complete disaster was avoided only by revoking the thoughtless policy.

Still, the Mongol conquests encouraged international trade. Silk and other products from China moved across the steppe to Il-Khanid lands and beyond. Iranian silk also occupied a central place in trade with Italian merchants via Mediterranean and Black Sea ports of Anatolia. Indian spices came to Hormuz, at the opening to the Persian Gulf, and went overland to Tabriz—thus bypassing Iraq and accelerating its decline—and on through Anatolia. Russian furs and Turkish slaves met sugar and other products from the Arab world along trans-Anatolian routes or on the Italian-dominated sea lanes. Direct Chinese shipping to the Persian Gulf gained importance briefly in the early fifteenth century.

The Mongols increasingly converted to Islam and melted into the Middle East. The distinction between Mongols and Turks tended to fade, while Persian remained the chief language of high culture.

With the accession of Ghazan to the throne in 1295, the Il-Khans became a Muslim dynasty. Symbolically, the Mongols' brimmed hats were replaced by turbans, while the formal allegiance to Beijing was dropped. Ghazan also introduced reforms, particularly in taxation, that brought economic improvements. Non-Muslims were persecuted for a short period, and Buddhism vanished from the Middle East, while Nestorian Christians shrank to a small minority.

The Il-Khanid realm slowly disintegrated during the fourteenth century. There was a severe famine in 1318 as well as a series of bitter rivalries among leading officials. Later il-khans were mere tools of one faction or another. While the Golden Horde encroached on northwestern Iran, local dynasties proliferated. Such were the Muzaffarids, who eventually ruled from Shiraz. The Jalayirid family, of Mongol origin, established its rule in Baghdad and held sway over parts of western Iran for a while. Such minor dynasties tended to be heavily exploitative, and their emphasis on feudalism brought further agricultural decline. The great outbreak of the plague in the mid fifteenth century may have decimated the population here as it did in Mamluk lands.

THE RISE OF THE OTTOMANS

In the last quarter of the thirteenth century, the Saljuq sultans of Rum fell under increasing Il-Khanid domination and eventually disappeared. In turn, the decline of the Il-Khanids left a power vacuum in Anatolia. This made way for the rise of what in some ways was ultimately to be the greatest of all Islamic states.

Nomadic Turkish tribes (Turkomans) began to pour westward into Anatolia in the eleventh century. Founding little ghazi principalities on the Saljuq frontier, they warred against Byzantium for the sake of Islam and for land and booty. In the mid thirteenth century, one Turkoman chief, Ertogrul, established his control over a small area of northwest Anatolia, perhaps as a vassal of the Saljuq sultan. Ertogrul's son, Osman, succeeded in 1280 and gave his name to the Osmanli (Ottoman) dynasty. During his forty-four years of ghazi warfare, Osman extended the new state's sway over a much larger chunk of northwest Anatolia, including the city of Bursa.

Osman's son, Orhan (1324–1359), not only expanded his territory in Anatolia but also crossed the Straits to Gallipoli. At first merely intervening by invitation in an intradynastic squabble in Constantinople in 1346, the Ottoman forces stayed on in the fragmented Balkans.

Murad I (1360–1389), who took the titles "sultan" and "emperor," pushed his boundary into north-central Anatolia and then concentrated on the Balkans. Amidst calls in Rome for a crusade, the armies of Hungary and several smaller states suffered disastrous defeats. Some Balkan rulers, including the Byzantine emperor, accepted tributary status at least temporarily, as did the Ottoman's longstanding rivals, the central Anatolian amirate of Karaman, after being defeated in 1387. In a renewed campaign, Christian Balkan rulers, aided by troops from Hungary and Poland, had some initial success but were crushed at Kossova in 1389. Most of the area south of the Danube came under Ottoman aegis. With their capital at Edirne (Adrianople), the Ottomans' center of gravity was long to be in their European lands, which they called Rumelia.

Bayezid I (1389–1402) was nicknamed Yildirim ("lightning") because of the speed of his conquests on two distant fronts. The state now had lost its original simplicity, and the ruler was no longer merely the first among a group of equal chieftains. The Turkoman tribes had already been supplemented by feudal cavalrymen, slave troops, and auxiliaries contributed by Christian vassal states. The ghazi spirit was making way for assimilation to Byzantine imperial forms and even for the use of Christian advisors. The conquests in the Balkans were rounded out, and the Byzantine emperor, now controlling little more than the city of Constantinople, was forced to establish a Muslim quarter. Another crusade met defeat by the Ottomans at Nicopolis in 1396. But while the ghazi tradition of the Turkomans limited their value largely to use against non-Muslims, the availability of other forces allowed Bayezid to concentrate on the conquest of Anatolia. During the 1390s his forces subdued Karaman and several eastern Anatolian states. All this warfare against fellow Muslims instead of "infidels" stirred up resentment among the Turkomans and made them look hopefully to another Muslim conqueror.

TIMUR'S SWEEP OVER EURASIA

In 1369 a Turkish Muslim warrior, Timur Leng ("Timur the Lame," "Tamerlane"), came to power in Samarqand. Then the "Great Wolf," as the crippled but magnetic "conqueror of the world" called himself, led hundreds of thousands of tribesmen to conquer areas as far apart as India and Russia. As he moved on, pyramids of human skulls or prisoners buried alive en masse perpetuated the terror that bolstered his invincibility.

A decade after Timur came to power, his armies swept through Iran and Iraq to subdue the petty dynasties that had succeeded the Il-Khans. A Mamluk sultan executed the emissary from Timur, who then sent forces into Syria. Now weakened by epidemics, famine, and high taxes, the Mamluks fell back south of Damascus in 1400. Egypt was saved only because Timur turned in another direction.

The Great Wolf entered Anatolia and repeatedly defeated the Ottomans. Turkoman disaffection with Bayezid's policies played into his hands. The Timurid host utterly routed the Ottomans at Ankara in 1402, and Bayezid was carried around in a cage as a trophy of war. Before long the conqueror reached the Aegean coast. Local rulers, including two of Bayezid's sons and also some former victims of Ottoman conquests, as in Karaman, became vassals of Timur. A third son of Bayezid ruled in Rumelia.

Timur returned to Samarqand, where he died in 1405 as he was preparing for a campaign to China. His descendants ruled until 1469 in Transoxania and Iran, while another Timurid continued the line at Herat, in Afghanistan, during the late fifteenth century.

The Jalayirids restored their control in Baghdad for a while but soon succumbed to a Turkish Shi'ite tribal confederation known as the Black Sheep (Kara-Koyunlu). Based in Mosul, the Black Sheep controlled Iraq and adjacent areas. A second Turkish confederation, the Sunni White Sheep (Ak-Koyunlu) of eastern Anatolia, which formed an alliance with Venice against the newly resumed expansion of the Ottomans, reached its height in the mid fifteenth century by conquering the Black Sheep and the Iranian Timurids but then soon disintegrated. All of this proved to be a transition period to two great states, a revived Ottoman Empire and a new dynasty, the Safavids, in Iran. But meanwhile developments were taking place in the cultural field.

RENEWED VITALITY OF ISLAMIC CIVILIZATION

There is a widespread idea that Islamic civilization virtually ended with the advent of the Mongols. In reality, the next three centuries brought cultural accomplishments that in some ways surpassed those of the former, "classical" age. Admittedly, Mongol decimation set back an already declining Iraq, but Egypt was able to increase its already emerging cultural primacy in the Arab world.

The post-1260 period saw a growing dichotomy between the Arabic and the Persian cultural zones. Except in fields closely connected with religion, including law, which continued to use the Arabic medium everywhere, the language of high culture in non-Arab-inhabited regions was Persian. This was true in later realms as far apart as those of the Ottomans and the Moghuls of India, with the semi-Persianized forms of local languages, Ottoman and Urdu, only slowly gaining recognition.

The notion that Islamic cultural greatness was in serious decline is a result of giving one's main attention to the Arab zone. With some spectacular exceptions, such an assessment is valid for that region. This is paradoxical in light of the fact that the Arab world, with the sad exception of Iraq, either avoided Mongol conquest or, like Syria, experienced it only for short periods. The regenerative consequences of nomadic conquest of declining civilizations in the case of the thirteenth-century Mongols was hardly comparable to that of, say, the seventh-century Arabs but, its savagery notwithstanding, does help explain some of the Persian-based culture of the age. What decreasing momentum can be discerned in Islamic civilization was due to tendencies at work in the region before the Mongol eruption more than to the destruction wrought by the invasion.

The ecumenical sweep of the Mongols threw all the great civilizations, including those of the Middle East and the Far East, willy nilly against each other. Middle Eastern Muslim artisans and craftsmen were taken captive to the Far East, while Chinese scientists, engineers, and administrators appeared in the Il-Khanid lands. Chinese inventions, including gunpowder and printing, spread and ultimately had a revolutionary impact on both the Middle East and the West; Far Eastern influences permeated Islamic art.

Hulagu had hardly finished destroying before he began to pick up the pieces. He established an observatory in 1259 in western Iran, where a great scholar who had entered his service, Nasir al-Din Tusi, made important astronomical discoveries. Besides the natural sciences, history was a field that benefited from both Il-Khanid patronage and the wider world view of the age. The Persian Ata Malik al-Juwayni's *History of the World Conqueror,* an account of Chingiz Khan and of the Mongols generally, is of particular note. Another writer who stands out was Ghazan Khan's court physician, Rashid al-Din, whose two-volume *Collection of Histories* has been deemed by some scholars to be the nearest thing to an authentic world history before the twentieth century and the greatest of all Persian prose works. The author deals with peoples from the Far East to the usually neglected western Europe and used informants and source material from all these regions.

Some of Persian poetry's revered geniuses appeared during the era of the Il-Khans or of their petty successor states. The poetry, particularly odes, of the fourteenth-century mystic, pantheistic Hafiz of Shiraz, who wrote at the Muzaffarid and Jalayirid courts, represents another high point in Persian literature.

The Mongols sparked a renewal of the Middle East's creative spirit in the visual arts by enhancing trade and cultural contact with the Far East. The motifs of the Chinese lotus, Chinese-looking faces, dragons, phoenixes, and cloud scrolls entered Middle East art patterns but were stylized in an Islamic way. This was evidenced particularly in the many miniature paintings produced to decorate manuscripts.

The Il-Khanid mausoleums were octagonal, with minarets at each corner, reminiscent of the great Mongol tents. Blue faience tiles or bricks decorated their exterior. Like the Saljuqs, the Mongols also used stucco for decoration. The most significant building of the Il-Khans probably was the Congregational Mosque east of Isfahan. Built in the fourteenth century, it has the typical four aisles opening onto a courtyard, an octagonal dome, and a single cylindrical minaret.

Islamic arts flowered even more extensively during the Timurid period, which has been compared to the simultaneous Italian Renaissance. Timur himself was intent on making Samarqand the showplace of the world. Persian architectural style soon reached its zenith. The fantastic mausoleum at Samarqand demonstrated a new dome style, involving lobes and tile work. Landscapes predominated in the new painting style. Shiraz became the manuscript center where paintings were collected for illustrating copies of classic books. Herat claimed the greatest Islamic painter, Bihzad, who was the first to begin a practice of signing miniatures.

Timurid accomplishments extended to the field of literature. Several of the rulers of the dynasty were poets, and they eagerly patronized other writers. The last of the great medieval Persian poets, Jami of Herat, lived until 1492 at the Timurid court. Jami used the highly ornate style that increasingly became the norm in Persian writing. A member of the Naqshabandi order of dervishes, his mysticism is expressed in symbolic erotic terms.

Architecture flowered in the Mamluk sultanate. The Mamluks built ornamental mosques and copious mausoleums which were influenced by their Fatimid predecessors as well as by Turkish styles. Also, the stained glass of European churches was adapted to the many stucco lattice windows to soften the brightness of the Cairo sun. Mamluk mosques were characterized by six-aisled sanctuaries and central courtyards. Ornate decorations typified this period, which was also famous for the use of elaborate geometric patterns. Another innovation brought to Mamluk buildings was the ever-present beautiful sunken fountains.

Aside from architecture, the Mamluks were successful in Cairo and Syria with the minor arts, such as glassmaking and pottery. Metalwork and wood carving also flourished, while textile weaving was unsurpassed. Damask cloth and fine linens were much sought after in Europe.

In general, this was an age of little greatness in science and letters in the Arab world, but intellectual effort never ceased in any field. The Mamluk sultans patronized learning, and students came from distant lands to study at al-Azhar and other mosque-colleges. Historians in Egypt, such as the fifteenth-century al-Maqrizi, continued to write valuable chronicles in the traditional style, and the massive biographical encyclopedia of ibn-Khallikan in the late thirteenth century has preserved important information. In the field of popular literature Mamluk Egypt saw the final development also of *The Thousand and One Nights*. In the natural sciences a remarkably overlooked name is that of the fourteenth-century Damascene astronomer, ibn-Shatir, who made some of the discoveries that Copernicus repeated a century afterward.

The most spectacular exception to the picture of an Arab civilization in decline was ibn-Khaldun, who died in 1406 after a career as royal advisor, chief judge, and teacher in his native North Africa, Spain, and Egypt. He is usually described as a historian, but his lengthy chronological account, mainly of North Africa, is not what made him distinctive. His greatness is revealed in the three-volume *Preface (Muqaddimah)* to his history, which in effect was a pioneer work in social science. Among his many other generalizations about human society, ibn-Khaldun explained history in terms of the social solidarity (*asabiyyah*) of tribal communities based on kinship. He said that it is groups with intense solidarity, especially when supplemented by a religion, who found new states through conquest. Each dynasty, according to this analysis, lives out a natural life lasting for three generations (120 years), during which solidarity erodes to make way for a repetition of the cycle.

Brilliant exceptions notwithstanding, Islamic civilization in both the Arabic and the Persian zones was now less creative in one sense than before. As Marshall Hodgson stresses, this was an age beset by a "conservative spirit," that is, one that focused on working within classic patterns. Although new ideas sometimes slipped in, the general assumption was that the early Islamic period had been the high point of history and that the most one could do now was to ward off decline. There was suspicion of innovation, and education consisted mainly in having students memorize the works of the past.

The Islamic receptivity to innovation provided a mixed story during these centuries. Aside from Far Eastern influences in the fine arts, the same Chinese inventions that helped European Christendom gather momentum on its road to modernization (after an early start partly resulting from Arab influences in the twelfth century)—namely gunpowder and the printing press—provide especially instructive examples in the case of the Middle East. Gunpowder was adopted by Muslim armies in some cases, notably by Ottoman infantrymen at an early date. Those bodies of troops that rejected the new weaponry, mainly cavalry forces, may have been evincing an instinctive conservatism, but this was largely a matter of protecting their own kind of warfare. No one seems to have rejected gunpowder weapons on the ground that Islam did not permit them, and the *ulama* were not the center of opposition. The case of the printing press is different, for the *ulama* resisted this innovation, seemingly to protect vested interests of copyists and calligraphers. Although printing was known in the Islamic world in the Mongol period and continued to be used by some Middle Eastern Jews and Christians, it was forbidden to Muslims in the Ottoman Empire until the eighteenth century. By contrast, the pre-Mongol Islamic world had readily adopted such Chinese inventions as the compass.

OTTOMAN RESTORATION
AND RENEWED OFFENSIVE

As for the Ottomans after their defeat by Timur, the restoration of the empire required a complicated, decade-long process. But in the struggle with three other sons of Bayezid, Mehmed I became the sultan of a newly restored empire by 1413. The Ottoman state now resumed the momentum of conquest. Mehmed I (1413–1421) and Murad II (1421–1451) suppressed numerous revolts and warred in Europe and Asia. Control over much of the Balkan peninsula was restored, and Ottoman forces raided as far as Hungary. Wars with Venice, Hungary, Serbia, and Wallachia (which, with Moldavia, forms Rumania today) were recurrent, and all these states periodically became Ottoman tributaries. The most troublesome problem in the Balkans was long the revolt of the indomitable Skanderbeg of Albania. Alternately resisting and paying tribute was the little remnant of the Byzantine Empire. Murad II besieged Constantinople and nearly reduced it but was diverted by troubles across the Straits.

Ottoman control in Anatolia immediately after the restoration was limited to a small area in the west. Numerous principalities that Bayezid I had ruled were now independent. Some of these gradually fell under Ottoman dominion during the second quarter of the fifteenth century, while Karaman remained a major challenge.

An offensive by Christian Europe in the 1440s severely tested the Ottoman mettle. King Ladislaus of Poland and Lithuania ascended the throne of Hungary as well, and a great Hungarian general, John Hunyadi, led a Crusade that brought together armies from much of Christendom. Advancing southward from Hungary, Hunyadi repeatedly defeated the Ottomans while Murad II was diverted by conflict with Karaman. In a ten-year truce, agreed to in 1444, the Ottomans relinquished control over Serbia and Wallachia. But when the Pope convinced Hunyadi that a treaty with an "infidel" was not binding, the Crusade soon resumed. Now the tide turned, as the Ottomans utterly routed the Crusaders at the great battle of Varna (1444). Another Crusade led by Hunyadi was demolished at Kossova in 1448.

Far from being turned back, the Eastern tide gained a new impetus that was to leave the West long on the defensive. For Byzantium, time was about to run out, and the desperate attempt by the ruling class to unite the Greek Orthodox Church with Roman Catholicism in the face of the Turkish threat did it no good. Such had been the Greeks' hatred of the Latins since the Crusader sacking of Constantinople in 1202 that the slogan of the day in that city was: "Better the turban of the Prophet than the tiara of the Pope."

The accession of the courageous, able twenty-three-year-old Mehmed II ("the Conqueror") in 1451 ushered in a period of accelerated expansion. His most dramatic achievement was to fulfill the centuries-old Islamic dream of wresting Constantinople from Christendom. After a fifty-four-day siege and one of the first large-scale uses of gunpowder in warfare, the Ottomans breached the walls of a city defended mainly by unpopular auxiliaries from the Latin West. Following the customary looting, a period of reconstruction began as the new rulers encouraged diverse peoples to settle in a long-declining, underpopulated metropolis. While the Byzantine emperor chose to perish in battle rather than to endure defeat, the general reaction of the populace was one of relief that a tolerant Islamic empire, which nominated a new Greek Orthodox patriarch and protected the Church, had saved it from the Latins. But now the Hagia Sophia was to be a mosque, and Constantinople—or Istanbul, a Turkish variant on the city's name—became the Ottoman capital.

Mehmed II's forces advanced in all directions. He defeated the White Sheep and took much of their territory, and he completely subdued and annexed Karaman in 1474. He clashed with Karaman's ally, the Mamluk Sultanate. Genoa's outpost in the Crimea fell, and the Crimean Tatar khan, representing a surviving branch of the Golden Horde, accepted a vassal status that was to endure for three centuries. There were clashes with the Kingdom of Poland and Lithuania, wars with Hungary and Venice, and another Crusade in 1464. Except for the failure to take Belgrade from the Hungarians, holdings in the Balkans were rounded out, and outright Ottoman rule superseded looser arrangements as far away as the Danube. Mahmud II expanded the Ottoman navy, which took much of Greece and several Aegean islands. Skanderbeg was finally subdued, bringing the Ottomans to the Adriatic coast. Ottoman armies penetrated to the outskirts of Venice, which accepted tributary status. With the dream of conquering Italy in Mehmed's mind, Ottoman troops landed at Otranto, at the "heel" of the peninsula in 1480, and the Pope prepared to flee. Only the sultan's death the next year brought withdrawal from Italy.

Mehmed II's death led to a struggle between his two sons, Bayezid and Jem. The former, an ascetic, scholarly man backed by slave troops and other forces favoring a less active policy of expansion for a while, prevailed over his more warlike brother. After taking refuge in Rhodes, where he expected to lead another expedition against Bayezid, Jem found himself a virtual prisoner. He was tossed from one Christian ruler to another for thirteen years, with the hosts receiving handsome payments from Bayezid in return for not unleashing him.

Bayezid was a weak ruler who preferred to leave matters of state to his grand vizir. But even now, victories and minor territorial acquisitions continued in wars in Europe. Rivalry for control of Turkoman border principalities brought war with the Mamluk Sultanate in 1485–1489. An Ottoman naval buildup was under way. War with Venice, which was supported by Crusading forces, ended that city's supremacy on the seas. Instead, "sea ghazis" asserted Ottoman domination of the western Mediterranean.

RISE OF THE SAFAVIDS

By now, a new empire, that of the Safavids, had arisen in Iran and was to remain for two centuries a second Middle Eastern power alongside the Ottomans. Fiercely devoted to Twelver Shi'ite Islam, the Safavid dynasty imposed the doctrine on a hitherto largely Sunni country. Henceforth, Iran was to be an overwhelmingly Twelver country, with about 90 percent of its population adhering to this doctrine today. Aside from a few enclaves elsewhere, only southern Iraq, where Twelver Shi'ism has deeper historical roots than anywhere else, shares the same religious affiliation. This became an important fact in setting Iran off from the countries around it and particularly in providing ideological coloring for its relationship with the Sunni Ottomans. The subversive nature of the Safavids' creed dictated a fierce, almost unremitting struggle between the two.

Suggestions that there was something in Iran's ancient heritage that caused it to adopt a relatively distinct form of Islam are fanciful. After all, earlier Islamic dynasties there had tended to be staunchly Sunni. Still, Shi'ism helped to reinforce Iranian identity and to prepare the way for the modern nation-state. Actually, the Safavids were Turkish in origin; early members of the dynasty wrote Turkish poetry while their Ottoman contemporaries paradoxically composed verses in Persian. The language of the Safavid court continued to be Turkish into the seventeenth century. But, while we should avoid projecting back the expectations of our own age of nation-states, the Safavids increasingly took on the appearance of an Iranian dynasty. By uniting the country under one monarchy, they reasserted its ancient identity in a way that made them heirs to the pre-Islamic Sasanians.

Not born until the first decade of the sixteenth century, the Safavid state had undergone a two-century period of gestation. The Safavid movement, as a Sufi order rather than a state, emerged at about the same time as the Ottoman dynasty from the disorder ensuing in the aftermath of Hulagu's conquests. The proliferation of Shi'ite and other heterodox Sufi orders was a characteristic feature of this period, although ironically the Safavids seem originally to have been Sunnis.

The Safavid movement took its name from Shaykh Safi al-Din, who was born in the late thirteenth century. An intensely devout young man, he found guidance from the elderly *shaykh* of a Sufi order in the northwestern Iranian town of Ardabil and later became the head of the group. Ardabil remained the center of a movement that directed Shi'ite propaganda over wide areas during the next century. Turkoman tribesmen tended especially to heed the Safavid appeals. Opposed by the local power, the Black Sheep, the Safavids moved their activities to the territory of the White Sheep, with whom a series of intermarriages occurred.

Following a period of disorder after the White Sheep decline, the leadership of the Safavid family fell to the inspiring young Isma'il at the end of the century. Establishing a base in Gilan, he attacked and overwhelmed the decaying White Sheep state in 1501. Assuming the title of *shah an-shah,* the Safavid ruler soon extended his control over all of Iran and Iraq. Another Turkoman dynasty, the Shaybanis, who now headed a new Uzbek state centered in Transoxania, was driven from eastern Iran but not from the region further north. The Uzbeks remained a hostile Sunni power on the Safavids' northeastern flank.

OTTOMAN-SAFAVID WARS

The Safavid-Ottoman showdown was not long in coming. In Anatolia, thousands of Shi'ite Turkomans, known as *Kizilbash* (''Red Heads'') from the red hats that symbolized their movement, rose up against the Ottomans under the leadership of one who called himself Shah Kuli (''the Slave of the Shah'') but whose foes called him Shaytan Kuli (''the Slave of Satan''). Many Ottoman soldiers joined in the revolt.

Sultan Bayezid's forces suppressed the rebels, but there was widespread demand for a more warlike ruler to take the helm against the Safavid threat. Such was Bayezid's son, Salim I (''the Grim''), who succeeded in a palace coup in 1512. The fanatical but capable Salim I proceeded with ruthless cruelty to exterminate Shi'ites in his territory. As Shah Isma'il prepared to overthrow the sultan in favor of another member of the Ottoman family, Salim initiated a holy war against the Safavids. The Mamluks sealed their own fate by a policy of nonintervention that was inevitably to put them at the mercy of a newly preponderant victor, as Salim led a great army of 100,000 men to northwestern Iran.

Meeting the foe at Calderan in 1514, Salim's army was well equipped with cannon, which the Safavids lacked. The Safavid army was mainly cavalry and had long resisted firearms, as did the Ottoman sipahis. Following some initial successes by the Safavids on one side, the superior Ottoman forces repulsed them on the other side, and this decisive battle soon turned into a disaster for the shah, himself now wounded. Some of his fanatical followers had believed he possessed divine qualities; their faith in him had been so great that they sometimes dispensed with armor when fighting for him. But now his halo was gone. The anticlimactic remaining decade of his reign saw him succumb to military inactivity and to alcoholism. After Calderan, Salim entered Tabriz, Isma'il's capital, but soon left with plans to return and conquer Iran in the spring. Dissatisfaction among his troops prevented him from carrying through with this second campaign, but Shah Isma'il's defeat brought about the absorption of most of eastern Anatolia into the empire and paved the way for expansion into Syria and Egypt.

CONQUEST OF THE MAMLUK SULTANATE

A series of blows to the Mamluk state in the fifteenth century contributed to its fall into Ottoman hands. Many Syrians and Egyptians were ready to welcome a more stable and hopefully more just ruler with open arms, and dissatisfied factions of *mamluks* were also eager to collaborate with an outside force. The Burji sultans were oppressive, and political chaos prevailed. Famines and the plague, which seems to have decimated the *mamluks* more than the indigenous people, had severely reduced the population, and wars were a further drain on the economy. Christian European pirates raided Mamluk seaports several times. Inflation got out of hand as demand for silver in Europe resulted in the substitution of copper coins in the Mamluk Sultanate. The *mamluks* were unwilling to adopt new military techniques that might have helped them to survive. As horsemen, they were wedded to a kind of warfare that artillery seemed to threaten, and they scorned such weapons as worthy only of weaklings. Only a few cannon were acquired and entrusted to low prestige units.

The first phase of modern European overseas expansion also helped to undermine the Mamluks. The Portuguese imposed a crushing blow on the Egyptian economy by rounding the Cape of Good Hope in 1498 to begin direct commercial relations with India that bypassed Mamluk territory. Receiving Ottoman assistance, partly because the Safavids and the Portuguese were working together, the Mamluk navy defeated the latter in one engagement. But a Portuguese victory in 1513 sealed the Mamluks' fate.

The Portuguese success did not represent any decisive superiority of Europe over the Middle East as a whole. The Indian spice trade was not completely diverted from this area for another two centuries. Portugal could occupy relatively primitive or underpopulated areas, as in the Americas, and was supreme on the seas for a while, but it was hardly a serious menace to the great land empires of the Far or Middle East. The beneficiary of the economic damage it did to the Mamluks was to be the Ottomans, who in turn continued on the offensive against Christian Europe.

Salim's incorporation of some Anatolian Turkoman principalities that had been tributaries of Cairo brought strains in Ottoman-Mamluk relations. The Mamluks were suspected of working with the shah, and such actions as giving sanctuary to Jem also antagonized Istanbul. When Salim led an army eastward in 1516, the Mamluk sultan feared that it would turn south in his direction. And so, a Mamluk army advanced to northern Syria. Even supposing that Salim's real purpose was to march on Iran again, he could not do so with the Mamluks in a position to attack him from the rear.

Mamluk fears were confirmed when Salim turned south into Syria. The Mamluk governor of Aleppo, Khayr Bey, who was secretly in league with the enemy, pulled his forces back, and the largely pregunpowder Mamluk army suffered a crushing defeat in the vicinity of Aleppo. As the last Mamluk sultan refused to submit to Ottoman suzerainty, Salim moved on to defeat the "Egyptian" forces again near Cairo in 1517 and to annex the Mamluk realm.

Salim did not see fit to establish direct control over all of the new territories. He left an Ottoman force in Egypt, but the *mamluks* were not destroyed, and Khayr Bey became an Ottoman vassal there. The next three centuries saw an ever-shifting rivalry between Ottoman governors and the *mamluks*. While southern Syria was also left under its own local notables, the north was put under an Ottoman governor.

The end of the Mamluk Sultanate also terminated the line of titular Abbasid caliphs. Salim took the last of them to Istanbul, and a story later emerged that the right to the office was turned over to the Ottoman house. In the nineteenth century, this was to be the basis for the dynasty's claim to a special position in the Islamic world. In fact, this was contrary to the Sunni theory, according to which the caliph had to be elected and from Qurayshi descent. Except for the occasional use of the title in a loose sense (not unique to the Ottomans), no claim to the caliphate seems to have been made for centuries.

THE OTTOMANS AS A GREAT WORLD POWER

The conquests of Salim I heralded the zenith of the Ottoman Empire. The next sultan, Sulayman (variously surnamed "the Great," "the Magnificent," "the Lawgiver," and "the Lord of His Age"), who reigned from 1520 to 1566, came to be synonymous with a period of Islamic glory that in some ways surpassed that of the early Abbasid era. The momentum of conquest and the power of the Ottoman state and its efficient military force in relation to the other kingdoms of the time were enough to guarantee this. But Sulayman's wise leadership and his devotion to justice—although he could also be merciless, as in having his own son assassinated—provided new ingredients for imperial success.

As he led great armies alternately to his eastern and western frontiers, Sulayman remained the great ruler of the age. He was at the center of a pattern of international politics that extended at least from western Europe to India and found himself the arbiter in conflicts among the others. To the northwest of Sulayman's Rumelian domains lay one of his persistent enemies, the Hapsburg ruler of Austria, and head of the Holy Roman Empire, who had also inherited the throne of Spain. The Ottomans' former foe, Hungary, was now reduced to the position of being a mere object of Ottoman-Hapsburg competition. A second great Christian European ruler was the king of France, whose rivalry with the Hapsburgs dictated that the periodic professions of Christian solidarity would be mere window dressing for an alliance, sometimes tacit and sometimes more or less open, with Istanbul. Venice was, as before, alternately to join anti-Ottoman Christian coalitions and then to come to terms with its great Eastern neighbor.

Christian naval expansion notwithstanding, Islamic states constituted the great land powers of the sixteenth century. Contrary to the widespread image of Western supremacy that dates back half a millennium, Hodgson rates most Christian kingdoms in this period alongside the lesser Islamic states of southern India and points out that Persian was the nearest thing to a world language.

The Safavids, under the strong leadership of Shah Tahmasp during much of this period, were the Ottomans' great Islamic enemy. Perhaps more than the equal of any Christian European power, the Safavids were natural allies of the Hapsburgs and were threatened by both the Ottomans and the Uzbeks. The early sixteenth century also saw the establishment of another major Islamic empire, that of the "Moghuls," founded by Babur, a refugee Transoxanian Timurid prince who had lost in the struggle at home with the Uzbeks. The Moghuls sometimes were allied with either the Safavids or the Uzbeks but tended to stay out of these conflicts.

Though still only irritants to the Islamic powers, Europeans were outflanking the Middle East. Portuguese naval power in the Indian Ocean was still not an insuperable threat, but the emergence of the Dutch and English in the same waters during the following century was to pose a more serious challenge.

Completing Europe's encirclement of the Islamic world, Russia advanced eastward at the expense of Muslim khanates. The Russians were eventually to look toward the Black Sea and the Straits as an outlet to the Mediterranean. Having adhered to Orthodox Christianity and in some ways representing an extension of the Byzantine version of European civilization, they posed as protectors of their coreligionists. After the fall of Constantinople to the Ottomans, one Russian ruler married a Byzantine princess and took the title czar (caesar). The "Third Rome" (Moscow) devoted itself to liberating Constantine's city from the "infidel." But, while the czars sometimes clashed with the Ottomans' Crimean vassals during the time of Sulayman, they were only beginning to cause worry in Istanbul.

Sulayman's reign began with a drive deeper into Europe. The two places where Mehmed II's forces had failed, Belgrade and Rhodes, were quickly captured. Though Ottoman eyes were at first directed to a projected conquest of Italy, French calls for aid against the Hapsburgs channeled efforts northward. The Hapsburgs had placed their own favorite on the Hungarian throne, and Sulayman entered on behalf of the Hungarian peasants and Prince Zopolya, who represented resistance to Austrian control. The Ottomans also came as protectors of a widespread Hungarian Protestant movement, which they generally favored against the Catholics throughout Europe. They crushed the Hapsburgs at Mohacs in 1526 and occupied the Hungarian cities of Buda and Pest (today's Budapest) but then left Zapolya as their vassal. With the subsequent restoration of the pro-Hapsburg candidate, Sulayman entered Hungary again three years later with a quarter of a million men. And, while some of his troops raided deep into Germany, the sultan proceeded to besiege Vienna. This city nearly succumbed but was saved when Sulayman's troops demanded to return to Istanbul for the winter. In 1541, as a result of Sulayman's fourth Hungarian campaign, most of the country was transformed into Ottoman provinces, and the Hapsburgs were forced to pay tribute to the sultan. It was in his final campaign in Austria that the aging Sulayman died in 1566.

Meanwhile, religious and military conflict with the Safavids continued. Another Kizilbash revolt in eastern Anatolia was suppressed, and Sulayman led several major campaigns into western Iran. A pattern emerged in which Shah Tahmasp withdrew to allow the invader to enter areas of scorched earth. Tahmasp generally eluded Sulayman's army, which eventually withdrew each time in order to get home for the winter. But Iraq and some parts of Armenia and Kurdistan fell under Ottoman rule. In order to concentrate on repelling a simultaneous Uzbek invasion, the shah concluded a peace treaty with Istanbul in 1555 that accepted the new Ottoman conquests.

The Ottomans derived both a strength and a weakness from the practice whereby the sultan led the whole army on each campaign. With some exceptions, conquest was not left to subordinates, who could have established their de facto independence, and not many years passed before the sultan himself appeared on opposite frontiers in Europe and Iran. Within that sweep, the Ottoman Empire retained an unusual degree of central control. However, the troops liked to spend the winter in Istanbul, and so campaigns were limited to the period from April to September of each year. An enemy army that could evade the sultan until the end of the fighting season had succeeded, in effect, in defending its territory. Another potential drawback of the Ottoman practice was that it required one quiet front while a campaign proceeded on the other one and a combination of skill and luck to prevent the Hapsburgs and the Safavids from acting in concert.

Despite its primary concern with expanding on land, the Ottoman Empire was also a great sea power. A Turkish privateer, Khayr al-Din, entered the service of the sultan and became the grand admiral of the empire. Khayr al-Din's forces established tenuous Ottoman control over the whole North African coast except for the then-vigorous Kingdom of Morocco. Parts of the newly acquired coast had previously fallen under the control of Spain, which itself had only recently (1492) ended the Muslim Kingdom of Granada. Muslim refugees from Spain were especially avid sea ghazis in the Ottoman navy. Most of the Aegean Islands were now under Ottoman control.

Though Khayr al-Din failed to take Malta, he made Ottoman naval power dominant in the Mediterranean throughout most of the sixteenth century. Crusader fleets were defeated on several occasions, and the coasts of Spain and Italy were raided by the Ottoman navy, whose maps even dared to label the New World one of the empire's provinces.

Ottoman naval forces based in Egypt and Basrah also challenged the Portuguese east of Suez. The Ottoman admiral Piri Ra'is drove the Portuguese from Socotra and established the sultan's control over Aden, much of Yemen, and parts of the Horn of Africa. There were Ottoman expeditions to India and as far away as Sumatra. But the Portuguese were able to hold onto Hormuz, at the entrance to the Persian Gulf, thus preventing Ottoman egress from that waterway.

INTERNATIONAL TRADE

The sixteenth century saw active commerce crisscrossing the Middle East. Bursa, near the Sea of Marmara, was long a main center of international trade, where Italian merchants traded various European products, like woolens, for Iranian silk, Anatolian iron, Indian spices, and Chinese porcelain, all funnelled along the regular caravan routes through Anatolia. Silk and other Iranian goods were also exported via Russia, while the Black Sea provided important routes for Ottoman trade with the Crimea and Russia. Indian spices reached Bursa by way of the Red Sea and Damascus, and products such as sugar from the Arab lands were exchanged for Anatolian timber and the like.

Iranian silk remained a basic item of trade. Heavy taxes on it provided the Safavids a major source of revenue, and the silk trade even became a royal monopoly under Shah Abbas. This business was later to fall almost entirely into the hands of an Armenian community, whose ancestors were transplanted to the Isfahan area by Shah Abbas. By the end of the sixteenth century, English merchants and the Dutch East India Company were taking Iranian silk from ports on the Persian Gulf.

PATTERNS OF OTTOMAN RULE

Now that the rise of the Safavid and the Ottoman empires has been traced, it is necessary to look at their internal dynamics. Both represented a marriage of older Islamic patterns with Turkish and Mongol traditions. Both took on new forms in response to the great technological development of the age, gunpowder, which they ardently accepted. In keeping with older patterns of the Islamic world, each "gunpowder empire," as Hodgson calls them, developed a military and political elite continuously replenished through slavery but with new characteristics.

In each state, an emperor (*padishah,* a Persian title that largely superseded the term "sultan" in Ottoman usage) ruled through a vast household. Although both dynasties survived many centuries, rival members of the family, who served as provincial governors during their father's lifetime, repeatedly struggled to succeed to the throne. In the Ottoman Empire, this developed into a pattern in which the victorious member of the dynasty had his brothers strangled to prevent further struggle; backed by a religious ruling (*fatwa*), Mehmed II officially condoned this un-Islamic procedure.

Those whose luck brought them close to the emperor were able to exert vast influence. The harem (i.e., female quarters) was often the real center of power. This was where the sultan's mother and other female and young male relatives, his concubines (picked by the queen mother), potential wives of important officials, and female servants lived and received their own exclusive kind of education. During much of Sulayman the Magnificent's reign, his Russian concubine, Hurrem Sultan (Roxelana) was perhaps the most powerful person in the empire, but the queen mother always outranked the other women and wielded the greatest influence during her lifetime.

Besides the harem, the Ottoman sultan's slave household was divided into an "inner" and an "outer" service. The former, dealing with purely internal matters of the palace, was a small, potentially influential group of "white eunuchs." It included garment-carriers, cup-bearers, and the like and was in charge of educating pages, who were young slaves of the sultan destined for high office. The larger outer service included religious functionaries, court physicians, astrologers, guards, and officers in charge of the garden, the kitchen, the mint, educating princes, and the like.

The Ottoman sultan headed the formal structure of government. He governed through an imperial council (*divan*), to which cases of miscarriage of justice could be appealed. The sultan originally presided over the council but later left this duty to his grand vizir (prime minister). The "Sublime Porte" (or "Porte"), which came to be a common term in the West for the Ottoman government, at first referred to the high doorway in which the sultan conducted state affairs and then later to the grand vizir's residence. Other members of the council included the imperial treasurer, the chancellor (who prepared documents, certificates, etc.), chief judges for Rumelia and Anatolia, the commander of the Janissaries, the chief admiral, governors (*beylerbeys*) of important provinces (*eyalets*, including several *sanjaks*), and the *shaykh al-Islam* (Mufti of Istanbul and head of the *ulama*).

Europeans called the Ottoman Empire "Turkey," a term that would have been incomprehensible to the Ottomans. Admittedly, Europeans sometimes inaccurately described all Muslims as "Turks" (and "to turn Turk" meant to become a Muslim), and only with this even more distorted meaning in mind did the word properly describes the Ottoman Empire, which besides being a dynastic state, was a Sunni Muslim one. This was not an empire in which the Turks as such ruled over others. With their slave mothers, the sultans' Turkish blood was increasingly diminished to the vanishing point. A form of Turkish was used as the court language, and the whole ruling class as well as the dynasty were known as Ottomans. But admission to the Ottoman class did not require Turkish background. When this class was open to free-born Muslims, such peoples as Arabs were equally eligible and provided some high officials almost to the last days of the empire. Paradoxically, the ruling class—"men of the sword" and "men of the pen"—used the word "Turk" pejoritively for tribesmen, peasants, and other persons of low status. In Ottoman terminology, the nonelite people of whatever ethnic background—though sometimes with specific reference to non-Muslims—were the "flock" (ra'aya).

In the earliest Ottoman period, the ruling class was composed of Turkoman chieftains. These evolved into a body of fief-holders whose expansionistic enthusiasm could still be directed mainly against non-Muslims. But such chiefs were not malleable subjects of a lofty autocrat, and they resisted centralization.

Increasingly clashing with and eventually replacing the tribal leaders were the "slaves of the Porte," (kapi kulis). Such individuals, recruited as youths and hence lacking competing family or regional ties, were intensely loyal to their master. Most notable among the slave institutions was the Janissary corps (yeni cheri, "new troops"), first created during the fourteenth century. The Janissaries, who maintained a close interrelationship with the ultra-heterodox Bektashi dervish order, with its shades of Shi'ism and Christianity, were outnumbered by other troops but long remained the elite fighting force.

Although slavery had been the route to military and ruling-class status for centuries, the pattern in the Ottoman Empire was different. Unlike the mamluks, who were manumitted after being trained, the slaves of the Porte remained the property of the sultan throughout their lives. Also, unlike the mamluk horsemen, the Janissaries were infantrymen and evolved in response to the need for artillery forces, although there were kapi kuli cavalrymen, called sipahis of the Porte, in the Ottoman army too. Also unlike previous freedmen regimes, the Ottoman slave oligarchy remained subject, if sometimes later only formally, to a dynastic sultanate.

By the time of Sulayman the Magnificent, the victory of the slave element was nearly complete. The grand vizir in particular came almost invariably to be a slave of the sultan. Likewise, nonslaves, including the descendants of the slave-elite, were barred from all offices except those of a basically religious nature, which were filled by ulama.

Another innovation in the Ottomans' slave-elite class was the method of recruitment. The main route to slave status was through a practice known as the devshirme. This was a pattern whereby (in violation of Islamic rules that forbid enslavement of Muslims or dhimmis) rural Christian boys within the empire, typically in their teens, were periodically taken as a tax on their families. Most of these boys were sent to serve provincial governors and other officials and, after receiving physical, military, and vocational training and learning to speak Turkish, generally became Janissaries. The most promising group became pages in the palace, received a rigorous education, and at the age of twenty-five were given important offices.

Naturally, Christian families were of a mixed mind with regard to the devshirme. Some religious people were surely heartbroken to have their sons invariably turned into Muslims, although technically there was no forced conversion. But this meant access to high positions. Sometimes Christian peasants would learn years later that their son was the grand vizir. The devshirme was often regarded as a privilege, and some Muslims are known to have disguised their sons as Christians in order to get in on this opportunity.

Besides the Janissaries, feudal cavalrymen (*sipahi*s) were an important (and numerically significant) part of the Ottoman army. Although some provinces, such as Egypt, were turned over to tax-farmers, the most common arrangement was for land to be divided into fiefs (*timar*s in the case of the typical small ones). Such lands supported and provided homes for *sipahi*s, who were called into the service of the sultan when he needed them for a military campaign. The fiefs were sometimes hereditary but, unlike the medieval European pattern, were kept under the effective control of the central government and helped to mobilize the agricultural wealth of the empire to support a massive war machine.

The surplus produced by the largely self-sufficient peasants was what supported the *sipahi*s, usually in the form of a tithe and other taxes paid in kind, as well as certain types of labor. In addition, the fief-holder collected taxes based on both Islamic law and decrees by the sultan. Peasants were tied to the land and, if they left it, could legally be forced to return any time within the following fifteen years. Nearly all the land they tilled was technically owned by the state. However, the lot of the Ottoman peasant during the period of military expansion was clearly enviable compared to that of European serfs. Many cases are recorded in which the latter crossed into Ottoman territories, and they generally welcomed the conquering armies of the sultan. The changed conditions of the Balkan peasantry under the Ottomans has been described by both Turkish and Western historians as a social revolution.

While the *devshirme* class predominated in one sphere, free Muslims filled the religious elite. By the latter is meant those *ulama* employed in schools, colleges, and mosques and as judges and muftis. Although in large part supported by pious endowments, they too were part of the government. The judges (*qadi*s) who applied religious law were also generally in charge of their districts, which were the smallest administrative units.

The *shari'ah* was the supreme law in the Ottoman realm, perhaps more than in any previous major Islamic state. The sultan issued decrees (*qanun*s), and some rulers, like Mehmed II, enacted a collection of imperial rules when they came to the throne. But such rules were valid only if the *shaykh al-Islam,* the highest religious authority, issued a ruling (*fatwa*) confirming that they were not in violation of the *shari'ah*. In practice, the *shaykh al-Islam* was usually able to exercise such power only when he was backed by powerful cliques. He was an appointee of and normally subservient to the sultan.

The millet (literally "nation") system provided a framework for religious toleration and sectarian self-government. Besides the Muslim millet, headed by the *shaykh al-Islam,* the Grand Rabbi headed the Jewish community, and separate patriarchs were appointed for the Greek Orthodox and Armenian Christians. The Armenian patriarch also had loose jurisidiction over miscellaneous sects, like Copts and Nestorians. As in all Islamic systems, each religion had its own law and courts governing relations among its members. The millet head was the intermediary between the sultan and the members of his flock in such matters as collecting taxes. The clergy's control over their communities long gave them a vested interest in perpetuating Ottoman rule. In the cities each sect normally inhabited its own quarter. Some Christian areas, like Moldavia and Wallachia, were vassal principalities not under direct Ottoman control.

Despite being second-class subjects, the Christian and Jewish population enjoyed a kind of toleration rarely known by religious minorities in other parts of the world. Non-Muslim groups naturally preferred to be ruled by people of their own persuasions, but their second choice tended to be incorporation into a Muslim state. Invariably, Greek Orthodox Christians looked to the Ottomans as liberators from Roman Catholic rule. Also, thousands of Jews fleeing Christian persecution in Spain found refuge in Ottoman territories. Both Jews and Christians were especially important in industry and commerce and sometimes served as tax-collectors. One group of Greeks, called the Phanariotes from the name of the district they inhabited in Istanbul, gained a key role as translators and mediators in Ottoman dealings with Europeans. Perhaps the greatest case of intolerance was the treatment of Shi'ites and Sunnis in the Ottoman and Safavid empires respectively.

In the cities, guilds of artisans and merchants were a central aspect of life. Each craft guild allocated raw materials and labor and controlled standards and levels of production, prices, training of apprentices, admission to master status, and the right to open shops. Within limits set by some degree of state control (including, as in all Islamic states, the employment of a supervisor of the market) the guilds provided an important arena for local self-government in an Islamic world that lacked corporate municipalities. The masters in each guild elected several officers, including a *shaykh,* and all the guilds of the city chose an overall *shaykh.* Both these guild leaders and the *ulama* provided vital intermediaries between the state and the populace.

The Muslim guilds doubled as *futuwwah* brotherhoods, with their codes of chivalry. They were also closely linked with dervish orders, like the Naqshabandis, whose lodges provided another nucleus of life, urban and village alike. In fact, for a Muslim not to be a member of such an order was a rarity.

SAFAVID INSTITUTIONS
AND SOCIETY

The Safavid shahs ruled much like their Ottoman counterparts in some ways. The main difference was the near divine status given to early Safavids. Although more orthodox Shi'ite influences eventually wore this away, the shah's claim to represent the Hidden Imam—in addition to a mythical descent from another one of the Twelve Imams—exemplified a continuing theocratic tendency.

The Safavid pattern of division between basically governmental and essentially religious offices evolved in a distinctive way. The early shahs ruled through a Turkoman vicegerent (*wakil*), whose authority in both religious and secular matters obliterated any possible distinction between the two spheres. The position of vicegerent eventually vanished, leaving the grand vizir (*sadr-i azam*), who was always a Persian, as the main person in charge of the bureaucracy. In part, this change represented the gradual ascendancy of Persians, whose coexistence with the Turkoman leaders had long been uneasy.

Another Persian official appointed by the shah, the *sadr*, was the counterpart of the Ottoman *shaykh al-Islam*. The *sadr* continued to have some control over mosque colleges, pious endowments, the judiciary, and the like. But religious leadership began to take on a different form even in the sixteenth century, although this did not fully develop until the late 1700s. The most influential religious authorities came to be a group of *mujtahid*s, each of whose authority to exercise *ijtihad* depended on general acceptance by a body of followers rather than on official appointment. *Mujtahid*s apparently did not challenge the principle of monarchy or assert a right to rule directly; however, they claimed that they, not the shahs, had the right to act in the name of the Hidden Imam. Thus there arose a separate center of authority, quite unlike the religious bureaucracy subservient to the Ottoman ruler. The Iranian *mujtahid*s sometimes exercised great influence at the court but were also often in active opposition.

During the sixteenth century, the Turkoman tribesmen were a powerful force who intermittently became the real rulers of the state. They repeatedly decided who would ascend the throne as their puppets, though sometimes eventually to turn against them. Only after a nine-year interregnum of Kizilbash domination was Shah Tahmasp able to assert his power in 1533 and to become the second great ruler of his house. In 1588 an eleven-year period of Kizilbash control made way for the accession of another strong ruler, Shah Abbas the Great.

The Safavids increasingly depended on a slave elite, or *ghulams*. Consequently, the shahs were able to free themselves from the influence of independent-minded Turkoman tribesmen. The process started with Tahmasp and was more fully implemented by Abbas. The *ghulams*, though at least superficially converted to Islam, were mainly of Georgian, Circassian, and Armenian origin, usually prisoners of war. While Turkoman cavalrymen were retained and supplemented by Iranian peasant musketeers, the elite group in the Safavid army became a corps of *ghulams*. Slaves of the same origin also gained top governmental posts such as governorships. They predominated in the harem and occupied influential roles as queen mothers and concubines, the latter vying in turn to gain the throne for their sons. But Persians always occupied most of the posts in the bureaucracy.

Agricultural land, generally owned by the shah, was administered in two ways. One part, known as state provinces, was in the hands of governors who supported tribal forces and local militias and also sent part of the agricultural produce to the shah. The second division, the demesnes, was under the direct control of the royal household, through agents, compensated by enfeoffment, who had the right connections or paid bribes at the court. Paralleling the emergence of a centralized slaveocracy, the latter pattern increasingly predominated.

Typically, the old pattern prevailed: A person who provided only the labor got one-fifth of the produce; if he used his own oxen, he received another fifth. But while conditions naturally varied, some European travelers presented a picture of an unusually prosperous peasantry in Iran.

The guilds seemingly performed the same functions as those in Ottoman lands. One unique feature was that they had to provide certain kinds of free labor for the palace. Also, there was a large element of state capitalism in crafts such as weaving, with many craftsmen employed by royal workshops.

OTTOMAN AND SAFAVID CULTURE

Almost as though time was dimming the glow of creativity, the rise of large, relatively stable empires paradoxically was accompanied by a drop in some cultural fields. Thus a deeper malaise in Islamic civilization made way for eventual political and military decline as well. Arnold Toynbee blamed this on the bifurcation of the "Iranic" world into the mutually hostile sectarian empires and the subsequent "collision" between the Ottomans and the "Arabic" zone. Indeed, with no independent courts to patronize intellectual and artistic efforts, the already-diminished creativity of the Arab Middle East dipped further during the next three hundred years, as did the size of a population ravaged by tax-farmers.

The termination of the political chaos of the Mongol-Timurid age coincided with the relative decline of literary florescence in Iran. This has been attributed to the Safavids' opposition to mysticism, formerly a basic inspiration for poetry. It is ironic in light of the dynasty's origin as a Sufi order. However, a recent study argues that the extent of the literary vacuum has been exaggerated and points out that the Safavids sometimes patronized poets. Also, poets of Iranian origin continued to flourish in India at the Moghul court. Hodgson extends the period of "Persianate flowering" to include the sixteenth century, but excluding the visual arts, it was mainly in the field of philosophical theology—with the elaborate ideas of the early seventeenth-century Mulla Sadra in particular—that the Safavids left much of note.

Although the Ottomans produced a major body of fine literature, little of it could be called great. Originally limited to Persian, later poets also employed Ottoman Turkish. Commonly labeled "divan" poetry because of the collections (divans) in which they were gathered, the verses of numerous men like the sixteenth-century Muhammad Ahmad al-Baki followed all the classic Persian forms and the ornate styles. There was also a body of folk literature, like Dede Korkut's epics, in the Turkish vernacular. But the great age of Islamic world power failed to produce another Hafiz or ibn-Khaldun.

Partly representing Byzantine influence, the Ottomans created a new architectural style. A central dome with a series of connecting buildings and smaller domes dominated Ottoman structures. The sixteenth-century Sinan was the great Ottoman architect who devised this type of interconnecting structure, which was both functional and visually striking. Such buildings contained the mosque, mosque-college, library, hospital, and rooms for the students. Decorative tiles covered the exterior.

The seventeenth-century Sultan Ahmad Mosque (or Blue Mosque), with six tall minarets, exemplifies this style and is in fact regarded as the last truly great monument of the dynasty.

The famous Isnik tiles were unique. The design was painted on first, and then a transparent lead glaze was applied. Isnik potters imitated Chinese porcelain by using the popular blue and white; turquoise and green later became more common.

The floral drawings that dominated the tile paintings also were subjects for cloth design. The Ottoman artists imitated the designs on imported Italian silks and velvets. Book illustrators, however, used the Persian miniaturists as their models.

While Safavid art and architecture do not show any great originality, they were productive and magnificent. Popularly described as "half the world," Isfahan had many mosques, mosque-colleges, caravanserais (inns), and at least two hundred baths. The showplace of the period was the seventeenth-century Shah Abbas Mosque. It included the typical four halls (*iwan*s), which opened onto an open court where the fountain was located. The entrance was strikingly beautiful, with faience tiles and mosaics in blue. The Safavids encouraged painting and succeeded in bringing the great Bihzad from Herat to Tabriz. The Safavid-Ottoman era certainly was one of great accomplishments.

OTTOMAN DECLINE AFTER SULAYMAN

The death of Sulayman the Magnificent in 1566 marks the beginning of a long period of gradual decline for the Ottoman Empire. The roots of weakness may go back even earlier, but some should be mentioned here, starting with more or less superficial ones.

Among the obvious reasons for decline was a degeneration in the quality of rulers. The first ten members of the dynasty had been exceptionally capable men. But now Sulayman made way for his only surviving son, Salim II, whose most revealing nickname was "the Sot." Salim II did not bother to lead his armies, as his predecessors had done, and preferred to leave matters of state to the grand vizir. Luckily for the Ottomans, Sulayman's able grand vizir, Muhammad Sokullu, stayed on for more than a decade and provided some continuity.

For the most part, Ottoman rulers continued to fit into this new pattern. Sometimes a child, a lunatic, or some other totally incompetent prince ascended the throne, and the real rulers were the shifting cliques of courtiers, military commanders, queen mothers, and concubines. Overlooking the fact that some of the most capable figures in Islamic history were women and that men provided their share of bad rulers, some past writers mistakenly treated the influence of the harem as a major factor in the Ottomans' decline. The relevant point is that the sultan had always been the keystone of the state, and a bad one, who relied on cliques of either sex, weakened the whole structure.

The way the problem of succession was resolved aggravated the problem of leadership. The early Ottoman method of letting the sons of the dead sultan fight it out and for the victor to have the others executed had its practical as well as moral drawbacks. However, this system did allow the princes to gain important experience as provincial governors during their fathers' lifetimes. While fratricide continued sporadically throughout the seventeenth century, now the rule was accepted that the eldest member of the royal family would succeed, thus avoiding a struggle. Instead of holding governorships, potential successors to the throne were kept confined in a "cage" in the palace, in effect as prisoners. The mid-seventeenth century Sultan Ibrahim ("the Mad"), who turned out to be one of the most tyrannical and incapable rulers, had been imprisoned so long that when a delegation appeared to inform him that he was to take the throne he thought his executioners had arrived and tried to keep them out.

The *devshirme* system began to break down. Levies of boys became less common over the years and completely stopped in the late 1600s. Sons of Janissaries were enrolled in the corps, as were other unqualified persons. Unlike the earlier pattern, Janissaries in active service were allowed to marry and to engage in business. They were no longer the disciplined crack force intensely devoted to the sultan. Hardly an army at all any more, the Janissaries proved uncontrollable. As early as 1622, a sultan met his end when they heard of his secret plan to create a Kurdish tribal force for use against them.

The timar system also degenerated. In many cases fief-holders evolved into mere tax-farmers or their lands became pious endowments. The timars no longer served to support cavalrymen of high quality or to manage the economy efficiently. Corruption became commonplace. Offices were regularly bought and sold without regard to ability. To most Ottomans, corruption seemed to be the real villain.

Economic problems undermined the empire. Silver of Mexican origin poured into Ottoman lands in the late sixteenth century, and the consequent severe inflation had devastating effects on the society and its institutions. Also, the increasing diversion of trade by Dutch and English merchants to sea routes furthered Ottoman economic decline. Perhaps even more basic was the fact that conquest—with its accompanying booty and opportunities to acquire new fiefs—had reached its limits, and war now was an expensive rather than a lucrative activity. A decline in sources of revenue brought excessive, arbitrary taxation and debased coinage. An upsurge of population growth produced a shortage of land in some areas and brought an influx of unemployable people into the cities. All these factors fed the rebellions that flared up more and more frequently throughout Anatolia.

Ottoman control over the Arab regions was weak. North African provinces became virtually independent, and their corsairs raided as far away as Iceland. Mamluk beys became the real powers in Egypt and periodically overthrew Ottoman viceroys who tried to exercise power. However, a viceroy restored considerable control over the mutually hostile mamluk factions in the 1660s. In the Lebanese mountain region, the Ma'ns, a local Druze dynasty, were under only nominal central authority during the early 1600s, as was a newly dominant family, the Shihabs, later in the century. The Lebanese chieftains sometimes asserted control over adjacent regions. Military commanders repeatedly revolted in Baghdad, nullifying the governors' authority. A local dynasty dominated Basrah from 1567 until 1668. Tribesmen in southern Iraq resisted Ottoman control in the late seventeenth century and even occupied Basrah for a while.

From time to time strong individuals attempted to restore Ottoman grandeur. Several sultans were helpless in the face of opposition from *ulama* and Janissaries, but some carried out campaigns of reform through ruthless cruelty against the corrupt. Sultan Murad IV brought an upturn in Ottoman fortunes with large-scale executions that became more and more arbitrary, allegedly claiming 100,000 victims.

From 1656 to 1661 an octogenerian "slave" strongman, Mehmed Koprulu, became grand vizir. He accepted the office only on the condition that everything he did would be accepted in advance by the sultan and the *shaykh al-Islam*. Again a campaign on behalf of honesty and austerity was pursued through bloodthirsty means. Much of this was repeated by a series of Koprulu's descendants, who gave the grand vizirate a nearly dynastic character throughout the rest of the century. But no reformer at this time sought to make any basic changes in the Ottoman system. The assumption was always that the machine of government had simply to be restored so it would work again as in the days of Sulayman the Magnificent.

THE MIDDLE EAST AND EUROPE: A REVERSAL OF ROLES

The gradual decline of the Ottoman state after the late sixteenth century and the subsequent rapid deterioration of the Safavids cannot be understood simply in terms of incompetent individuals and misdirected institutions. Rather, it basically reflected the ebbing fortune of Islamic civilization while Christian Europe's edge grew to indisputable predominance by the late eighteenth century.

The emergence of a fundamental gap between the capabilities of the West and the world at large was a product of abnormal vitality in European civilization. For centuries all spheres of life in much of the West were transformed at ever faster rates, eventually making each generation primitive in comparison with the next. The conventional term for this has become "modernization," with "modern," mainly Western, societies contrasted with more "traditional" ones in which human control over nature is less accelerated. Indeed, the West's industrialization was to have an adverse impact on the Middle East by undermining the latter's traditional industries and crafts (a process already initiated by Mongol devastation) and turning it into a producer of raw materials for the new "world market." In effect, it created a kind of "underdevelopment" that previously did not exist.

When Europe was undergoing these developments, the Middle East found itself in a relatively unflorescent period. The basic conservatism of Islamic society at the time of its post-Mongol zenith—or even earlier—may have provided the seed for decline, and the dazzling nature of recent politicomilitary achievements may have blinded Middle Easterners to long-term dangers.

Receptivity to imported innovation waned. In the fifteenth and sixteenth centuries, the Ottomans often were aware of Europe's most recent military technology and geographic findings, but such new knowledge ceased to be of interest to Middle Easterners just as it was mushrooming.

To a certain extent mutual insularity was normal for two different civilizations. Ideas and styles did not usually percolate freely across civilizational lines. Scholars who wrote in Persian and Arabic and in terms of their own cultural tradition simply lived in a different intellectual world from their Christian European counterparts.

Everyday things crossed civilizational lines more freely. The introduction of maize, potatoes, tomatoes, and other Western Hemisphere plants met no resistance. Even tobacco was accepted after some initial opposition. Spreading from Ethiopia and Southern Arabia in the sixteenth century, coffee drinking rapidly became a conspicuous feature of Middle Eastern life, and the *ulama* did not hold out against it for long.

Military innovations were usually acceptable to the *ulama* on the grounds that they would help in the defense and expansion of Islam. Even here, Islamic efforts eventually lagged. The Ottoman navy, which had previously kept astride of the newest developments in Europe, belatedly found its galleys outclassed by European "tall ships" in the late sixteenth century. By the next century, it was commonplace for Ottoman and Safavid weapons to be outdated. Shah Abbas's acceptance of help from English miitary experts shows a receptivity to new ideas but also demonstrates that the Safavid army had fallen behind.

Middle Eastern Christian minorities were less aloof from European developments. Trade with Europe came to be almost exclusively in their hands. Missionaries in the eighteenth-century soon learned that the conversion of Muslims was out of the question and instead concentrated on local Christians. Missionary schools were an early channel of transmission for European civilization to a few. Some Middle Eastern Christian groups—mostly fragments of older sects—kept their own liturgies while merging with the Roman Catholic Church. The most notable example of such "uniate" churches is the Maronites of Lebanon, some of whom studied in Rome even in the sixteenth century. The impact of modernity thus got a head start among many Christians, and the Maronites in particular have recently sometimes regarded themselves as "Westerners."

Islamic creativity reached its nadir in the eighteenth century. Even the revisionist historians who have rightly refuted overstated versions of this statement are unable to deny its essential accuracy. Indeed, the Islamic world never knew a "Dark Age"; its civilization was alive but now lacked much vitality. Mosque schools and colleges continued to transmit old religious and legal learning by memorization. Books were written in traditional patterns, with few signs of originality, although some new styles emerged in a still-flowering Ottoman poetry. None of the mosques and palaces being constructed compared with the great earlier ones. The "conservative spirit" had just about spent itself. Only in the last part of the century were there signs—pointed to in one recent study—of a slow intellectual revival in some places, particularly Egypt. Western supremacy in the economic, cultural, political, and military fields had still left Middle Eastern empires largely intact. Although its logical consequences were not to be fully felt until the end of the century, it seemed to immobilize a civilization whose internal dynamics had already reduced its creativity.

SLOWED MILITARY MOMENTUM

Returning to the story of Ottoman wars with Christian Europe after the death of Sulayman the Magnificent, we find setbacks beginning to occur, but the day of expansion was not yet over. The reign of Selim II witnessed the failure of an ambitious plan to push the Russians back and to dig a canal between the Don and the Volga to provide a waterway to the Caspian and permit an attack on the Safavids from a new direction. Soon afterwards, the Ottomans' Tatar vassals raided Moscow, but in the long run they could not stop czarist expansion.

War in the Mediterranean brought mixed results in the 1570s. Venetian-held Cyprus fell to the Ottomans, but the sultan's navy suffered its first major setback in 1571 at the hands of a Crusader armada at Lepanto, near the Greek coast. Still, an intense building program restored the decimated Ottoman fleet within a year. As it proceeded to raid southern Europe, the prospect of a landing and conquest seemed likely, but Christian naval domination of the Mediterranean soon became a basic reality.

A "Long War" (1593–1606) with the Hapsburgs provided another indication of relative decline in Ottoman power. With several Balkan peoples revolting against Istanbul's rule, the fortunes of war alternated, but the Ottomans were able to hold their own. A peace treaty generally restored the territorial status quo ante. But Vienna's former tribute to Istanbul ended, and for the first time the Ottomans recognized the Hapsburg ruler as a fellow emperor instead of a mere king.

The only enemy capable of posing a dire threat to the Ottoman heartland was still the Safavids. This was because the Safavid zenith, under Abbas the Great's new slave armies, came at a time when the Ottomans were already in decline.

The Ottomans went on the offensive in the east during the struggle for power in Iran after Shah Tahmasp's death. The Uzbeks compounded the Safavids' problem by invading eastern Iran. When Shah Abbas took the throne, he needed peace with the Ottomans in order to deal with the peril from the north. And so, in a peace treaty of 1590, the Safavids acquiesced in Ottoman conquests as far east as the Caspian. But after driving the Uzbeks back at the end of the century, Abbas moved westward again and soon restored the old boundary. He continued to advance, taking Iraq in 1623 and then penetrating into Anatolia. It was not until 1638 that the Ottomans, strengthened by Murad IV's reforms, were able to roll the Iranians back, after which the peace treaty of 1639 established a frontier that generally corresponds to Iran's western boundary today.

A rapid deterioration of Safavid strength after the death of Abbas saved the day for the Ottomans. Almost all subsequent Safavid rulers virtually duplicated the vices and weaknesses of their worst Ottoman counterparts. Most were victims of alcoholism. In part, this was a result of confining princes in the palace—at least those who were not killed or blinded by their fathers and brothers—for fear that they would usurp power. Rulers with this kind of preparation were content to be mere instruments of intrigue involving concubines, queen mothers, eunuchs, and other people around them. Only the *ulama* and tribes sometimes challenged the degenerate, corrupt order that ate into the military power and prosperity of the realm.

The last half of the seventeenth century saw a mixture of victories and setbacks for the Ottomans. They took Crete from Venice, but in another Ottoman-Hapsburg war, started in 1663, they were unable to resume the offensive on that front, and Christian Europe was heartened. However, new advances were possible for the Ottomans in their campaign against Poland in the 1670s. A peace treaty with Poland in 1676 left the Ukraine divided into areas of direct Ottoman control and of Ottoman suzerainty. But Russia was able to hold the Ottomans back and force them to accept the Dneiper as their northern frontier.

A new offensive in Europe began in the 1680s. Grand Vizir Kara Mustafa led a huge army into Hungary and took the Hapsburg-ruled part of the country. With the Pope calling for a crusade, armies from various European states eventually joined in a War of the Holy League against the Ottomans. Vienna came under a three-month Ottoman siege in 1683, and the city could undoubtedly have been taken by storm if Kara Mustafa had not so confidently planned for it to surrender without a fight. When the Polish king led in a relief force, the Ottomans neglected to intercept it in time. An Ottoman force diverted to meet the Poles was defeated, and the sultan's army fell back from Vienna, never to return.

The rest of the war was largely one of Ottoman losses. The Hapsburgs drove their foe from the region north of the Danube. With Muslim refugees pouring out of the lost territories, the Ottomans' economic problems multiplied. Venice conquered southern Greece and part of the Adriatic coast; the Russians, under Peter the Great, occupied Azov, on the northern coast of the Black Sea; and Poland held the Ukraine.

Ottoman defeats, confirmed in the Treaty of Karlowitz (1699), marked a watershed in the relationship between Christian Europe and the Islamic world. The fearful Ottoman government had no choice but to accept its losses of territory. A separate treaty with Russia the next year confirmed the boundary changes on that front. Although the Ottomans were still too strong for almost any single European state and actually reversed some of the territorial changes a few years later, the trend generally became one of slow withdrawal from Europe. The old fear of an Islamic onslaught ceased to haunt Christendom.

OTTOMAN AND SAFAVID EMPIRES

Approximate Boundaries in A.D. 1683

MOGHUL EMPIRE

Arabian Sea

UZBEKS

Aral Sea

Herat

Ghaznah

Kirman

Yazd

Isfahan

Hormuz

Muscat

Qum

OMAN

Caspian Sea

Shiraz

Ardabil

GILAN

KHUZISTAN

Persian Gulf

Astrakhan

Hamadhan

Volga R.

Tabriz

GEORGIA

Karbala

Najaf

NAJD

Dar'iyyah

CIRCASSIANS

Calderan

Don R.

Azov

Red Sea

Dnieper R.

CRIMEA

Black Sea

Aleppo

Hama

Homs

Damascus

Bug R.

Konya

Varna

Istanbul

Bursa

EGYPT

PODOLIA

Pruth R.

MOLDAVIA

Nicopolis

Dniester R.

TRANSYLVANIA

WALLACHIA

Salonica

MOREA

HUNGARY

Pest

Buda

Mohacs

Belgrade

Mediterranean Sea

Ionian Is.

Danube R.

Vienna

Otranto

Ionian Sea

Benghazi

TUNISIA

Venice

Tripoli

TRIPOLITANIA

CYRENAICA

EIGHTEENTH-CENTURY OTTOMANS:
REFORM AND DEFEAT

The early eighteenth century brought considerable success to the Ottomans. In another Russo-Ottoman war, czarist troops entered Moldavia in 1710, but they moved too far ahead of their supplies and failed to get the active help they expected from the Moldavians. Suffering from famine, the Russians tried to withdraw but were trapped at the River Pruth. The two powers concluded the Treaty of Pruth (1711), whereby Russia relinquished the gains it made in 1700.

In a war with Venice in 1713 the Ottomans recovered the Morea (southern Greece). But Austria entered the struggle and soon made considerable gains, occupying the rest of Hungary and large slices of the Balkans, including Belgrade. Then the Treaty of Passarowitz (1718) confirmed both the Ottomans' losses to Austria and their gains on the Venetian front. In still another conflict, in 1736, the Russians met setbacks in the Crimea, again because of the shortage of supplies, while the Tatar Khan raided deep into the czar's empire. Austria's initial gains in this war brought an Ottoman offensive and, according to the Treaty of Belgrade (1739), a regaining of territories lost twenty one years earlier. Russian successes in Moldavia were endangered by this separate peace, and a Russo-Ottoman treaty restored the earlier frontier and excluded Russian vessels from the Black Sea.

Despite their sporadic successes and a certain continuing self-confidence, the post-Karlowitz Ottomans realized for the first time that they could profit from learning some of Europe's secrets. Not only did western Europe now prove powerful, but Peter the Great's eager emulation of this region had seemingly worked for Russia and might do the same for Islam. Thus a series of Westernizing reforms initiated a recurrent, later to be accelerated, Herodian pattern whereby Middle Eastern rulers selectively imitated those European powers that defeated them, if only to ward off further losses.

The years from 1718 to 1730 in the Ottoman Empire came to be known as the "tulip era," as gardens in which that plant was cultivated became the rage among the ruling class. Along with this came an aping of European buildings, furniture, clothing, and other superficial matters that would have been inconceivable in former times. Only a century before, awe for the East had induced King Charles II of England pretentiously to adopt Persian dress at his court for a short time. Even now the notion of Eastern inferiority was not so completely jelled in the West as to prevent some craze for Ottoman styles and for tulips.

Not all the reforms of the tulip age were so superficial, although the idea still prevailed that no basic changes in Islamic civilization need accompany the adoption of specific European techniques. The Ottoman ambassador to Paris was instructed to seek out useful knowledge, and he wrote in approving tones about some of the exotic social customs there, including the appearance of women in public. A few individuals bothered for the first time to learn French. Among numerous Western-inspired reforms, the most notable was the establishment of a printing press on the initiative of Ibrahim Muteferrika, a Hungarian convert to Islam. A ruling from the *shaykh al-Islam* approved this innovation, but only on the condition that books on religion be excluded from such reproduction. In turn, Western science and ideas seeped in faster by way of printed translations. Another convert to Islam, a French renegade, the Comte de Bonneval, was instrumental in bringing about several reforms in the army, including the establishment of schools for teaching modern mathematics and medicine for military use. Even a conservative reaction, which brought a Janissary revolt and the fall of Sultan Ahmad and his modernizing grand vizir in 1730, could not stop the Herodian trend in the long run.

Neither could the piecemeal eighteenth-century reforms so easily contain the tide of decline and defeat. More wars weakened the economy. Taxes became unbearable, and the coinage was debased. There were numerous popular rebellions and cases of flight of peasants from the land.

Control over the provinces weakened further during the eighteenth century. In Egypt from 1711 on, rule by particular factions of *mamluk* beys alternated with times of anarchy during which *mamluk*s, Janissaries, and sometimes rebellious tribes and peasants struggled for power. After 1757, one *mamluk*, Ali Bey, became the ruler of an essentially independent state. His control even extended to the Hijaz. In an alliance with Shaykh Zahir al-Omar, a Galilean notable who established another de facto state in northern Palestine, Egypt's ruler marched through Syria and held Damascus for a while. One of his *mamluk*s, Abu-Dhahab, overthrew him in 1772 and defeated him the next year in his attempted comeback from exile in Shaykh Zahir's territory.

In Baghdad, an Ottoman governor, Hasan Pasha, founded a de facto dynasty in 1704. Then, after 1747, a series of *mamluk* rulers rapidly succeeded each other amidst an intermittent series of coups.

Even in Anatolia and eventually in Rumelia, local notables asserted their control during the early eighteenth century. The Ottoman army became heavily dependent on the contingents they contributed. Anatolia was lucky in comparison with most Arab provinces in that its *derebeys* ("valley lords"), as the notables there were known, had local roots and had the welfare of their own regions at heart. But the sultan enjoyed little control over what the map now so misleadingly showed to be his empire.

The third quarter of the eighteenth century demonstrated European supremacy still more convincingly. With Istanbul objecting to Russian encroachment on Poland and the resultant shift in the eastern European balance of power, war broke out again in 1768. Although the Tatars once more raided Russia, the Russians soon prevailed and established a puppet regime in the Crimea. Other Russian forces crushed the Ottomans in 1770 and sliced through the northeastern part of the Balkans. The prospect that they would reach Istanbul seemed real for a while. At the same time the Russian navy, with English help, sailed from the Baltic to the Mediterranean to destroy the Ottoman fleet and join forces with Ali Bey and Shaykh Zahir. Only civil strife and other problems in Russia, plus the pressures of European countries who realized that excessive gains for the czar would strengthen him too much relative to themselves, saved the Ottomans from disaster.

The Treaty of Kuchuk Kaynarja ended the state of war in 1774. The two powers recognized the independence of the Crimean khanate, over which the Ottoman rulers would retain the role of caliph in a purely religious capacity. This distinction, inexplicable in terms of Islamic political theory, was seemingly the first of a series of Ottoman attempts to assert their weak claims to the caliphate. While Russia was to withdraw from much of the conquered territory, the Ottomans ceded it several fortresses, the district of Azov, and the area between the Bug and the Dneiper. Russia, whose ruler was also dignified by recognition as a *padishah,* was thus a Black Sea littoral power. The right of its merchants to use this sea and the Straits was guaranteed. The treaty also gave Russia the right to build and keep under its protection a church in Istanbul and to remonstrate in favor of Christians in the evacuated areas, rights which the czars later succeeded in stretching to mean a general role as protector of the Greek Orthodox Church in the Ottoman Empire. Thus began a now nearly inexorable process, restrained only by the jealousies of other European powers, of czarist encroachment on former Ottoman lands. More broadly, this was a world in which Islamic lands increasingly were subject to the whims of European Christendom.

IRANIAN INTERREGNUM

Unlike the Ottomans' more gradual decline, the disintegration of the Safavid Empire took place in the early eighteenth century. It began in 1711, when two groups of Afghan tribesmen rebelled and established their independence. Safavid forces sent against the Ghalzay Afghans, led by Mahmud, were decimated eight years later after mistakenly firing cannon on their own men. And actions of the incompetent Husayn Shah, such as having his grand vizir's eyes torn out before discovering that charges of treachery against him were false, helped to ripen the Safavid Empire for conquest. Following earlier raids, Mahmud reached Isfahan in 1722, a city now reduced by disease and famine to cannibalism. The large Safavid army quickly fell apart in its encounter with a small group of tribesmen, and few Persians had the will to resist Mahmud as he ascended the throne.

The Afghan conquest of Iran brought anarchy and economic decline. Magnificent Isfahan nearly vanished, and other great cities shrank to little more than villages.

Both the Ottomans and the Russians saw a chance to gain territory and agreed in 1724 to partition much of the old Safavid lands between themselves. While Peter the Great occupied parts of the north, the Ottomans incongruously posed as supporters of the deposed Safavids against their fellow Sunni Afghans and conquered much of western Iran, which the Afghan dynasty ceded to Istanbul.

A Safavid claimant, Tahmasp II, gained the support of some large tribes whose importance went back to their *Kizilbash* days. These included the Qajars and the Afshars. A dauntless warrior of the latter tribe, Nadir Khan Afshar, soon became the leader of the Safavid restorationist camp. The Afghans were defeated by Nadir in 1729, and a continuing series of reverses rapidly brought about their demise. With Iran now seemingly getting hold of itself, the Russians agreed to withdraw from the conquered territory, and victories over Ottoman forces in the early 1730s led to a treaty restoring the status quo ante. A year later, the Afshar strongman ended all pretense by declaring himself Nadir Shah.

The new shah obscured Iran's fundamental decline with a whirlwind of military victories. He took Iranian armies deep into Central Asia to defeat the khanates that had succeeded in some of the Uzbek lands. Another drive took Nadir into Afghanistan and on through Khyber Pass to rout the forces of a declining Moghul Empire. Although Iranian forces occupied Delhi in 1739, Nadir did not try to hold India permanently. Nadir also inflicted another serious defeat on the Ottomans in 1745. Within Iran he tended to centralize the state by avoiding feudal grants and by confiscating pious foundations, as well as through the forcible settlement of some tribes.

But the Afshar dynasty's success proved ephemeral. Nadir imposed high taxes. Moreover, victory seemingly evoked sadism in him, and his style of rule soon came to be symbolized by the pyramids of suspected Iranians' heads, which only intensified opposition to him. In a country where chaos—which he admittedly ameliorated—had brought so much economic loss, the shah simply hoarded the wealth he took from India and other conquered areas. The masses suffered from famine.

The shah's religious innovation proved to be another important source of resentment as he attempted to turn Iran again to Sunnism. Perhaps calculating that this would help win acceptance for his leadership in the larger Islamic world, he tried to get Iran's Twelver form of Shi'ism accepted as a fifth *madhhab* (school) of Sunni law. Few Shi'ite *ulama* were willing to accept such an idea except under the threat of death.

With Nadir Shah's assassination in 1747, anarchy returned. Other members of his dynasty were able to hold some areas, but not for long. By the 1750s the benevolent and politically adept Karim Khan of the Zand tribe prevailed in most of Iran and ruled from Shiraz as the vicegerent of a figurehead Safavid shah. For now, he subdued his main rival, the later ascendant Turkoman Qajar tribe. Although Karim Khan brought some improvement, the country was economically exhausted, and recurrent starvation, disease, emigration, and war had halved the population of some cities. The Ottomans, who were retreating on other fronts, were in no position to take advantage of Iran's misfortune, but European penetration was evident as the Russians gradually gained preponderance in Georgia and as the English East India Company became active in the Persian Gulf.

THE CAPITULATIONS

Western economic power furthered the decline of lagging Middle Eastern economies. European merchants became more and more active, and their products began to undermine local manufactures and put artisans out of work, although the decline did not nearly reach the serious proportions of the next century. Trade and shipping between Christian Europe and the Islamic world were entirely in the hands of the Europeans, whose merchants also were active in trade between different Ottoman ports.

European economic penetration was enhanced by agreements known as capitulations. Islamic states had always not only allowed religious minorities to live under their own law but also granted non-Muslim outsiders (*harbi*s, "people of the lands of war") special permission to enter Islamic territory in security. The Ottoman Empire concluded agreements with Italian city-states allowing their subjects such rights in the fourteenth century, and they extended these rights to France in the sixteenth century. In a related matter, France began to pose as the protector of the sultan's Catholic subjects, and other powers claimed responsibility for their own chosen minorities.

Over the centuries, both the Ottomans and the Safavids concluded a series of such capitulation agreements with various European states. In general, the agreements provided for trading privileges, including low customs duties, and exempted merchants from local jurisdiction (i.e., provided extraterritoriality). Even in cases involving Ottoman or Safavid subjects, the foreign merchant was granted certain privileges, such as trial on criminal charges only in special courts outside the regular judicial system.

At first the capitulations did not involve submission to somebody more powerful. The word *capitulation* originated in reference to the "chapters" (Latin, *capitula*) into which each treaty was divided and only later took on its present connotation in keeping with what the treaties had come to represent. The first capitulation agreements were entered into by a powerful Ottoman Empire in a somewhat condescending spirit toward Europeans and contained reciprocal rights for the sultan's subjects. But as the empire became weak, the extraterritorial provisions, which European powers could even extend to local people, particularly *dhimmi*s, increasingly belied the Ottomans' and Iranians' control over their own territory.

REVIVAL IN ARABIA

Central Arabia, or Najd, had never fallen under Ottoman control, although Istanbul claimed a vague overlordship. Instead, various nomadic tribes maintained their independence, as did small amirates centered on the villages and towns that were supported by oasis agriculture and trans-Arabian commerce and pilgrimage traffic. As with many bedouin, Islamization tended to be more or less superficial. Widespread Sufi practices like pilgrimages to saints' tombs smacked of idolatry to some. Reverence for sacred trees and the like may have been carry-overs from pre-Islamic days.

In this situation, a movement arose in the eighteenth century that in some ways presaged other attempts at reform that would be made during the next two hundred years. A pious young Najdi, Muhammad ibn-Abd al-Wahhab, who pursued religious studies in Madina and Basrah, embraced the strict Hanbali school of law and the teachings of the fourteenth-century Syrian Hanbali theologian, ibn-

Taymiyyah, with such ardor that he was expelled from several places. In 1745 he took refuge in the hitherto petty amirate of Dar'iyyah, ruled by the house of Sa'ud. He converted Amir Muhammad ibn-Sa'ud to his doctrine and, marrying the latter's daughter, became a virtual coruler; the descendants of the two men have since been closely intertwined. Ibn-Abd al-Wahhab's "Unitarian" movement—or the "Wahhabis," to use a term originally adopted by detractors—was now backed by Sa'udi political and military power, and it began a career of enforced purification and expansionism that, following one abortive mushrooming in the early nineteenth century, finally culminated in the Kingdom of Sa'udi Arabia in the twentieth.

Wahhabism was a radical rejection of then-current trends in Islam and of all un-Islamic practices. In keeping with Hanbali doctrine, Wahhab demanded the reopening of the gates of *ijtihad,* unrestrained by the consensus of the Islamic community after the first three centuries. Otherwise, only the Qur'an and the *sunnah* were to be accepted without question, with the idea that this would lead not to a freer but rather to a stricter interpretation as part of a return to a long-corrupted faith. Tobacco, jewelry, silk, and the like were banned, as were domed tombs of saints and other objects of veneration. By 1774 the Sa'udi-Wahhabi state was well on its way to uniting Central Arabia. But it had still hardly attracted the attention of the wider Islamic world.

CONCLUSIONS

The devastation inflicted by the Mongols proved to be a prelude to continuing cultural greatness under Mongol and Turkish dynasties. This was particularly true of the northern Middle East, the zone of Persian culture, but even the Arab region under the Mamluk Sultanate showed some flashes of creativity. Still, a general wariness about innovation—although the acceptance of Chinese influence brought by the Mongols provides a brilliant exception—tended to bring a diminution of florescence in the long run.

Then a network of mutually hostile Islamic states, including the Ottoman and Safavid empires, became the greatest centers of world power. The Ottomans in particular outdid all other Middle Eastern conquerors in invading and ruling much of Europe. This great eruption of Middle Eastern power was accompanied by two paradoxes. First, it came just as the civilizational flowering of the anarchical Mongol age began to fade. Second, it came at a time when Europeans were encircling the region by virtue of their supremacy on the oceans—including, in the case of the Russians, the "dry sea" of the Eurasian steppe—and expanding into underpopulated lands.

Using their not-yet-abnormal cultural florescence as a base, Europeans began a take-off incomparable to anything since the Middle East–nurtured Neolithic Revolution ten millennia before. By the eighteenth century, Europe was indisputably ahead of where it had been two centuries earlier and equally ahead of its contemporaries elsewhere. Not only did the world at large remain outside the positive impact of this economic, politicomilitary, and cultural revolution, but the developing "world market" produced by Europe's Industrial Revolution was already undermining Middle Eastern industries. The Islamic world had reached a low point in relation to its former achievements. Internal disintegration and defeats by European powers, including the beginning of the Ottomans' slow retreat from Europe by 1774, were telling signs of the emerging relationship between the West and the Middle East. So far, the Middle East had made only minor attempts to learn Europe's secrets, but more drastic efforts were to follow as increasingly unbearable blows and the insufficiency of selective borrowing eventually awakened more Middle Easterners to a sense of their civilization's fundamental inadequacy.

5

The European Tide

1774-1914

From the late eighteenth century on, a Europe whose cultural vitality and military and economic power knew no rivals began to close in on the Middle East. The latter, like the other civilizations of Asia, had more often than not previously been at least the equal of the West, whose abnormal transformations now however put the rest of the world increasingly at its mercy. The condition of the Ottoman ''sick man of Europe'' was exceeded only by that of an enfeebled Iran, leaving Europeans bedeviled by the ''Eastern question''—how to dispose of each without upsetting the European balance of power. Unlike most of the non-Western world, the two major Middle Eastern states retained their formal independence throughout the period. For that matter, the Ottomans only slowly relinquished their colonial Christian territories in the Balkans, a curious relic of an age when the relative capabilities of the Islamic and Christian worlds had been radically different. Yet, especially by the latter half of the nineteenth century, Ottoman and Iranian sovereignty had become empty shells preserved only by the mutual rivalries of European powers.

Russia recurrently encroached on both Middle Eastern states. But other European governments' concern for the balance of power always frustrated St. Petersburg's[1] greater ambitions. Great Britain, the dominant imperial power of the age, was usually not much interested in annexing Middle Eastern territories as long

[1]Today's Leningrad, then the Russian capital.

133

as other powers did not threaten its "road to India." And so such powers as Britain, though sometimes carving out de facto colonies for themselves, served as a check against czarist expansionism.

Besides the specter of European political and military power, the issue of Westernization engrossed Middle Easterners during this period. Rulers saw that Western military techniques were their only hope of salvation. Once introduced, such innovations produced demands for Westernization in other spheres of life. While the Zealots' loyalty to their own heritage remained at one pole, Middle Eastern nationalists increasingly adopted a Herodian stance that called for further Westernization to save themselves. Some began to claim that the wholesale adoption of Western civilization was the only alternative to weakness and backwardness; others took a new look at Islamic ideals to legitimize the selective adoption of some of the secrets of European power.

AFTER KUCHUK KAYNARJA: MORE PRESSURES AND REFORM

The immediate aftermath of Kuchuk Kaynarja saw accelerated reform in the sultan's realm in the face of continuing danger from European, particularly Russian, encroachment. Some earlier innovations like the printing press, were now reinstated. In the early 1780s under Sultan Abd al-Hamid I's reformist grand vizir, Halil Hamid Pasha, there were several attempts to modernize the army and navy, including the establishment of a new school of mathematics. Even before the peace treaty was signed, one significant departure from traditional reform was the employment of Christian French army officers as advisers. In turn, the opposition of conservative Janissaries and *ulama* led to the execution of the grand vizir in 1785 and the interruption of the trend.

The youthful Sultan Salim III (1789–1807) initiated a more radical stage of reform as soon as a respite from still another war with Russia permitted him to concentrate on internal matters. The New Order (*Nizam-i Jadid*) which the sultan pronounced in 1792 included a variety of attempts to reform the administration of the Empire, but it was identified primarily with an infantry corps that reflected despair with proposals to improve existing troops. Modeled on European armies, even in matters of clothing, the New Order troops required numerous other innovations, such as a medical service and Western-style schools for officers. French books, not all of which were devoted to purely military matters, were used, and French officers provided instruction and enjoyed a kind of informal personal relationship with Ottoman subjects that Westerners had not experienced before. What started as an attempt to learn from the West in the military field brought a long train of unexpected consequences in other aspects of life.

Another channel for Westernization was diplomacy. In 1793, for the first time in Ottoman history, Salim III established permanent diplomatic relations with several European countries. The ambassadors were instructed to seek useful information, and young men were sent specifically to learn the languages of the host countries.

As the growth of provincial independence continued and as both Russia and Austria demonstrated expansionist designs, the Ottomans' international position deteriorated further. Istanbul was helpless as the czar violated the peace treaty by annexing the Crimean Khanate in 1779. Catherine the Great of Russia was soon working to implement a project to restore the Byzantine Empire, with her grandson prepared for the role of emperor in the Second Rome from the day he was baptized as Constantine. War with both Russia and Austria began in 1787, and the allies advanced rapidly into the sultan's European territories. With a war against revolutionary France forcing Austria to withdraw from the conflict in 1791, Russia continued to press on and to impose the humiliating Treaty of Jassy on the Ottomans the next year. The annexation of the Crimea and other territories was legitimized, while the Russians withdrew from the Balkans.

The old Franco-Ottoman friendship eroded somewhat in the 1780s as it proved unable to prevent Russian encroachment on the sultan's lands. Still, it survived the French Revolution of 1789, which precipitated a series of wars between France and shifting groups of European powers that lasted until 1815. Then, in 1797, France and Austria concluded a peace treaty that partitioned the Venetian territories between them. As part of this deal, France got control of the Ionian Islands—near the western coast of Greece—and some enclaves on the Albanian coast. This put the French too close for Istanbul's comfort, as some rebellious notables in the sultan's Balkan territories began to connive with French agents and as Paris gazed greedily toward other Ottoman lands.

BONAPARTE IN THE EAST

General Napoleon Bonaparte, whose popularity in the French Republic recently had been buoyed by conquests in Italy, pushed for acceptance of his characteristically grandiose proposal for an invasion of Egypt. Bonaparte, then in his late twenties, had been assigned to lead an assault on Britain, the only major country then in the enemy camp. But he saw the establishment of a French colony in Egypt as a more feasible alternative, one that would allow him to cut Britain's communications with its empire in India, where the French had lost out in the early 1760s. French commercial interests in Egypt had recently grown in importance, while British dealings with Ibrahim and Murad, the duumvirate of *mamluk* beys now in power there, posed a threat. Also, the arbitrary exaction of taxes by the beys provided an official justification for the invasion. But Bonaparte's dreams carried him far beyond Egypt. His reading of ancient history told him that the "East" was where all the great "glory" had been won, and he once proclaimed Europe a mere "molehill" unworthy of his effort. He hoped to march on to India much like Alexander the Great—even, in his wild dreams, to ride an elephant and found a new religion. Presumably both the Ottomans and the Iranians would be reduced to the status of French vassals. The five-man Directory, which then ruled France, eventually accepted Bonaparte's plan, perhaps in part to get rid of a dangerous threat to their own power.

Stopping to take Malta on the way, a great armada of four hundred ships carried Bonaparte and his 50,000-man army to their top-secret destination in 1798. The British knew something was underway, and their superior fleet, commanded by Lord Nelson, now was in the Mediterranean after a recent absence. It took a measure of good luck for the French armada to reach Alexandria. The *mamluks* received the news of the landing with derision, for they assumed that they could easily defeat "Frankish" armies, which, after all, had not dared attack the Islamic heartland for so many centuries. But the invaders were able to push on to Cairo during the same month they landed and to defeat the *mamluks* decisively at the Battle of the Pyramids. Still, the ease with which the French won can be exaggerated, for the *mamluks* withdrew to Upper Egypt, where Bonaparte's troops never fully subdued them.

Bonaparte's expedition in many ways was a turning point in relations between the West and the Middle East. For one thing, the Western world learned a great deal about Egypt, as Bonaparte aped Alexander the Great to the extent of taking a corps of five hundred scholars with him. Constituting the Institut de l'Égypte, they represented virtually every field of study, from zoology to Eastern languages. Their findings were published years later in the twenty-four-volume *Déscription de l'Égypte,* a work of unprecedented thoroughness. One notable discovery was the Rosetta Stone, with its parallel inscriptions in Greek and Egyptian scripts, which provided modern scholars the key to deciphering hieroglyphics and thus gave birth to the science of Egyptology, the study of ancient Egypt.

More important was the beginning of the modern Western impact on the Arab East. The area could no longer remain confident of its own superiority, and it was inevitable that future rulers of Egypt would seek what the militarily superior West had to offer. *Ulama* from al-Azhar visited the French scholars and in some cases were highly impressed with their scientific procedures. The printing press is an example of what the French expedition introduced to Egypt for the first time.

Bonaparte soon began to experience setbacks. Lord Nelson found the French armada soon after it reached Egypt. A great naval battle ensued, which ended in the devastation of the French fleet. A British naval blockade virtually isolated the French forces from their home base. Also, Bonaparte seriously miscalculated Sultan Salim III's response to his occupation of Egypt, which was, after all, an Ottoman province, though not under the central government's actual control. No one was impressed with Bonaparte's claim that he was there as a friend of the sultan and to suppress the latter's enemies. There was great anger among the people of Istanbul because of this "infidel" encroachment and also because the disruption of imports from Egypt produced a food shortage. The sultan entered into alliances with both Britain and Russia and declared war on France. Enthusiastic Turkish crowds applauded as a Russian fleet passed through the Straits.

As for the Egyptians, Bonaparte announced that he was there to deliver them from *mamluk* oppression. In what he later privately admitted to be pure "charlatanry,'' he even proclaimed that he was a "true Muslim.'' He offered his conflict with the Pope and with the Knights of Malta, whose centuries-old piracy against the Muslims was a holdover from the Crusades, as weak evidence. The stilted, faulty Arabic in his proclamation—composed by one of the French scholars—added ridicule to the Egyptian people's hatred of their conqueror. In any case, his heavy taxation and other oppressive policies soon turned the *ulama*-led populace against him. A series of rebellions and repression followed. Admittedly, the *mamluk*s were a despotic ruling group, and Bonaparte made the innovation of encouraging the Egyptians to help govern themselves through representative councils, but the French were not seen as an improvement over even the worst Muslim rulers. Bonaparte, perhaps inspired by Alexander's worship of Amon and seeing the advantages he might gain in the East, seems to have flirted with the idea of converting to Islam, but he told a group of leading *ulama* that his men would never agree to be circumcised or to give up wine. Again imitating Alexander, Bonaparte once tried Eastern clothes but dropped the idea after evoking ridicule from his men.

Cut off from France by sea, the "great sultan,'' as Bonaparte sometimes was dubbed, opted to break out of isolation by moving overland into Syria. He still hoped to go on to India and dreamed of returning home via Istanbul. A Bosnian soldier, Ahmad al-Jazzar, who had come to dominate much of Syria, nominally as an Ottoman governor, was about to move on Egypt. Also, the "great sultan'' may have hoped to escape from the bubonic plague; however, it continued, as in Egypt, to strike at his men as they moved on. He defeated some Turkish forces in Palestine, carrying out a massacre of over three thousand prisoners in Jaffa and piling up their bodies to form a barricade. But Jazzar, with the aid of the British fleet and with his defenses actually organized by a French renegade (a former classmate that Bonaparte detested for his better marks), thwarted the conquest of Acre. Finally giving up the siege of the city, Bonaparte retreated to Egypt. Before long, he deserted his men by slipping through the British blockade—again with amazing luck—and returned to France to compete in the renewed struggle for power there. Within months, he carried out a coup d'etat and eventually became emperor.

After the Syrian debacle, the French still easily defeated two Ottoman forces sent against them. But Bonaparte's successors in command—General Jean-Baptiste Kléber and later General Jacques Abdallah Menou, who at least pretended to convert to Islam—were concerned mainly with getting their demoralized army out of its hopeless predicament. A Franco-Ottoman agreement allowing the French to evacuate Egypt was concluded but fell apart after the British demanded that they first surrender and become prisoners of war. Then, in 1801, British and Ottoman armies landed near Alexandria and, after a series of engagements, forced the French to surrender. The French were allowed to return home according to the terms of the earlier agreement. Their mission accomplished, the British also left two years later to allow local and Ottoman forces to pursue their own internecine struggle for control of Egypt.

The Ottomans—and also the British and Russians, though only temporarily—soon made peace with France. By 1806 the Ottomans had resumed their traditional role as an ally of the French, now against both Britain and Russia, with the latter invading the Principalities (Moldavia and Wallachia). Then, in 1807, Napoleon concluded a separate peace with the czar at Tilsit and for a while even considered a plan to partition Ottoman territories. He still dreamed of returning to Egypt and marching on to India. Now increasingly concerned about the possibility of Russian control of the Straits, Britain made peace with the sultan in 1809. Napoleon's invasion of Russia in 1812 made it imperative for the latter to have peace on its southern front, and so the Russo-Ottoman Treaty of Bucharest, in the same year, provided for Russia's withdrawal from almost all of the occupied Ottoman territories. Napoleon's final demise three years later ended a complicated phase of international politics but left British and other European concern for limiting Russian expansion into Ottoman territories as a perennial theme.

RIVAL REFORMERS:
ISTANBUL AND CAIRO

In Istanbul, Salim III's reforms evoked a conservative backlash. During 1807 an alliance of Janissaries, *ulama*, and local notables whose independence was endangered by strengthened central authority overthrew the sultan and put a weak, conservative member of the Ottoman house on the throne. The New Order was abandoned. Soon afterward, a Balkan notable, Bayrakhtar Mustafa Pasha, who was embittered by not getting an important position in the central government, embraced the cause of reform and tried to restore Salim. When the latter was murdered, only one member of the ruling dynasty, soon to become Sultan Mahmud II, was left. At first under Bayrakhtar's aegis, the new sultan began to restore the reform program, but the Janissaries again intervened to overthrow the strongman. In the absence of an eligible rival for the throne, the ardently reformist sultan's life was spared, but for the most of two decades he dared not take a stand against the powerful conservative groups.

It was left to Muhammad Ali Pasha, who emerged as ruler in Egypt in the aftermath of the French invasion, to carry out the Middle East's first intensive program of modernization. An Ottoman soldier and former tobacco merchant born in Macedonia of Albanian or possibly Turkish extraction, he succeeded to the command of an Albanian regiment sent against the French. A clever, ruthless man of unexcelled cunning (he later had a translation of Machiavelli's writing prepared only to find out that he had nothing to learn from the seemingly overrated Florentine), Muhammad Ali adeptly played off the rival *mamluk* factions against each other and the Ottoman governor. He gained the support of the populace and their leaders from among the *ulama*, who proclaimed him governor in 1805, a position that the sultan soon formalized. The *mamluk*s retreated to Upper Egypt, and Muhammad Ali finally broke their power in 1811 by inviting their commanders to the Citadel in Cairo, where his artillery exterminated them as they passed along a narrow passageway. Repeating the pattern of eighteenth-century *mamluk* beys,

Muhammad Ali established his virtual independence in a personal empire centered in Egypt. With no loyalty to Egypt as such, he maintained autocratic control until 1848 and started a dynasty that survived until 1953.

Muhammad Ali's central concern was the development of a powerful army. Depending at first on his Albanian force and other heterogeneous troops, his army invaded the Sudan in the early 1820s, primarily to find recruits for a new slave army, otherwise organized along Western lines, following Salim III's example. In order to train his officers and to provide the necessary medical care for the troops, the beginnings of modern education emerged in the form of a school for officers, a medical school, and the like, all staffed by French instructors. When the black slaves succumbed to disease, Muhammad Ali sought another source of military manpower and finally fell upon an option that seemed not to have been thought of before—Egyptian peasants. For millennia, the latter had been governed by alien military classes who assumed that they were unfit to be soldiers. Using cruel means that resembled the capture of wild animals, the governor's men conscripted large numbers of Egyptian villagers. Many fled their villages or mutilated their bodies to avoid this fate, but those who were conscripted were molded into the most effective military force in the Middle East. This also began a pattern in which Egyptians— known as "peasants" regardless of social background—provided the common soldiers and eventually some junior officers. Turks and Circassians long remained at the top of the army and the society but tended gradually to melt into the general population.

A broad program of modernization provided the foundation for this military power. In order to squeeze what he could out of the country more efficiently, Muhammad Ali gradually abolished the tax-farms and pious foundations, leaving Egypt as essentially one big estate, much as in Ptolemaic days. The peasants, in turn, continued to have customary rights to, but not ownership of, particular pieces of land and could be punished and forced to return if they fled their villages, which many did as a result of severe exploitation. In a pattern of monopoly, the peasants had to sell their produce to the government at artificially low prices that left them ever deeper in debt and impoverishment, while the ruler was able to get handsome profits to pay for his military adventures.

Muhammad Ali opened an important channel for Western influence by sending student missions to France. Perhaps more receptive than the students to what he saw and read there was the *imam* accompanying them, Shaykh Rifa'ah Rafi al-Tahtawi, who left us an exciting account of his experiences and also other works that argue in favor of reopening the gates of *ijtihad* and of popular government and even socialism. Tahtawi has the distinction of being the first Middle Easterner to articulate a strong patriotic sentiment, in this case a purely Egyptian loyalty expressed in the poetic gems scattered throughout his works. In addition, Tahtawi became the director of Muhammad Ali's Translation Bureau which transmitted about two thousand diverse Western books into Arabic.

A pattern of landlordism eventually emerged as Muhammad Ali granted land to members of his family and to other important men around him. All land remained technically under state ownership, with the grants often in the form of new tax-farms, but the emergence of private ownership eventually was formalized.

Besides assuming direct control over the land, various steps were taken to enhance productivity and thus to increase government revenue. New crops, notably long-staple cotton, helped enable Egypt to become increasingly dependent on the sale of agricultural products to Europe. After centuries of deterioration the irrigation system was greatly improved. Ruthless measures succeeded in settling most of the relatively small bedouin population.

Muhammad Ali made an unsuccessful attempt to industrialize Egypt. Numerous factories were established, and peasants and craftsmen were brutally forced to work in them. But maintenance of machinery was poor, and a lack of other kinds of power forced reliance on oxen to turn the wheels, which did not work well. Those Europeans who initially felt some apprehension lest Egypt's industry eliminate part of their own export market soon had their fears allayed.

At first Muhammad Ali offered his service to his weak overlord in Istanbul. Even while he was establishing control in Egypt, he was called on for help in suppressing the Wahhabi Sa'udis of Najd, who had by now occupied the Hijaz and were uncontrollably raiding into Syria and Iraq. Under the command of Muhammad Ali's sons, notably the capable Ibrahim, a campaign in Arabia succeeded in conquering most of the peninsula between 1811 and 1820. While the Sa'udis restored their control of central Arabia after the forces from Egypt withdrew, the Hijaz and coastal Yemen remained in Muhammad Ali's empire a little longer.

Then, in 1821, Muhammad Ali's troops were needed in Greece to suppress a rebellion that typified a growing nationalism among Christian Balkan peoples. (A series of revolts starting in 1804 had already led to autonomy for Serbia in 1817.) Promised the governorship of Crete and the Morea, Muhammad Ali succeeded in his mission. But the real arbiters were the powers of Europe, where much one-sided moral indignation was evoked by Ottoman but not Greek atrocities. Also, Britain and France feared unilateral Russian intervention, and the fleets of these three powers joined to destroy the Ottoman and Egyptian fleets in 1827. Muhammad Ali's forces withdrew from Greece, while the sultan was unable to resist a Russian invasion of the Balkans and eastern Anatolia.

Only the apprehension of other European powers about the czar's expansionism induced the Russians to withdraw from most of the occupied territories (while acquiring numerous privileges in the Balkans). Recognition of Greek independence, though within a much smaller territory than today, was left as Istanbul's main concession in the peace treaty signed at Adrianople (Edirne) in 1829.

Mahmud II finally was able to carry out reforms that in part were in emulation of his vassal in Cairo. With the end of one war with Russia in 1812, the sultan concentrated on consolidating his control of the empire, and this was achieved, with the exception of places like Greece, Egypt, Arabia, and parts of the Fertile Crescent. By 1826, he dared create modern military units, thus evoking rebellion by Janissaries and their supporters among the artisans and *ulama*. In turn, he was able to massacre the Janissaries—the ''auspicious event,'' as this break with medievalism came to be known—and to create a new army that was in effect the restoration of Salim's previous attempt. The Bektashi order of dervishes, which was closely associated with the Janissaries, was also banned. The remaining timars were finally abolished, and the state took control of pious foundations. Provincial administration was modified, and road building, conducting a census, starting a regular postal service and an official newspaper, and the like helped to bolster central control.

With the creation of a powerful army in mind, Mahmud II started the Westernization of education. Schools of engineering, medicine, and military science emerged, with French and Prussian army officers as instructors. And students were sent to study in France. A program of translating European books ensued. Some European-style schools, even for adolescent boys, began the "bifurcation" of Middle Eastern culture between its traditional and Westernized forms.

Although such fundamental Western institutions as secular law or representative government still had virtually no beginnings in the Ottoman Empire, Mahmud II began a pattern of superficial Westernization. Western nomenclature was adopted for government offices. Western-style furniture was put in the palace, and the sultan started appearing on the street at various public events like a European king. Not only did he adopt Western clothes and cut his beard to conform to European styles, but he tried to revolutionize the dress of his subjects by legal fiat. Instead of the traditional turbans, a new kind of headdress, the fez, was decreed for nonclerics. This round red hat with a tassel—permitting the Muslim to touch his forehead to the floor during prayer—had previously appeared in North Africa and may have been of European origin but eventually caught on so as to become a distinctive part of Middle Eastern attire.

Still, the sultan was no match for his titular subordinate in Cairo, who came close to taking over the empire in the 1830s. Allying himself with the Shihab amir in Lebanon, Muhammad Ali's troops, commanded by Ibrahim Pasha, invaded Syria with ease in 1831 and, within two years, moved on through Anatolia to within 150 miles of Istanbul. Muhammad Ali's armies could almost surely have made him the strongman, or perhaps sultan, of the whole empire except for European intervention.

The challenge of the rebellious vassal forced the sultan into the arms of the czar. The Russian fleet sailed to the Golden Horn, and Russian soldiers got permission to march overland to help defend Istanbul. The Treaty of Hunkiar Iskelesi (1833) established an alliance between Istanbul and St. Petersburg. This obligated the former at the latter's request to close the Straits to the warships of third powers. By implication, Russian warships were to gain access to the waterway, in contrast to the "ancient rule" of the Ottoman Empire excluding all alike. In effect, this constituted a de facto Russian protectorate over the Ottomans and evoked protests from other capitals.

One of Muhammad Ali's initial advantages—being welcomed with open arms in Syria because of his seemingly more orderly administration and emphasis on religious toleration—vanished as the same oppressive methods known in Egypt appeared in Syria and bred rebellion. But when the sultan tried to push the pasha's army back from Syria in 1839, the latter's superiority was proved all the more. Perhaps in part because of the fear of Russia's embrace, the Ottoman fleet mutinied and transferred its loyalty to Muhammad Ali.

Again, the European powers decided the outcome, leaving an emasculated empire for Muhammad Ali and a sultan no longer dependent on St. Petersburg. Meeting in London in 1840, the representatives of the great powers decided that Muhammad Ali's forces must leave Anatolia and Syria. Austrian and British naval forces temporarily occupied Beirut and encouraged a renewal of the Syrian revolt to force the pasha's hand. In accordance with the "ancient rule," the London Straits Convention of 1841 forbade the use of the Straits to foreign warships, and the czar renounced the Hunkiar Iskelesi Treaty. In the same year, the sultan awarded a consolation prize to Muhammad Ali: the hereditary governorship of Egypt and the Sudan for his family. Annual tribute to Istanbul was required, but the sultan henceforth had little say over his vassal's affairs. Now that his more grandiose dreams were shattered, Egypt's ruler lapsed into mental depression and then senility before his death in 1849.

TRADITIONAL ECONOMIES DISRUPTED

An often overlooked feature of the settlement imposed on Muhammad Ali was the effective extension of the Anglo-Ottoman Commercial Treaty of 1838 to Egypt. With other European states' getting the same privileges as Britain, this removed barriers to the importation of goods into Ottoman lands. It hastened the already ongoing process whereby traditional Middle Eastern industries and the guilds that had been such an important aspect of urban life were undermined by industrial goods imported from Europe. As for Egypt, where the state monopolies were now banned, this in fact provided a final blow for Muhammad Ali's industrialization program. Throughout Ottoman lands, there were dramatic decreases in the number of factories during this period matched by equally dramatic increases in foreign trade, possibly fiftyfold during a hundred-year period. Middle Easterners even sometimes became dependent on agricultural goods imported via Europe, as when Western Hemisphere coffee replaced the Yemeni product in many places.

The other side of the coin was the increasing dependence of Middle Eastern countries on exporting agricultural goods and other raw materials for the world market, with the terms of trade always favoring European goods. Self-sufficient peasant villages with hereditary rights to state-owned land made way for the emergence of private ownership in the hands of big landlords and production of cash crops. Although some traditional industries and guilds survived into the twentieth century and village life retained some of its age-old characteristics in less accessible regions, the older coherence of society was generally shattered. According to one current interpretation (that of the "dependency," or "political economy," school), it was the emergence of the European-centered world market from the sixteenth century on, with regions like the Middle East on the disadvantaged "periphery" that created "underdeveloped" societies. According to this school of thought, today's industrialized countries—the "core"—actually acquired their wealth at the expense of the "periphery." Whether or not one accepts this controversial theory, it is clear that a grotesque gap between the standard of living of much of the West and that of what is today called the Third World was emerging by the nineteenth century.

Despite some abortive earlier attempts, the beginnings of modern industries were left for the twentieth century. Some new industries—the production of thread in Bursa for European factories, for example—were developed in the nineteenth century, but by European, especially British, interests. Most European investment—on a large scale later in the nineteenth century—was in raw materials, particularly mines, or in communications, most of all railroads, sometimes with the Ottoman government providing subsidies. European bank loans at high rates of interest also started Istanbul, Cairo, and Tehran on the road to bankruptcy. Thus did the impact of the Western economic tide devastate the Middle East in ways that may be deemed more fundamental than the more obvious political subordination.

RUSSIAN AGGRANDIZEMENT AND THE EUROPEAN BALANCE OF POWER

Russian pressures repeatedly led to new collisions with the Ottoman Empire after 1840. Each time other European powers frustrated czarist aggrandizement, but they increasingly took territories for themselves and imposed a kind of collective protectorate on the empire.

In the early 1850s growing rivalry over the Holy Places in Palestine created a new crisis. Russia claimed the right to protect the sultan's Greek Orthodox subjects, and France asserted the same responsibility for Roman Catholics. Monks of the two faiths sometimes resorted to violence in their rivalry over particular shrines, and this dragged in their foreign patrons. As the Ottomans rejected Russian demands on this issue, the Russians proposed to Britain that "the sick man is dying" and should be partitioned. Perhaps not understanding that Britain firmly opposed the suggestions, the czar's forces invaded the Principalities in 1853. Another Russian army penetrated eastern Anatolia, and the Russian navy obliterated its Ottoman counterpart in the Black Sea. In turn, British and French forces landed in the Straits region to protect the Ottomans. But the major theater of battle came to be the Crimea, with British, French, Sardinian, and Ottoman forces landing there and after a long siege eventually taking the city of Sevastopol.

A conference convened in Paris, and the resulting peace of 1856 ending the Crimean War brought withdrawal of all occupying forces. The Principalities were restored to Ottoman sovereignty but with their autonomy protected by the powers, and a growing sense of Rumanian nationalism soon led to their gradual merger. Several Balkan peoples revolted during the next two decades. No further territorial changes occurred, although autonomy in some cases, like that of Serbia in 1867, became little less than independence.

The Black Sea was largely neutralized. The Peace of Paris restricted naval activity to light Russian and Ottoman vessels, but another international agreement in 1871 restored Russian rights to maintain a fleet there and allowed other navies to enter the Straits under certain conditions during peacetime. The Peace of Paris also opened the Straits, the Black Sea, and the Danube to merchant ships of all nations.

The Ottomans' military dependence on the great powers was matched by a new financial dependence. Beginning with the need to finance the Crimean War, the foreign debt got out of hand. By the 1870s, inefficient collection of revenue and a series of bad crops led to a situation in which most of the money was committed to paying the debt. Neither civil servants' salaries nor interest on loans could be met. Eventually, the powers agreed to a major reduction of the debt and in 1881 set up an Ottoman Public Debt Administration that included European representatives in charge of collecting specific taxes.

A new round of international crises over the Balkans culminated in another Russo-Ottoman War in 1877. Despite some early Ottoman successes, the Russians eventually pushed through the Balkans to the vicinity of Istanbul, where the British fleet again appeared. Another Russian force occupied much of northeast Anatolia. The harsh Peace of San Stefano followed, in which the sultan was forced to cede parts of the Balkans and of northeastern Anatolia, including Kars, Ardahan, and Batum, to Russia and to accept independence for Serbia and Montenegro and autonomy for an extremely large Bulgaria, still to be Russian-occupied.

The other powers would not stand for such big gains by Russia. An international congress met in Berlin and forced a revised peace that was much less favorable to St. Petersburg. The most significant change was a reduction in Bulgaria's territory. In addition to Serbia and Montenegro, Rumania also became independent. Bosnia and Herzegovina were assigned to Austrian administration while technically remaining Ottoman territories. Britain occupied Cyprus on a similar legal basis.

The few remaining areas of the Balkans still under Ottoman control subsequently were scenes of revolt, like Macedonia and even heavily Muslim Albania in the 1880s. A Greek attempt to take Thessaly in 1897 failed, but a bloody revolt in Crete, aided by the Greek army and involving massacres by all sides, led to intervention by the powers and autonomy for the island, which was finally annexed by Greece in 1912.

THE TANZIMAT

As for the Ottoman Empire's continuing process of Westernization, the death of Mahmud II initiated a period of accelerated reform known as the Tanzimat (''Reorganization''). Extending through the reigns of Abd al-Majid (1839–1861) and Abd al-Aziz (1861–1876), this in part represented efforts, sincere or otherwise, to satisfy

European demands and prevent the further intervention for which abuses provided a rationalization. Consequently, the promulgation of two important documents, the Noble Rescript of Gulhane in 1839 and the Imperial Rescript of 1856, declaring an end to arbitrary practices not coincidentally appeared at the time of great international crises, when the fate of the empire was at the mercy of European power. But, while this was an important catalyst, the drive for change was fundamentally fueled by the convictions of a series of devoted reformers, particularly Mustafa Rashid Pasha and later Ali Pasha and Fu'ad Pasha, all of whom recurrently held the grand vizirate and the dominant role in shifting political coalitions.

The principle of equality for all the sultan's subjects, regardless of religion, occupied a prominent place in Tanzimat decrees. The relative tolerance of Islamic practice notwithstanding, this was a radical idea that contradicted the concept of *dhimmi*s as protected peoples subject to certain disabilities, and full application was perhaps too much to expect at once. Indeed, opposition to equality came from the *dhimmi*s themselves. Some Christian church leaders were wary of losing their special position as millet leaders. And although the end of the *jizyah* (poll tax) on *dhimmi*s was welcome, the prospect of being conscripted into the army just like Muslims was not. A compromise that was worked out—allowing non-Muslims to opt to pay a special tax equivalent to the *jizyah* in return for their old privilege of exemption from military service—was a reversion to Islamic principles in disguise that pleased everyone.

Major reforms in the administration of the empire were carried out. The abolition of tax-farming was a main promise of the 1839 decree. But the practice was restored two years later. A land law of 1858 resulted in the tax-farms and various customary rights to the soil being transformed into freehold titles and thus the emergence of a landlord class and a sharecropping peasantry. Among other reforms, a beginning was made toward establishing municipal government. A law of 1864 provided for a new provincial unit, the vilayet, and a slow move toward a uniform provincial administrative system ensued.

New developments in communications spread to the Ottoman Empire. In 1854 the telegraph appeared and steamship companies began to form. Foreign-financed railroads slowly began to connect Ottoman cities. All of this enhanced centralization and accelerated foreign influences.

The gradual secularization of the legal system began at this time. The Noble Rescript, perhaps the Ottomans' first open break with theocratic principles, announced "new rules" as though to defy the traditional Islamic concept of an immutable body of law, and no *fatwa* (ruling) by the highest religious authority was sought to legalize it. A criminal code, enacted in 1840, was based on Islamic rules, but a subsequent series of codes, such as the commercial code of 1850, brought a large degree of Westernization of law. Published in stages between 1870 and 1876, the Majallah (Digest) codified Hanafite civil law, covering contracts and related matters, thus giving this aspect of Ottoman jurisprudence a European form while retaining Islamic substance. Only the law of personal status was too sacrosanct for tampering. The subsequent legal system reflected the growing duality in the Islamic world between aspects of life governed by Western-style law and by traditional Islamic courts.

Modern education gained a new impetus. From the late 1850s on, there was a vast increase in the number of modern elementary schools and an even greater increase in secondary schools. An elite institution, the Lycée of Galatasaray, emerged in 1860. With its instruction in French and a totally Western-style curriculum, this school was to play a central role in the growth of a modern-educated class.

The appearance of a new kind of intelligentsia—in contrast to the graduates of traditional mosque colleges—pushed modernization in new directions. Private newspapers began to appear from 1840 on, and they initiated a simplified kind of journalistic Turkish that avoided much of the older pomposity and use of Persian and Arabic vocabulary. Translations from French literature made way for the imitation of European literary styles. Turkish literature from this time on has been labeled more European than Asiatic. Even the drama, a literary genre formerly alien to the Islamic world (aside from Shi'ite passion plays), was introduced with the plays of Ibrahim Shinasi.

THE YOUNG OTTOMANS
AND THE CONSTITUTION

Some of the new intellectuals began to demand new reforms. For the first time, reform was not something only pushed from above. The early modernizers had seen the emulation of Western military techniques and then administrative reform as the way to defend the empire. This kind of change, however, only led to further European interference. Now, other facets of Western societies were pointed to as their secret. The real key to success was thought to be "freedom," limitations on the power of the ruler, and popular control through an elected parliament. Another idea new to the Ottomans was that of love for the fatherland—a territorial nationalism that encompassed all peoples in the empire—although this idea tended still to be incongruously mixed with the concept of an Islamic *ummah*.

Ideas such as these inspired the formation in 1865 of an organization that later became known as the Young Ottoman Society. Shinasi, Ziya Pasha, and perhaps most important, Namik Kemal were among the writers and journalists who pushed for reform. They even had some support in the Ottoman royal house, and a member of the ruling family in Egypt, Mustafa Fazil Pasha, became a leading Young Ottoman. The latter was apparently miffed over a new rule relating to succession to the Egyptian throne that left him out, and he hoped instead to head a constitutional government for the whole Ottoman Empire.

The Young Ottomans opposed both the authoritarianism and the secularism of the Tanzimat. They realized that reform had created a highly autocratic, centralized state, in contrast to earlier practices that let many groups participate in political decisions. Also, Islamic injunctions about consultation and the right of the people to approve the ruler (the *bay'ah*) provided indigenous rationales for the kind of Westernization that the Young Ottomans wanted. Superficial, slavish imitation was scorned. This movement has the distinction of being the first that worked to reconcile Islamic and Western civilizations, indeed to embrace much of the deeper aspects of the latter on the ground that they were in accord with a rightly interpreted Islam.

Other forces for a while seemed to push the empire in the direction called for by the Young Ottomans. Sultan Abd al-Aziz's wastefulness got blamed for the hopeless financial situation. And a new conflict with Russia renewed incentive for reform. Student demonstrations brought matters to a head. Midhat Pasha, a capable official who had become known for his effectiveness in implementing administrative reforms in the Balkans and Iraq, came to the fore as the spokesman for a constitution. A *fatwa* authorized the deposition of Sultan Abd al-Aziz, and another prince, who agreed to support a constitution, eventually ascended the throne as Sultan Abd al-Hamid II.

After being drawn up by a committee headed by Midhat, the constitution was promulgated by Sultan Abd al-Hamid II. In accordance with its terms, a parliament was elected. To many, the establishment of a European-style democratic regime seemed to be on its way, even though the parliament had limited authority and the sultan was left with much arbitrary power, for example, to banish any person or to dissolve the parliament.

Abd al-Hamid II soon made full use of the constitution's loopholes to create a new absolutism. In 1878 he dissolved the parliament, which did not meet again during his long period of rule. Dismissed from office and exiled, Midhat later was permitted to return, but only to be imprisoned and finally murdered by the sultan's agents. The Young Ottoman movement withered, eventually to be replaced by a new generation of reformers.

ACCELERATED MODERNIZATION AND DESPOTISM

The long reign of Abd al-Hamid II (1876–1909) turned out to be the antithesis of constitutionalism. Instead, tyranny reached its zenith as the suspicious sultan employed spies and informers and as modern communications allowed despotism to penetrate to all corners of his domain. Although two plots to overthrow him in 1878 failed, they helped to intensify his suspiciousness and cruelty.

Contrary to what often is believed, Abd al-Hamid II's reign was a period of intensified modernization along the lines of the Tanzimat period. The population continued to grow, with that of Anatolia reaching about 12 million by the early twentieth century. Modern education progressed rapidly as schools of all levels were established, and the University of Istanbul (to use its later name) was started in 1900. Censorship sometimes bordered on the ridiculous, such as covering up news of assassinations of foreign heads of state by attributing their deaths to fictitious diseases. Still, more newspapers and other periodicals were started, and the number of readers vastly increased. Scientific knowledge was disseminated through popular articles written in an increasingly simplified Turkish. Another literary medium, the novel, emerged in Turkish. Railroads tripled their previous length to nearly six thousand kilometers by 1913, admittedly still small in comparison with European countries. From 1888 on, the Orient Express provided an unprecedented connection between Istanbul and western European cities. The Hijaz Railway, connecting Damascus and Madina, was financed with contributions from all over the Muslim world at the start of the twentieth century.

The beginnings of a great tragedy for the Armenian people appeared at this time. The Armenians had been regarded as one of the most fortunate groups under Ottoman rule, and they filled many important positions after the growth of nationalism caused the Greeks to lose favor in the early 1800s. But the growth of education and cultural activities among the Armenians also fed their own political nationalism. In addition, Armenian officers in the czar's army were prominent among the invaders of eastern Anatolia in 1877, and this enhanced the natural appeal of this Christian power as a liberator. Armenian nationalist societies began to engage in terrorist activities, such as holding hostages in a bank in 1896. Such incidents provoked countermeasures by Turks, particularly those increasingly numerous refugees from persecution in places formerly under Ottoman rule. Several thousand Armenians were massacred in the 1890s, but this was only a precursor of worse events to come. All of this was the nearly inevitable consequence of a Christian separatist nationalism near the heart of the empire among a people who formed only a minority of the population even in most parts of their traditional homeland.

THE YOUNG TURKS

By the 1890s, a combination of despotism and external threats to the empire helped to inspire a new opposition movement to the sultan among his Turkish subjects. Various intellectuals and again some dissident members of the Ottoman family became active in exile in Europe. Divergent attitudes with regard to issues of Westernization and the question of Turkish nationalism versus a multinational federal empire split the ranks of such people. But these "Young Turks," the name that came to be applied to them although they never used it themselves, were united in demanding the restoration of the constitution and opposing despotic rule. A network of Masonic lodges provided another medium for spreading revolutionary ideas. Opposition groups were also being formed among army officers and among those in strategic positions as telegraph operators. In 1907 some older civil and military groups came together to form the Ottoman Committee of Union and Progress (CUP).

In 1908 there was widespread popular unrest in many places, with food shortages and high prices leading to riots and strikes. Salonica, in Macedonia, became the key to revolution, as a leading CUP army officer, Enver Bey, suspecting a crackdown by the sultan, escaped to the hills and drew increasing numbers of his fellow soldiers to his side. As other troops in Macedonia mutinied against generals loyal to the sultan, the sultan gave in to CUP demands for restoring the constitution. Though not officially assuming power, CUP became a major force influencing the state. The next year a revolt led by *ulama* and theology students brought Abd al-Hamid back to power. But soon afterward an "Army of Deliverance" restored CUP influence and removed Abd al-Hamid from the throne in favor of a sultan more amenable to its will. Amid several splits and the appearance of other opposition groups, CUP increasingly became the real rulers. In fraudulent parliamentary elections in 1912 CUP candidates took nearly all of the seats. Although another group of officers temporarily overthrew the growing despotism of CUP, the latter again took control in 1913. The hopes for real constitutionalism were finally dashed as the arbitrary will of a CUP triumvirate of three beys (soon elevated to pashas)—Enver, Tal'at, and Jamal—tightened its grip.

The early CUP period found the Ottoman Empire still on the defensive against local nationalism and European imperialism. Tripolitania and Benghazi (i.e., Libya), the last North African territory over which Istanbul exercised even loose control since the establishment of French rule in Algeria (1830) and Tunisia (1881), fell prey to an Italian invasion in 1911. Ottoman troops were left to aid in the continuing resistance of the Sanusis, a puritanical religious group dating back to the early nineteenth century. Italy also occupied the Dodecanese Islands in the Aegean.

In 1912, four Balkan states—Bulgaria, Greece, Montenegro, and Serbia—joined together to attack their former overlord. What had been left of Ottoman territory in the Balkans shrank to Istanbul and its immediate hinterland. In a Second Balkan War later in the same year, the Balkan states turned on each other, allowing the Ottomans to enter and retake Thrace and Edirne from Bulgaria, but this hardly represented a basic reversal of fortunes.

With almost all European powers encroaching on Ottoman territories, the one with the cleanest hands seemed to be Germany. All the Ottoman eggs were still not put in the German basket, for as late as 1914 Istanbul looked forward to receiving two warships it had purchased in Britain, and many realized that Britain was their only real hope for restraining the more blatant expansionism of the other powers. But CUP committed itself increasingly to Germany. Enver, in particular, ever since he served as the Ottoman military attaché in Berlin, was an admirer of the Germans.

From the 1880s on, Berlin was engaged in an avid courtship of Istanbul. Kaiser Wilhelm II visited Istanbul in 1889 and 1898. German capital began pouring in, the most notable example being financing for an Istanbul-to-Baghdad Railway, which, with its western connections, would, if completed, constitute a Berlin-to-Baghdad line and further tie Germany to the Ottoman Empire. Berlin sent a military mission to Istanbul as early as 1883. Following defeats in the wars with Italy and the Balkan states, the Ottomans' concern with improving their armed forces led to further dependence on Germany, with General Liman von Sanders and fifty-two other German officers gaining key positions in the sultan's army in 1913.

TURKISH NATIONALISM

The modern Western concept of nationalism infiltrated the Middle East during the late nineteenth century. According to nationalist thinking, which had dominated Europe for the past hundred years, the individual owed his supreme loyalty to a nation. Especially in central and eastern Europe this was often defined along ethnic lines, with separate statehood the goal of those peoples that had not already achieved it.

This was in contrast to the traditional Middle Eastern concept, according to which, aside from personal loyalty to a ruler and an emotional attachment to a restricted locality, people had identified themselves primarily with the religion to which they belonged. In Islamic doctrine, all Muslims were one community (*ummah*), regardless of their tribe, language, or race. Ethnic differences had, in practice, been divisive many times throughout the history of Islam, but the multiethnic Ottoman Empire had not been based on the principle of domination by one particular ethnic group. On the other hand, identity never transcended religious divisions.

One alternative for the Ottoman Empire during the nineteenth century was "Ottomanism." This idea, urged by liberals, was that of one Ottoman people without religious or ethnic distinctions. It proposed to solve the problem of identity in keeping with another Western idea, equality. But this never really caught on, and even its advocates often expressed contradictory sentiments.

The religious identity was still deeply rooted and now took the form of pan-Islamism. The Ottoman dynasty began to assert its dubious claim to the title of caliph. And since the Ottoman Empire was the only major Sunni Muslim state retaining any degree of real independence, Muslims outside the empire, particularly those under Western colonial rule, tended to accept the claim. Turning the tables on those who saw Islam as the basis for constitutionalism, Sultan Abd al-Hamid II exploited pan-Islamic sentiment in order to suppress liberalism within Ottoman territory and to assert his leadership in the Islamic world. Though mixed with contradictory ideas, emphasis on pan-Islamism even survived the CUP revolution of 1908.

Turkish ethnic nationalism gained official acceptance after 1908. In addition to the general influence of central and eastern European nationalist movements, the writings of several nineteenth-century European scholars on the pre-Islamic Turks of Central Asia nurtured a new pride in Turkishness. The influx of Turkish refugees from Russia, influenced by the pan-Slav movement, further strengthened the new Turkish ethnic identity, as did the development of Arab separatism. For the first time poets proclaimed the glorious history of the Turks. A Turkish Society, designed to emphasize Turkish greatness, was established in 1908. A network of local clubs, called the Turkish Hearth, spread after 1912 and with it the new pride in Turkish culture.

Since there was no concept of a homeland within boundaries approximating the later Republic of Turkey, this ethnic movement took the form of pan-Turkism. The idea was sometimes called pan-Turanism, from *Turan*, a term with strong romantic connotations used for the original Central Asian homeland. The "Turanian" peoples whose unity was sought supposedly included Hungarians, Finns, and Mongols too, but in practice pan-Turanian goals were limited to the Turks. Although at first this was a purely cultural nationalism, it also assumed political aspects and called for the unity of all the Turks of the world. The Turks of the Russian Empire were more numerous than those of the sultan's domain, and there were Turkish areas in Iran and China as well. All such Turkish-inhabited areas, according to the new nationalist movement, formed one homeland.

AFGHANI AND MODERNISM

An enigmatic Islamic scholar, Jamal al-Din al-Afghani (1839–1897), appeared in nearly every Islamic capital during the late nineteenth century. Even his origin is unknown. Although the designation "al-Afghani" indicates that he was from Afghanistan, he may have been an Iranian named al-Asadabadi trying to disguise his Shi'ite background. For that matter, his sincerity as a Muslim has been questioned by some recent historians. Although he sometimes became an adviser to rulers, each time he fell into disfavor. But wherever he went, he spellbound numerous followers with his pan-Islamic appeals—for the solidarity of all Muslims regardless of state or sect against the increasing danger of European imperialism.

Afghani's concerns went much further than with pan-Islamism; they extended to the whole problem of the encroachment of modernity on Islamic society. Often considered the founder of "modernist" Islam, Afghani saw that modern ideas and institutions were emerging alongside—and gradually displacing—Islamic ones. Instead of this, he preached the need to integrate the two. Much in the spirit of medieval Islamic philosophers, Afghani rejected charges that Islam was inconsistent with human reason in general or with modern science in particular. Taking reason as his guide, he insisted that any seeming conflict with religion must be reconciled by reinterpreting the latter. Afghani gave special impetus to the idea that the "gates of *ijtihad*" must be reopened. Otherwise, rigid adherence to what had been settled a millennium earlier would stand in the way of progress and the ability of the Islamic world to defend itself, or else change would leave Islam bypassed and irrelevant. From the point of view of later secularists, who wanted simply to throw out the religious basis of society, such ideas seem like precursors of "fundamentalism," but to traditionalists this sounded like dangerous innovation.

EGYPT AFTER MUHAMMAD ALI

The quarter century following the death of Muhammad Ali (1849) saw new strides in the development of Egypt under his descendants. But the period turned into one of disappointment and led to bankruptcy, European financial control, and finally occupation.

Ibrahim Pashsa took the reins for a while during his aging father's last days but preceded him in death. The ultrareactionary Abbas came to the throne and let much of Muhammad Ali's transformation lapse, but the next ruler, Sa'id, was greatly enamored of Europeans and favored accelerated modernization and Westernization. This outlook continued under Isma'il (1863–1879), the early part of whose reign represented a new high point for the dynasty but then made way for its ruin.

Important changes were now occurring in Egyptian society. More and more land came under perennial (year-round) irrigation,[2] and agriculture came to be dominated by cash crops, especially long-staple cotton, for the world market. As it did elsewhere, privately owned agricultural land developed, but in Egypt the change took place much faster. Big landowners of Circassian origin were part of the picture, but some Egyptian peasants acquired smaller holdings and tended to predominate on a local level as village headmen. Especially as the sons of headmen lost their exemption from military conscription during the reign of Sa'id and began to enter officer ranks, this indigenous landholding class was eventually to assert itself against the Turco-Circassian oligarchy and growing European influence.

Geography made Egypt an increasingly important focus for European ambitions. Britain's need for fast communication with its empire in India was of special importance. Steamships sailed from Britain to Alexandria and from India to Suez, at the northern tip of the Red Sea, in the 1830s; the short overland connection was made by British-built railways in the 1850s.

The old idea of a canal to connect the Mediterranean and the Red Sea now became a reality. Using his long-standing friendship with Sa'id, the French engineer and entrepreneur Ferdinand de Lesseps won a concession in 1854 that made unlimited quantities of Egyptian labor available for the project. Shares in the Suez Canal Company were owned partly by the Egyptian government but mainly by French stockholders. Despite the initial misgivings of the British government and the sultan, the 101-mile Suez Canal was completed and opened to traffic in 1869 amidst an extravagant celebration to which Isma'il invited European royalty.

Isma'il's reign saw the appearance of a modern veneer. Railroad mileage multiplied, and such innovations as the telegraph were introduced. Street lights and modern buildings gave sections of major Egyptian cities a European look, although the rapid growth of urban population did not take place until after 1880. Banks and new schools, including some for girls, appeared. Isma'il was determined to make the country a "part of Europe."

Perhaps 100,000 Europeans, including Greeks and Italians, lived in Egypt by the 1870s. As in Ptolemaic and Roman days, parts of Alexandria seemed to belong more to a European-oriented Mediterranean world than to Egypt. Such minorities, as well as Armenians, Syrian Christians, Jews, and Copts, were virtually to monopolize the world of commerce and finance for several decades. This paralleled the preponderance of non-Muslims in such fields in other parts of the Ottoman Empire.

---

[2]In contrast to basin irrigation, in which water is collected during the annual flood for one crop, perennial irrigation allows Egyptians to raise as many as three crops per year.

The international status of the Muhammad Ali dynasty soared for a while during Isma'il's rule. Expeditions into southern Sudan and East Africa, where, however, Ethiopia imposed defeats on Egyptian forces twice in the mid 1870s, put Egypt alongside European powers in the ongoing competition to partition the continent. The ruler's nominal superior, Sultan Abd al-Aziz, came to Egypt as a guest and granted him a loftier title, "khedive," of Persian origin. A new rule of succession whereby the khedivate passed to the eldest son rather than to the senior member of the dynasty also bolstered Isma'il's prestige. The capitulations remained in force, but in 1873 the consular tribunals were replaced by mixed courts that included foreign and Egyptian members.

But Isma'il's successes gradually turned sour. The disruption of U.S. cotton exports during the American Civil War put Egyptian cotton at a premium on the world market, but the end of that conflict in 1865 deprived Egypt of this temporary source of prosperity. Meanwhile, khedivial grandiosity cost the country dearly and left it hopelessly in the throes of foreign indebtedness. Isma'il resorted to various desperate measures, including the shortsighted announcement that those who paid three years of taxes in advance would be given partial exemption in the future. Also, he sold Egypt's shares in the Suez Canal Company to the British government, which accordingly acquired a new interest in the country.

The independence of Egypt rapidly made way for European financial control. In 1878, the khedive had to accept an Englishman and a Frenchman in the cabinet as ministers of finance and public works. These "dual controllers" and the malleable Armenian prime minister, Nubar Pasha, took effective control of a large sphere of Egyptian affairs. Also, from 1876 on, a Debt Commission, including representatives of Austria, Italy, Britain, and France, made sure that most of the revenue, now necessarily increased by higher taxation, would be earmarked for the foreign debt.

European control led to growing opposition. Afghani stayed in Egypt during most of the 1870s, and his preaching inspired one brand of resistance. Khedive Isma'il also tried to resist, mainly by encouraging other anti-European forces, and international pressures finally induced the sultan to dismiss him in favor of the more subservient Khedive Tawfiq in 1879.

The nationalist forces also included Egyptian army officers and the Consultative Assembly, which Isma'il established in 1866. Both groups, who barely managed to paper over their other differences by virtue of joint opposition to foreign financial control and to the predominance of Circassians and Turks, tended to represent the new native Egyptian landed class. The Consultative Assembly, composed mostly of village headmen, had little power at first but increasingly attempted to assert itself until dissolved by the new khedive in 1879.

Led by Colonel Ahmad Orabi, Egyptian army officers became the vanguard of the nationalist movement. Besides a more general resentment against foreign control, the ire of this "peasants'" party was directed at the effects on them of the new financial stringency brought on by foreign indebtedness. While the Circassians and Turks remained in top ranks, reductions in the size of the army had brought the dismissal of some Egyptian officers. Others found themselves put on half-pay, or else their salaries fell far into arrears. As early as 1879 some officers led a demonstration outside the ministry of finance and insulted Prime Minister Nubar Pasha and Sir Rivers Wilson, the British member of the dual control.

In 1881 there were bigger demonstrations and mutinies by the Orabists. They succeeded in forcing the khedive to reconvene the Consultative Assembly and to dismiss several top persons and in getting their candidates appointed instead. Thus the leader of the Constitutionalists, Sharif Pasha, became prime minister in September, while the pro-Orabist poet-statesman, Sami Pasha al-Barudi became minister of war. Orabi himself later held the position of minister of war. So far, the nationalists were prevailing at the expense of foreign control; the prospects of the Muhammad Ali dynasty also appeared dim.

The first Egyptian national movement ended with British occupation. Foreign financial interests feared that their loans would not be repaid, and Britain became concerned over the security of the Suez Canal. An Anglo-French naval demonstration near Alexandria was accompanied by demands that Orabi leave the country and that Egyptian defenses in the Alexandria harbor be dismantled. As the nationalists defied such calls, the mood of the Egyptian people showed in riots against Europeans, and in turn European governments became more agitated. France had formerly taken the most hawkish position but now backed down from intervening. The British proceeded to bombard Alexandria and then to land their forces, among whom Khedive Tawfiq took refuge. The Egyptians were defeated in the battle of Tal al-Kabir, Orabi was exiled, and a period of British occupation and effective rule began. Still owing nominal allegiance to Istanbul, Tawfiq remained as the obliging puppet of the new conquerors. The British at first expected the occupation to end soon, and repeatedly gave assurances to that effect, but subsequent developments perpetuated it until 1956.

A puritanical religious movement under the leadership of Muhammad Ahmad, proclaimed to be the "Mahdi," overthrew Egyptian rule in the Sudan in 1881. For a while, it even seemed possible that the Mahdi would invade Egypt and be joined by a mass revolt of Egyptian peasants. A ten-thousand-man Egyptian force led by General William Hicks was sent against the Sudanese zealots in 1883, only to be wiped out. The garrison at Khartum, together with General Charles Gordon, who had been sent to evacuate it, was also overrun. It was not until 1896–1898 that Sir Horatio (later Lord) Kitchener, commanding Egyptian troops, suppressed the Mahdist movement. In 1899 the Sudan gained the unusual status of a condominium, called the Anglo-Egyptian Sudan. In reality Britain dominated the country, and Egypt's role in the condominium was essentially a formality. French resentment over the British takeover of Egypt and a barely-avoided clash between the two powers in the southern Sudan made way in 1904 for an entente in which Paris acquiesced in the British role in the Nile Valley in return for a free hand in Morocco.

The occupation left Egyptians too dazed to resist. The religious scholar Muhammad Abduh, a disciple of Afghani and an ardent supporter of the Orabi movement, returned to Egypt after a period of exile ready to pursue modernist reform but not a seemingly useless struggle for independence. Avidly receptive to the writings of such Europeans as Tolstoy and Spencer, Abduh expanded on Afghani's emphasis on the need to interpret revelation in the light of reason, going so far as to reject the value of much of the corpus of *hadiths*. As chief mufti of Egypt he issued innovative rulings, and as a member of al-Azhar's supreme council, pushed for a modernized curriculum. After Abduh's death in 1905, his colleague Rashid Rida dominated the modernist movement but gave it an increasingly conservative tone.

The British "consul-general," Sir Evelyn Baring (soon to become Lord Cromer) assumed real rule over Egypt in 1883. Authoritarian and condescending toward his subjects and allowing them only a nonelective Legislative Council, Lord Cromer— and his successors, including Lord Kitchener from 1911 to 1914—ruled through British "advisers" scattered throughout the Egyptian administration. His greatest success was in straightening out the financial mess by the 1890s. In part, this was the result of other achievements, especially an increase in agricultural productivity. Irrigation was improved by such steps as the construction of a dam at Aswan, in Upper Egypt (not to be confused with the more recent High Dam). Also, such age-old brutal practices as forced labor for peasants and the use of the whip were gradually abolished.

A new phase of Egyptian nationalism soon became evident. Khedive Abbas Hilmi (1892–1914) was of a different mettle from his predecessor and schemed to undermine British power. He aspired to get French and Ottoman support and also encouraged nationalistic expression. Perhaps the most important nationalist leader was a French-educated journalist, Mustafa Kamil, whose bombastic speeches and articles in his Patriotic party's newspaper expressed an amalgam of Egyptian nationalism and solidarity with the Islamic world. He also emphasized the need for democracy and the adoption of Western civilization. Although he was careful not to violate the law, Kamil was intransigent in demanding an end to the occupation.

Some Egyptians countered the anti-British agitation with what they considered to be a more positive program. Such were Ahmad Lutfi al-Sayyid and his Ummah party, which stood for a purely Egyptian identity and liberal democracy and stressed the importance of education and Westernization. This party, which appealed to big landowners, was friendly toward and favored by the British.

The year 1907 brought an event that embittered a previously apathetic peasantry against British rule. Some British officials were hunting pigeons in the village of Dinshaway when one of their bullets hit an Egyptian woman. Indignant villagers attacked the hunters, and the soldiers then fired at Egyptian crowds. This was climaxed by brutal punishment—including four executions—of the Egyptians involved in the incident. Dinshaway long continued to symbolize Egyptian bitterness over the occupation. The Coptic prime minister, Butrus Ghali Pasha, who presided over the largely British tribunal that imposed the sentences and who also later supported an unpopular scheme to prolong the Suez Canal Company's concession for fifty years after its scheduled expiration date (1968), was assassinated in 1909 by a Muslim Egyptian. Nationalism thus threatened to disrupt relations between the two religions.

Cairo became a growing center of Arabic culture, with key roles played by Syrian emigrés, mainly Christians, for whom Egypt both before and after the British occupation was a welcome refuge from the more oppressive Ottoman regime. These emigrés were especially important in the proliferation of newspapers during this period. Journalistic requirements tended toward simple writing styles. Poetry flourished at the hands of such writers as Ahmad Shawki, and Western literary forms, such as the drama and the novel, began to catch on.

THE FERTILE CRESCENT
AND ARAB NATIONALISM

The nineteenth century brought important developments in the Fertile Crescent, only some of which paralleled the course of other Ottoman regions. Almost for the first time, Istanbul imposed real control in some areas. For example, the *mamluk* regime in Baghdad finally succumbed to the central government in 1831, but it was left to the governorship of Midhat Pasha in 1869–1872 to establish real order by suppressing the ever-marauding bedouin tribes. Although the Egyptian route for east–west commerce won out, British steamships became active on the Tigris and Euphrates. Iraq, however, remained a backwater in comparison with the western Fertile Crescent.

Muhammad Ali's occupation was a turning point for Syria. The mosaic of local chiefs was replaced by an effective government, and the position of non-Muslims was enhanced by their membership on local consultative councils and the removal of some traditional restrictions. The application of the Tanzimat later perpetuated the same tendencies.

By mid-century, there were signs of a literary revival in Syria. This has sometimes been credited to the arrival of American missionaries in 1820, as has subsequent Arab cultural and eventual political nationalism. Actually, the revival had already begun in both Syria and Egypt, but such Syrian Christians as the poet Nasif Yaziji and Butrus Bustani, whose accomplishments included an encyclopedia and an Arabic dictionary, worked closely with the Americans. Missionary schools, including the Protestant College, later called the American University in Beirut, and its French Jesuit counterpart, later called the Université Saint-Joseph, continued to be major educational influences.

Mount Lebanon was experiencing traumatic changes. The Druze sect had long predominated in the area, particularly the south; Maronites lived in the north. But, reflecting prosperity derived from the production of silk for the world market, the Maronites were increasing in numbers and moving south. Even the dominant clan, the Shihabs, had taken the unusual step of converting to the Maronite religion, apparently in order to maintain their positions. But as Muhammad Ali's most ardent Syrian collaborators, the Shihab amirs did not long survive the restoration of the sultan's power.

Clashes between Maronites and Druzes began in 1841. The Ottoman response was to partition Lebanon into two districts, but that left an unhappy minority in each place. Trouble broke out in 1857 in the north, ironically with a revolt of Maronite peasants against their Maronite landlords. By 1860 the conflict had spread south and turned into a clear-cut civil war between the two sects, soon overflowing into other parts of Syria, with Muslim mobs attacking Christians in Damascus.

The European powers decided to intervene, and French troops landed in Beirut. In 1861 the Ottoman government proclaimed a special regime for the Mountain that was to last until 1914 and to serve as a precursor to parallel patterns later in the twentieth century. According to this arrangement, the sultan, in consultation with the European powers, appointed a governor, who was assisted by a council representing the various sects.

Syria became the breeding ground for Arab ethnic nationalism, a movement that asserted the unity of Arabic-speaking Christians and Muslims and eventually called for independence from Turkish rule. Christian Arabs played an important role in this movement, especially in its early stages. After all, nationalism was a Western virus that Christians were more susceptible to catching, and the bonds of religion and loyalty to the sultan-caliph continued to unite Turks and Muslim Arabs.

Some beginnings of Arab nationalism appeared in the first half of the nineteenth century, particularly among Christians. Again, the cultural revival and the American missionaries have been given credit for this. Founded in 1857, the Syrian Scientific Society has been described as a manifestation of Arab national consciousness. It was where Ibrahim Yaziji (son of Nasif) read a poem calling on the Arabs to "arise and awake." A secret society established in Beirut in 1875 protested against Turkish rule; some earlier writers called it the first movement for Arab independence, but this now seems to have been an exaggeration. Such movements apparently represented local particularism and especially Christian opposition to Ottoman rule more than Arab nationalism.

However, other evidences of Arab nationalism did appear. In part reflecting resentment over the Ottoman claim to the caliphate, a Muslim Arab from Aleppo, Abd al-Rahman al-Kawakabi, wrote a book extolling the virtues of his people and blaming the Turks for the backwardness of the Muslim world. He called for an Arab caliph but not for a state limited to the Arab-inhabited region. It has been suggested that he was working for the khedive, who may have aspired to lead the Arabs. The distinction of having been the first writer to call for Arab independence belongs to Najib Azouri, a Christian Palestinian exiled in Paris and possibly receiving French support. Azouri's book, published in French in 1905, stressed the unity of Muslim and Christian Arabs and called for an Arab sultan as the constitutional ruler of the proposed Arab state and for an Arab caliph, with secular power in the Hijaz, as the head of Islam.

It was not until Turkish nationalism began to supplant older identities in Istanbul that Arab separatism gained any substantial support. To the extent that Ottoman or pan-Islamism prevailed, Turks and Muslim Arabs continued to feel a sense of unity. But Turkism left the Arabs out or, worse still, posed the threat of assimilation. After an initial period in 1908 when the CUP revolutionaries seemed to have ushered in a spirit of interethnic brotherhood, the pan-Turkism of the new regime revealed itself to the Arabs. The government soon banned the Arab-Ottoman Brotherhood, an organization founded by Arabs in Istanbul to stress the unity of the two peoples. The Young Turks proceeded to try to centralize the Empire. They made Turkish the official language. Despite their numerical preponderance, the Arabs were allowed only 60 seats in the newly elected Parliament in comparison to 150 for the Turks.

Arab nationalist societies began to proliferate after the 1908 revolution. Perhaps because its location was conducive to Western influence, Syria was the center of Arab nationalism, but several Iraqi officers in the Ottoman army also joined the movement. One of the most notable of the Arab nationalist societies was al-Ahd ("the Covenant"), consisting of Arab officers under the leadership of the popular Egyptian Major Aziz Ali al-Misri, a hero of the Italo-Ottoman War of 1911. Al-Misri has the distinction of being the only Egyptian to play an important role in the early Arab nationalist movement; at the time, his countrymen were wavering between Egyptian and pan-Islamic identities but rarely thought in terms of Arabism. Arab students in Paris organized another group, al-Fatat ("Youth") in 1911. Both organizations officially called for a dual Arab-Turkish monarchy on the model of Austria-Hungary, but they were turning increasingly toward the goal of full independence. An Arab congress representing various groups met in Paris in 1913; it called for decentralization and for Arabic as the official language in the Arab provinces. Istanbul sent a representative to agree to the demands, but when the CUP did not implement the agreement, the embitterment of Arab nationalists became more intense. Even in 1914, however, there were still only a few Arab nationalists, and Arabs remained overwhelmingly loyal to the empire.

Although distinct from the nationalists, the princes of Mecca were also restive under Turkish rule. As members of the clan of Hashim, to which the Prophet Muhammad belonged, they were known as Hashimites, and as the Prophet's descendants through the line of his grandson Hasan they were *sharifs* ("noble men"). For almost a thousand years Hashimites had filled the office of amir and sharif of Mecca, usually simplified as "Grand Sharif" by Westerners. They were keepers of the Holy Places, sometimes also controlling the adjacent region, the Hijaz. The Ottomans, after imposing their hegemony over the area in the 1500s, designated amirs from the rival branches of the sharifial family and left the Hijaz largely to them.

Sharif Husayn, the headstrong and ambitious old man who held the office after 1908, saw his position threatened by centralization. So distrustful had Sultan Abd al-Hamid II been of Husayn that he kept him as an involuntary "guest" in Istanbul for fifteen years before the 1908 revolution. Following his appointment Husayn warded off Ottoman control by winning the loyalty of the Hijazi tribes and forced one Ottoman governor to kiss the hem of his garment. He dreamed of higher things—of becoming king of the Hijaz or of all the Arabs, or even caliph of Islam. But, with a railroad now connecting Madina with the rest of the empire, the central government was becoming a greater threat. The Ottomans were making plans, bitterly opposed by Husayn, to extend the railroad to Mecca.

Arab nationalists in the Fertile Crescent began to think of Husayn as a potential leader. Thirty-five Arab members of the Ottoman Parliament notified him in 1911 of their willingness to "rise with him" against the Turks. Encouraging

Husayn's ambition was his impatient son, Amir Abdullah, who wanted to work with the Arab nationalists. When Abdullah, a member of the Ottoman Parliament, passed through Cairo on his way to Istanbul in February 1914, he met Lord Kitchener and inquired whether his father could expect British assistance against the Turks. Kitchener replied that Britain could not interfere in the internal affairs of a friendly power but only laughed when Abdullah pointed to previous intervention in Kuwayt, which was also an Ottoman territory. Two months later, when Abdullah was in Cairo on his return trip to the Hijaz, he pursued the matter further with Sir Ronald Storrs, the Oriental Secretary. However, another son of Sharif Husayn, the more cautious Amir Faysal, was still persuading his father to remain loyal to Istanbul.

IRAN: RISE OF THE QAJARS

To resume the story of Iran so abruptly interrupted in the midst of Karim Khan Zand's sway over much of the country, this ruler's achievements reached their zenith with an invasion of Ottoman territories and the occupation of Basrah in 1775. But with his death four years later the Iranians withdrew, and the Zand dynasty also succumbed to intrafamilial conflict.

This made way for the advances of a Turkish tribe, the Qajars, located just south of the Caspian Sea in the region of their future capital, Tehran. Agha Muhammad Khan Qajar, who escaped from detention by the Zands and whose vindictiveness dated back to his childhood castration by Afshar captors, eventually subdued his rivals throughout the country. Reflecting patterns that had recurred since Mongol days, his troops presented him with 20,000 eyes plucked from his opponents' heads in Kirman. The Qajar forces also built pyramids of human skulls. The new ruler's coronation in 1796 formally inaugurated a dynasty that was to last until 1925. But the peace that was harshly imposed by the new shah and by his successor, Fath Ali Shah (1797–1834), after so much anarchy was soon to make way for the accelerated disintegration of a country whose population was perhaps half tribal.

THE IRANIAN ULAMA
IN OPPOSITION

Besides the emergence of the new ruling dynasty, the late eighteenth century saw important developments in Twelver Shi'ism. The previously important school of thought, the Akhbaris, who rejected *ijtihad,* gave way to the overwhelming predominance of its rival, the Usulis. The latter accept the right of a few leading *ulama,* known as *mujtahids,* to reinterpret Islamic law. According to this doctrine, other people are bound by *taqlid* (imitation), but not in the sense that Sunni Muslims follow the details of one of the centuries-old schools of jurisprudence. Instead, each person voluntarily chooses a living *mujtahid* as his *marja-i taqlid* ("source of imitation") on the basis of the *mujtahid*'s great learning. This was quite in contrast with

Sunni religious leaders in the Ottoman Empire, who were chosen by and subservient to the sultan. Sometimes one Twelver *mujtahid* gains preeminence as the sole *marja*, but usually he is only one of several such persons whose authority is accepted by varying proportions of the community. In any case, while the *marja*'s views are not considered infallible, he is at least theoretically in a position to mold religious teachings in a way that would be impossible for Sunni *ulama*.

Much more than under the Safavids, the *mujtahids* tended to reject the legitimacy of the shahs' rule, particularly from the mid-nineteenth century on. This sometimes was matched by a quietist attitude based on the idea that all governments are necessarily illegitimate during the twelfth *imam's* absence. But at other times the prevailing tendency has been to stress the need to work for justice and to oppose tyranny, with less concern sometimes even for the details of Islamic law prior to its future full implementation when the *imam* returns as the Mahdi. Shi'ite passion plays depicting the Umayyad Caliph Yazid versus the martyred Husayn sometimes implied opposition to all tyrants and perpetuated the stress on martyrdom.

Several factors enhanced the *ulama's* power. These included the location of some of their religious centers in Ottoman-controlled Iraq beyond the shah's reach, the important role they played as funnels for charitable contributions, and their close alliance with merchants. The feebleness of the Qajars was another factor, at times allowing clerics to maintain their own private armies. Also, unlike the Safavids, the Qajars could not legitimize their role by pretending to be descendants of one of the twelve *imams*, and a myth sometimes surfaced that they had fought with the Umayyads at Karbala. Iran was thus the only part of the Islamic world in which one could find something like the church-state dualism of medieval Latin Christendom. The Shi'ite ''church'' was to play a major role during the nineteenth and twentieth centuries as leader of the populace against both local tyranny and foreign domination.

EUROPEAN IMPERIALISM IN IRAN

Now wedged between British India and the Russian Empire, which progressively incorporated the Islamic peoples of Central Asia during the nineteenth century, Iran's independence increasingly lost its reality. Britain and Russia repeatedly decided which prince would ascend the throne. Formal independence became largely a product of the two European empires' mutual jealousy. Concerned with protecting its commercial interests and the security of the ''road to India,'' Britain rarely evinced interest in actual territorial aggrandizement at Iran's expense and sometimes even promoted the kinds of reforms that might enable the country to resist blatant expansionism. In a sense Iranians could find satisfaction in the ability of Great Britain (or more precisely, of the British colonial government of India, which oversaw matters east of Suez) to check the czars. But although the Iranians often appreciated Britain's position during the nineteenth century, both imperialisms eventually earned more nearly equal shares of their animosity.

Russian encroachment on Iran became intense in the early nineteenth century.

Georgia switched from Iran's to Russia's sphere of control in 1783, but during the next decade Russian and Iranian armies alternately dominated this area. Russian victories in 1812 led to the Treaty of Gulistan (1813), in which Tehran renounced its right to have naval vessels on the Caspian Sea and its claim to Georgia and other parts of its former domain. In reality, Iran's territorial losses were greater than the extent of its military defeat made necessary, for the commander (and governor of Azarbayjan), Abbas Mirza, successfully bargained for Russian support as heir to the throne. He did not live long enough to claim his prize, but as would often happen later in the century, the personal interests of a member of the ruling dynasty were given priority over those of Iran.

Further Russian encroachments brought a new war in 1826. Before long the enemy occupied northwestern Iran, including Tabriz. In the resulting Treaty of Turkomanchay (1828), Iran ceded further territories to its northern neighbor (who withdrew approximately to today's border) and agreed to pay a large indemnity. The subsequent extensive extraterritorial privileges for Russian subjects, later extended to other powers, further ate into Iran's independence. Led by religious leaders, who had inspired many people with calls for *jihad* during the war, Iranian anger against Russian imperialism—and particularly over the refuge given to a eunuch and two Muslim women of Christian origin, captives of earlier wars— culminated in an attack by the populace on the Russian legation in 1829. Several people were killed, including the minister. In turn, the shah apologized to St. Petersburg and agreed to further indemnities.

Tehran began a persistent pattern of looking for a third imperial power to use as a lever against Russia and Britain. In 1807, following Britain's successful negotiation of a treaty with Iran in 1801, Napoleonic France became the first such third state with the conclusion of a Franco-Iranian Treaty of Alliance that seemed to offer France a base for an attack on British India and to give Iran an alternative to Russian encroachment. But Napolean left the shah out in the cold by entering into an alliance with the czar at Tilsit soon afterward, and the Franco-Iranian treaty made way in 1814 for an Iranian alliance with Britain in the form of the so-called Definitive Treaty. A bribe to Abbas Mirza allowed Britain to abrogate relevant provisions of this treaty fourteen years later, during the Russo-Iranian war.

BEGINNINGS OF IRAN'S WESTERNIZATION

Defeat evoked some "defensive modernization" in Iran, but to a much smaller extent than in the Ottoman Empire. The introduction under Abbas Mirza's leadership of modern weapons and drill and European instructors—a faint imitation of Ottoman military reforms—seems to have had little positive impact but served mainly to undermine the age-old patterns of tribal cavalrymen. Nasir al-Din Shah's able minister, Amir-i Kabir, attempted a program of reform and industrialization, but he was dismissed in 1851 and later killed, as his popularity seemed to make him a possible rival to the monarch. Nasir al-Din Shah created a Dar al-Funun ("House of Knowledge''), a European-style college with European teachers, to train army officers and civil servants. A few students were sent to Europe from 1875 on, and the foreign sectarian schools that were established had some impact, but educational modernization hardly developed a momentum comparable to that in Ottoman lands.

A printing press appeared in 1812 under Abbas Mirza's aegis, and an official gazette was started in 1851. The translation of European works and the development of less obscure writing styles also proceeded. The introduction of the telegraph in 1858, followed by an Indo-European Telegraph Line in 1865, helped to open the country to outside influences. Still, Iran remained relatively primitive, with only eight miles of railroad as late as 1900.

As in other non-European regions, although more slowly than in the Ottoman Empire, the ever-growing world market produced by Europe's industrial revolution drew Iran into the role of exporting primary (i.e., nonindustrial) products. The development of widespread private land ownership paralleled this during the late nineteenth century, and landowners concerned with getting large pfofits from market crops brutally exploited the peasants. Still, the overall impact of modernity, including the world market and medical advances, brought a net improvement in living conditions, as reflected in the approximate doubling of the population during this period (several devastating epidemics of cholera notwithstanding) to about 10 million in 1914.

Partly reflecting the slower impact of modernity, craft guilds retained their vitality longer in Iran than in many other places. In an exception to the general trend, considerable development occurred in some handicrafts, especially carpet making, and craft products supplemented the stream of agricultural sales to Russia, India, and Ottoman territories. Some merchants grew increasingly prosperous.

The merchant class spawned new ideas and movements. One such development was that of Sayyid Ali Muhammad, who in 1844 declared that he was the *bab* (door) to the Hidden Imam. The Babis emphasized equality, world brotherhood, and the importance of education. Soon asserting themselves as an entirely new religion, they attempted to supersede Islam altogether. This new heresy met heavy persecution, especially after several revolts and after one of its adherents tried to assassinate the shah. The main portion of the movement accepted the leadership of a man who called himself Baha Ullah. This group, the Baha'is, continued to exist as a small minority in Iran and to engage in worldwide missionary activity, with its center in Acre, in Palestine.

DESPOTISM, NATIONALISM, AND CONSTITUTIONALISM IN IRAN

The country's administration retained brutal features. Tax-farming continued to be a general practice, and the collectors exacted all they could from the peasants. Those villages that resisted paying were sacked and their people massacred or taken captive. Even such practices as keeping hostages from their members could not keep the numerous tribes under control, and the peasants recurrently bore the brunt of this Hobbesian world.

Spendthrift shahs imposed an intolerable drain on the treasury. The reparations to Russia after 1829 and continuing military campaigns created a financial strain; primitive methods of collecting taxes and expenses such as those incurred by a series of royal visits to Europe from 1873 on aggravated the situation.

The sale of concessions to European businessmen with little regard for the country's overall interests became a quick but shortsighted source of revenue. In 1872 a British subject, Baron Julius de Reuter, obtained exclusive rights to mines, a railway, and a national bank, with the bulk of Iran's revenues designated for payment. In this case Russian indignation brought cancellation. But then in 1890, in return for an annual percentage, the tyrannical Nasir al-Din Shah (1848–1896) granted another English company a monopoly over the production and sale of tobacco.

Such concessions brought on popular anger led by merchants and clerics. The former's economic interests were threatened, and the *ulama* were embittered by shahs who seemed to cooperate with the Christian European onslaught against the Islamic world. Following the 1890 concession, the leading *mujtahid,* Hasan-i Shirazi, issued a ruling forbidding the use of tobacco under these circumstances. Iranians showed incredible solidarity in putting aside the practice of smoking until the monopoly was terminated. But the concessionaire had to be compensated, and the government fell deeper in debt to Britain and Russia. Customs receipts were pledged in payment, and the need for efficient collection led to customs houses' being farmed out to Belgian officials.

Concession hunters continued to find prizes. In 1901 a British subject, William Knox D'Arcy, obtained an oil concession that led to the creation of the Anglo-Iranian Oil Company (AIOC). The first commercial discovery of oil in Iran (or anywhere in the Middle East aside from the Russian-ruled part of Azarbayjan) came in 1907. The British navy switched from coal to Iranian oil by 1914 and gained a controlling interest in AIOC in the same year.

Agitation against foreign penetration and local corruption and absolution continued to intensify. Afghani came to Iran in 1866 and was later in the forefront of opposition to the tobacco concession. Escaping from Nasir al-Din Shah's agents, Afghani fled to London to direct an opposition newspaper. One of his followers assassinated the shah in 1896.

Another Iranian, Malkom Khan, originally an Armenian Christian but at least formally a convert to Islam, led a wing of the opposition that included many graduates of modern schools. In exile in London, Malkom Khan published a newspaper that strove to simplify and modernize the Persian language and called for an end to corruption and despotism, even for the adoption of secular law.

Though destined not to succeed, a constitutional revolution, fundamentally an expression of the growing Iranian nationalism, seemed for a while to win out over a monarchy whose despotism and ineffectiveness were matched by a readiness to succumb to European imperialism. Beginning in December 1905, two thousand merchants and religious leaders took refuge (*bast*) in a mosque, which custom forbade the government from violating, and demanded various reforms. This occurred again in January 1906, and each time the shah merely pretended to agree to some of the demands as the withdrawal of the merchants from their usual activities brought the economy to a halt. During the following summer, over 12,000 joined in the *bast*. These included *ulama* in a mosque in Qum, the holy city south of Tehran, and a large number of merchants on the grounds of the British legation. A network of committees throughout Iran supported the demands for reform. The weak Muzaffar al-Din Shah (1896 –1907) was forced to give in and grant a constitution providing for an elected Consultative Assembly (Majlis) and the principle of ministerial responsibility to that body. As a concession to the vital religious wing of the revolution, the constitution provided for a committee of *mujtahids* to determine whether acts of the new assembly were consistent with the *shari'ah,* but this provision came to be ignored in practice.

IRAN STRANGLED

Aided by the Russians, Muhammad Ali Shah came to the throne in 1907 and conspired to overthrow the constitution. In 1908 the Russian-officered Cossack Brigade, which dated back to 1879, shelled the Majlis building and declared martial law in an attempt to restore despotic rule. But constitutionalists took control of Tabriz, while many of the religious leaders continued their opposition to autocracy from the Shi'ite holy cities of Iraq. Deciding that constitutionalism, particularly the idea of popular sovereignty, was a dangerous innovation, one leading *mujtahid,* Fazlullah Nuri, shifted to the shah's camp, later to be executed by temporarily victorious constitutionalists. Ironically, it was Bakhtiyari tribesmen, led by a chief Sardar Asad, who had been influenced by Western ideas while studying in Paris, who turned the tide by occupying Isfahan and Tehran in support of the constitutionalists and permitted the Majlis to convene again in 1909. Britain and Russia allowed Muhammad Ali Shah to be deposed in favor of the twelve-year-old Ahmad Shah. A comeback attempt by the ex-shah from his Russian exile later was nipped in the bud.

Meanwhile, betraying those who saw it as a supporter of constitutionalism and a bulwark against expansionism, Britain agreed with Russia in 1907 on a plan to divide Iran into spheres of influence. Although the country's formal independence was unaffected, the agreement gave Russia a free hand to penetrate the north economically, with the British enjoying similar rights in much of the southeast. Both powers could compete for concessions in a third zone.

In another expression of its tendency to seek ties with a third state, Iran looked to the United States as a country whose hands were free of imperial designs there. An American banker, Morgan Shuster, was recruited to put Iran's finances in order. Supported by the ardently nationalist, intellectual-led, Democratic party, Shuster became Treasurer-General and was entrusted with full control over the country's finances. But a financially sound Iran was not acceptable to those who were looking for prey, and in 1911 Russia demanded Shuster's dismissal. The Iranian government had no choice but to comply as the czar's troops occupied Tehran and ended the constitutional regime.

The constitution and the struggle for independence that motivated it had now lost out. The constitutionalists' efforts to abolish such practices as tax-farming had been dissipated. Iran was a country whose only army, aside from anarchic tribes, consisted of the Russian-dominated Cossack Brigade and a pro-British, Swedish-officered gendarmerie, and the country seemed destined for formal annexation by the two imperial powers. There were now British troops in the south and Russian troops in the north, with provincial governors their puppets. The Russians and British even manipulated elections in an attempt to keep Iranian nationalists from being elected to the Consultative Assembly. The Democrats, including many now in exile, could only feel agony. Their hope was that another power, Germany, whose imperialism could not seem more than hypothetical despite its recent concession-hunting in the Persian Gulf region, would come to the rescue.

CONCLUSIONS

The 140 years ending in 1914 saw repeated attempts by Middle Easterners to come to terms with a European civilization whose capability grew more and more overwhelming. Much of a European-originated modernity penetrated the region. Westernization started with attempts to modernize armies and seemed to spread uncontrollably into other areas of life. Western-style education took its place alongside traditional schools to produce a dual civilization, partly indigenous and partly Westernized. Western ideas such as democratic and constitutional government took hold, although without much success. The relatively recent development of nationalism in Europe also led to similar movements among Muslim peoples.

Modern technology—the railroad, the telegraph, and the like—appeared in the Middle East but penetrated the society at a vastly slower pace than in most of the West. While Japan's uniquely successful modernization allowed it to defeat Russia in 1905, thus inspiring Middle Eastern nationalists with proof that Asians were not inherently weaker than Europeans, the gap between the Middle East and the West continued to grow, leaving the Middle East more vulnerable than ever. Significant population growth everywhere in the Middle East testifies to the improvement of living conditions in some ways. But the irresistible tide of a "world market" where the West's industrial products commanded high prices in exchange for the raw materials of the larger world undermined the latter's own crafts and its social structures and created dependent economies.

None of the many attempts by Middle Eastern rulers to put their houses in order had succeeded. The task would have proved formidable even under the best of circumstances. Now those who were trying to bridge the gap between their own societies and those of the West were themselves beset by a babel of conflicting ideas—narrow traditionalism versus blind imitation; constitutionalism versus autocracy; theocracy versus secularism; religious versus ethnic, dynastic, and local identities—that crippled the effort. With provinces struggling to break away and with European powers rivaling each other in encroaching on the area, successful modernization efforts by Istanbul, Cairo, or Tehran would have provided cause for wonder.

By the late nineteenth century Asians and Africans were rarely not under some form of European domination. European power seemed to be closing in on what little was left of Middle Eastern independence in 1914. Egypt was already a province of the British Empire in all but name. What remained of the Ottoman Empire was receding in the face of continuing European designs. After a remarkable constitutional revolution of 1906, Iran was experiencing renewed strangulation at Russian and British hands.

6

The East Engulfed

1914-1920

The summer of 1914 found most of the nations of Europe aligning themselves in two rival warring camps. The peace had long been fragile, and the aspiration of an increasingly powerful Germany to obtain a "place in the sun" alongside Great Britain and France polarized the Great Powers. Then the assassination of Austrian Archduke Francis Ferdinand by South Slav irredentists in June unleashed a flood of rivalries. By August Germany and Austria-Hungary, known as the Central Powers confronted a coalition, the Allies, that included Great Britain, France, and Russia. World War I, as the struggle came to be known, raged for more than four years and involved growing numbers of nations. In comparison with Western countries, Middle Easterners possessed little weight to affect the scales. But they found themselves pulled into the war as clients of one Western camp or the other, and in the end they were to be at the mercy of whoever prevailed.

The First World War was a watershed in the relationship between the Middle East and the West. The Ottoman Empire, which had ruled most of the area for four centuries, fell apart as a result of its defeat by European powers and of separatist nationalisms among its peoples. Arabs and Turks, previously united by a common faith and a common government, would henceforth go their separate ways. The political map began to take its contemporary form, with European powers gaining control over most of the fragments of the Ottoman Empire. The end of the war was to leave the Middle East, particularly the Arabs, with new grievances against the West that would remain a major preoccupation for many years. The Arab-Zionist (or Arab-Israeli) conflict, which was further to poison Arab-Western relations, also emerged at this time.

THE OTTOMAN ENTRANCE
INTO THE WAR

The possibility of helping Germany defeat the Allies attracted many Turks. It seemed to be a chance to shake off the Capitulations. In September 1914, even before it had entered the war, Istanbul unilaterally abrogated the Capitulations, but only a victory over the Allies could make this permanent. Some Turkish leaders also hoped to reconquer lost territories, from North Africa to the Balkans. Moreover, it was natural for the Turks to ally themselves with the enemies of Russia, which had habitually encroached from the north and openly hoped to control the Straits and to restore the Ottoman capital city to Orthodox Christendom. Both pan-Turkism and pan-Islamism, which were now at their height, provided further incentives for the Turks to join the Central Powers. In a war against Russia, the Ottomans could hope to liberate the Turkish areas of the Transcaucasus and Central Asia. And pan-Islamism, besides its value in rallying the Muslims of the Ottoman Empire against the Allies, was potentially a powerful weapon for undermining Western colonialism in such places as India and North Africa and might lead to the expansion of Ottoman control over these areas.

Many leading Turks, however, admired British and French liberalism. More important, they realized that Britain, despite its occupation of Ottoman territories such as Cyprus and Egypt, had been largely responsible for preserving the Ottoman Empire during the previous century. They perceived that, to the British, the existence of the Ottoman Empire was an important asset to prevent Russian expansion into the eastern Mediterranean and to provide stability in the territories that lay along the vital route to British-ruled India. The British commitment to this longtime policy had already weakened. But to go to war against Britain, especially now that it was allied with Russia, would be an invitation for it to change its policy. And even the German embrace seemed more and more to be a stranglehold.

Yet Istanbul, despite an initial declaration of neutrality, stood alongside Berlin and Vienna. Enver's vanity, ambitiousness, and recklessness made him especially vulnerable to the urgings of German diplomats. Now as the minister of war and increasingly the dominant figure in the CUP triumvirate, he worked to bring the Ottomans into the war and soon overcame the doubts of his colleagues.

The Allies gave momentum to Turkish pro-German sentiment. They rejected Turkish requests for border rectifications in the Balkans and for the abolition of the Capitulations. It is possible that an agreement to end the Capitulations would have prevented the Ottomans from joining the Central Powers. In addition, the British government, as part of its mobilization for the war, sequestered two warships that had been built by a British company for the Ottoman navy and were due for delivery. This was a hard blow for the Turks, who were deeply concerned with ending Greek naval supremacy in the Aegean. Voluntary contributions from the Turkish people had paid for the ships, with women even donating their hair.

Then the Ottomans discovered an alternative to the British ships, although one with fateful consequences. When the war started, two German battle cruisers, the *Goeben* and the *Breslau,* were stranded in the Mediterranean. Barely eluding capture by the British navy, the ships surprised nearly everyone on August 10 by sailing to Istanbul, which had concluded a secret alliance with Berlin eight days earlier. In violation of Turkish neutrality, the ships were given sanctuary under the pretext that they had been sold to the Ottoman navy. In reality, the Germans had obtained control of the Ottoman navy; the two ships were given Turkish names, and the German officers simply exchanged their hats for fezzes.

With the ships' guns pointed at the Ottoman capital, the choice of war was no longer in Turkish hands. A German general ordered the closure of the Bosporus and the Dardanelles, Russia's vital outlet from the Black Sea to the Mediterranean and to the other Allied Powers. In October the Ottoman navy launched an attack on Russian Black Sea ports and sank several Russian ships. Aside from the members of the triumvirate, even the Ottoman cabinet did not know of the attack in advance, but it was too late to turn back as Russia and its allies declared war. In keeping with pan-Islamism, the shaykh al-Islam declared the war to be a *jihad*—holy war. The incongruity of a *jihad* fought by a junior partner of Christian Germany limited its appeal, though Istanbul spread the fictitious story that Kaiser Wilhelm II had converted to Islam and had, following a pilgrimage (*hajj*) to Mecca, changed his name to Hajji Muhammad Wilhelm.

IRAN AND THE WAR

Encroachment by Britain and Russia had left Iranian independence as little more than a formality when the war started. Although Prime Minister Mustaufi al-Mamalik declared his country's neutrality, most Iranians supported Germany and the Ottomans. If given a chance, Iran would have joined the Central Powers. Prince Ruess, the German minister, assiduously cultivated hatred of British and Russian imperialism. The tribes, who constituted about a fourth of the population, staunchly opposed the Allies. German agents, the most famous of whom was Colonel Wilhelm Wassmus (the so-called German Lawrence), helped to organize tribal rebellions. Religious leaders called for *jihad*. Most of all, the liberal intellectuals, the core of the Democratic party, strongly supported the Central Powers. But many of the leading nationalists were in exile, mainly in Germany, leaving inordinate influence in the hands of opportunists whose sympathies changed with the tides of war.

In November 1915 Prime Minister al-Mamalik was ready to conclude an alliance with Germany. As rumors spread that Russian forces were planning to occupy Tehran, the prime minister and most of the members of the Majlis slipped out of the capital city to go south to Qum. Those fleeing included not only nationalistic Democrats but also opportunists who, foreseeing a German victory, wanted to be on the winning side. In fact, thousands of people were soon joining the flight to Qum. There were plans to proceed further south to Isfahan to establish a temporary capital. Young Ahmad Shah was ready to join the exodus, but as he was getting into his carriage, the British and Russian ministers kept him from leaving, assuring him that Tehran would not be occupied. This thwarted the nationalist plan to move the capital. However, many pro-German members of the Majlis moved from Qum to Kirmanshah, closer to the Ottoman border. There they established a provisional government and organized a military force of Lur tribesmen.

THE BRITISH PROTECTORATE
IN EGYPT

The guns had barely begun to fire in 1914 when European statesmen started to make plans for disposing of the Ottoman Empire. With the Turks in the enemy camp, the former British policy of upholding the empire was no longer viable. And aside from the need to secure local allies during the war, London had to consider postwar arrangements along the route to India.

Egypt had been under British occupation and de facto rule since 1882 but remained legally under Ottoman sovereignty. London terminated this anomaly in December 1914 and declared Egypt a protectorate. The independent-minded Khedive Abbas Hilmi lost his throne to his more pliable uncle, Husayn Kamil. With the ties to Istanbul now broken, the new Egyptian ruler took the title of sultan.

While the formality of a protectorate changed the reality little, the war made British rule a heavier burden for Egypt. The country was under martial law and became an armed camp for British troops. The assembly of five or more people became illegal, and press censorship was strict. The Legislative Assembly, established in 1913, did not meet after the beginning of the war. Admittedly, Egypt avoided the ravages of war that much of the Middle East suffered. Hostilities on Egyptian territory were limited to Turkish attacks on the Suez Canal, the occupation of a border post in the Western Desert by tribesmen from Cyrenaica heeding the Ottoman call to *jihad,* and in rare instances the penetration of German warplanes. The British did not force the Egyptians to fight in the war. But they turned to the Egyptian peasantry as a source of labor for building roads and railroads and for digging trenches in the war zones. Local Egyptian officials cooperated with the British by furnishing their quotas of forced laborers. The number of peasants harshly uprooted reached more than a million and a half, some of whom were sent as far away as France. The British also requisitioned animals and fodder, often with inadequate compensation. A few Egyptians benefited financially from the war as a result of the influx of British troops and the soaring cotton prices. But food became scarce and prices more than doubled, while most incomes remained on a prewar level. The poor suffered heavily.

Egyptian resentment against British rule was growing. It spread to the peasantry, who had tended to be apathetic. But the iron hand imposed by the British during the war kept most of this resentment below the surface. Informed Egyptians found some cause for hope in a vague British commitment, when the Protectorate was declared, to work for a revision of the Capitulations and to hasten the development of self-government. Furthermore, in January 1918, President Woodrow Wilson of the United States, which had entered the war on the Allied side during the previous year, outlined Fourteen Points, including the principle of self-determination, for a future peace settlement. With the other Allies agreeing to accept most of Wilson's proposals, Egyptians were heartened. But without progress toward independence, suppressed Egyptian feelings would explode after the war.

PLEDGE TO THE ARABS

The First World War strengthened Arab nationalism, which had previously had only a few adherents. Arab nationalists could now hope for British assistance against the Turks, and repressive Turkish policies in Syria, evoked by fears of Arab collaboration with the British, multiplied anti-Turkish sentiment.

At the beginning of the war, Enver sent Jamal to command the Fourth Ottoman Army in Syria. Jamal seemed a suitable commander for the Arab region, since his pan-Islamic inclinations might have enabled him to gain the confidence of Muslim Arabs.

But following the failure of his attack on the Suez Canal in 1915, evidence of Arab nationalist sentiment brought out the harshness and despotism of Jamal's personality. He sent scores of leading Syrians into exile and had others, twenty-two in one day, hanged for treason. Jamal was in touch with the Allies, scheming to establish himself as the sultan of a breakaway state, but the need to cover up his own activities made repression of Arab nationalists even more expedient for him.

The war provided a new opportunity for Sharif Husayn to work with the British. Even now he carefully maintained a wait-and-see attitude, while stalling on persistent Ottoman efforts to get his endorsement of the *jihad* and to get him to send Hijazi tribal forces to fight against the Allies. But in January 1915 he accidentally learned that Istanbul was planning to depose him.

Amir Faysal also embraced the Arab nationalist cause, removing a major pro-Istanbul influence from Sharif Husayn. Faysal stopped in Damascus in 1915 on his way to Istanbul, where he sought assurances that his father would not be deposed. Meeting with Arab nationalists, Faysal learned that they shared his suspicions of the Allies and would join them only if given firm guarantees of independence. Having failed to obtain satisfaction in Istanbul, Faysal stopped in Damascus again on his way home and became a member of two Arab nationalist organizations, al-Ahd and al-Fatat. While he was away, the leaders of the two societies had drawn up a document stating the terms under which they would agree to join the Allied camp. The Damascus Protocol, as the understanding was later known, asked for British recognition of Arab independence, with boundaries specified to include the whole Arabian Peninsula (except for Aden, already under British rule) and the Fertile Crescent, extending north to embrace a thin slice of present-day Turkey as far west as Adana and Mersin, on the Mediterranean coast of Anatolia. In return, the Arab nationalists were willing to conclude a defensive alliance with and grant economic concessions to Britain. Faysal transmitted the Damascus Protocol to his father, who was now also ready to negotiate with the British.

Early in the war, the British began to think about working with the Arabs. An Arab revolt against the Turks, especially if led by the grand sharif of Mecca, might undermine Istanbul's attempt to rally the world's Muslims, most of whom were under Allied control. Furthermore, some British officials envisaged one or more Arab client states that would replace the Ottoman Empire as their means of securing imperial communications. On instructions from London, Sir Henry McMahon, the British high commissioner in Egypt, began to exchange letters with Sharif Husayn.

The Husayn-McMahon correspondence, consisting of letters exchanged between July 1915 and March 1916, prepared the way for the Arabs to enter the war on the British side. In return for Arab support against the Turks, the British promised to recognize Arab independence. Husayn accepted a fifteen-year alliance and the obligation to depend on British advisers and to give preference to British economic enterprise. As for the boundaries of the future Arab Kingdom, Sharif Husayn asked for the area specified in the Damascus Protocol but later agreed to exclude the Turkish-inhabited region of Mersin and Adana. McMahon, pointing to French interests, also excluded those "portions of Syria lying west of the districts of Homs, Hama, Damascus, and Aleppo"[1] from his promise. Husayn refused to relinquish the Arab claim to this area but agreed to defer a final agreement on the matter until the war was over. Although Iraq was included in the area of Arab independence, Husayn agreed to a temporary British occupation of the southern part of the country.

Another loophole in the British commitment to Husayn was a stipulation that agreements with other Arab chiefs would not be prejudiced. The colonial government of India had entered into treaty relationships with the rulers of Southern Arabia, Kuwayt, Bahrayn, the Trucial States, and Muscat and Oman during the nineteenth century, making these states essentially British protectorates. Reflecting concerns that sometimes put British officials in New Delhi and Cairo in conflict, the Indian government concluded a similar arrangement with Asir, in the Red Sea coastal region north of Yemen in 1915, as well as one with Qatar, on the Persian Gulf, in 1916. However none of these rulers participated in the Arab Revolt.

Aside from Sharif Husayn, the most important potentate in Arabia was Amir Abd al-Aziz ibn-Sa'ud of Najd, also in the Indian Government's sphere of concern. The Sa'udis' hereditary enemies, the Rashidi dynasty of Shammar, in northern Arabia, had temporarily driven them into exile in Kuwayt in the late nineteenth century, but Ibn Sa'ud restored Sa'udi control over his homeland in 1902. By 1913 he had expanded, at Ottoman expense, into the al-Hasa region on the Persian Gulf.

---

[1]Whether Palestine, lying to the south of the four specified cities, was part of the excluded area has been a matter of unending debate ever since.

Captain W. H. I. Shakespear, the British political agent in Kuwayt, traveled to Najd in 1915 for negotiations with the amir but died while participating in a Sa'udi military campaign against the Rashidis. Then Sir Percy Cox, the British political adviser in the Persian Gulf region, continued the talks and formalized an alliance with ibn-Sa'ud in December 1915. Amir ibn-Sa'ud, unlike Sharif Husayn, did not fight against the Turks during the First World War, but he provided assistance to the Allies by continuing periodically to battle with the pro-Ottoman Rashidis. The latter, together with Imam Yahya of Yemen, were the only rulers in the peninsula to support Istanbul.

THE WAR IN THE ARAB LANDS

Following the conclusion of his correspondence with McMahon, Sharif Husayn launched an Arab revolt against Turkish control on June 5, 1916. The original Arab nationalist plans had called for the mutiny of Arab troops in Syria, joined by a general uprising, but this was thwarted when Jamal, fearing that possibility, transferred Arab units to other fronts and when his repressive actions removed many potential leaders and deterred others. Instead, the revolt, begun in Mecca, was primarily one of Hijazi (and later Transjordanian) tribal forces led by Husayn's sons. But some Syrian and Iraqi officers in the Ottoman army also joined the revolt after deserting or being taken prisoner. In addition to British subsidies to the tribes, the British navy provided important assistance in the capture of towns along the Red Sea coast, enabling the Arabs to drive the Turks out of much of the Hijaz during 1916.

The Arab revolt seemed to have lost momentum toward the end of 1916, when Allied liaison officers, mainly British but also including a few Frenchmen, arrived in the Hijaz. One of these officers was an enigmatic and flamboyant young man, Lieutenant (later Colonel) T. E. Lawrence. The Arab forces moved further north in February 1917. A small group of bedouins, led by Lawrence, rode on to Transjordan, where they recruited a tribal force that captured Aqaba, at the northern end of the Red Sea, in July. Turkish forces continued to occupy the city of Madina until the end of the war. They also held the Hijaz Railway, which allowed them to send provisions to Madina, although the Arabs, sometimes led by Lawrence, periodically sabotaged it. However, the Ottoman call to *jihad* was thwarted, as were German plans to establish a submarine base on the Red Sea coast.

The British army in Egypt was now preparing for an offensive into Palestine. Jamal Pasha launched an attack on the Suez Canal in 1915 but was driven off, succeeding neither in disrupting the canal nor in inciting Egypt's Muslims to support their caliph against the British. Smaller Turkish raids on the waterway during 1916 were equally unsuccessful. The major impact of the Turkish threat to the canal was to inspire British wartime diplomacy with an obsession for its security and to accelerate the military build-up in Egypt.

Two British attacks on Gaza in early 1917 failed. But then the capable General Sir Edmund Allenby took command, providing superior leadership and inspiring great confidence in his men. Allenby's army now cut into Palestine, taking Beersheba in October and Jerusalem in December and continued to advance northward.

Following the capture of Aqaba, the British brought Faysal and his troops there by ship to form the "right wing" of Allenby's army. The Arab forces, with Faysal and Lawrence, moved north on the eastern side of the Jordan River, though with no spectacular military victories. Some of Lawrence's raids on the Hijaz Railway at this time were notably unsuccessful. The tribes along the way joined Faysal, and as the Turks moved out, Arab governments emerged in various cities. In October 1918 Faysal, at the head of a thousand Arab horsemen, entered Damascus, a city now in a joyous frenzy as the starving Turkish army withdrew. All of Syria was in Allied hands by the end of the month.

Meanwhile, a British invasion was ending Ottoman rule in another Arab land, Iraq. The British navy's new dependence on oil dictated concern for the security of the oil fields of southwestern Iran, adjacent to Iraq. A British force landed at the head of the Persian Gulf in November 1914 and soon occupied Basrah but did not find it easy to push much further. General Sir Charles Townshend moved 12,000 troops upriver by boat and reached the town of Kut al-Amara, south of Baghdad. With the Turks besieging the town for 143 days, the British troops, now starving and disease-ridden, surrendered in April 1916. The British eventually made a comeback and pushed the Turks out of the southern two-thirds of Iraq before the war ended, but only with strenuous efforts involving nearly half a million men.

SECRET INTER-ALLIED AGREEMENTS

Meanwhile, the European powers made secret plans, based on their own interests, that ignored the aspirations of Middle Eastern peoples. Russian Foreign Minister Sergei Sazanov proclaimed in a note to the British and French Ambassadors in St. Petersburg in March 1915 that "the time-honored aspirations" of his country must now be realized. He asked for the incorporation of the Ottoman capital city and other specified territories adjacent to the Straits into the Russian Empire. In an exchange of notes during the following month, generally known as the Constantinople Agreement, the British and French governments accepted the Russian proposal. This also stipulated that the spheres of influence into the which the British and Russians had divided Iran in 1907 would be extended to cover the whole country. According to this agreement, most of the central area would be joined to the British (southeastern) sphere, while Russia was given liberty of action in its area (the north), which seemed to mean eventual annexation.

The Allies promised southwestern Anatolia to Italy as a postwar prize. The Treaty of London, concluded in 1915 to induce Italy to join the Allied camp, provided that Rome would acquire sovereignty over the Dodecanese Islands and get a "just share" of territory in southwest Anatolia. The St. Jean de Maurienne Agree-

SECRET AGREEMENTS
DURING WORLD WAR I

RUSSIAN EMPIRE

- Kabul

RUSS. SPHERE, 1915 AFGHANISTAN

RUSSIAN SPHERE, 1907

INDIA
(Br.)

BRITISH
SPHERE
1907

BR. SPHERE, 1915

Caspian
Sea

MUSCAT and OMAN
(Br. influence)

Persian Gulf

Trucial
States

Br. protectorates
(undefined borders)

INDIAN OCEAN

RUSSIAN
EMPIRE

TRANSCAUCASUS

- Erzerum

- Kirmanshah

- Kut

BR. (Direct)

ADEN (Br.)

Black Sea

RUSS.

FR.
(Direct)

FR.
(Indirect)

BR. (Indirect)

Red
Sea

Unassigned

RUSS.

- Edirne

IT. Sphere
of Influence
IT. (Direct)

CYPRUS
(Br.)
International

EGYPT
(Br.
protectorate,
1914)

ANGLO-EGYPTIAN
SUDAN

SERBIA
ALBANIA
GREECE

Gallipoli

Dodecanese
Islands

Mediterranean Sea

LIBYA
(It.)

ment, concluded by Britain, France, and Italy in 1917, clarified this ambiguous commitment by allotting the whole southwestern quarter of Anatolia to Italy.

Greece wanted to annex Thrace (European Turkey) and parts of western Anatolia, including the port city of Smyrna, with its large Greek population. During the early part of the war, Great Britain made several offers to Greece. Greek Prime Minister Eleutherios Venizelos, later dismissed from office, was favorable to the Allied cause, but King Constantine supported a policy of neutrality. When Greece entered the war in 1917, after Venizelos had returned to power at the head of an Allied-supported rebellion, there was no promise of territory.

The most important secret commitment was the so-called Sykes-Picot Agreement, concluded by Britain, France, and Russia. Great Britain named Sir Mark Sykes, an Orientalist then serving in the War Office, to negotiate with France on the division of the Ottoman Empire. His French counterpart in the negotiations was François Georges-Picot, a career diplomat who, as a former Consul-General in Beirut, was particularly concerned with Syria. Sykes and Georges-Picot reached a tentative agreement in February 1916 concerning the Arab provinces. Then they went to St. Petersburg for talks with Sazanov and concluded a tripartite agreement in May. As for Anatolia, the Sykes-Picot agreement added the eastern part to the area already reserved for Russian annexation and earmarked much of south-central Anatolia for French administration.

Despite Britain's prior commitment to Sharif Husayn, the Sykes-Picot Agreement provided for partition of the Fertile Crescent. It reserved southern Iraq and the Palestinian port cities of Haifa and Acre for British administration and the Syrian coastal region north of Palestine for French rule. It stipulated that the region between French Syria and British Iraq would be under Arab rule but would be divided into French and British spheres of influence.

Palestine was a special problem. It was part of the whole region of Syria, for which France had had a concern for several centuries. France saw itself as the protector of the Catholic minority, mainly the Maronites. French cultural interests (including numerous French schools) and investments in Syria were extensive. On the other hand, Russia was concerned with the interests of the Orthodox Church in Palestine. Sazanov adamantly rejected French control over the Holy Places. And Franco-British rivalry, despite a rapprochement since 1904, was still alive in matters relating to the Middle East. London was uneasy about the possibility of French control of Palestine, not so much for religious as for strategic reasons. Palestine was important to the British because of its closeness to the Suez Canal. Consequently, the Sykes-Picot Agreement designated a large part of Palestine, including the Holy Places, for international administration.

THE ZIONIST MOVEMENT
AND THE BALFOUR DECLARATION

The claim of European Jews to Palestine now also entered the picture. The Jews had been one of the peoples of ancient Palestine, particularly of Jerusalem and the adjacent area, known as Judea. But by the Hellenistic period emigration and conversion had made Judaism worldwide. Since Rome's ruthless expulsion of the remaining Jewish population, only a few Jews remained in Palestine, including those in areas outside Judea, such as Galilee. The conquest of Palestine by Muslim Arabs in the seventh century A.D. resulted in immigration by Arabs from Arabia and— undoubtedly of greater importance—in the gradual Arabization of the indigenous Aramaic-speaking population. Palestine became part of a larger and relatively homogenous Arab world, and so it remained until the twentieth century.

Yet the Jews kept their emotional and religious ties to Palestine, which they called the "Land of Israel." Some modern Jews see themselves as simply a religious group rather than as a nationality. But Jews have more often identified themselves (and have been identified by others) as a people, "the people of Israel," the "descendants," in "diaspora" (dispersion) or "exile" of the people of ancient Judea. This sense of being a people was perpetuated both by the persecution that the Western, Christian world meted out to the Jews and by the autonomy that they and other religions enjoyed in the more tolerant Eastern, Islamic world under the millet system. The dream of "returning" to "the Land of Israel" never died. Throughout the centuries, small groups of pious Jews trickled to Palestine. At each Passover, Jews vowed to be "next year in Jerusalem."

A new movement, political Zionism, joined this older, religious Zionism toward the end of the nineteenth century. The political Zionists called for the establishment of a Jewish state, or, as they often put it for tactical purposes, a "national home." This more ambiguous term evoked less opposition, particularly among Jewish opponents of Zionism. The new Zionists were modern nationalists, influenced by the other emerging national movements of eastern Europe. Many were not religious at all. Political Zionism was a religious movement only in the sense that membership in the Jewish "nationality" was usually defined in terms of adherence (perhaps only formally) to the Jewish religion. Some highly orthodox Jews rejected it as contrary to Judaism, since they believed that only the Messiah, not the political Zionists, could reestablish the Jewish state. Some early Zionists thought that the Jewish state could be established in any available land, but the majority, in rejecting a British offer made in 1903 of territory in East Africa, would accept only Palestine, a decision that permitted political Zionism to mesh with traditional religious sentiment.

The best known figure in the early Zionist movement was a brilliant Viennese journalist named Theodor Herzl. Although Russian persecution of Jews had led to some Zionist colonization in Palestine during the 1880s, political Zionism gained popularity after Herzl's publication of *The Jewish State* in 1896. His powerful personality mesmerized many eastern European Jews, who saw him as a savior. In 1897 Herzl convened the First Zionist Congress in Basel, Switzerland, which adopted a program calling for a Jewish "national home" and established the World Zionist Organization. Yet only a tiny proportion of the Jews of the world were Zionists.

A future Arab-Zionist conflict was in the making. On one side were those Zionists who, though coming from Europe and belonging to Western civilization, thought they were returning to the ancient homeland from which the Romans had driven them. On the other side were the indigenous Arab Palestinians, supported by their fellow Arabs in neighboring countries. The Arab Palestinians saw the Zionists as European intruders—indeed, as another manifestation of Western colonialism—whose stated aspiration to establish a society that would be "as Jewish as England is English" threatened their own right to Palestine. Although supporters of Zionism today reject this interpretation of their movement, since "colonialism" and "imperialism" have become derogatory words (and since Oriental Jews have become Israelis and staunch Zionists), early Zionists were proud of their movement's "colonial" nature. Herzl described the future Jewish state as "a rampart of Europe against Asia."

Up to 1917 Zionism had achieved little. Herzl (who died in 1904) and his successors had, hitherto without success, tried to gain the support of European governments and of the Ottoman Empire. But despite Ottoman opposition to a Jewish national home, more Zionist colonization took place, bringing Palestine's Jewish population from about 24,000 in 1880 to about 80,000 in 1914. The deportation of Russian nationals as enemy aliens during the war reduced the number to 56,000 by 1917. The Arab Palestinians numbered well over 600,000. Perhaps the most remarkable Zionist achievement was the beginning of a revival of the Hebrew language, which had not been a spoken tongue for more than two millennia, as the common language of the immigrants.

World War I presented a problem for the Zionist movement but also gave it its first great opportunity. Zionists divided along national lines. Some saw the war as a conflict between Russia, the country of pogroms against Jews, and Germany, a country that many Jews had idealized as particularly hospitable to them. Others supported the Allies, foreseeing an Allied victory that would give the British control over Palestine. Most notable among the pro-British Zionists was Chaim Weizmann, an immigrant from Russia and a chemist at Manchester University. Even before the war, Weizmann had developed friendships with key British journalists and politicians, including David Lloyd George and Arthur James Balfour, and had skillfully won their sympathy for Zionism. His discovery of a new method of producing acetone, an ingredient in explosives, contributed to the British war effort, gaining him gratitude and valuable publicity.

It was partly through Weizmann's efforts that the British government offered to support some of the Zionist objectives. Balfour became foreign secretary in 1915, and Lloyd George became prime minister the following year. With these and other pro-Zionists in the Cabinet, a declaration favorable to Zionism was not long in coming. In November 1917 Balfour addressed a letter, every word of which had been carefully weighed by the Cabinet, to Lord Rothschild, head of the British Zionist Federation, announcing London's support for "the establishment in Palestine of a national home for the Jewish people." The Balfour Declaration did not offer all that the Zionists wanted. While the members of the British Cabinet may, at least vaguely, have understood "national home" as a step toward eventual Jewish statehood, the declaration carefully avoided mentioning a Jewish state. By using the phrase "in Palestine," the government did not clearly propose all of Palestine as a

Jewish national home. Finally, the "civil and religious [albeit not political or economic] rights of existing non-Jewish [i.e., Arab] communities" were guaranteed. Yet this was a foundation on which Zionists could later build.

Many writers have tried to explain why Britain issued the Balfour Declaration. The British may have been influenced by guilt over the West's persecution of Jews, by a familiarity with the Old Testament that created a romantic attitude toward Jews, and even by a belief that Zionism was a fulfillment of Biblical prophecy. On a more practical level, British leaders saw the desirability of rallying Jewish support for their side in the war. But their major motivation was strategic. Great Britain wanted a postwar arrangement to secure its vital lines of communication. A Jewish national home, so British leaders reasoned, might become a useful ally on the eastern flank of the Suez Canal.

THE ARAB RESPONSE

The Arabs were shocked when, in the wake of the Balfour Declaration, the new revolutionary regime in Russia revealed the Sykes-Picot Agreement in November 1917. When the news got to Jamal Pasha, he called a meeting of leading people in Damascus and gleefully publicized the fact that the British, after promising Arab independence, had then agreed with France and Russia to partition Arab territories among themselves.

There is some inconclusive evidence that Sharif Husayn had known about the Sykes-Picot Agreement all along and accepted it, but other evidence contradicts this notion. Husayn had been aware of French claims in Syria and had heard rumors of an Anglo-French agreement. But as late as May 1917 Sykes and Georges-Picot traveled to the Hijaz to meet with Husayn, who again rejected French aspirations. And the two men left Husayn with the understanding that French influence would be limited to the Syrian littoral, with France merely supplying advisers even there. For Husayn, these terms were more favorable than McMahon's original promises had been. The Arabs have since seen themselves victims of a betrayal. In any case, the contradictions between the Husayn-McMahon Correspondence, the Sykes-Picot Agreement, and the Balfour Declaration caused the first of a series of Arab nationalist grievances against the British and the West.

The Allies continued to reassure the Arabs. The British Foreign Office sent a telegram to Husayn in February 1918 claiming that what the Bolsheviks had published were preliminary discussions held before the Husayn-McMahon correspondence. A British statement in June 1918 (Declaration to the Seven) assured Arab nationalists that all territories already liberated by the Arabs would have full independence and that areas liberated by Allied armies would be governed according to "the principle of the consent of the governed." Britain further committed itself to work for the "freedom and independence" of Arab territories then still under Ottoman rule. A widely publicized Anglo-French Declaration of November 1918 stridently denied any aim of imposing foreign control over Arab territories and proclaimed that the Arabs would be allowed to choose their own governments. A British representative sent to the Hijaz in January 1918 told Husayn, to his satisfaction, that Jewish immigration would be permitted only to the extent that it was consistent with the Arab Palestinians' "political and economic freedom." President Wilson's Fourteen Points also seemed to point the way toward Arab independence.

THE WAR IN NON-ARAB LANDS

The Ottoman Empire, although eventually crushed, proved to be a formidable adversary for the Allies, not only in the Hijaz, Syria, and Iraq, but on other fronts as well. This was more than one might have expected of an underdeveloped Eastern society pitted against some of the greatest industrial powers of Europe, even allowing for the fact that the Allies were exerting their primary effort against Germany at such places as the Marne and Verdun. Although the Ottoman army was already exhausted by the recent Italo-Turkish and Balkan wars and was poorly armed and clothed from the start, it inflicted hundreds of thousands of casualties on the Allies and sometimes defeated them. The training and leadership of German officers helped make this possible, as did supplies from Germany, particularly after Bulgaria's entry into the war on the side of the Central Powers in 1915 facilitated transportation. However, the Turks' main successes were in defending their own territory from impregnable positions against Allied onslaughts.

The Ottoman grip on the Dardanelles and the Bosporus proved unbreakable. Early in the war the Allies decided to land troops on the fifty-two-mile-long Gallipoli Peninsula, on the western side of the Dardanelles, and to proceed from there to Istanbul. For this purpose they (primarily the British) assembled a great naval armada in the Aegean and made the planned landing in April 1915. The people of Istanbul thought the British would soon be there. Women and children were being moved to Anatolia, and a special train was ready to evacuate Sultan Mehmed V and his family.

The Turks thwarted Allied avances in May and in August. Of the half million Allied troops and the 800,000 Ottoman troops participating in the campaign, nearly half were killed or wounded on each side. The heat of summer proved unbearable to the Allied soldiers, accompanied, as it was, by flies and disease, a scarcity of water, and the constant odor of decaying human flesh. In November came snow and sleet, with men freezing to death and dying of influenza. In December the British Cabinet decided to withdraw and end the campaign. The Allied troops were lucky to be able to escape undetected on small boats, leaving behind vast stores of food and equipment for the Turks. The war would probably have ended by 1916 rather than two years later if the Turks had not succeeded in defending the Straits.

Eastern Anatolia and Transcaucasia, the adjacent Russian-ruled area south of the Caucasus Mountains provided another major theater of combat. Transcaucasia is a formidable mountainous area swept by blizzards during much of the year, which might ordinarily have precluded a winter offensive. But Enver became intoxicated by the idea that pan-Turkism was attainable and proceeded to eastern Anatolia with hopes of becoming a great conqueror by personally heading an invasion of Russia. His troops, who attacked in December, were repelled by Russian forces and Armenian volunteer units, and most of his men were killed or froze to death. Enver slipped back to Istanbul, vainly hoping to suppress the news of his failure from his own people. Then the Russian army entered northeastern Anatolia and occupied large areas. By March 1917 the Ottomans had lost 300,000 men on the Russian front. Those who survived were on the verge of starvation.

But the Russian Revolution gave the Turks another chance. The March Revolution, which overthrew the czar, started the disintegration of the Russian army in Anatolia and the Transcaucasus. The October (Bolshevik) Revolution completed the process. Although unexpected, this was not an entirely unearned opportunity for the Turks, as the successful closure of the Straits had been an important factor in undermining the Czarist regime.

Turkish forces again crossed into Transcaucasia. In the Treaty of Brest-Litovsk (February 1918), the new Bolshevik government of Russia made a separate peace with the Central Powers and ceded the Transcaucasian regions of Kars, Ardahan, and Batum, parts of Russia since 1878, back to the Ottoman Empire. However, the peoples of the region (Georgians, Armenians, and Azaris) had taken advantage of the chaos in Russia to establish their independence and form a Transcaucasian Federation. The Turks, for the time being, imposed their terms by force. In the face of the Ottoman invasion the Federation disintegrated, with the Azaris and other Muslim and Turkish groups generally supporting the Ottoman advance and rallying to form a pan-Islamic army. By September 15, 1918, the Turks had conquered Baku, on the Caspian Sea. With the Muslim, Turkic peoples across the Caspian attempting to establish their independence from Russia and presumably ready to greet the Ottoman armies as liberators, pan-Turkism seemed to be near realization. But with the Turks losing on the other fronts and now on the verge of surrender, the Transcaucasian victories turned into a mirage.

A gruesome tragedy for the Armenians, who numbered almost 2 million people in the Ottoman Empire in 1914, accompanied the Turko-Russian phase of the war. Although Armenian leaders shrewdly proclaimed their loyalty, few Ottoman Armenians had any enthusiasm for the Turkish war effort. Thousands of Armenians in Russia eagerly volunteered to fight against the Turks. In this frantic situation, in which the Turks feared their own destruction, the authorities ordered the deportation of all Armenians from Eastern Anatolia, and hundreds of thousands of men, women, and children were subsequently driven for hundreds of miles, with many dying of thirst and starvation along the way. In other cases the Turks simply took groups of Armenians from their villages and slaughtered them. The army systematically massacred a quarter of a million Armenian men who had been drafted to form labor batallions. Tal'at, as minister of the interior and later as prime minister, supervised the pogrom with terrible efficiency. Nearly a million Armenians perished. In turn, Armenians organized to massacre Turks whenever they had the upper hand, as during the Russian occupation of northeast Anatolia. Thousands of Turks, fearing the Armenians, died of hunger or cold as they fled from their homes in the face of Russian advances.

In a less clear-cut battle zone, contending forces fought for control of "neutral" Iran. The Russians augmented their troops in the north and moved closer to Tehran. The Turks occupied parts of western Iran, particularly the northwestern province of Azarbayjan. Fearing that the Central Powers would inspire a rebellion in India, the British established a series of bases in eastern Iran along the Afghan and Indian borders early in the war. Even then, a small group of Turks and Germans eluded capture and crossed the whole breadth of Iran to Afghanistan in an unsuccessful attempt to induce that country to join the Central Powers.

Pro-German tribes took control of southern Iran. The major exceptions, aside from some coastal towns, were the oil fields in the southwest, which the British occupation of southern Iraq safeguarded. Elsewhere in the south, tribesmen assassinated several British consuls and businessmen, leading to a general flight of British officials. However, in 1916 the British dispatched Sir Percy Sykes and a small group of Indian troops to southwestern Iran. Sykes organized a local force known as the South Persia Rifles and restored British control over much of the country during 1917.

Kuchik Khan, an Iranian nationalist and reformer who was determined to end his country's exploitation by Europeans and its own upper class, organized a rebellion in Gilan province, on the Caspian coast, in 1915. Within two years, the *jangali* ("jungle") movement, as his group was known, controlled the thick Gilani forests and jungles that are so atypical of the Middle East and gained a Robin Hood-like fame, robbing the rich to give to the poor. Although Kuchik Khan accepted German and Turkish aid, he was subservient to no one.

THE END OF THE WAR

The Ottoman war effort (except in Transcaucasia) was in a state of collapse by the fall of 1918. The Turkish army had suffered almost 1,500,000 casualties. Except for northern Iraq, it had lost the Arab portions of the empire. In September an Allied force advanced from Greece into Bulgaria, which then capitulated, disrupting Turkish access to the Central Powers. Germany and Austria-Hungary would also sue for peace in November. With all hope ended, the Young Turk government resigned, and its leaders, including Enver, Tal'at, and Jamal, hastened to flee from Ottoman territory aboard German ships. Istanbul's bid for peace led to the signing of an armistice, in effect a surrender, on October 31 in the Aegean harbor of Mudros. Among other provisions, the Mudros Armistice called for the disbanding of Ottoman forces and authorized the Allies to occupy any strategic point in the empire whenever their security was threatened.

The war had deeply disrupted civilian life in the Middle East. Scarcity brought soaring prices for food and other necessities. The British blockade hindered foreign trade. In some cases, as in Syria, authorities withheld food supplies from certain areas to punish people suspected of disloyalty. In other places, including parts of Iran, nomads were able to plunder at will, and with roads unsafe, supplies were unobtainable. Hunger and disease were widespread during the war, later leading to massive Western relief efforts. According to very conservative estimates, wartime conditions caused 200,000 deaths in Syria alone. Anatolia's population fell from 12 million in 1914 to 9.5 million at the end of the war. Travelers reported misery everywhere they went. Millions of peasant women toiled in the fields during the war, and most of their husbands never returned. There were hundreds of thousands of orphans, and after the war it was often impossible to determine whether they were Turks or Armenians.

The war set back economic and social progress. Little time or energy remained for such matters. Instead, the rival armies were busy destroying what already existed. Soldiers chopped down ancient olive trees in Syria to obtain fuel for military trains. Russian and Turkish troops in Iran tore down buildings to use their beams as fuel. Railroads were destroyed. The struggle for survival meant delays for many reforms.

But some positive changes occurred. For instance, the Ottoman Law of Family Rights of 1917 brought modifications, favorable to women, in the law of marriage and divorce. This was the aspect of the traditional Islamic legal system that Westernization had previously left untouched. And wartime necessity led to the employment of women by the Ottoman government and by private businesses, undermining their traditional seclusion in Eastern society. Women were instrumental in maintaining continuity in the educational system and in establishing new schools. Still another change at this time was the improvement of roads by the various armies. The British built hundreds of miles of roads in Iran over which automobiles could pass for the first time, as well as more than a thousand miles of usable railroads.

Indeed, one cannot ignore the broader effects of Western armies on the Middle East. The end of the war left about one million British troops there. More than 2 million British soldiers had served in the area during the war. Admittedly, many of these were Indians and other non-Westerners. But in the long interaction of the two civilizations, neither had ever before made itself so directly and intensely felt in so many of the lands of the other.

Only a shadow of the Ottoman Empire now remained. The loss of the Arab provinces was complete when the Turks relinquished northern Iraq to the British. Much of southern Anatolia also came under British occupation but was later turned over to Italian and French troops. British troops also landed at other points on the Anatolian coast. A joint Allied force occupied Istanbul itself. A French general symbolized the Christian West's defeat of the Muslim Turks by riding into the city on a white horse, as Mehmed the Conqueror had done when he took it from the Byzantines in 1453. Local Greeks and Armenians, feeling that their day had come, pushed Turks off streetcars and tore off Turkish fezzes and veils. The Turks were

bitter and helpless. The reactionary Sultan Mehmed VI had reasserted royal authority in pre-1908 fashion and meekly accepted Western protection against nationalists
and reformers. He hoped for a permanent British protectorate like the one in Egypt.

The sultan was even ready to acquiesce when the Greeks, former Ottoman
subjects who now aspired to create a Hellenic empire on both sides of the Aegean,
landed a force (under Allied authority and from Allied warships) at Smyrna in May
1919 and began to penetrate the interior. But most Turks, aside from their contempt
for the Greeks, felt that this was a betrayal of the spirit of the Mudros Armistice,
since Allied security had not required it. Stories of massacres and plundering by the
Greek troops further horrified the Turks. To the Turkish people the Greek occupation was the greatest humiliation of all, and it finally stimulated general resistance
against the Allies.

By the end of the war, Iran was also part of the British Empire in all but name.
The country was in chaos. In 1915 the British and Russians had planned to complete
the partition of Iran. But with the collapse of Russian power in 1917 and the Bolsheviks' subsequent repudiation of previous Russian imperialism, the British had the
field to themselves.

THE PEACE CONFERENCE

The Allied leaders, meeting in Paris in January 1919, tackled the problem of peace
settlements with the Central Powers, which had capitulated during the previous au-
tumn. The Allies' primary concern was to devise a settlement with Germany, resulting in the Treaty of Versailles. The Peace Conference imposed separate treaties
for the other defeated states, including the Ottoman Empire. Hoping to preserve
peace and security and to promote international cooperation, the Peace Conference
also established the League of Nations and incorporated its Covenant (constitution)
into the Versailles Treaty. Among other provisions, the Covenant established the
"mandate system," designed as a compromise between proponents of self-
determination and colonialism as a means of governing territories detached from the
Central Powers. According to this plan, various territories, all non-Western, that
were considered insufficiently prepared for independence would be assigned, as "a
sacred trust of civilization," to the tutelage of "advanced [mostly Western] nations."

The Peace Conference contended with a tangled network of conflicting claims
to Ottoman territories. The Greeks asked for European Turkey and the Smyrna region. The Italians demanded the share of Anatolia that their allies had promised
them in 1917. The Armenians, who had established an independent state in
Transcaucasia, presented an exaggerated claim to eastern Anatolia, very little of
which had an Armenian majority even before the recent massacres and deportations.
Amir Faysal, astute when among Arab tribesmen but bewildered by European diplomacy, appeared at the conference (officially as the representative of the Hijaz) to
present the case for Arab independence. Lawrence, still in Arab dress, came to the

conference as Faysal's translator and adviser, fervently supporting him against the French but not against the Zionists, whose interests coincided with those of the British. The Zionists, represented by a delegation headed by Weizmann, asked for a Jewish national home in a Palestine that would have included large parts of present-day Jordan, Lebanon, and Syria and much of Egyptian Sinai. Meeting in London, Weizmann and Faysal had reached an agreement in January for cooperation between a future Jewish national home and the Arabs, but Faysal made this conditional on immediate Arab independence.

The French were suspicious of the British, who, as the main foe of the Ottomans during the war, had emerged as the preponderant power in the Middle East, allowing other Allied nations to participate in the occupation only as a courtesy. Before the Peace Conference convened, Prime Minister Lloyd George persuaded French Premier Georges Clemenceau to accept a revision of the Sykes-Picot Agreement. According to the Lloyd George-Clemenceau Agreement, Palestine, instead of being internationalized, as the Sykes-Picot Agreement stipulated, would be assigned to Great Britain. Northern Iraq, rather than being part of the area under French influence as the Sykes-Picot Agreement provided, now was assigned to Britain, along with the rest of Iraq. Clemenceau thought that Lloyd George had, as part of the bargain, agreed to full French control over all of Syria, including the interior, which, according to the Sykes-Picot Agreement, was to be merely a French sphere of influence. The British were torn between their desire to cooperate with France and their reluctance to ignore completely their commitments to the Arabs, not to mention their longstanding rivalry with the French in the area. The French equated demands for Arab self-determination with a British desire to renege on the Sykes-Picot Agreement and to perpetuate their own dominance through Hashimite protégés.

THE SETTLEMENT IN ARAB LANDS

Arab Asia was now a patchwork of independent and foreign-ruled areas. The Ottoman collapse left local dynasties in control of Shammar, Yemen, Asir, Najd, and the Hijaz, over all of which Istanbul's suzerainty had previously been weak or non-existent. Sharif Husayn had unrealistically assumed the title of "King of the Arab Countries" in 1916 but obtained international recognition only as "King of the Hijaz." To the north both Iraq and Palestine were under British occupation. The Syrian littoral north of Palestine, at first occupied mainly by British troops, was turned over to French administration in 1919. Arab forces under Amir Faysal in Damascus ruled the interior of Syria.

On the insistence of President Wilson, the champion of self-determination, the Allied leaders agreed to send an international commission to determine the wishes of the former Ottoman provinces. When the other governments failed to carry out this agreement, Wilson sent an American commission, consisting of Henry King, the president of Oberlin College, and Charles Crane, a leading businessman. The King-Crane Commission, which conducted an intensive investigation, found that the Syrians overwhelmingly rejected French control. The Syrians were determined to establish their own independence and refused to accept the severance of any part of their country, including Palestine or Lebanon. They were willing to accept a mandate, preferably American, but with Britain as a second choice, only if this was to be limited to temporary aid. The commission accordingly recommended a temporary American or British mandate over a united Syria, with Faysal as king. After interviews with Iraqi leaders, it recommended a similar British mandate for Iraq. Initially favorable to Zionism, the commission was surprised with the extent of Arab opposition to the movement, as numerous conferences with Zionists revealed that they aspired to ''a practically complete dispossession of the present non-Jewish inhabitants, by various forms of purchase.'' The American investigators recommended a rejection of the Zionist program for unlimited Jewish immigration and for a Jewish state. The Peace Conference, however, ignored the commission's report, which was not published until 1922.

Arabs in the Fertile Crescent were meanwhile making plans for independence. A General Syrian Congress, composed of representatives from all parts of geographic Syria, met in Damascus in 1919. In March 1920 the congress declared the independence of a united Syria, with Faysal as the constitutional monarch. A meeting of Iraqi leaders chose Abdullah as their king, even though Iraq was still occupied by British troops.

The Paris Peace Conference disregarded Arab sentiment and Britain's previous commitment to Arab independence. The Allied Supreme Council, representing the leading Allied Powers, met in San Remo, on the Italian Riviera, in April 1920 and awarded a mandate for Syria and Lebanon to France. It awarded separate mandates for Iraq and Palestine (including Transjordan) to Britain. These were to be ''Class A'' mandates, a designation restricted to relatively advanced areas whose independence, according to the League of Nations Covenant, was ''provisionally recognized subject to the rendering of administrative advice and assistance for a limited time.'' Some Arabs wondered, however, whether such arrangements would really differ from old-fashioned colonialism. Furthermore, the mandate for Palestine incorporated the words of the Balfour Declaration, which had provided for a Jewish national home. The declaration had heretofore been merely a statement of British policy, without international legal status.

France was now free to uproot the Arab government in Damascus. The French commander in coastal Syria presented an ultimatum to King Faysal, demanding acceptance of the mandate and other terms that would, at best, have reduced the king to a figurehead in a French-dominated country. Faysal, breaking with more intransigent Syrian leaders, accepted the ultimatum at the last minute. This did him no good. Claiming that his reply had arrived too late, French forces moved eastward from the coastal region. The small and poorly armed Syrian army made a futile stand at Maysalun Pass, outside Damascus. The French army quickly prevailed and occupied the Syrian capital. Faysal, his kingdom ended, went into exile. The ''Day of Maysalun'' came to symbolize the sorrow of Arab nationalists.

THE POST–WORLD WAR I
PEACE SETTLEMENT

—— TURKISH FRONTIER, 1923

INCLUDING TERRITORIES
DESIGNATED IN 1920 AS:

1 — Part of Syria
2 — A Fr. Sphere of Influence
    (Overlapping with 7)
3 — An It. Sphere of Influence
4 — Greek
5 — Internationalized
6 — An Independent Armenia
7 — An Autonomous or Independent
    Kurdistan (Overlapping with 2)

NZ — Neutral Zones, 1922
  *Najdi – Iraqi
 **Najdi – Kuwayti
****States Conquered by Najd During the 1920s
    to form Sa'udi Arabia

Black Sea

BULGARIA

USSR

Samsun

Inonu

Sakarya R.

Sivas

Izmir
(Smyrna)

4

5

3

4

2

2

2

7

Batum

Ardahan

Kars

6

7

7

Mosul

Alexandretta

SYRIA and
LEBANON
(Fr. Mand.)

PALESTINE
(Br. Mand.)

IRAQ (Br.
Mand.)

TRANSJORDAN
(under Br. Mand.)

KUWAYT
(Br. Protect.)

AL–HASA
(Najdi rule)

*NZ
**NZ

***SHAMMAR

***HIJAZ

NAJD

***ASIR

Red Sea

YEMEN

ASIR

MUSCAT AND OMAN
(Br. Influence)

Arabian Sea

HADRAMAUT

Br.
Protectorates

ADEN (Br.)

INDIAN OCEAN

IRAN

EGYPT
("Independent,"
1922)

LIBYA

ANGLO–EGYPTIAN SUDAN

187

THE TREATY OF SÈVRES

Following the San Remo Agreement, the Allies drew up a peace settlement, the Treaty of Sèvres, for the Ottoman Empire. The terms the treaty tried to impose on the Turks (unsuccessfully as it later turned out) were harsh. Istanbul gave up all claims to the Arab provinces. Armenia was to be independent, and President Wilson was designated to determine its boundaries. The treaty gave autonomy to Kurdish-inhabited southeast Anatolia, with the option of complete independence within one year. It permitted Greece to annex most of European Turkey and several Aegean islands and put Smyrna and the adjacent area under a five-year Greek administration, with the possibility of formal annexation to Greece at the end of that period. The Ottomans renounced their title to the Dodecanese Islands in favor of Italy. Britain, France, and Italy signed a separate agreement providing for the division of most of southern Anatolia into spheres of influence, the boundaries of which approximated those established in the secret wartime agreements.

The few remnants of Turkey, after all these truncations, were subjected to restrictions that undermined its independence. The treaty continued the Capitulations, which the occupying powers had already reimposed. It included humiliating provisions to assure fair treatment of various minorities. It set up a three-power commission, not including Turkey, to exercise extensive financial control. It limited the Turkish army to 50,000 men and imposed numerous other military restrictions. It established an international commission to control the Straits.

NEW ARRANGEMENTS FOR IRAN

The British government was planning to determine Iran's future. The British would not permit an Iranian delegation to attend the Paris Peace Conference, using the excuse of Iranian "neutrality" in the war. But the real reason was that London did not want interference from other powers. Sir Percy Cox became the British minister to Tehran in 1919 and proceeded to negotiate a treaty. An Anglo-Iranian Treaty, concluded in August 1919, provided for a British loan and for British advisers to train the Iranian army. The treaty, which essentially imposed a protectorate over Iran, infuriated most nationalists. Although Iran's ratification of the treaty had become uncertain by 1920, the British were so confident about the new arrangement that they were already sending the advisers.

The Communists, despite their attacks on imperialism, now demonstrated that they were not much different from the czars or other powerful European nations. In 1919 the Russians began to extend aid to the now-beleagured *jangalis* in Gilan Province. Kuchik Khan, as a devout Muslim and Iranian patriot, was reluctant to work with the Soviets, but some of his colleagues eagerly welcomed their help. Then, in May 1920, a Soviet force landed on the Caspian coast. Kuchik Khan prayed for guidance, but his colleagues finally persuaded him to conclude an alliance with the newcomers. His worst fears were realized when the Soviets and a few

Iranian Communists reduced him to a figurehead and declared a "Persian Soviet Socialist Republic." Having temporarily lost one province, Iranians feared that they would lose the entire country.

CONCLUSIONS

By 1920, Western domination had submerged the Middle East. European powers had parceled out northern Africa and various peripheral lands during the nineteenth century, and more subtle forms of penetration like the Capitulations and spheres of influence had long undermined Ottoman and Iranian sovereignty. Now, however, the victorious Allies were partitioning the Turkish heartland with the acquiescence of a sultan whose capital was under Allied occupation. Arab nationalists, who had joined the Allied side in return for a promise of independence, now found their lands in the Fertile Crescent divided into British and French mandates and the concept of a Jewish national home imposed on Palestine. Iran was seemingly becoming a veiled British protectorate. The British in Egypt, having formally established a protectorate, seemed more determined than ever to stay. Only in the Arabian Peninsula were local rulers left independent, themselves under degrees of British tutelage.

Yet, even as this was true, a reaction against Western imperialism was setting in. A mass uprising was underway in Egypt. A determined nationalist resistance movement was gaining momentum among the Turks. Iranians were standing their ground against the Anglo-Iranian Treaty. Iraq was in revolt. Amir Abdullah was threatening to avenge his brother Faysal's expulsion from Syria. Anti-Zionist riots were beginning in Palestine. Even in countries where nationalism appeared to have been crushed during the summer of 1920, it would, in most cases, achieve partial success within the next two years.

7

Rebellion, Emulation, and Reaction

1920-1939

The confrontation with European power and civilization continued to permeate all the concerns of the Middle East during the 1920s and 1930s. This relationship had two aspects. First, Middle Easterners struggled to free themselves from Western domination, which had reached its height by 1920. This fight for independence consumed an inordinate share of the energy of all Middle Eastern peoples. Although nationalism would force Western imperialism to recede in some places during the early 1920s, further Middle Eastern successes came slowly.

A second and perhaps more fundamental concern for a still underdeveloped region continued to be how to catch up with the modern society of the West. Nearly all agreed on the desirability of attaining the West's level of material progress, if only to provide the means for defense against the West. But to what extent was it necessary to adopt nonmaterial facets of Western civilization? Some leaders wanted to make a total transformation of their countries; others sought to preserve or to return to traditional Islamic values. Many wavered or tried to find a middle path between the two extremes.

THE TURKISH STRUGGLE
FOR LIBERATION

The Turks, against seemingly hopeless odds, put up the most valiant resistance and achieved the most conclusive victory in the struggle against Western imperialism. This was partly because the Treaty of Sèvres that the Allies tried to impose on them was so unbearable. But the Turkish nationalist success was also the result of capable military and political leadership. Setting limited goals, Turkish nationalists achieved them by skillfully exploiting rivalries among the European powers and these powers' unwillingness, particularly just after an exhausting war, to risk using their full capabilities, disproportionate to any possible gain, for suppressing a determined people.

A major factor in the repulsion of European rule from Turkey, pointing the way for other Eastern lands, was the leadership of Mustafa Kemal, who later took the name Kemal Atatürk. The brilliance and daring of this iconoclastic young man had enabled the Ottoman army to foil the Allied campaign in Gallipoli in 1915 and had brought his forceful personality to the attention of the Turkish people. Despite Enver's jealousy, Kemal rapidly rose from the rank of lieutenant-colonel to become a general and a pasha. Although he had strongly opposed the alliance with Germany in 1914, he was the only Turkish hero to emerge from the war. And as he returned from the Syrian front to Istanbul in November 1918, he more than anyone else saw that the battle for his homeland must go on. Taking his own greatness for granted, he awaited the chance to act.

Feigning a willingness to accept defeat, Kemal had the good fortune to be sent by the sultan's government to eastern Anatolia as Inspector General of the Ninth Army in 1919. He landed at Samsun, on the Black Sea coast, on May 19, just as the news of the Greek landing at Smyrna four days earlier was readying the Turkish people for struggle. Since the 1918 armistice, local societies for the defense of rights had sprung up in some parts of the Turkish heartland. And, in eastern Anatolia, many army units, victorious in Transcaucasia to the end of the war, remained intact. Kemal's assignment was to demobilize Turkish forces; instead he proceeded to weld soldiers and civilians together into an iron-willed resistance movement. When the government recalled him, he resigned his commission in order to stay in Anatolia. He called two congresses, at Erzerum and Sivas (both in northeastern Turkey), out of which emerged a nationwide revolutionary organization, the League for the Defense of Rights in Anatolia and Rumelia. The congresses adopted a National Pact, which accepted the loss of the Arab provinces but insisted on the integrity and independence of the area "inhabited by an Ottoman Muslim majority." (Despite the previous upsurge of Turkish ethnic pride, some members of the two congresses still were not inclined to use the traditionally pejorative word "Turk"; the term "Ottoman Muslim" also had the advantage of including both Turks and Kurds.)

At one point, the sultan's government seemed ready to work with the nationalists. The sultan's incompetent brother-in-law resigned as prime minister in October 1919. His replacement claimed to lead a "Ministry of Conciliation." Elections were held, resulting in an overwhelming nationalist majority in the Ottoman Parliament, which adopted the National Pact. The Allies reacted by imposing a full-fledged occupation of Istanbul. Scores of nationalist leaders were arrested, some by British troops in the lobby of the Ottoman Parliament, and were exiled to Malta. Those who had avoided arrest now began to steal away at night, making a long trek to Ankara, a remote town protected by the mountain fastness of central Anatolia and yet connected to the outside by railroads and telegraph lines. It was here that Kemal had meanwhile set up the center of Turkish resistance.

Kemal called for the establishment of a new parliament, the Grand National Assembly. This met in Ankara in April 1920 and declared that sovereignty belonged to the nation, as represented in the Assembly. Thus began a fierce struggle, not only against foreign occupation but also against the royalist government in Istanbul, although the nationalists still insisted that they were loyal to the sultan himself, whom they described as being under duress. The Treaty of Sèvres, imposed in July, reinforced nationalist resistance against the Allies and the Ottoman government that had accepted it.

The Kemalists' foremost concern was the Greeks, who advanced deep into Anatolia in 1920. In January of the following year Turkish forces commanded by General Ismet repelled the advance at the Battle of Inönü, and again at a second battle of Inönü in March. But a renewed Greek offensive in July forced the Turks to retreat almost to Ankara. After the Grand National Assembly granted him full dictatorial powers, Kemal took personal command of the army. He proceeded to mobilize the people and resources of the country, requisitioning 40 percent of the cloth, food, and other articles. Even Turkish women were organized to bring supplies by donkey cart or on their backs over mountains to the front lines.

Kemal's forces stood against the advancing Greeks at the Battle of the Sakarya River in August and September. After twenty-two days of unceasing ferocity over a sixty-mile front, possibly the longest pitched battle that had ever been fought and certainly one of the most decisive encounters between the Islamic world and Europe, the Greeks finally fell back. The tide had turned. The Greeks were not conclusively defeated, but the Turkish nationalist movement gained new momentum. Kemal gained the rank of field marshal and the title of ghazi, warrior for Islam (implicitly against Christendom). Then a final Turkish offensive in August 1922 drove the Greeks to the sea. Turkish forces entered Smyrna in September, as the enemy troops and thousands of Greek civilians boarded British warships. The Greek section of Smyrna, longtime center of Greek Anatolia, was soon in flames, as though to symbolize the final victory of the Islamic East in the Anatolian Penisula.

Meanwhile, the Turkish nationalists approached other European powers. After defeating small French forces in eastern Anatolia in 1920, Kemal reached an agreement with France, who had begun to see the Turkish nationalists as a lever against its British rivals, considered to be the real power behind the Greeks. The

French had also decided to limit their ambitions to Syria. They withdrew from Anatolia and even agreed to a modification of the Turko-Syrian border in Turkey's favor. Thousands of Armenians, who had collaborated with the French occupiers, fled to the sanctuary of Arab lands. Similarly, the Italians, who resented the Allies' awarding part of southwestern Anatolia to Greece, decided to undermine Anglo-Greek designs by cooperating with the Turks and withdrawing from Anatolia. Both the Italians and the French settled for minor economic concessions. This freed Turkish troops to face the Greeks, and they also acquired large stores of military equipment left behind by the French. A Soviet and Turkish pincers movement defeated the Armenians in northeast Anatolia and the Transcaucasus in 1920, just as President Wilson futilely awarded a large area of eastern Anatolia to the Armenians. Although Kemal was anti-Communist, he joined forces with the Soviets, who were also resisting an Allied invasion, and Soviet weapons and other aid gave the Turks another advantage. The Treaty of Moscow, which Ankara and the Soviets concluded in 1921, left Kars and Ardahan, both of which had been under Russian rule from 1878 to 1917, in Turkish hands.

When, following the Greek defeat in Anatolia, the Turkish nationalists turned toward Istanbul and European Turkey, only the British stood in their way. British Prime Minister Lloyd George's government had staked its life on support for the Greeks against what he called the "Asiatic barbarians." Lloyd George saw this not only as an expression of European Christian solidarity but also envisaged an expansionist Greece as a useful protégé on Britain's route to India. But the other Allies backed down. After a short confrontation, during which a war between Britain and Turkey (and possibly the USSR) seemed imminent, the British government lost the backing of a war-weary public and also gave in to the Turks. The Armistice of Mudanya allowed the Turks to cross the Straits into Europe and recognized their sovereignty over Istanbul. Lloyd George's resignation was final proof that the Turks had shaken the greatest imperial power of the West and broken the pattern of Europeans' manipulating the East with impunity.

A new Peace Conference met at Lausanne, Switzerland, in November 1922. Months of negotiations ensued, during which General Ismet, now the Turkish prime minister, relentlessly pursued every point, even using his hearing deficiency to wear away the patience of the Allied negotiators. The Treaty of Lausanne, concluded in July 1923, enabled Turkey to achieve essentially the objectives spelled out in its National Pact. Foreign occupation would end. Turkey regained control over the Straits, although with provisions for demilitarization and free access by other nations. It was freed from all the other restrictions, including the Capitulations, that the Sèvres Treaty had imposed. Even the loss of the Arab provinces, to which the nationalists had been reconciled from the start, was an advantage in that it helped to create a homogeneous Turkish nation. A separate Greco-Turkish agreement further enhanced this homogeneity, though at the cruel price of uprooting people from their ancestral homelands. It provided for an exchange of population, with over a million Greeks in Turkey exchanged for almost half a million Turks living in Greece. Rising from utter defeat, the Turks had snatched their emancipation from Western imperialism.

THE EGYPTIAN REVOLUTION OF 1919
AND FORMAL INDEPENDENCE

Egyptians also resisted Western control, though with less clear-cut success than Turkey. Egypt's relative calm during the First World War could not last. Its people were bitter over the imposition of a British Protectorate in 1914. The presence of thousands of soldiers from all parts of the British Empire, restrictions on civil liberties, wartime shortages, inflation, and forced peasant labor in the war zones all combined to unite the country against colonial domination.

On November 13, 1918, only two days after the Armistice in Europe, a self-appointed three-man nationalist delegation met with Sir Reginald Wingate, the British high commissioner. The delegation (soon generally known by the Arabic word, *wafd*) asked for an end to the Protectorate and to martial law. Furthermore, the Wafd requested permission to travel to London to present its demands to the British government. Thus began a new phase in Egypt's struggle for independence and the emergence of the Wafd as the leading political party in this national struggle during the next three decades.

The leader of the Wafd was Sa'd Zaghlul, often regarded as the "father of the Egyptians." The son of a small landowner and mayor of a village in the Egyptian Delta, he studied in traditional religious schools and al-Azhar, where he became a disciple of Afghani and Abduh. He later studied at the French School of Law, adding a modern Western-style education to his traditional, Eastern one. As a collaborator with the British in Egypt, he was highly regarded by Lord Cromer, the British Agent, who had him named Minister of Education in 1906. In this and other positions, Zaghlul worked for legal and educational modernization rather than for independence. But as Britain's rule in Egypt became more blatant during World War I, Zaghlul emerged as the nationalist leader.

The movement that Zaghlul led was a liberal, secular, purely Egyptian nationalism. It wanted Egypt's independence under a representative government, with the monarch's powers curtailed and with civil liberties guaranteed for the people. While the old Patriotic party, now in decline, had diluted its Egyptian nationalism with pan-Islamic solidarity, the Wafd's object of loyalty was unambiguously Egypt.

Furthermore, there was no idea of Egypt's being part of a wider Arab nation. The Arab nationalist movement had grown up under fundamentally different circumstances. While Egyptians, resentful of British rule, had sometimes supported the Ottoman sultan-caliph (without actually wanting to be under his control) before the First World War and had seen the Ottoman Empire as a potential safeguard against British colonialism, the Asian Arab nationalists had allied themselves with Britain during the war in order to throw off the Turkish yoke. To many Egyptians, the Arab nationalists were traitors to Islam. And, since the Egyptians typically considered themselves more advanced than the Fertile Crescent Arabs, not to mention those of Arabia, the Allies' promises of independence for Arab Asia, while Egypt had just become a Protectorate, were galling.

The only country outside Egypt that the Wafd wanted to control was the Sudan, which Egyptians had long considered to be an integral part of their country. Nationalist slogans thus called not only for the evacuation of the British from Egypt but also for the unity of the Nile Valley.

To get back to November 1918, the British refused to reconsider the Protectorate or even to permit Zaghlul and his colleagues to go to London. In turn, Zaghlul organized a nationwide movement to collect funds and gathered hundreds of thousands of signatures on petitions designating the Wafd as the representative of the Egyptian people. He sought support from foreign representatives in Egypt, appealed to President Wilson, and continued to denounce the Protectorate. Prime Minister Husayn Rushdi, though willing to work with the British, had also wanted to head a delegation to London to request greater independence. But by this time Zaghlul had become so unmistakably the spokesman for the Egyptians that, when Rushdi and his colleague, Adli Yakan, got permission to go, they refused to make the trip without him. They knew that the Egyptian people would think that they were undercutting the authentic national movement and would reject any partial settlement that they might obtain. Finally, on March 8, 1919, the British arrested Zaghlul and some other Wafdist leaders and deported them to Malta in the hope that their absence would calm Egypt.

The British were mistaken. Zaghlul's arrest enraged the Egyptians. There were strikes and student demonstrations in Cairo, and before long, disorder spread to the villages. Sabotage disrupted railroads and telegraph lines, and British soldiers were murdered. For a while most of the country lay outside effective British control. The movement was truly national, as Copts and Muslims, rich men and poor men, and even women marched in the streets to demonstrate their support for Zaghlul.

In the hope that a leading general might intimidate the Egyptians, the British government replaced Wingate with Allenby. But Allenby tried to appease the nationalists. Zaghlul was released. Free to go wherever he wished, he proceeded to Paris to put Egypt's cause before the Peace Conference. There he met bitter disappointment, as the victorious Allies, even Wilson, recognized the Protectorate. Turbulence in Egypt continued, as Egyptians considered Zaghlul's release a sign of further British concessions.

Britain appointed a commission of inquiry, headed by Lord Milner, to study the situation in Egypt and to make recommendations on new arrangements, but only within the scope of the existing Protectorate, which was what the Egyptians had been demonstrating against. The Wafd boycotted the Milner Commission, which arrived in December 1919, and nearly all Egyptians followed its lead. So impressed was the commission with the mood of the country that its report went beyond the mandate given to it. Milner recommended that the Protectorate be replaced by an Anglo-Egyptian treaty of alliance that would safeguard British interests. Zaghlul now entered into negotiations with the commission in London but could not reach an agreement. Then the Egyptian government sent a delegation to London, headed by Adli Yakan, who was now the prime minister. Adli, too, could not make the compromises demanded by the British, lest his government be denounced by the Wafd. As new riots broke out in Cairo, the British arrested Zaghlul again and sent him into exile.

Since Britain could not conclude a treaty, Allenby pressed his government into ending the Protectorate unilaterally. On February 28, 1922, he formally declared Egypt's independence from Britain. Sultan Fu'ad (who had succeeded to the throne in 1917) took the title of king, and a group of Egyptian legal experts began to draw up a liberal constitution. But the British reserved four matters for their own discretion: (1) the security of British communications; (2) the defense of Egypt against all foreign aggression; (3) the protection of foreign interests and of minorities; and (4) the Sudan. This was acceptable to subservient, pro-British politicians like Abd al-Khaliq Tharwat, now the prime minister, who had not really wanted complete independence but who had not dared to accept anything less. For many rich Egyptians, who feared that continued anti-British agitation would lead to a social revolution, Allenby's unilateral declaration was quite convenient. But to Egyptian nationalists, 1922 was only the first step toward real independence.

IRAN: A NEW DYNASTY

Meanwhile, the tide of European imperialism was also receding from Iran. The 1919 Anglo-Iranian Treaty had become increasingly repulsive to the Iranian people and to the Majlis, which would have to ratify it. As British public opinion became ever more hostile to foreign military involvements, London chose not to force its will on Iran and gradually withdrew its troops.

Instead, Britain quietly worked to set up a new regime that could effectively govern Iran and preserve its independence from the USSR. General Riza Khan, who had gained command of the 15,000-man Cossack Division (formerly the Russian-officered Cossack Brigade), was ready to engineer a coup. A shrewd, if uncouth, young man of modest origin and scanty education, Riza ardently wanted to put an end to the anarchy, foreign penetration, and backwardness of his country. For this purpose, he formed an alliance with a leading journalist, Sayyid Ziya al-Din al-Tabataba'i, and proceeded, with some help from British troops, to move his forces to Tehran in February 1921. He took control of the government, becoming commander-in-chief of the army, with al-Tabataba'i as prime minister. Within three months, he squeezed al-Tabataba'i out of power and in 1923 became prime minister. Two years later, Riza Shah Pahlavi, as he subsequently was known, began a new dynasty, called the Pahlavis.

Meanwhile the USSR pulled out of Iran. A Soviet-Iranian Treaty of Friendship, already being negotiated before the 1921 coup, was soon concluded. Tehran recognized Moscow's right to send troops into Iran whenever a third power used its territory to plan an attack on the USSR. The Soviets formally repudiated all Russian privileges and concessions in Iran. The troops, from the Azarbayjan Soviet Socialist Republic, for which Moscow claimed no responsibility, withdrew from Iran's Gilan Province. Only then did Tehran ratify the Soviet-Iranian Treaty. It is unclear why the Soviets renounced their foothold in Gilan. Perhaps they were there primarily to counter British control, and after the British withdrew the USSR had no reason to stay. There may have been disagreement in Moscow all along on whether to control Gilan at the expense of antagonizing Iran as a whole.

With Soviet troops gone, Riza Khan's forces crushed the Jangali movement. Its leader, Kuchik Khan, who had broken with the Soviet forces during the fall of 1920 and had even fought against them, had joined forces with them again. When the Soviets withdrew, he fled into the mountains and died of exposure.

IRAQ, TRANSJORDAN, AND THE HASHIMITES

Iraq and Transjordan acquired limited self-government during the early 1920s. The end of the war had left Iraq under British military rule, with acting Civil Administrator Colonel A. T. Wilson (in the absence of Sir Percy Cox, the civil administrator, who was transferred to Iran in 1918) responsible to the military authorities. Wilson headed a largely Anglo-Indian administration and strongly opposed giving self-government to Iraq, as Iraqis became increasingly bitter against British rule. Finally, the tribes of the middle Euphrates rose in rebellion in June 1920, and the Shi'ite religious leaders proclaimed a *jihad*. Soon most of the country was out of Britain's control. The British managed to suppress the insurrection only at great expense. Cox now returned to his position in Baghdad. Seeing the need for some Iraqi participation in the government, he set up a Council of State, with limited power, headed by an Arab Iraqi.

The Hashimites, angry over Faysal's expulsion from Syria, also made trouble for the British. In November 1920 Amir Abdullah, heading a Hijazi force, arrived in southern Transjordan. Originally part of Faysal's Syrian kingdom, Transjordan had been included in the Palestine mandate. But the British established only loose control over the largely desert, tribal area. Abdullah threatened to use this territory as a springboard for an attack on the French in Syria.

Winston Churchill, now the colonial secretary, called together the leading British officials concerned with the Middle East to meet in Cairo in March 1921. The conference worked out a solution to the problems of Iraq and Transjordan. Faysal would become king of Iraq and Abdullah, amir (prince) of Transjordan. After obtaining the consent of notables in each country, plus popular approval in a carefully managed plebiscite in Iraq, these two sons of King Husayn of the Hijaz took their respective thrones. An Anglo-Iraqi Treaty of Alliance followed in 1922, but among other restrictions on independence, it provided that Iraq, which was still subject to the British mandate, would accept British advice on important matters. Transjordan, now a separate entity but still technically part of the Palestine mandate, was exempted from the area designated for a Jewish national home, a unilateral British action that angered many Zionists but was legitimized by the mandate document that the League officially adopted in 1922.

FURTHER STEPS TOWARD INDEPENDENCE

Several Middle Eastern countries gradually won more independence from European control during the late 1920s and the 1930s. The 1922 Anglo-Iraqi Treaty was slightly modified in 1926 and 1927. Another Anglo-Iraqi Treaty, in 1930, substituted a 25-year alliance for the mandate and gave Iraq formal independence. However, among other limiting provisions, the British kept two air bases in the country, the right of transit across Iraqi territory, and the exclusive right to provide military advisers. The treaty went into force in 1932, when Iraq was admitted to the League of Nations. But to increasing numbers of Arabs the Hashimite "Anglo-Arab" monarchies in both Iraq and Transjordan appeared to be mere client regimes dependent on London.

The development of Arab unity was slow. Iraq aspired to be an "Arab Prussia" to undo the largely artificial postwar division of the Arabic-speaking world. But Iraq's remote location and political instability were handicaps. Egypt was still preoccupied with its own nationalism, although by the late 1930s it had become more interested in Arab Asia and even other Muslim areas as young King Faruq, who succeeded his father in 1936, dreamed for a long time of becoming caliph. But apart from rudimentary separate nationalisms in other Arab countries (and the more deeply rooted local identity of Lebanon's Maronite Christians), pan-Arabism was also stymied by continuing French rule over Syria and distrust between the Sa'udi and Hashimite families.

Britain's limited grant of independence to Egypt in 1922, with its "four reserved points," did not satisfy the nationalist movement. Egyptians faced further humiliation in 1924, following the assassination in Cairo of Sir Lee Stack, the British governor-general of the Sudan. As British troops occupied the customs house in Alexandria, the Egyptian government bowed to British demands, including the withdrawal of Egyptian troops and civilian officials from the Sudan.

After several unsuccessful attempts to settle Anglo-Egyptian differences, the threat to both sides posed by the Italian invasion of Ethiopia in 1935 induced London and Cairo to compromise. The Anglo-Egyptian Treaty of 1936 officially put an end to the British occupation of Egypt and established an alliance between the two countries. But the treaty actually perpetuated the occupation on a more limited basis by letting Britain keep ten thousand troops in a specified Suez Canal Zone. Even then, British troops retained the right to stay in other parts of Egypt until the Egyptian government provided certain buildings and communications facilities for the Suez Canal Zone. Egypt also agreed to turn over all its means of communication to Britain in case of war. The treaty gave Britain the exclusive right to provide military advisers. The joint administration of the Sudan was confirmed, to be safe-guarded by both British and Egyptian troops. Britain renounced its responsibility for foreigners and minorities and agreed to support the termination of the Capitulations, which was accomplished by an international conference at Montreaux in 1937. Egypt became a member of the League of Nations in the same year.

With Riza Shah effectively controlling Iran and developing its economic and military capacity, Iranian independence gained increasing respect. The powers went along with the shah's termination of the Capitulations in 1928. To protect Iranian independence, he avoided borrowing money from abroad and restricted foreign ownership of land and businesses. In a further assertion of national pride, the shah decreed in 1935 that foreign governments must use the name Iran, the country's real name. Iranian postal officials were ordered to send back mail addressed to "Persia." As the worldwide depression led to declining royalties from the Anglo-Iranian Oil Company, the shah cancelled its concession in 1932 and managed to get a new one the next year, with increased royalties for Iran. The once-customary British and Russian control had become a thing of the past, although it would return in 1941. Yet in the 1930s Iran continued to suspect these powers of trying to under-mine its independence and sometimes picked quarrels with them. It was in search of an outside protector against Britain and the USSR that Iran turned to Nazi Germany, toward which it directed much of its trade during the 1930s. Riza Shah admired the apparent efficiency of Hitler's regime, and some Iranians were flattered to be re-garded by German racists as fellow "Aryans."

With its victory over Western imperialism by 1923, Turkey was the one Mid-dle Eastern country that no longer had reason to bear a grudge against the West. Even relations with Greece became normal. The only country whose expansionist policies threatened Turkey was Mussolini's Italy, causing Turkey to conclude a Bal-kan Entente with Greece, Rumania, and Yugoslavia in 1934. Fear of Italy was also one motivation for concluding the Sa'dabad Pact, a nonagression treaty signed by Turkey, Iran, Iraq, and Afghanistan in 1937.

Turkey pursued two territorial claims after 1923. The Treaty of Lausanne had temporarily left Mosul, a province inhabited largely by Kurds that Turkey was then unwilling to renounce, as part of British-mandated Iraq. After the League of Nations Council awarded Mosul permanently to Iraq in 1925, Turkey reacted by reviving its ties with the USSR, with which it concluded a Treaty of Friendship and Neutrality. This reaction proved temporary, for the Ankara government soon decided that it had too much to lose from a confrontation with London. In a treaty with Iraq and Britain, Turkey settled for 10 percent of the royalties on oil from the Mosul region over a twenty-five-year period. Later on, though, Turkey did obtain Alexandretta, previously the northwestern part of Syria, as will be explained later. Also, an inter-national conference meeting at Montreaux in 1936 replaced the Lausanne Straits Convention. Although a complicated set of rules continued to govern navigation through the Bosporus and Dardanelles, Turkey managed to get rid of several restric-tions, including the provision for demilitarization, which had meant that it could not defend a vital part of its own territory.

CONTINUED FRENCH RULE IN
SYRIA AND LEBANON

Syria and Lebanon, which together came to be called the "Levant States" during the period of French rule, faced frustration in their attempts to gain independence. French colonial policy usually allowed little self-government, and the Levant States were no exception. Martial law prevailed much of the time. An attempt was made, particularly through the educational system, to perpetuate French at the expense of the Arabic language and culture. The separation of Palestine and Transjordan from the rest of geographic Syria had left a truncated country, and the French further divided Syria. To be sure, predominantly Maronite Mount Lebanon wanted France to protect its long-standing autonomy against Muslim domination. But France increased Lebanon's territory, at Syria's expense, to form a Greater Lebanon containing large numbers of Sunni and Shi'ite Muslims and non-Maronite Christians. This act antagonized the Syrians and many non-Maronite Lebanese and laid the basis for future turmoil.

The French even divided up what was left of Syria into states of Damascus and Aleppo, which were reunited to form the State of Syria in 1925. They established separatist governments for the predominantly Alawite (a heterodox offshoot of Twelver Shi'ite Islam) district of Latakia and for the mainly Druze (another Shi'ite offshoot) area near Transjordan. The partly Turkish region of Alexandretta also obtained a separate government. Thus, in a classic policy of divide-and-rule, the French played off one religious and ethnic minority against another to facilitate colonial control.

Syria, for most of the time, was tense and hostile to French rule. Beginning with a Druze uprising, a general revolt spread over the country in 1925. Harsh suppression followed, including two bombardments of Damascus.

Constitutional development was slow. A constitution for Lebanon, providing limited self-government, went into effect in 1926. A Syrian Chamber of Deputies, elected in 1928, also drew up a constitution. The French first rejected the proposed document because it refused to accept the mandate or the separation of any part of geographic Syria from the country but then unilaterally enacted it after omitting the objectionable provisions.

A new sympathy for nationalism in the Levant States emerged in Paris when the leftist Popular Front government took power in 1936. The fear of Italian imperialism also evoked a spirit of compromise. France proceeded to conclude treaties, similar to the 1930 Anglo-Iraqi Treaty, with both Lebanon and Syria, providing for their independence within three years. The Alawite and Druze areas were to be united with Syria. The Lebanese and Syrian Chambers of Deputies approved the treaties, but France, with a new government inpower, changed its mind. By 1939, it had abandoned the treaties entirely and even suspended the Syrian constitution.

Meanwhile, France acceded in 1937 to Turkish demands to give increasing autonomy to Alexandretta. Elections in the province followed in 1938, after Turkish troops had been allowed to share in the maintenance of order. Although about 60 percent of Alexandretta's population was Arab and presumably pro-Syrian, the Turks won control. With another war imminent and with France anxious to win Ankara to its side, France ceded Alexandretta to Turkey in 1939, providing a new and lasting grievance for Syria and the Arabs.

CONFLICT IN PALESTINE

Palestine had not achieved even partial independence by 1939. Moreover, the ethnic makeup of the country was changing as a result of Britain's commitment to building a Jewish national home. During most of the 1920s, the flow of Jewish immigrants from Europe into Palestine was a mere trickle. In 1931 the Jews still formed only 17 percent of Palestine's population. But the rise of Hitler in Germany in 1933 created a new situation, as German Jews were deprived of their civil rights, their professions, and often their property. Jews throughout Europe were fearful. Few countries were willing to open their doors to large numbers of Jewish refugees from Nazi persecution. The Zionists, for their part, wanted to encourage Jewish immigration to Palestine and discouraged Jews from going elsewhere. In one year, 1935, more than 66,000 Jews, still mainly from eastern Europe, entered Palestine. The Arab population was also rapidly increasing, mainly because of a high birth rate. By 1939 the country's population of one and a half million was almost one-third Jewish.

From the start, the British were ready to offer rudimentary self-government, but on terms that seemed totally inadequate to the Arab Palestinians. In 1922 the mandatory government proposed the establishment of a Legislative Council, consisting of two Christians, two Jews, eight Muslims, and ten British governmental officials. This plan would have put ten Arabs and two Jews on the Council, and the Christian Arab Palestinians were no less anti-Zionist than the Muslims. But the Arabs rejected the plan, pointing out that it would give the supporters of the Balfour Declaration, the Jews and the British, a permanent majority. The plan would also have required Arab Palestinians to acquiesce in the concept of a Jewish national home, which they understood to mean an eventual Jewish state. The Jews were unenthusiastic about any development of representative government for Palestine as a whole while they were still a small minority. But the Jewish community (the Yishuv) adroitly indicated its acceptance of the British plan, seemingly confident that it would be rejected by the Arabs and not be implemented. Many Arab Palestinians later believed that their refusal to accept a tactical compromise, which might have eventually given them a greater voice in their country's affairs, had been a mistake. Pointing to the strength of the Zionists and the existence of an international climate favorable to settler societies and colonial rule, others deny that greater moderation would have helped the Arab cause.

The Yishuv had its own political institutions. First of all, there was the World Zionist Organization, to which the British gave responsibility in matters relating to the "ingathering" and the settlement of Jews. In 1929 a Jewish Agency for Palestine was set up to take over these functions. The creation of the Jewish

Agency, headed by the president of the Zionist Organization, was intended to provide representation for "non-Zionist" Jews, who nevertheless could be counted on to support the development of the national home. The Jewish Agency, with diminishing "non-Zionist" representation, soon became virtually indistinguishable from the Zionist Organization. It even maintained a clandestine military force, the Haganah. In addition, the Yishuv established an Elected Assembly, which chose a National Council and an Executive to govern the community between sessions. Another vital organization was the General Confederation of Trade Unions, or Histadrut, which was closely linked with the Elective Assembly, because both institutions were dominated by the Mapai (Workers') party. The Histadrut not only represented workers' interests but also ran a health service, a newspaper, schools, and business enterprises.

The British proposed the establishment of an Arab Agency in 1923. But the Arabs refused the offer, indignant at the suggestion that they, who still made up nearly 90 percent of the population, could be treated as merely one of the two Palestinian communities. Each Arab religious group did, however, retain control over its strictly religious affairs, a carry-over of the Ottoman millet system. Thus the Supreme Islamic Council supervised Sunni Muslim schools, law courts, mosques, and religious endowments.

The Palestinian Arabs were not simply against foreign rule. Immigration on such a large scale by a group of people who did not identify with the existing population of the country would have caused disturbances anywhere. In this case, the hostility was compounded by the cultural and political differences between the newcomers, almost all of whom were Europeans, and the indigenous Arab population. The Arabs feared that they would become a minority if Jewish immigration continued. Besides, they believed that the creation of a Jewish state would require their own expulsion from Palestine.

The acquisition of land by the Zionists added another dimension to the struggle for Palestine. The Arab Palestinian peasants, like rural people everywhere, had a deep emotional attachment to the land they tilled, aside from economic dependence on it, but they found themselves without any say in its disposition. Until the nineteenth century, the title to land had been vested in the state, although the peasants had customary rights to it and considered it theirs. The Ottoman Empire, in trying to westernize its legal system, had established private titles to land, but the peasants feared that land registration would enable the government to tax them more heavily and conscript more of their sons for military service. Many peasants realized that a powerful and wealthy man would not likely be overtaxed, and so they registered their land in the name of some local notable, thereby enhancing his wealth and power. In other cases, peasants did nothing to obtain land titles, which wealthy persons later managed to buy cheaply. Hence even before the rise of political Zionism, a situation developed that would later facilitate Zionist objectives.

The World Zionist Organization had set up a Jewish National Fund to purchase land in Palestine. One of the goals of the Zionists was to create a "new Jewish man," a worker or, better still, a farmer, unlike the urban middle class Jews of eastern Europe. Although most of the European Jewish immigrants settled in cities, Zionism placed an almost mystical emphasis on establishing ties to the land. Collective Jewish agricultural settlements, the Kibbutzim (singular: Kibbutz), with their total sharing of land and other property, and the Moshavim (singular: Moshav), which permitted greater private ownership, developed in Palestine. Arab landowners, particularly those who lived in Damascus and Beirut and found the new political borders inconvenient, were tempted to sell, and many did. Although the Zionists still had bought only about 6 percent of the land by 1948, this land tended to be in the most fertile areas.

As Zionists acquired land, many Arab peasants were uprooted. Arabs could not even stay on the land as tenants or hired labor, since the Jewish National Fund forbade the use of non-Jewish labor (a rule that was sometimes violated in practice). At least in part, this was because the Zionists hoped to create a totally Jewish society, but socialists explained it in terms of opposing the exploitation of cheap labor. In this way, Jewish settlement did not entirely fit the pattern of most other Western settler societies in Africa and Asia, which was based on cheap "native" labor, but the consequences for the Arab Palestinian peasants were even more severe. The fund's rules provided that the land it purchased must remain the inalienable property of the Jewish people. Once Arab-owned land was sold to Zionists, the process was irreversible. Although the fund, with its available capital and Western technical skills, developed much marshland and desert, it also took possession of lush Arab farmland in the Vale of Esdraelon and eastern Galilee. On one occasion, in 1921, the Sursuk family of Beirut sold 50,000 acres, comprising twenty-two Arab villages, to the fund.

Anti-Zionist violence in Palestine became endemic. There were Arab riots in 1920 and 1921. Then in 1929 an incident arising from the construction of a temporary screen by Jews at the Wailing Wall (the western remnant of Herod's temple, which is also a part of the Haram al-Sharif or Noble Sactuary, an Islamic holy area) got out of hand, leaving 472 Jews and 268 Arabs dead.

As Jewish immigration increased, a large-scale Arab rebellion broke out in 1936 against the British and the Zionists, turning into a three-year civil war. All Arab Palestinian factions now united to form a Higher Arab Committee led by the fiery and intransigent mufti of Jerusalem (and president of the Higher Islamic Council), Hajj Amin al-Husayni, who had emerged as the leader of the struggle against the British and the Zionists during the 1920s. The Husayni family had been dominant in Jerusalem since Ottoman times. Its main rival, the Nashashibi family, was much more willing to work with the British, in the hope of winning them over from the Zionist side, but it was less influential. Demanding an end to Jewish immigration and land transfers and the establishment of an independent Palestine, the Arabs declared a general strike and an economic boycott of the Yishuv. Emotions flared throughout the Arab world in sympathy with the Arab Palestinians. It was a Lebanese, Fawzi al-Qawuqji, who led the anti-British and anti-Zionist guerrilla campaign in northern Palestine.

The British found themselves in an impossible situation. The mandate had committed them to virtually irreconcilable principles, and their policies wavered. Their attempt to be impartial antagonized both Zionists and Arabs. Colonial Secretary Winston Churchill issued a White Paper in 1922 that reiterated British support for Zionism but reassured Arabs that this would not mean their subordination to the Zionist movement. He stated that the Jewish National Home did not mean a Jewish state and that immigration would be limited by Palestine's "economic absorptive capacity." Following the reports of two British commissions in 1930, the Passfield White Paper announced that government-owned lands would be set aside for landless Arab peasants, not for Jewish immigrants, and that Arab unemployment would henceforth be considered in determining economic absorptive capacity. But following strong protests from Zionists in Britain, Prime Minister Ramsey MacDonald issued a statement that essentially nullified the Passfield White Paper.

Another commission, sent to Palestine in 1936, concluded that conflict between the "predominantly Asiatic" Arabs and the "predominantly European" Zionists was "irrepressible" and proposed a plan for partition: Palestine would be divided into an Arab and a Jewish state, with a smaller international area, including Jerusalem. Some Zionists reluctantly accepted the concept of partition, but the Twentieth Zionist Congress rejected this particular proposal in 1937. The Arabs refused the plan outright, pointing out that almost half the inhabitants of the proposed "Jewish state" were Arabs and that most of the land was Arab-owned. They also objected to the commission's proposal that the bulk of the Arab population be removed from the Jewish state, by force if necessary, and they believed that the influx of Jewish refugees from Europe would lead to further Zionist expansion.

London now decided to make important concessions to Arab Palestinian nationalism. Further attempts to work out a settlement, including three alternate partition plans proposed by another British commission in 1938 and an Arab-Jewish conference in London in Feburary 1939, had all come to naught. The Arab rebellion was intensifying, while gathering war clouds in Europe made pacification in Palestine imperative. To many British leaders, it also seemed foolhardy to alienate Egypt and Iraq, two Arab states where Britain had strategic interests. A White Paper of May 1939 stipulated that Jewish immigration to Palestine would be limited to 75,000 during the next five years and that further immigration would depend on Arab consent. Land transfers to Jews would be forbidden in some areas and limited in others. After ten years, unless circumstances required postponement, Palestine would obtain its independence, with certain safeguards for the Holy Places, British interests, and the protection of the various communities, but presumably as a predominantly Arab state with a Jewish minority. Although recent studies refute this interpretation (which insinuates that Arab demands were unjust), the Zionists saw the White Paper as a case of appeasement comparable to Munich and a betrayal of the Balfour Declaration, just at a time when the Jews of Europe were in mortal peril. Nor did it satisfy the Arab Palestinians, whose leaders, including Hajj Amin, were in exile. But although it did not guarantee their independence, it gave some of them hope that the British commitment to Zionism was weakening and that the European Jewish tide would finally recede.

OUTRIGHT WESTERNIZATION IN TURKEY

After leading Turkey to victory over European imperialism, the Ghazi Mustafa Kemal proceeded to implement a drastic "Herodian" program of westernization. In his view, Western civilization was the only one that mattered. He dismissed Islamic civilization as an amalgam of "age-old rotten mentalities," inferior in every way, not just technically, to the West. As a Turkish nationalist he also saw Islamic civilization as something foreign, borrowed from the Arabs, which should now be cast off. Unlike later Middle Eastern nationalists, he did not even bother to clothe westernization in the more acceptable guise of modernization.

Kemal aspired to adopt Western civilization as a whole; he believed that it could not be acquired piecemeal. This outlook was heavily influenced by the writings of the Turkish nationalist sociologist, Ziya Gökalp, who had distinguished between culture, defined as the nonmaterial aspects of life, and civilization, the material aspects. Gökalp, influenced by the failure of earlier reformers to stem the decline of the Ottoman Empire, advocated the adoption of Western civilization. While he wanted the Turkish people to have their own culture, he rejected the one they then had, which he saw as Arab and foreign, in favor of his romantic vision of a pre-Islamic Turkish culture. He believed that this culture had in many ways been like that of the modern West. To advocate westernization in such areas as emancipating women or secularizing society was really to seek a return to the authentic Turkish culture.

In particular, Kemal believed that the ills of the Islamic world were a result of the influence of religion. Himself an agnostic, he rejected religious discipline and indulged in sexual promiscuity and drunkenness, which he sometimes flaunted to show the people his contempt for the Islamic prohibition of alcohol. He was apparently not hostile to Islam as such or to religion in general, and he at least did not contemplate turning his people into non-Muslims. What he opposed was religious influence on society and the brakes it allegedly put on progress. But the distinction was not clear to many Turkish—let alone non-Turkish—Muslims.

Kemal's first priority was to abolish theocratic institutions. This actually began with the 1919 National Pact's attribution of sovereignty to the people, which fundamentally contradicted the Islamic concept of the sovereignty of God, working through His viceroy on Earth, the caliph. Despite his protests to the contrary, Kemal had long awaited the opportunity to abolish the sultanate and caliphate. When the Allies invited representatives of both the nationalists and the sultan to the Lausanne Conference, Kemal took advantage of the occasion to push the abolition of the sultanate through the Grand National Assembly. It was not until the following year that he dared to prod the Assembly into formally declaring the establishment of a republic, a word that to Muslims still carried an "infidel" ring. When Sultan Mehmed VI was exiled, he was succeeded in the role of caliph by Abd al-Majid II. Then in 1924 the Assembly also abolished the caliphate and other theocratic offices, including that of shaykh al-Islam. The religious schools and law courts were also abolished, along with the Ministry of *Waqfs* (religious endowments). In 1928 the reference to Islam as the state religion was deleted from the Constitution.

The Kemalist program of secularization meant a complete revamping of the legal system along Western lines. Previous Ottoman attempts to modernize law had led to the adoption of European-style codes of secular law, partly in substance and partly in form, replacing the immutable God-given law. But the rules of personal status, relating to marriage, divorce, inheritance, and religious endowments, had remained Islamic. The only change in the law of personal status had been the Ottoman Family Law of 1917, which had introduced a few reforms. Kemal rejected any continuation of this gradualist approach. Instead, the Grand National Assembly completely westernized Turkish law by adopting European codes in all fields, including personal status. Among other changes, polygamy became illegal, and men could no longer arbitrarily repudiate their wives, while women acquired equal rights in the areas of divorce, child custody, and inheritance.

The Kemalist period witnessed a whole series of symbolic changes. To be like Europe, Turkey adopted Sunday (and Saturday afternoon) as a weekly holiday (called the *vikend*). Turkish writing took on a ''Western'' appearance as Arabic letters were replaced by a slightly modified form of the Latin alphabet. The Qur'an was translated into Turkish, and the call to prayer—which had always been in Arabic throughout the Muslim world—now had to be recited in Turkish. While Middle Eastern men had increasingly adopted Western clothing, they had always kept their traditional headgear. A turban, skullcap, or fez permitted the forehead to touch the floor during prostrations for prayer. For a Muslim to put on a hat with a brim was virtually a symbol of apostasy. Yet Kemal wore such a hat publicly in 1925, and before the gasps ceased, the Assembly outlawed the fez and made wearing hats with brims compulsory. Kemal attempted to discourage women from wearing veils, but stopped short of actually forbidding them. The ''international'' (Gregorian) calendar replaced the Islamic one. Every Turk was required by law to adopt a family name, something that was still uncommon in the Islamic world. The Assembly awarded the surname Atatürk (''Father of the Turks'') to Kemal. General Ismet, his eventual successor, took the name Inönü in commemoration of his victories over the Greeks in 1921. Dervish orders, long an important facet of Turkish life, were outlawed.

Some of Kemal Atatürk's reforms seemed comical to Westerners. Some Muslims were offended by what seemed to them his superficial aping of ''infidel'' ways. To Kemal, however, these changes signified Turkey's entrance into the Western world and removed the marks of being Oriental that had prevented its acceptance as a modern country. Internalizing the ethnocentrism of the West, he saw these discarded symbols of his own civilization as stigmas of barbarism. As a Turkish nationalist he rationalized that the Islamic influences that he was abolishing were foreign.

In addition, it was possible to show, at times perhaps by forcing the argument, that many of the reforms would have practical benefits for Turkey. For example, the Arabic alphabet is difficult and time-consuming to learn, even for Arabs. It is much harder for peoples whose languages are unrelated to Arabic. The Arabic letters did not even fit the sounds of the Turkish language. Having Sunday as a day of rest would facilitate commerce and communication with Europe. Kemal even pointed out that the fez required more material than the hat and was too expensive for a poor country. But these were rationalizations, not fundamental reasons, for such drastic changes.

Kemalism included an intense Turkish nationalism that adopted some far-fetched versions of history. Paralleling nationalists in other countries, the Kemalists wanted to purify Turkish, insofar as possible, of words of Arabic and Persian origin, as well as to change foreign place names, like Constantinople (to Istanbul), Angora (to Ankara), and Smyrna (to Izmir). When they found that some words had no Turkish equivalents, European (mainly French) words had to be substituted. To justify such borrowing, Kemal—and Turkish schoolbooks—propounded a pseudoscientific theory that all languages were derived from Turkish and consequently that these adopted European words were really Turkish. According to this "sun-language" theory, all past civilizations were the result of Turkish immigration from Central Asia to the Eurasian periphery. Any cultural borrowing could thus be justified as a resumption of some primordially Turkish trait.

Although Kemal's version of Turkish nationalism had an ethnic basis, it lost its former pan-Turkish aspect. It was a devotion to the "Anatolian Homeland," that is, the territory essentially within the existing boundaries, which had no meaning historically. But by claiming that ancient Anatolian peoples, particularly the Hittites, were also Turks, the Turkish nationalist could annex the whole history of Anatolia to that of his people and thus foster a new territorial identity. Even the one significant linguistic and ethnic minority, the Kurds of eastern Anatolia, were euphemistically called "mountain Turks."

The formal structure of government, according to the Constitution of 1924, was based on the model of European parliamentary democracy. A basic slogan of Kemalism was "populism," which made "the people" the theoretical source of authority. Populism was sometimes given more specific meanings, such as opposition to economic privilege, which the regime actually did little to combat. In reality, the commitment to Westernization was matched by suspicion of the traditionalistic masses, and Turkey's government was an authoritarian single-party system dominated by Kemal. The aura he had obtained as the leader of Turkey's liberation, in addition to his personal persuasiveness or charisma, enabled him to rule virtually as he wished. He was not only the president of the Republic but also the leader of the People's Republican party, the real center of power, which was essentially a continuation of the League for the Defense of Rights under a new name. He was able to select the prime minister, usually Ismet Inönü.

Kemel's dictatorship was generally not harsh. Sometimes vigorous debates took place within the party and the Assembly. And Kemal's ideal form of government was liberal democracy, for which he viewed his period of tutelage as paving the way. On two occasions, in 1925 and 1930, he allowed opposition parties to form. But each time dissent turned into disorder. Conservative, antisecularist forces still represented the dominant sentiment within Turkey and threatened to undo Kemalist reforms by co-opting any opposition party. Kemal then had to restore single-party government.

A final principle of Kemalist Turkey was etatism (statism, meaning government control over the economy). Kemal instituted a series of government plans, state banks to promote industrial development, state-owned industries (including government monopolies in some fields), and high protective tariffs. Communist and fascist practices may have influenced him to move in this direction, but practical considerations were more important. Etatism seemed to fill the vacuum left by the departure of the Greeks and the destruction of the Armenians, who had predominated in commerce and industry. Private capital was scarce. The world depression intensified the emphasis on etatism, which the People's Republican party adopted as one of the six principles of Kemalism in 1931, along with nationalism, revolutionism, secularism, populism, and republicanism.

When President Kemal Atatürk died in 1938, he left a deeply changed country. Yet he had not transformed it into a modern nation, certainly not a Western one. The villagers, particularly in eastern Turkey, were still traditional Middle Easterners. The secularizing reforms were not understood and were evaded whenever possible. Marriages in the villages continued to be conducted without regard to the new law, and again and again the Assembly retroactively legalized such unions and legitimized their offspring. When one political leader unintentionally raised his brimmed hat at a meeting, the people in the crowd mistook the act as defiance against westernization and began throwing their own hats to the ground. If economic advances had pushed Turkey slightly ahead of most of the Middle East, it remained clearly an underdeveloped country by Western standards.

It is ironic that, despite Kemal's emphasis on secularism and his rejection of pan-Islam or any special ties with the Islamic world, the Turkish national identity remains more closely bound to Islam than any other Middle Eastern nationalism. While general usage recognizes the existence of Christian Arabs, most Turks could not conceive of a "Christian Turk," except in the legal sense. Such a person is popularly called a "non-Turkish Turk." At the time of the exchange of populations with Greece during the early 1920s, religion was the criterion for distinguishing between the two peoples, even in the case of Turkish-speaking Christians and Greek-speaking Muslims. Religion never ceased being an important touchstone for Turkish nationality.

EMULATION OF KEMALISM IN IRAN

With the example of Atatürk in mind, Riza Shah attempted to westernize Iran, but with less success. First, whereas Turkey's geographical position had long exposed it to Europe, there were fewer beginnings of westernization in Iran. Second, lacking the aura of heroism that Atatürk had gained from his triumph over European imperialism, Riza Shah was less able to impose unpopular reforms on a conservative population. In addition, the shah's lack of education or exposure to the West hardly prepared him to be a Persian Atatürk. Nor did the political structure he established facilitate changes in Iran similar to those effected by the Turkish government.

At first, Riza planned to declare Iran a republic. But this evoked so much furor among the *ulama*, who associated a republic with Kemalism, that he backed down and opted to start a new dynasty. As the new shah, he gave lip service to the 1906 Constitution but assumed the role of an autocrat. He became increasingly authoritarian and paranoid. His closest associates were in frequent danger of arrest or murder by his agents. The only organ somewhat analogous to Atatürk's People's Republican party was the Society to Guide Public Opinion, a propaganda organization inspired by Nazi and fascist models. Established in 1939, it might have developed into an authoritarian party had Riza Shah remained in power.

Riza Shah devoted great effort to reviving a strong Iran that could resist foreign control. The tribes, who had long defied the government in Tehran, were crushed by 1925, as were subsequent tribal revolts. The government forcibly settled some tribes, an action that turned them from proud warriors and herders into poor and dispirited peasants. But at last there was an effective central government. And Riza Shah created a national army, starting conscription as early as 1925. The army, almost 400,000 strong by 1941, was an awesome means for controlling the country, though too poorly armed to ward off an invasion by Britain and the USSR.

Furthermore, the new regime attempted to modernize Iran. Aside from the roads and railroads built by the British during World War I, the country still had a primitive communications system when Riza Shah seized power. One of his greatest achievements was the construction of a Trans-Iranian Railway between 1927 and 1938, more impressive because the Iranian government refused to finance it with foreign loans but raised the necessary funds from taxes on sugar and tea, two staples in the diet of even the poorest Iranians. By 1941 Iran also had 15,000 miles of new roads. Government monopolies established factories for producing textiles, sugar, and cement, and the construction of a steel mill began in 1929. A modern school system started to develop, at least in the cities and towns. But little was done to change drab village life or to develop agriculture.

There was no fundamental transformation of Iranian society under Riza Shah's rule. Very little was done to improve the economic conditions of the masses. While much of the old aristocracy declined, Riza Shah's sale of state lands led to the growth of a new landlord class. The tax that he imposed on staples weighed heavily on the poor, and few of them, especially the humiliated, impoverished, and embittered ex-nomads, had any admiration for him.

Riza Shah emulated Atatürk's attacks on religious influence. Since there had been virtually no prior westernization of law in Iran, the government began in 1928 by instituting a new civil code, based largely on French law except in matters of personal status. Reform in family law followed, including a 1931 statue permitting women to begin divorce proceedings. In another effort to break with tradition, European-style hats were required in 1935, following an earlier attempt to replace traditional Islamic headgear with a new "Pahlavi hat." Iranians were required to wear Western-style clothes. Riza Shah further shocked traditionalists when he gave a tea and ordered officials to bring their wives. In 1936 he outdid Atatürk by out-lawing the veiling of women in public. Women who could not bear to expose their faces had no choice but to stay at home. By adopting the name "Pahlavi," the name of an ancient form of the Persian language, for the dynasty that he founded, Riza Shah stressed his country's ties with pre-Islamic Iran rather than with the Islamic World.

THE ZEALOT APPROACH:
THE ARABIAN PENINSULA

The Arabian Peninsula had long been the area of the Middle East least affected by the modern world. As Westernization and secularization proceeded elsewhere in the Middle East, Arabia actually reinforced the Islamic character of its society. In Toynbeean terms, this was the "Zealot" approach to an encroaching civilization.

The puritanical Wahhabi movement that had been identified with the Sa'udi amirs of Najd since the eighteenth century did not merely stand for traditional Islam against westernization. It insisted on returning to its own version of pristine Islam, uncorrupted by centuries of accretions of non-Islamic practices. To these unitarians, as they called themselves, traditional reverence for saints and even the marking of graves were anathema, and less strict Muslims were really idolaters. The Wahhabis rejected such generally accepted practices as wearing silk, shaving beards, and smoking tobacco. They denounced the laxity of Muslims who drank alcohol or ac-cepted westernized, non-Islamic systems of law, which, in late Ottoman times, had even penetrated the Hijaz. After restoring Sa'udi power in Najd in 1902, ibn-Sa'ud gave renewed impetus to Wahhabism. By creating agricultural settlements he trans-formed bedouins, who had generally taken religion lightly, into *Ikhwan* (brethren) whose dedication to Wahhabi doctrine had priority over tribal ties and who fanatic-ally fought for their faith.

King Husayn of the Hijaz had become stubborn and unrealistic in his later years, and this helped to bring about his fall from power. His claim to being "king of the Arab Countries" had antagonized other Arab rulers in the peninsula, espe-cially ibn-Sa'ud, whose Wahhabi followers considered his rule over the Holy Places a sacrilege. He had antagonized much of the Islamic world by rebelling against the caliph during World War I. The failure of his regime to protect pilgrims from ma-rauding tribes, as well as abominable health conditions in the Holy Cities, cost him further support. He was bitter over the partition of the Fertile Crescent, seeing this as a betrayal of Britain's promises to him during the war. The British offered him a treaty of alliance, which might have protected him against the Wahhabis, but only on condition that he accept British policies in Palestine, which he refused to do. Even in 1918 the Sa'udis and the Hashimites were resuming their struggle for mas-tery of Arabia. When Husayn sent Amir Abdullah to occupy a disputed border oasis in 1919, his force was waylaid by Najdis and almost wiped out. By 1921, ibn-Sa'ud had conquered Shammar and part of Asir, the rest of which became a Sa'udi Protectorate in 1926 and was annexed in 1930.

The big prize, though, was the Hijaz. In 1924, following the abolition of the Ottoman caliphate, Husayn climaxed his folly by assuming the title of "caliph" himself. Most of the Islamic world greeted this claim with scorn, and the Wahhabis began a rapid advance into the Hijaz. Ibn Sa'ud's troops entered Ta'if and massacred more than three hundred of its people. Even though Husayn abdicated in favor of his eldest son, Ali, the Wahhabis occupied Mecca and Madina and finished their conquest of the Hijaz by taking Jiddah in December 1925. Adding to his title of sultan of Najd and its Dependencies, ibn-Sa'ud now also became "king of the Hijaz." The two realms were consolidated as the kingdom of Sa'udi Arabia in 1932.

But ibn-Sa'ud did not prove to be the inflexible fanatic that many Hijazis had feared. The Wahhabis did not repeat their massacre at Ta'if, as ibn-Sa'ud kept his most ferocious warriors out of the Holy Cities. To be sure, he began a stricter enforcement of Islamic law under the supervision of Committees for the Commendation of Virtue and the Condemnation of Vice. The five daily prayers were enforced by policemen with long canes. He reinstated the practice of cutting off the hands of convicted thieves, as enjoined by the Qur'an. Many tombs, including one alleged to be Mother Eve's, were destroyed, although the Wahhabis prudently stopped short of desecrating the Prophet's grave. But, while alcohol and music were forbidden, ibn-Sa'ud finally agreed not to destroy the merchants' stocks of tobacco. Once he had reached what were to become the boundaries of his kingdom, ibn-Sa'ud saw fit in 1930 to suppress the fanatical Ikhwan. While foreign Muslims were at first appalled by Wahhabi domination over the Holy Places, ibn-Sa'ud's essential moderation, plus the improved security and health conditions that he instituted, allayed their fears and won their eventual acceptance.

Ibn-Sa'ud welcomed the material innovations of the modern West, like automobiles, medicine, and telephones, despite the opposition of the more rigid Wahhabis. Perhaps they realized that once modernity entered the door it could not be stopped. Ever able to think of clever arguments, ibn-Sa'ud once convinced some *ulama* that the telephone could not be the work of Satan by using it to carry the words of the Qur'an. He even set up a few small but modern schools.

Even in 1939, however, Sa'udi Arabia was scarcely affected by westernization. It had a patriarchal government that made no distinction between the private purse of the king and the finances of the state. The monarch was "democratic" in the traditional tribal sense of being accessible to everyone. Indeed, he could not disregard the opinions of tribal and religious leaders or the advice of other members of the royal family. Nevertheless, ibn-Sa'ud made all the major decisions himself.

An event took place in 1935 that seemed insignificant at the time, yet would ultimately lead this stronghold of traditionalism to becoming part of the westernized world. Standard Oil of California, which had been given a concession in 1933 when ibn-Sa'ud needed money to supplement his income from a declining pilgrim trade, discovered oil at Dhahran, in the Eastern Province. Little did anyone dream that Sa'udi Arabia possessed the world's largest oil reserves, which would eventually bring incredible wealth and power but would also undermine an ancient Eastern way of life.

Except for the British-protected states of the Persian Gulf and southern Arabia, Yemen was the only part of the Arabian Peninsula that ibn-Sa'ud failed to absorb. His army actually invaded Yemen in 1934 but withdrew after the two countries concluded a mutually satisfactory peace. Ibn-Sa'ud was too shrewd to try to annex this densely populated country whose towering mountains and distinctive Zaydi branch of Islam made it virtually impregnable to foreign invaders.

Under Imam Yahya, Yemen survived as a medieval Islamic society. The *imam*, whose absolute rule was administered through an oligarchy of *sayyids* (descendants of the Prophet), wanted nothing that the West had to offer. He once proclaimed bluntly that he did "not like alcohol and parliaments and things like that." Yet even he inadvertently paved the way for a republican revolution of 1962 when he sent a young man, Abdullah al-Sallal, to Baghdad for military training and second-hand exposure to Western ways and ideas.

THE MIDDLE ROAD: EGYPT
AND THE FERTILE CRESCENT

Along the spectrum ranging from a Western-inspired secularism to a rigorous adherence to Islam as the basis of society, Egypt and the Fertile Crescent countries came to occupy a middle ground. Their leaders were Herodians, but gradualists. Constitutions (except in Lebanon, where a multisectarian rather than a nonsectarian system emerged) invariably proclaimed Islam to be the official religion. But they also proclaimed the sovereignty of the nation, thus perhaps unwittingly repudiating the Islamic concept that the ruler is God's agent for the enforcement of His unchanging law. Indeed, few people realized that a break with Islamic concepts had occurred. When the Turkish government abolished the caliphate in 1924, a storm of protest ensued throughout the Islamic world, not least in an Egypt whose constitution had already proclaimed national sovereignty. Egyptians had failed to draw the logical conclusion that this was a rejection of the authority of the caliph, who was not, according to Islamic doctrine, simply a spiritual leader but rather the successor to the Prophet Muhammad in his capacity as ruler of the Isamic community. Representatives from throughout the Islamic world met in Cairo in 1926 in an effort to restore the caliphate, but national and dynastic rivalries made it impossible to reach any agreement on this subject.

While there was no constitutional obligation in these countries to retain the Islamic *shari'ah,* parliaments treaded softly. Thus the earlier pattern persisted, in which Western-style codes were adopted except in matters pertaining to personal status. In Egypt and Lebanon, French-style civil codes were adopted; elsewhere, the nineteenth-century Ottoman *Majallah* (European-style codification of Islamic civil law) continued to prevail. No serious consideration was given to abolishing the *shari'ah* on the Kemalist pattern, and the only modification of Islamic family law accepted in the Fertile Crescent countries was that which the Ottoman Parliament had enacted in 1917. The Egyptian Parliament, carefully justifying its actions by eclectically citing rules from various schools of jurisprudence or the minority opinions of some legal scholars, enacted several laws during the 1920s modifying the rules on marriage and divorce slightly more radically than the Ottoman law of 1917 had done. For example, Egyptian women could now apply to a court for divorce under some circumstances, contrary to the previous rule that allowed only husbands the prerogative of divorce. More radical changes, such as the Egyptian cabinet's proposal in 1927 for restrictions on polygamy, were rejected by the Parliament.

At first there was an intellectual trend toward greater secularization and westernization. A book by an Egyptian *shari'ah* judge named Ali Abd al-Raziq appeared in 1925 which went so far as to assert that the caliphate had always been incidental to Islam and thus that the true Islamic conception of the relationship between religion and state did not differ from that of the Christian West. A blind Egyptian, Taha Husayn, who had studied in what he considered to be stultifying traditional mosque schools and at al-Azhar before blossoming at the modern Cairo University and at the Sorbonne, was emerging as the great figure in modern Arabic literature. In a book published in 1926 on the subject of pre-Islamic Arabic poetry, Taha Husayn fundamentally challenged orthodox Islam. Aside from ridiculing certain Islamic doctrines, he attempted to show that some of the supposedly pre-Islamic poetry had actually been written at a later date. Since the Arabic usage in this poetry had been a foundation for the interpretation of the Qur'an, his assertions stirred up a hornet's nest, but other liberal intellectuals came to his defense.

Such writers were obviously out of tune with the masses, or indeed with most traditionalist *ulama*. Al-Raziq's unorthodoxy lost him his license as a religious scholar. Husayn's book was withdrawn from publication, although it was later printed in a slightly revised form. Even the reformist tradition of Muhammad Abduh, out of which the liberal intellectual movement had branched, developed in a conservative direction. Abduh's successor, Rashid Rida, while continuing to criticize the rigidity of traditional Islamic thinking, was urging a return of the Islam of the *Salaf* ("predecessors," i.e., early Muslims). The movement, known as the Salafiyya, had begun to identify itself with the Wahhabis, the very antithesis of the liberal camp.

By the mid-1930s, the liberals' position was also less clear-cut. They were beginning to write about religious subjects in tones that seemed to contradict their earlier writings. Although Taha Husayn, in his *Future of Culture in Egypt,* published in 1939, clearly placed himself among the modernists by proclaiming the need to westernize and even by arguing that Egypt had always been part of Europe, there was a time during the early 1930s when the tone of his own writing typified the conservative trend.

A popular revulsion against westernization culminated in new religious movements, the most notable of which was known as the *Ikhwan al-Muslimin* (Muslim

Brethren). Hasan al-Banna, a young Egyptian schoolteacher of strict religious up-
bringing who had been concerned with religious causes from his youth, founded the
movement in 1928. It was a reaction against both Western political domination and
the Western influence that had eroded Muslim life. Combining the Herodian and
Zealot approaches, the Brethren did not blindly reject all innovations. Like the
earlier modernist movement, they agreed on the need to rethink Islamic doctrines
(i.e., to reopen the gates of *ijtihad*) but nevertheless to interpret strictly the Qur'an
and the *hadiths* of Muhammad. They did not object to modern technology or to such
superficial matters as Western-style clothing. Nor did they stand for the seclusion of
women, whom they organized as "Muslim Sisters," whose members were
permitted to attend the modern universities to prepare for careers as teachers and
nurses. They supported Egyptian and Arab nationalism insofar as it was directed
against Western rule, although in principle they rejected the Western-inspired concept of separate nations that did not include all Muslims. Actually, by stressing ties
with the Islamic world, which in practice meant mainly the neighboring Arab lands,
the Brethren may have helped bring Egypt into the pan-Arab movement, which is
basically a secular, ethnic nationalism. But the Muslim Brethren demanded that society be restored to an Islamic basis, with the Qur'an as the constitution, and the
reinstatement of the *shari'ah* in every sphere. The "fundamentalism" of the Brethren resembled that of the Wahhabis but was the reaction of a more westernized society. Far from simply being reactionary, they stressed social justice and sometimes
even "Islamic socialism."

The movement appealed to the poor and increasingly to almost all segments of
society, in part because it expressed deep-seated popular resentment against Western influence. Success was also the result of the constructive activities that the
Brethren organized—hospitals, food for the poor, and even factories—and to the
tight hierarchical organization, comparable to that of a totalitarian political party,
from cells composed of a few members up to the General Guide (al-Banna), who
dominated it. Not least, the movement was the result of Hasan al-Banna's magnetic
personality and brilliant mind. The Muslim Brethren later became still more important, but by 1939 it had become a mass organization in Egypt, with a membership
numbering in the hundreds of thousands, and it had spread to the Sudan and the
Fertile Crescent.

EUROPEAN-STYLE
PARLIAMENTARY GOVERNMENT
IN THE ARAB WORLD

One Western idea that took hold in Egypt and the Fertile Crescent during this period
was parliamentary democracy. Western-style constitutions were adopted in Egypt
(1923), Iraq (1924), Lebanon (1926), Transjordan (1928), and Syria (1930). Each
provided for civil liberties much like those included in Western constitutions. In
each case there was some sort of popularly elected parliament and a cabinet headed

by a prime minister. Except for Transjordan's, each constitution provided that the cabinet would be responsible to the parliament.

Later Arab radicals have called this system a sham. In reality, parliaments did function in some countries, but they were limited in what they could do and in how truly they represented the people. Much power remained in European hands, even after formal independence. The politics of "independent" Egypt consisted of shifting alliances between the king, the Wafd (the popular political party), and the British. Parliamentary government was even less meaningful in Syria and Lebanon, where the real ruler continued to be the French high commissioner. Furthermore, the Egyptian, Iraqi, and Transjordanian monarchs, rather than being merely formal heads of state, were at the center of the political process. The Egyptian king, for example had the legal power to dissolve the Parliament, to dismiss a cabinet that had the Parliament's support, or to reject bills passed by the Parliament. He appointed two-fifths of the members of the upper house. The position of the king of Iraq was even stronger; he had the right to appoint all the members of the upper house. The amir of Transjordan appointed six of the twenty members of his country's rudimentary representative body, the Legislative Council, whose powers were merely advisory.

Monarchs went beyond their constitutional authority. The Wafd party, led by Zaghlul until his death in 1927 and then less ably by Mustafa al-Nahhas, won large majorities in each Parliament for which elections were relatively free. But the party controlled the cabinet only for a few short periods. Zaghlul's government, after the Wafd won 90 percent of the seats in the 1924 election, lasted only nine months. The king simply dismissed each Wafdist cabinet, dissolved the Parliament, and installed his own men. Some of the "king's men" organized their own short-lived parties, such as the Unionist party in 1925, headed by Prime Minister Ahmad Ziwar. In 1928 Nahhas was dismissed after heading the government for two months, and the king dissolved the Parliament to rule by decree. After the Wafd won 212 out of 235 seats in the 1929 election, Nahhas became prime minister in January 1930, but King Fu'ad soon replaced him with another of his men, Isma'il Sidqi, who founded the grossly misnamed People's party. For more than five years, the 1923 Constitution was replaced by an authoritarian one that made the cabinet responsible to the king alone. The Wafd won another free election in 1936, but young King Faruq replaced it in January 1938 with a cabinet that manipulated new elections to the extent that the Wafd won only twelve seats.

Much the same situation prevailed in Iraq, but without any political party analogous to the Wafd. The king (Faysal, up to his death in 1933, and then his son, Ghazi, until he died in a car crash in 1939) ruled through cabinets headed by various handpicked individuals, some of whom headed their own loosely organized parties based on personal loyalties to themselves. The government generally determined who would get elected to the Parliament. The real dynamics of power have been aptly explained in terms of a narrow oligarchy consisting of a few former Ottoman soldiers who participated in the Arab Revolt during World War I and a group of tribal *shaykhs* now turned into landlords. A law passed in 1933 in effect made peasant debtors into serfs by forbidding them to leave the land or to seek other employment.

The typical parliamentary party in these instances was formed by a politician who brought together a group of friends and relatives, with no ideological or popular basis. Egypt's Wafd was the exception, as it represented the nearly unanimous opposition of Egyptians to foreign rule and was highly organized throughout the country. In Syria, a National Bloc also opposed foreign rule but was itself a loose association of traditional notables. Such parties were committed to the social status quo. Clandestine ideological parties were also beginning to emerge—small Communist movements, the fascist Young Egypt, and the proto-fascist Syrian Nationalist Party that advocated a pan-Syrian (including the whole Fertile Crescent) as opposed to a pan-Arab or local nationalism. In Iraq, the Ahali (People's) Group of intellectuals that emerged in the early 1930s, though not organized as a political party, advocated a combination of democracy and socialism.

To the extent that Western-style democratic practices worked, they were getting a bad name. Democratically elected majorities, such as the occasional Wafd cabinets, retained the same restrictions on civil liberties that they had complained about when out of power. Neither the Wafd nor any other popularly supported political party cared much to improve the lot of the poor. Little thought was given to land redistribution or to ending the highly regressive system of taxation in a country like Egypt, in which most peasants lived on the verge of starvation while toiling to enrich their tax-exempt absentee landlords. And "democratic" procedures tended to have undemocratic results; illiterate peasants trooped to the polls to vote as their landlords directed them.

The usual prerequisites for democratic government did not exist. Democracy has rarely lasted in underdeveloped countries, particularly those without a substantial middle class. Industrialization in Egypt was beginning under the leadership of local capitalists who established the Bank of Egypt in 1920 to finance industrial projects. Most countries also made some progress in education, public health, and communications. But basic change was discouragingly slow. For example, illiteracy in Egypt only declined from 91 percent in 1917 to 85 percent in 1937, despite a 1923 law calling for free compulsory primary education. Living standards, already low, declined significantly as population grew, and, particularly during the depression of the 1930s, as prices for agricultural products exported to Europe declined. The gap between rich and poor became wider than ever.

A tradition of democratic government was also lacking. Admittedly, many Islamic concepts—the spirtual equality of believers, religious toleration, the absence of any rigid caste system, religious law as a limitation on rulers, and even the injunction to rulers to consult their subjects—seem conducive to democratic government. But the reality of Islamic history had been one of autocracy based on military power, without any of the institutions such as elected parliaments that required centuries to take root in the West. This Western tree, when transplanted full-grown to

Middle Eastern soil, produced strange fruit, even if it did not immediately wither, and few cared to keep it watered.

Iraq's attainment of formal independence was soon followed by the intervention of the army in politics. After the Ahali Group had reduced its socialism to a milder reformism, some of its leaders, particularly Hikmat Sulayman, a relatively liberal politician who had joined the movement, began to make contact with nationalist army officers. The dissatisfied officers, mainly younger ones, were led by General Bakr Sidqi, who had gained renown in Iraq from his suppression of a revolt by Nestorian Christian (so-called "Assyrian") refugees who had fled from Turkish control during the First World War. Sidqi led a coup d'etat in 1936 that installed him as chief of the General Staff and Sulayman as prime minister. But this coup led to others in 1937 and 1938. The 1938 coup installed General Nuri al-Sa'id in power. Nuri, who had previously headed two governments during the early 1930s, had been one of the Iraqi officers serving with Faysal during the First World War and was known for his devotion to the Hashimite house and cooperation with Britain. The series of coups was not finished, and by 1941, reverting to a centuries-old Middle Eastern pattern, Iraq had had seven.

CONCLUSIONS

The nineteen years preceding the Second World War witnessed profound developments in the Middle East. The Turkish-inhabited core of the former Ottoman Empire had reacted violently against humiliations at the end of the First World War and had emerged by the early 1920s as the Republic of Turkey. While pushing back European political domination, the Turks, led by President Kemal Atatürk, attempted wholeheartedly to transform their Eastern society and to make themselves a part of the West. Turkey lost much of its Oriental flavor, at least superficially, and while poverty was on the rise almost everywhere else in the Middle East, Turkey moved slowly in the direction of a European-style standard of living. Iranian independence had also acquired a new reality, as the British stopped trying to impose a semicolonial arrangement on Iran and as Riza Shah tried, though with limited success, to modernize the country along Western lines.

The achievements of the Arab countries were more gradual and limited. Egypt and Iraq had gained formal independence by the 1930s, but Britain retained much control. French rule in Lebanon and Syria had not receded, despite violent resistance. The Arabs of Palestine were being struck by a unique tidal wave from Europe that was threatening to submerge them completely. While a new British policy in 1939 threatened to halt the development of the Jewish national home and gave the Arab Palestinians some hope, the outcome of the Arab-Zionist clash was far from certain. In the Arabian Peninsula a new political order under the aegis of the Sa'udi dynasty was committed to purifying the Islamic character of society. Elsewhere in the Arab world the receptivity to westernization varied and vacillated. Experiments with Western style parliamentary government showed little success. And the westernizing intellectual trend of the 1920s gave way to a more conservative one during the 1930s. While, at the two extremes, Kemalist Turkey and Wahhabi Arabia knew whether they wanted to march resolutely westward or to turn toward their own Eastern heritage, most of the Arab world was divided and unsure of itself and seemed to wander in circles.

8

The Retreat of Europe

1939-1954

A storm was rising in Europe during the 1930s that would eventually sweep through the Middle East and leave a new situation in its wake. Germany, led by Adolf Hitler, was endlessly making territorial demands. After a futile attempt at appeasement, Britain and France declared war on Germany when it invaded Poland in September 1939. By 1941 this European conflict had turned into a Second World War in which the so-called Axis Powers—Germany, Italy, and Japan—confronted the Allied Powers, chiefly Britain, the USSR, and the United States.

Middle Easterners played a minor role in the Second World War. The area was crucial largely as a terrain for some of the duels of European armies, and European control in the Arab lands and Iran temporarily reached nearly a new zenith.

Yet the war left European colonial powers enfeebled and Eastern nationalists more resolute. Outright colonial arrangements were largely finished, and nominal independence became more real during the decade following the end of the war in 1945.

The same period witnessed stronger popular demands for social, economic, and political change. Existing regimes that often combined conservative monarchs with landowning cliques deferential to Western hegemony came under attack. The challengers came heavily from a generation younger than the one in power. They represented a "new middle class" of professional people, unlike the older, smaller commercial middle class. They often came from relatively poor families and owed their status to their Western-style education. A key element in this new class, and one with the necessary force at its disposal, was young army officers. This was a partially westernized group, one that was relatively unencumbered by tradition and sometimes truly committed to the modernization (though not complete westernization) of society and to ending corruption, social injustice, and the vestiges of Western colonialism.

MIDDLE EASTERN RESPONSES TO A EUROPEAN WAR

Most Middle Easterners did not consider the European war—and the Allied cause in particular—to be their concern. Aside from Italian-ruled Libya, the European imperial powers that Middle Easterners had resisted (at least after Turkey's and Iran's longtime foe, the USSR, entered the war in June 1941) were on the Allied side. Hitler's expansionism had focused on other regions, and many Middle Easterners looked to the Axis nations as possible deliverers. They often overlooked Germany's deference to an Italian imperialism that might, as the Libyan and East African experience showed, make British and French power seem benevolent by comparison. Although official commitments (still not public) by Berlin and Rome to Arab independence and unity were forthcoming by 1941, Italian designs long inhibited the Germans from making promises to Middle Eastern nationalists. Many also overlooked the Nazi race theory that put most Middle Easterners—Arabs in particular—in the bottom rungs of humanity.

And yet in the period just after September 1939 the Middle East appeared to be on the Allied side. Nearly everyone assumed that the Allies would win, and they were supreme in the Arab world. France tightened its control in Syria and Lebanon, suspending the constitution in Lebanon, as it had already done in Syria. The British army was still in the Egyptian Delta, since Egypt had not yet been able to build the roads and other facilities on which Britain's commitment in the 1936 treaty to withdraw to the Suez Canal area was contingent. Egypt broke diplomatic relations with Germany and interned German nationals. Iraq, under Prime Minister Nuri al-Sa'id, did the same, only more enthusiastically. Nuri even wanted to participate in the war against Germany, and the regent, Prince Abd al-Ilah, who ruled in the name of his infant nephew, King Faysal II, was equally pro-British. More nationalistic Iraqis were willing to support Britain only in return for concessions to the Arabs, including a definite commitment to Arab Palestinian independence. These ardent Arab nationalists were strongly influenced by Hajj Amin al-Husayni, the exiled Palestinian leader, who now made Baghdad his headquarters. He later took refuge in Iran and eventually in Germany, from where he broadcast anti-Allied messages to the Arab world during the last years of the war. Other Arab Palestinian leaders supported the British, as did Amir Abdullah of Transjordan.

The Jews in Palestine were bitter over the recent White Paper but had nowhere to turn except to the British. Except for a few extremists, they attempted a tightrope act of simultaneously opposing the White Paper and supporting the British war effort. Aside from their fears of extermination in a Nazi-dominated world, the Zionists hoped that support for the war against Germany would woo the British away from their current policy. They also hoped to gain military experience that could be ҫffective against the Arabs after the Second World War was over. With this in mind, they petitioned the British authorities to permit the formation of a Jewish Division. British fears of inflaming the Arab world blocked this, although a small Jewish Brigade was formed late in the war. But thousands of Jews served in the British army, as did smaller numbers of Arab Palestinians. Understandably, few Arab Palestinians were enthusiastic about the British war effort.

Turkey, now led by President Ismet Inönü, no longer had grievances against Britain and France. The Turks were apprehensive about Italian imperialism. The Soviet-German Treaty of Non-Aggression of August 1939, in which Moscow switched from a bitter opposition to fascism to an agreement with Berlin to partition Eastern Europe, put the Germans in more bad company in Turkish eyes. In October 1939 Ankara concluded an alliance with London and Paris, committing itself to support the other parties in a war that entered the Mediterranean area, though not if this would involve it in a conflict with the dreaded USSR.

Riza Shah's Iran was pro-German. Traditional anti-British sentiment (and anti-Russian feeling after the German attack on the USSR in June 1941) propelled Iran in this direction, as did the shah's admiration for Hitler's regime and Iran's close commercial relationship with Germany. Increasing numbers of German technicians were in key positions throughout Iran.

Then momentous developments in Europe shattered all expectations. The German army struck in May 1940, and within weeks continental Western Europe was at Hitler's feet. Most of France, including Paris, was occupied by Nazi forces. The French government, having fled to the city of Vichy, transformed itself into an authoritarian system headed by Marshal Philippe Pétain and made peace with Germany. Only a few "Free French," led by General Charles de Gaulle, escaped to England to continue the struggle. The British army in France was lucky to escape across the English Channel, and months of German bombing of British cities left little doubt that an invasion would follow.

To the peoples of the Middle East, the Axis victories made support for the Allies seem foolhardy. Turkey announced its neutrality. In June 1941 Germany and Turkey concluded a Treaty of Non-Aggression, but Ankara rebuffed pressures from both sides to enter the war. Turks were fearful that belligerency would lead to bombing and occupation either by the Germans or by Soviet "liberators." Some Turks hoped that Germany would destroy the USSR and liberate the Turkic peoples or else simply tended to identify with their old World War I ally. Otherwise, the predominant Turkish sentiment continued to be pro-Allied. Turkish leaders argued that neutrality was beneficial to the Allies in relieving them of the need to defend Turkey. But Moscow protested that the closure of the Turkish Straits handicapped the Soviet war effort and that Turkey's sale of chrome to Germany strengthened the Axis nations. Only as the tide turned toward the Allies would Turkey gradually come over to their side. Turkey would not declare war on Germany until February 1945, and then (like several Arab states) only in order to be invited to the San Francisco Conference of May 1945, where a new world organization, the United Nations (UN), was to be established.

The defeats of 1940–1941 undermined Britain's position in the Arab world. Aside from the Yishuv, only Transjordan stuck by Britain, although "neutral" Sa'udi Arabia continued to pursue pro-Allied policies. Nuri's arch-rival, Rashid Ali al-Gaylani, now headed the Iraqi government. Rashid Ali was not pro-Axis per se, but he was coming under the influence of the "Golden Square," four highly nationalistic colonels led by Salah al-Din Sabbagh. Even now, Rashid Ali was willing to bring Iraq into the war on Britain's side in return for immediate independence for Palestine under the rule of its Arab majority. But among other acts of defiance, he refused to sever diplomatic relations with Italy after it entered the war in 1940. Fear of being on the losing side led even Nuri to seek a secret deal with Germany, which, however, suspiciously spurned the reputed British "puppet." When Rashid Ali was temporarily replaced as prime minister, the Golden Square forced his reinstatement in February 1941. Nuri and Abd al-Ilah fled to Transjordan, as the new government planned to use German support to achieve Iraq's and the Arabs' national objectives.

Egypt reaffirmed its alliance with Britain but dragged its feet. The government of Ali Mahir, later replaced under pressure from the British, severed relations with Italy but did not expel Italian diplomats. Although Italian forces crossed the border from Libya and bombed Alexandria, Cairo chose to consider this a "border incident" rather than an invasion and refrained from declaring war until February 1945. King Faruq—apparently in order to insure more favorable treatment in case of an Allied defeat—secretly wrote to Hitler in April 1941 that he hoped to see the German army liberate Egypt.

THE DESERT WAR

Libya and the Western Desert of Egypt were becoming a major theater of the war. The Italian army crossed into Egypt from Libya in September 1940, but the British, under the Middle East commander, General Sir Archibald Wavell, mounted a counteroffensive in December. By February 1941 Wavell had driven his foe out of Cyrenaica (eastern Libya) as well as Egypt.

But the Germans, commanded by the daring and brilliant General Erwin Rommel, came to their ally's rescue and largely took over the Axis venture in this region. Despite Hitler's low priority for the Middle East, Rommel soon demonstrated his genius with tanks in the desert and got permission to mount a major effort to drive the British out of Egypt and beyond. Until late in 1942 the Allies faced the threat of a great German pincers movement closing in through Egypt and via the Soviet Union to Iran.

The two sides alternately advanced and retreated over vast distances. In May 1942 German forces were sixty miles from Alexandria, and the British grimly contemplated a last-ditch stand on the east bank of the Suez Canal. They were already burning documents in Cairo and preparing for the evacuation of British families. Many of the inhabitants of Alexandria were fleeing en masse.

The British forged their defenses along a line extending south from the little railway station of al-Alamayn, on the coast west of Alexandria. Two German offensives failed to break through. Then, in October, under the command of the tough, inspiring General Sir Bernard Montgomery, the reinforced British army began its drive. Rommel was lucky to escape as most of his tanks were wrecked and 55,000 of his men killed, wounded, or captured. The British now advanced quickly through North Africa, soon meeting the Allied forces that had landed in Morocco and Algeria. The tide had also turned in Russia as the Soviet victory at Stalingrad blocked the other prong of the German pincers. European powers again had determined the fate of the region, with Middle Easterners largely looking on.

ALLIED INTERVENTION

The Allies had meanwhile asserted their power in several Middle Eastern countries. In April 1941 Britain notified Iraq that troops from India would land at Basrah en route to Palestine. In accordance with the Anglo-Iraqi Treaty, Iraq agreed but, once the force had arrived, asked it to move on before other British troops arrived. With Britain rejecting such a restrictive intepetation of Iraq's treaty obligations, Iraqi troops besieged the British air base at Habbaniyyah, as nationalists throughout the Arab world applauded this attack on British imperialism and in some cases headed for Iraq to offer their services. Floods prevented British troops in Basrah from moving northward, but British planes bombed the Iraqi forces on the high ground overlooking the base and drove them back. A British force assembled in Palestine. Together with Transjordan's Arab Legion, a bedouin force commanded by Sir John Bagot Glubb, it crossed to Iraq to relieve the Habbaniyyah Base.

The Germans were too busy elsewhere to provide much help to the Iraqis. Arranging with Vichy France to refuel in Syria, they did manage to land about fifty planes at Mosul, in northern Iraq. But this limited aid came too late. By the end of May the British and Transjordanian force had arrived at Baghdad. Rashid Ali, Hajj Amin, and their leading supporters fled to Iran. As Abd al-Ilah, Nuri, and the other pro-British politicians returned from exile, the old order got a new lease on life under another British occupation.

Vichy's collaboration with Berlin spelled doom for its rule in Syria and Lebanon. British and Free French forces entered the two countries in June 1941 and soon overcame fierce resistance from the French Army. The Free French commander, General Georges Catroux, announced that Syria and Lebanon would get their independence, and the British, who had insisted on this declaration in order to reassure the Arab world, endorsed it.

Riza Shah's pro-German policies provoked a new Anglo-Russian occupation of Iran. The Allies were deeply concerned over the influence of German technicians, whose number there had surpassed two thousand. Even more, with the Soviets in the Allied camp, the Allies needed Iran as a supply route. Harsh British and Soviet notes in August 1941 demanded in vain the expulsion of the Germans from Iran. Eight days later Soviet forces poured in from the north and the British from Iraq. The Iranian army, Riza's proud accomplishment of two decades, rapidly collapsed. He finally abdicated in favor of his twenty-one-year-old son, Muhammad Riza, and went into exile. An Anglo-Soviet-Iranian Treaty of Alliance provided for withdrawal of foreign troops from Iran within six months after the end of hostilities. The rivalry of politicians in the Majlis replaced the shah's absolutism, but the real powers were again the British (later joined by American troops) in the south and the Russians in the north.

War transformed Egypt into an armed British camp and brought flagrant intervention in its politics. With King Faruq sympathetic to the Axis and Rommel at the gates, cheered on by demonstrators, the British decided (paradoxically, in view of Egypt's earlier political history) that it was time for the Wafd to come to power. The Wafd, it was reasoned, had shown no pro-Axis tendencies and was still the only party sufficiently organized and popular to control the mobs and too anti-royalist to work with Faruq against the Allied war effort. In February 1942 the British ambassador, Sir Miles Lampson, presented an ultimatum to the king, threatening "consequences" unless he immediately appointed Mustafa Nahhas as prime minister. British tanks then surrounded the palace, and the ambassador and British troops went in to demand Faruq's abdication. Only a shameless plea for "another chance" saved Faruq's throne, with Nahhas heading a new Wafdist government.

IMPACT ON LIFE
IN THE MIDDLE EAST

Fears that the suffering caused by the First World War in the Middle East would be repeated were not realized. Few Middle Easterners lost their lives in this war. There were food shortages, especially early in the war, but nothing comparable to the starvation in places like Syria during the First World War. This was partly the result of a unique experiment in regional integration under imperial auspices, the Middle East Supply Centre, established by Great Britain in 1941 and later joined by the United States. The Centre, based in Cairo, allocated scarce resources throughout the Middle East. The presence of foreign troops and wartime demand for Middle Eastern raw materials and manufactured goods even brought prosperity and industrial advance in some places. A few Middle Easterners gained great wealth, although inflation was a severe problem for the poor throughout the region. Prices at least doubled or even tripled in almost every country; they shot up an estimated 699 percent in Iran.

FRANCE'S DEPARTURE
FROM THE LEVANT

The blatant way in which the British intervened in the Arab world during the war necessitated special efforts to prove their good intentions toward Arab aspirations that antagonized both France and the Zionists. In particular, the British invasion of Syria and Lebanon could be justified to Arabs only by working for the two countries' independence.

After the defeat of the Vichy forces, the Free French soon began to qualify their promise of independence. General Catroux took firm control, appointing pliable presidents for the two republics. He specified that the mandate would continue until replaced by treaties, which would have left most important matters still in French hands. This met increasing British objections, French accusations of interference, and at least one threat by de Gaulle to use force against his ally. Only after an acrimonious meeting between British Prime Minister Winston Churchill and de Gaulle in September 1942 did France reluctantly permit elections for the Lebanese and Syrian Chambers of Deputies during the following year.

The elections returned nationalist majorities in both countries. So tarnished was France's image as a dependable protector that even most of the historically pro-French Lebanese Maronites opted to seek independence. With France unwilling to end the mandate without a treaty, the Lebanese decided to act unilaterally while the British were still there to support them. In November 1943 the Lebanese Chamber abrogated references to the mandate in the constitution, claimed all governmental power, and ended the status of French as an official language. The French then arrested Lebanese President Bishara al-Khuri, Premier Riyad al-Sulh, and other ministers and suspended the constitution. As general outrage found expression in strikes and the organization of rebel groups, Britain and the United States protested to France. Britain threatened to use force unless France restored the Lebanese constitution.

France had to give in, and the Lebanese leaders were released. When the Syrian Chamber made similar changes in its constitution, France did not challenge it. According to an agreement reached in December 1943, France gradually turned over most functions to the Syrian and Lebanese governments during the following year. The two main exceptions were control of the French schools and command of the 18,000 locally recruited Special Troops. France continued to insist on the conclusion of treaties to define its continuing privileged position in the two states.

In May 1945, after Germany's surrender, Paris reverted to a hard-line position and made additional demands on Syria and Lebanon. Rioting and attacks on French troops and property ensued. France reacted by bombarding a large part of Damascus, including major public buildings. Churchill, with U.S. support, sent a note to de Gaulle on May 31 demanding that all French troops return to their barracks, and the local British commander threatened to open fire on the French. With de Gaulle declaring to the British ambassador that London had "insulted France and betrayed the West," France nevertheless gradually withdrew without retaining any special rights. The slow pace of withdrawal, which resulted from a quarrel between Britain and France over whose troops would be the last to leave, led to a U.N. Security Council debate in February 1946, but all foreign troops were gone from both Syria and Lebanon by the end of the year.

ARAB UNITY AND
THE ARAB LEAGUE

London also sought to conciliate the Arab world by supporting Arab unity, though under the leadership of British clients. Foreign Secretary Sir Anthony Eden announced his government's approval of Arab unity in May 1941. Nuri al-Sa'id came forward the next year with a proposal for a Fertile Crescent union. Amir Abdullah, who would become king of a nominally independent Transjordan in 1946, suggested a similar plan for a united "Greater Syria," to be federated with Iraq. Such plans, however, met opposition from the Hashimites' blood enemies, the Sa'udis, and from an Egypt that saw a united Fertile Crescent as a threat to its primacy in the region, not to mention the apprehension of many Syrians. Egyptian Prime Minister al-Nahhas took the initiative away from the Hashimites by proposing a wider but looser grouping, which led to the formation of the League of Arab States in 1945. This organization, which perpetuated state sovereignty, would henceforth be a forum for inter-Arab cooperation and quarrels.

THE SHIFT FROM BRITISH
PREDOMINANCE

Victory for Great Britain in World War II left its wealth and energy depleted. It was no longer possible to hold on everywhere, especially as non-Western nationalism was intensifying. And by 1946 the influence of other West European states had nearly vanished from the Middle East (excluding French North Africa).

But the field was not left for local nationalists alone. The American presence in the Middle East was becoming apparent, at least temporarily, even before 1945. The U.S. wartime roles in Iran and in the Middle East Supply Centre, as well as the extension of Lend-Lease to several countries, were cases in point. There was extensive Sa'udi-United States cooperation during the war, including the construction of a U.S. air base at Dhahran. Of definite long-range significance, the Arabian-American Oil Company (ARAMCO), a corporation that had grown out of the original Sa'udi concession to Standard Oil of California, with the participation of other American oil companies, was becoming an important American private operation, and U.S. oil interests in the Arabian Pennisula rivaled those of the British in Iran. Elsewhere, as in Iraq and Kuwayt, U.S. oil companies held concessions jointly with

British (and sometimes French) firms. Despite the special relationship between the United States and Britain, it sometimes seemed to the latter that the Americans wanted to eliminate their presence in the Middle East because of either a historic aversion to colonialism or the intention of taking over the British imperial role.

Moscow also was making demands on Turkey and Iran that were viewed either as the legitimate pursuit, at least in part, of important interests or else as the revival of czarist expansionism. In any case, Soviet aspirations would soon be "contained" by the active involvement of the United States.

Nor did British power withdraw from the area entirely. Just as Britain was decolonizing in the Indian subcontinent—access to which was formerly the main reason for concern with the Middle East—the increasingly vital role of Middle Eastern oil for the British economy made it stubbornly cling to its position in the Middle East. This included oil concessions in the Persian Gulf area, protectorates along the Arabian periphery (and the crown colony of Aden), and the treaty relationships with Egypt, Iraq, and Transjordan that allowed British bases and access.

COMPETITION FOR IRAN
AFTER THE WAR

During the war the Soviet occupation authorities virtually cut northern Iran off from the rest of the country. The agricultural products that normally flowed southward were diverted to the Soviet Union. Iranian troops were excluded from the north. The Tudeh (Masses) party, a Communist organization under Moscow's patronage, was becoming a powerful force. A Soviet demand in 1944 for an oil concession made the Iranian government apprehensive. On the proposal of Muhammad Musaddiq, an elder statesman known for his integrity, his dedication to his country, his flair for the dramatic, and his longtime opposition to the Pahlavi dynasty, the Majlis made it a crime for any Iranian to engage in negotiations for a foreign oil concession without legislative authorization.

As the six-month deadline for evacuation passed, Soviet troops remained in northern Iran. Under their guidance a "Democratic Republic of Azarbayjan" took shape. With little popular backing, the regime was propped up almost entirely by Soviet power. Another separatist government, the Kurdish Republic of Mahabad, also emerged under Soviet auspices, but with greater popular support, in the Kurdish area of northwestern Iran.

When the clever, energetic seventy-year-old Ahmad Qavam became prime minister in January 1946, the way seemed paved for Soviet success. Qavam, though a landlord, had close ties with the Tudeh party, and many assumed that he would cooperate with Moscow. He brought several members of the Tudeh party into the Cabinet and dismissed key anti-Tudeh officials. Even when Iran's UN representative brought a complaint against the USSR in the Security Council, where his position found strong U.S. support, the prime minister disavowed his action. But the disavowal was apparently tongue-in-cheek, with Qavam glad to take advantage of the pressure and embarrassment that the UN debate was causing the USSR. Qavam flew to Moscow and concluded an agreement providing for a Soviet withdrawal (but giving autonomy to Azarbayjan) and the establishment of a joint, 51 percent Soviet-controlled oil venture. The oil arrangement, however, was contingent on approval by the Majlis, which Moscow thought was assured.

In fact, Qavam set about organizing his own party, the Democrats of Iran, as a counterweight to the Tudeh. He used a tribal insurrection in the south as an excuse to dismiss the Tudeh members from his cabinet. Following elections, the Majlis, led by Musaddiq, overwhelmingly rejected the Soviet oil agreement. Iranian troops moved to the northwest to suppress the Soviet-backed regimes, which soon collapsed, with their leaders fleeing to Soviet territory amidst an anti-Tudeh pogrom. Declarations of American support for Qavam's actions precluded any return of Soviet troops.

Iran was establishing closer ties with the United States and meeting Soviet hostility. U.S. military credits were forthcoming in 1947. The sending of a U.S. military mission in 1948 brought reminders from Moscow of its right to intervene in Iran under the 1921 treaty. Hostile diplomatic notes and Soviet propaganda kept the fires going. An American company was employed to advise Iran on carrying out a seven-year plan, and a technical assistance program began in 1950.

TURKEY JOINING THE ANTI-COMMUNIST WEST

Turkey, still led by President Inönü, became a key focus of Soviet-American rivalry. Before World War II ended, Moscow began making demands on Ankara and denounced the Turko-Soviet Treaty of Friendship in March 1945. In June Foreign Minister V. M. Molotov demanded Soviet bases on the Turkish Straits, which had been closed to Soviet ships during the war, and the return of Kars and Ardahan, which had been under Russian control until 1917. Moscow later asked for a revision of the Montreux Straits Convention and the cession of some Turkish territory to Bulgaria.

While the British and American governments initially showed sympathy for the Soviet desire for freer access to the Straits, they supported Turkey in resisting other demands. Soviet propaganda continued against the undemocratic nature of the Turkish government and its failure to join the Allies in the war. Soviet and Bulgarian troops were massed near the Turkish borders. The Turkish army, whose equipment and training had become obsolete as a result of its noninvolvment in World War II and also because of the country's general failure to keep up with European and Western technical and economic advances, was depending on numbers for strength. But three quarters of a million Turks under arms were imposing a severe strain on the economy.

Turkey had been receiving aid from Britain, whose economic exhaustion now forced its discontinuation. London announced that it could no longer support either Turkey or Greece, where a British-sponsored monarchy was attempting to suppress a Communist guerrilla movement that was backed by the Soviet bloc.

Washington was deciding to take London's place. The battleship S. S. Missouri sailed to Istanbul in a show of strength. In an early application of the "containment" doctrine, President Harry Truman proposed a program of military and economic assistance to Greece and Turkey in March 1947. With the rapid approval by Congress of what came to be known as the "Truman Doctrine," Turkey soon aligned itself with the United States and the anti-Communist coalition in the emerging cold war. Later in 1947 the United States announced that naval ships would be based in the Mediterranean, the beginning of the Sixth Fleet that would long remain a powerful American instrument in the area. Turkey later was included in the Marshall Plan for U.S. aid to Europe. It was admitted to the Council of Europe, an organization of non-Communist states, in 1949 and, after a delay that hurt the feelings of many Turks anxious to assert that they were "Western," to the North Atlantic Treaty Organization (NATO) in 1951. Although Stalin's successors renounced Soviet demands in 1953, Turkey, now with increased economic and military capability resulting partly from U.S. aid, remained a staunch member of the anti-Communist Western alliance.

THE RISE OF ISRAEL

During and immediately following World War II, the White Paper continued to form the basis for British policy in Palestine. Regulations laid down in 1941 restricted land transfers to Jews. And just as Nazi Germany was proceeding with the extermination of most of Europe's Jews, the doors to Palestine were almost closed to any who were able to seek refuge there. This helped to placate the Arab Palestinians but exacerbated the Zionist challenge to the British.

Violent opposition to Britain during the first years of the war came only from the most extreme Zionist faction, the Stern Gang. Established by the youthful Abraham Stern, a recent arrival from Poland, this organization carried out terrorist attacks on the British and more moderate Jews. A larger organization, from which Stern's group had split off, was the Irgun Zvai Leumi (National Military Society), which had grown out of the interwar Revisionist movement that had preached a hard-line policy against the Arabs and Britain. Led by another Polish immigrant, Menachem Begin, the Irgun had initially joined with the Haganah, the largest Jewish military organization, in its policy of wartime "self-restraint," but it also began a terror campaign after the war turned in Britain's favor. While the Jewish Agency condemned such acts, targets of extremist Zionist assassins included Lord Moyne, the British Secretary of State for the Middle East, who was gunned down in Cairo in 1944, and Sir Harold MacMichael, the High Commissioner for Palestine, who survived a similar attempt.

The Zionists pursued other clandestine activities. The Haganah, like the Irgun and Stern Gang, stole arms from British troops in preparation for a postwar confrontation. In an attempt to rescue the remnants of European Jewry, the Jewish Agency helped thousands of illegal immigrants to enter Palestine and evade the British authorities.

At a time when Hitler was not yet sure whether emigration or extermination would be used to solve his "Jewish problem," the Germans allowed shiploads of Jews to leave Europe. Germans sometimes cooperated with the Zionists by facilitating the transfer of Jewish property and funds. Dilapidated old vessels, overloaded with suffering human cargo, sailed toward Palestine. Some perished in shipwrecks on the way. Most of those who reached their destination were denied entry and were instead transferred to the Indian Ocean island of Mauritius or, later, to Cyprus. Nor would other countries accept them. On one occasion, the Jewish Agency blew up a refugee ship, which unexpectedly resulted in 240 deaths, and gained increased world sympathy by inaccurately presenting the incident as a collective suicide of the people on board. People in austere temporary relocation camps felt the anguish of living in limbo and could hardly comprehend why they were being turned away from Palestine.

Demands for the admission of large numbers of European refugees to Palestine increased the Palestinian Arabs' fears of being uprooted to make room for a Jewish state. They and other critics of Zionism suggested that other countries should accept these unfortunate people and accused Western Christian supporters of Jewish immigration to Palestine of using Zionism to divert refugees from their own shores. It was also maintained that Zionists were callously using the plight of their fellow Jews to achieve political objectives. While non-Jewish public opinion in such a country as the United States was adverse to admitting more Jews, some anti-Zionists said that this might have been overcome if Zionist leaders had not strongly opposed the creation of any alternative to Palestine. Arguments and counter-arguments thus ran endlessly.

The Zionist movement took a hard-line stand. The tough and brilliant David Ben-Gurion, a pre-World War I immigrant from Poland, was eclipsing the leadership of the more moderate Weizmann. At the same time such leaders as Ben-Gurion began to see the United States as the center of gravity of a postwar West and its Jewish minority as a vital reservoir of support. An important meeting of American Zionists, also attended by many Zionists from other parts of the world, took place in the Biltmore Hotel in New York in 1942. Dominated by Ben-Gurion, the Biltmore Conference demanded that Palestine be opened for Jewish immigration and that the whole country become an independent Jewish state. The Jewish Agency later adopted the Biltmore program. A rival but smaller movement among moderate Jews in Palestine, the Ihud (Union) called for Jewish immigration but for a binational Palestine. Led by such eminent men as Dr. Judah Magnes (the president of the Hebrew University) and the great philosopher and theologian, Martin Buber, the Ihud gained little support.

The end of World War II left a weakened Britain with an intractable problem in Palestine. The Zionist hope that the Labor Party victory in the 1945 elections would change British policies in favor of Jewish statehood was soon dashed. A quarter of a million Jewish survivors of Nazism were waiting in camps in Europe. Although some U.S. State Department officials pleaded that support for Zionism would drive an embittered Arab world into the arms of the USSR, American political leaders vied for the votes of Jews and others who favored the Zionist program. Many Christians as well as Jews believed that the Jews had a clear-cut moral, or even God-given, right to Palestine. The Arab claim to the country rarely seemed to be understood in the Western world. President Truman infuriated London by asking for the immediate admission of 100,000 Jewish refugees into Palestine.

Zionist terrorism increased. The Haganah reached an agreement with the more extreme organizations to coordinate their activities in November 1945. After the Haganah destroyed ten bridges in June 1946, Britain imposed martial law throughout Palestine and arrested seven hundred Zionist leaders. Then the Irgun blew up the King David Hotel, the site of the British civil and military headquarters in Jerusalem, leaving ninety-five people, mainly British, dead.

Britain's attempts to reach a solution were to no avail. In 1946 an Anglo-American Committee of Inquiry proposed the admission of 100,000 Jews to Palestine but not the establishment of a Jewish state. Another Anglo-American commission, composed of Henry Grady and Herbert Morrison, proposed a UN Trusteeship with autonomy for predominantly Jewish and Arab provinces, but met rejections from all sides. The British government invited representatives of the Zionists (who refused to attend), Arab states, and Arab Palestinians to a conference in London in September 1946, but again without results.

Faced with a hopeless task, London took the problem to the UN General Assembly in April 1947, although it did not bind itself to carry out the UN recommendation. A UN Special Committee on Palestine (UNSCOP) visited the country and proceeded to draft two alternate proposals. The minority plan called for a federal Palestine, composed of Jewish and Arab areas. The majority plan called for partition, in a complicated checkerboard pattern, into a Jewish and an Arab state and an internationalized area to include Jerusalem. Partition had the support of most Western states, Britain being the major exception. In a short-lived reversal of their traditional anti-Zionist policy, which may have been due to a desire to expel the British from Palestine, even the Soviet Union and the Communist bloc supported the partition plan. The main opposition came from Arab and some other Asian states. Still, a two-thirds vote was not assured, and it was only after the application of considerable pressure on several wavering delegations by Zionists and some of their influential supporters that a partition plan based on the UNSCOP majority report, with minor modifications, gained UN endorsement in late November.

Neither side was satisfied with the UN plan. The Zionists reluctantly accepted it as an "irreducible minimum," viewing as essential the creation of a state into which European Jewish refugees might freely come. The Arab Palestinians and the Arab states rejected it, pointing out that although the Jews formed only a third of Palestine's population they were awarded 54 percent of the country, including most

ISRAEL'S EXPANSION

Proposed Jewish State, UN Partition (1947)

Other Areas Occupied in 1948 – 1949

Areas Occupied in 1967

Mediterranean Sea

LEBANON
Beirut

Damascus
Sidon
SYRIA
GOLAN HEIGHTS
Yarmuk R.
Acre
GALILEE
Haifa
Nazareth
Jordan R.

Tel Aviv
Jaffa
Amman
Jericho
GAZA STRIP
Jerusalem
SINAI (occupation ended, 1982)
Gaza
WEST BANK
Port Said
Dead Sea
Suez Canal
Beersheba
Isma'ilia
Al-Auja
NEGEV
JORDAN
Suez
Mitla Pass
Eilat
Aqaba
Gulf of Suez
Gulf of Aqaba
SA'UDI ARABIA
EGYPT
Sharm al-Shaykh

of the fertile areas (but also most of the Negev desert in the south). They pointed out that the partition lines represented a double standard, drawn so that almost every Jew in Palestine would be within the Jewish state or the international area. On the other hand, the Jewish state would include large areas that were overwhelmingly Arab-populated, and almost 50 percent of its population would be Arabs. Arabs suspected that the Zionist ''acceptance'' of the partition plan was only tactical in nature and would be followed by attempts to take more territory. Arabs also objected to the fact that the establishment of a Jewish state would split the Arab world geographically and argued that the partition of Palestine was illegal. Their efforts to bring the question before the World Court were not heeded.

The partition plan was never implemented, since a full-scale Jewish-Arab civil war started immediately. Britain announced that it would terminate the mandate on May 15, 1948 and began pulling out its troops in stages. Zionist forces fought against Palestinian guerrillas led by Abd al-Qadir al-Husayni (who was killed in April) and an Arab Liberation Army that crossed over from Syria under Fawzi al-Qawuqji. The Zionists were better armed, especially after the arrival of weapons from Czechoslovakia, and unlike the Arab Palestinians, had a well-established community government. They were soon prevailing. Although some Jewish settlements were isolated, the Palestinian Arabs could not take them, while Arab cities and villages fell in rapid succession during April, leaving Jews in control of parts of the proposed Arab state.

Cruelty abounded on both sides. The Irgun, Stern Gang, and Haganah took the Arab village of Dayr Yasin, near Jerusalem, in April. The Haganah then withdrew in favor of the other Zionist forces, who proceeded systematically to slaughter 254 of its inhabitants. Arab forces in Jerusalem retaliated by waylaying a convoy of buses carrying Jewish doctors and nurses to the Hadassah Hospital, on Mount Scopus. The Jewish Agency condemned the Dayr Yasin massacre, which, however, helped to remove the basic impediment in the way of a Jewish state by accelerating a mass flight of Arabs from most of Palestine.

The departure of a few thousand well-to-do Arabs for safer places soon after the UN partition resolution started the exodus. The breakdown of order and essential services caused others to leave. After the Dayr Yasin massacre, major demographic changes occurred, with virtually the entire population of villages and whole cities, such as Jaffa, fleeing in terror. Both the eagerness of the Arab elite to escape and the dissemination of information about Jewish terrorism by both sides may have exacerbated the fears of ordinary people. However, there is no viable evidence for later allegations of evacuation orders from Arab leaders, and monitored Arab radio broadcasts reveal consistent Arab warnings not to leave. Although some rare Jewish leaders urged Arabs to stay, the Irgun and Stern Gang warned them that other massacres would follow if they did not flee. Later on, the Israeli army also expelled Arabs on a large scale, sometimes in accordance with explicit orders from Ben-Gurion.

On May 14, as the British withdrawal was completed, Zionist leaders announced the establishment of the State of Israel. The armies of the surrounding Arab states had already decided to intervene to support the Arab Palestinians. King Abdullah also wanted to annex as much of Arab Palestine as he could get, an ambition most other Arab leaders hoped to block. Egyptian troops moved into the southern Palestine coastal region and also crossed over to the area south of Jerusalem. The Transjordanian Arab Legion entered eastern Palestine, assisted by Iraqi contingents on its right flank. The minuscule Lebanese army even entered the war in token fashion, while the Syrians made slight penetrations in the northeast.

The Palestine War provided a unique crucible to demonstrate the weakness of Eastern societies. The Arabs confronted a largely European Jewish society, whose people were highly cohesive, literate, and proficient in modern technology. Middle Eastern nationalists had recently forced other Europeans to give in, but largely because they lacked determination when nationalistic opposition caused them excessive trouble or expense. Only in the case of the Zionists, whose modernity was matched by a fierce willingness to stand up for their objective of a Jewish state (and sometimes believing they had no other alternative), did Middle Eastern peoples face a truly determined European enemy. Characteristic of the gap between the two societies, Israel, with a population of only 650,000 Jews, was able to mobilize more troops than all the Arab states could send against them. Israelis possessed the technical skills to make weapons to supplement the war material that reached them (sometimes smuggled) from the United States and Europe. In addition, the Arab states acted at times as if they distrusted one another even more than the State of Israel.

Despite their lack of preparation, sometimes lacking maps or food supplies except those obtained locally, the Arabs initially had considerable success. But the Israeli army (in effect, the Haganah) increasingly prevailed. At one point Egyptian troops were sixteen miles from Tel Aviv, and Transjordanian and Iraqi forces came within ten miles of the sea. But before the Jewish state could be pinched in two, the Israelis were relieved by a UN-sponsored truce on June 11. They effectively used the truce to strengthen their forces, and the second round of fighting, which broke out briefly in July, brought Arab retreats. After small Israeli advances into the northern Negev at the end of September, a full-scale offensive began in October and was renewed in December. By the end of the year, the Israelis had penetrated Sinai and cut off the Egyptian forces in the Gaza region. British pressures forced them to pull back.

Armistice talks began in January 1949 on the island of Rhodes, with Dr. Ralph Bunche, the acting UN mediator, as the intermediary. (The original UN mediator, Count Folke Bernadotte, had been assassinated by members of the Stern Gang in September 1948, following his proposal for a modification of the UN partition plan that would have allotted the Negev to the Arabs and Western Galilee to the Israelis.) The Arab representatives at first refused to deal directly with the Israelis, whose state they did not recognize. An Egyptian-Israeli armistice was the first breakthrough. Another armistice followed with Lebanon. Then came Transjordan, after being driven out of the southern Negev in a last-minute Israeli truce violation and yielding another strip of territory in central Palestine under Israeli pressure, and finally Syria. The UN had already provided a small Truce Supervisory Organization (UNTSO), and an Egyptian-Israeli, a Jordanian-Israeli, a Syrian-Israeli, and a Lebanese-Israeli Mixed Armistice Commission (MAC) were composed of representatives of the UNTSO, Israel, and the Arab state concerned. The armistices were viewed as the first step toward a peace settlement, to be facilitated by a UN Palestine Conciliation Commission, composed of U.S., French, and Turkish representatives, and by a full-dress conference later in 1949 at Lausanne.

The armistices left Israel in control of about 78 percent of Palestine. And the general Arab exodus had resulted in an overwhelmingly Jewish country. Perhaps 770,000[1] Palestinians were now huddled in "temporary" refugee camps in surrounding areas, dependent on meager UN rations. Only two small fragments of Palestine were left to the Arabs. The narrow "Gaza Strip" in southwest Palestine, now overflowing with refugees, remained under Egyptian administration. The "West Bank," the portion of east-central Palestine held by Transjordan (from now on simply Jordan), including part of Jerusalem (notably the Old City, containing the Holy Places), was soon formally annexed, despite denunciations by other Arab states. The Arab-Palestinian Diaspora spawned a new kind of Zionist movement—in reverse—that would produce endless volumes of poetry and prose expressing its determination to return to its usurped homeland but would long remain unorganized, waiting for the Arab states to defeat Israel.

While Israelis considered their independence a victory against British colonialism in their own ancient homeland, Arabs viewed the Jewish settlers in Palestine as a product of the British mandate. To the Arabs, British opposition to Zionist demands during the last years was just another example of a colonial government opposing the extreme position of a colonial settler population, as later in Rhodesia or South Africa. To Arabs, the establishment of Israel seemed to represent the ultimate form of colonialism, previously exemplified only in the case of sparsely inhabited regions like North America, in which the local non-Western population is displaced by European settlers.

MUSADDIQ'S RISE AND FALL

Let us return to the story of post-World War II Iran. By 1949 Muhammad Musaddiq, although a member of the landed class, had come to symbolize nationalism and reform in the eyes of most Iranians. The main target was the Anglo-Iranian Oil Company (AIOC), which Iranians saw as a surviving instrument of British imperialism. Beginning with his earlier stand against a Soviet oil concession in northern Iran, Musaddiq espoused the slogan "negative equilibrium," which rejected the former practice of balancing privileges granted to Britain and the USSR in favor of

---

[1]Zionist sources typically put the figure at scarcely over 500,000, while Arab estimates sometimes reach one million. The UN reported that 904,122 refugees were registered in 1951, but, aside from the natural increase, the figure may have been inflated.

denying privileges to any foreign power. Musaddiq's movement, a loosely organized National Front consisting of several political parties, also favored domestic change. Muhammad Riza Shah, largely a figurehead when he first succeeded his father, had asserted his influence to a limited extent after the end of World War II in an alliance with the landed class that controlled the Majlis, though he later began distribution of Royal Lands to the peasants. Musaddiq aspired to weaken the shah's influence, possibly establishing a republic, and to break the power of the landlords.

Bitterness against the AIOC was growing. Iran had suffered economically for several years and badly needed increased revenues to finance its Seven-Year Plan for development, adopted in 1949. Iranians were shocked to learn that AIOC royalties paid to their own government amounted to little more than a third of the profits and taxes accruing to the British government from Iranian oil. In contrast, Venezuela had obtained the right to share profits on a fifty-fifty basis with the oil companies, an arrangement that spread to Sa'udi Arabia in 1950. Although in 1949 the AIOC agreed to more favorable terms for Iran, nationalists were not satisfied, and Iranian demands for nationalization became increasingly strident. In March 1951 this culminated in the assassination of Prime Minister Ali Razmara, who favored a compromise agreement, by a member of the fundamentalist Fida'iyan-i-Islam, which was roughly comparable to the Muslim Brethren in Egypt.

Musaddiq now came to the fore. Under his leadership, the Iranian Parliament (the Majlis and the recently established Senate) quickly followed up the assassination of Razmara by voting to nationalize the oil industry. Soon afterwards Musaddiq took office as prime minister, and another, more detailed law provided for the implementation of nationalization, with compensation offered to the AIOC. When British technicians refused to work for the newly created National Iranian Oil Company (NIOC), their residence permits were terminated, and they left Iran in October. During his two-year period of leadership, Musaddiq not only stood up against what he perceived to be British economic imperialism but also secured the enactment of domestic reforms. A law passed in August 1952 required landowners to earmark 20 percent of their shares of the crops for the peasants' use.

An Anglo-Iranian confrontation ensued, although London accepted the principle of nationalization. Anglo-Iranian negotiations that were held in August 1951—following appeals to the two countries from President Harry S. Truman and the efforts of his special representative, Averell Harriman—floundered over London's demand for a British role in the actual management of the oil industry. All efforts to reach a settlement failed, including British appeals to the Security Council, which took no action, and to the World Court, which eventually ruled that it lacked jurisdiction in the case. With Britain applying various kinds of economic pressures, such as freezing Iranian assets, and allegedly engaging in intrigues against the Iranian government, Tehran severed diplomatic relations with London in October 1952.

Nationalization brought hardship to Iran. Its people did not have the technical skills required to run the oil fields and refineries; the operations and Iran's main source of income ground to a halt. Western oil companies generally cooperated with the AIOC by refusing to buy Iranian oil. And other oil-producing countries in the

Middle East destroyed Iran's leverage by increasing their own oil production to meet Western demand.

The Iranian prime minister, who had long been favorable to the United States and expected its support, appealed to President Eisenhower for economic aid in 1953, pointing to the danger from communism. But Eisenhower interpreted this as a threat and refused his request. Actually, the U.S. position in the Anglo-Iranian dispute, though neutral at first, had been moving increasingly in a pro-British direction. The Tudeh, which until recently had been a fervent opponent of an allegedly U.S.-backed Musaddiq, was rapidly becoming more and more powerful in the streets, and, much to his distress, Musaddiq was coming to depend on it. His support was eroding as several of his opportunistic former allies were breaking with him. Though a liberal democrat, he finally resorted increasingly—if reluctantly—to authoritarian measures. In a rigged plebiscite in early August 1953, the voters overwhelmingly voted to dissolve the Majlis, leaving Musaddiq in sole control.

Later in August, the shah tried to dismiss Musaddiq, appointing a right-wing general, Fazlullah Zahidi, in his place. Musaddiq, amid massive demonstrations in his favor, refused to step down. The shah, now violently attacked in the press, fled Iran.

But the CIA, with some British help, engineered a coup that brought the royalists back. A large, CIA-paid anti-Musaddiq crowd, headed by professional mob leaders and joined by army units, surged out of southern Tehran to overthrow the nationalist government. Allied with the upper class and the U.S. government, the returning shah gradually established a royal dictatorship. His secret police penetrated everywhere, rounding up anyone who threatened his rule. Six hundred army officers were arrested in 1954 because of alleged links with the Tudeh. Iran came to terms with Western interests by turning oil production over to a consortium of companies (40 percent British and 40 percent U.S., a prime case of Americans taking over British privileges) that would technically act as an agent of the NIOC under a fifty-fifty arrangement.

TURKEY BECOMES A WESTERN-STYLE DEMOCRACY

In Turkey, under President Inönü, the People's Republican party (PRP) remained the sole center of power. In some ways authoritarianism became more blatant during the war years. The most notable example was the imposition of a special tax in 1942 on excessive business profits, which had resulted from burgeoning wartime exports. The law specified no tax rate, and special commissions were allowed to exact extortionate amounts from members of non-Turkish, non-Muslim minorities. Those who could not pay were sent immediately to labor camps. Only with the decline of Nazi Germany, whose racism had inspired this type of ruthless discrimination, did the Turkish government relax its application of the law and release those who had been arrested.

The end of the war brought a move toward Western-style liberal democracy.

With the Nazi-Fascist model gone, many Turks thought it necessary to become a democracy in order to be part of Europe. This move gained support from a prosperous new business class that disliked the statist policy of the single-party regime and from a rural elite that was less committed to secularism and resented the limited land reform instituted in 1945. Backing for change also came from peasants, who typically deplored PRP secularism. As Ankara relaxed its policies, new political parties were allowed to form to oppose the government. The Democrat party, established in 1946 by dissident PRP leaders, including Celal Bayar and Adnan Menderes, won a landslide victory in the 1950 elections. Menderes became the new prime minister, with Bayar the largely ceremonial president.

But by 1954 democratic government was facing setbacks. The Democrats enacted laws imposing penalties on newspapermen whose writing was harmful to the state and allowing the government to dismiss judges, professors, and civil servants without appeal. Once again it became clear that deep-seated patterns of authoritarian rule were hard to erase.

The general standard of living had risen only a little before 1945, but a substantial improvement took place during the postwar decade. Improvements in education, health, and communications laid the foundation for further economic development. The literacy rate, 30 percent in 1945, had reached 40 percent ten years later. Modernization was rapidly penetrating the villages, especially after the Democrats, with their strong peasant constituency, devoted much attention to rural improvements. Turkey was outstripping most of the Middle East and Asia in modernization, though at the cost of severe inflation and mounting government indebtedness.

Turkish secularist policies instituted by Atatürk remained in force but were not so rigidly enforced. In 1948 religious education returned to the schools, and the University of Ankara got a faculty of divinity in 1949. The Democrats, though they did not renounce secularism and even banned the religious Nation party in 1954, swung back further toward the center. One of their first acts after coming to power was to permit the restoration of the call to prayer in Arabic. They later permitted the reading of the Qur'an on the radio. Interest in Islam increased, as shown by attendance at Friday prayers and the volume of religious publications. Perhaps this was partly a result of a growing realization that westernization did not necessitate outdoing the West in secularism.

THE ARABIAN PENINSULA

The Arabian Peninsula was still the area least affected by westernization and its accompanying ferment. With a fifty-fifty profit-sharing arrangement with ARAMCO in effect after 1950, Sa'udi oil revenues soon reached a quarter of a billion dollars a year. This brought the country the material trappings of the West and the beginning of the breakdown of Wahhabi austerity and puritanism, as evidenced by the conspicuous consumption, even corruption, of the royal family. There was even some rumbling of discontent among an incipient modern-educated group and among ARAMCO employees. But so far, the Sa'udi dynasty was secure in power. The death of King ibn-Sa'ud in 1953 led to the succession of his weak, spendthrift son, Sa'ud, but with another son, the more capable Faysal, designated crown prince. There were faint signs of more modern political patterns, notably the establishment of an advisory Council of Ministers just before ibn-Sa'ud's death. But government remained a family affair, with the king's absolutism limited mainly by the need to keep the support of the tribes and his enormous family.

New wealth from oil was also beginning to transform some of the once poor and still (in certain ways) medieval shaykhdoms in the Persian Gulf region. Kuwayt, with tremendous revenues for a population of less than half a million, was becoming a welfare state with a patriarchal ruler and a conservative society.

Yemen was one of the world's least modern countries. But it bordered on the British Crown Colony of Aden, a modernized enclave whose hinterland, the Aden Protectorate, was still a medieval area under British-protected rulers. With thousands of the *imam's* subjects finding jobs in Aden, it had become a window for Western influence. Yemenis in Aden organized a Free Yemen party to plot against despotism in their home country. Revolutionaries assassinated the aged Imam Yahya in 1948, and a member of a dissident branch of the royal family temporarily took power. But after leading loyal tribes in a march on the capital, Yahya's son, the ruthless Ahmad, became the new *imam*.

CONSERVATISM AND UNREST IN IRAQ

The old order seemed to be well fortified in Iraq. Prince Abd al-Ilah was a dominant figure as the regent until 1953, when King Faysal II came of age, and then informally as his adviser. So was Nuri al-Sa'id, whether or not he happened to be prime minister at the moment. Both were bastions of close ties with Britain and of a landlord-dominated oligarchy.

But unrest was not far below the surface. Demonstrations and strikes were recurrent, sometimes leading to workers' being killed by the police. Several new political parties rose to challenge the oligarchy. In varying degrees they supported social reform or socialism, antiimperialism, democracy, neutralism in the cold war, and Arab unity. These groups were gradually driven underground, and in 1954 Nuri's government forbade all political parties, including the oligarchical factions organized around such men as himself. The Arab defeat in Palestine in 1948 increased dissatisfaction with the ruling group, as did the failure to obtain a more favorable treaty with Britain. A compromise agreement, signed in 1948, only intensified hostility against the government, and massive rioting blocked its ratification. Economic growth accelerated, as 70 percent of the oil revenues resulting from a new fifty-fifty sharing agreement with the Iraq Petroleum Company in 1951 was allocated to a Development Board. But even this seemingly progressive measure evoked accusations of graft and favoritism and tended to increase popular expectations faster than national income.

JORDAN: ENLARGEMENT AND CHALLENGE

The aftermath of the Palestine War left Jordan in a state of shock. Formerly a quiet desert principality, it suddenly found itself with a population tripled by annexing the West Bank and by the influx of refugees. The more modern, westernized, aggrieved, and nationalistic Palestinians were a new breed of subjects for the Hashimite ruler. Accused of planning to make peace with Israel, Abdullah was killed by a Palestinian supporter of Hajj Amin al-Husayni in 1951. His son, Talal, succeeded him, but the new king's severe mental disorder soon forced him to abdicate in favor of his seventeen-year-old son, Husayn. Although a new constitution in 1952 and subsequent amendments created the formal framework of a Western-style parliamentary government, the monarch, strongly supported by bedouin tribes, continued in effective control. The kingdom remained under British tutelage, formalized by a new treaty of alliance in 1948 that allowed Britain air bases and exclusive rights to equip and train the Jordanian army, even to provide commanding officers.

INSTABILITY IN SYRIA

Western-style parliamentary institutions in independent Syria were influenced by traditional Middle Eastern social patterns. The conservative representatives of leading families, who dominated the Chamber of Deputies during the late 1940s, formed loosely organized factions that differed on few major issues. With the Arab states competing for Syria's loyalty, the overriding question was inter-Arab alignments. The Peoples' party, based in Aleppo, favored unity or close ties with Iraq, while the Damascus-based National party, led by President Shukri al-Quwatli, was generally aligned with the Hashimites' rivals, Egypt and Sa'udi Arabia.

But new forces were rising. Two young Syrian schoolteachers, the Christian Michel Aflaq and the Muslim Salah al-Din al-Bitar, both of whom had studied in France and first espoused but then rejected communism, formed an Arab Renaissance (Ba'th) party. While emphasizing democracy and socialism, the Ba'th was foremost an Arab nationalist party whose main concern was to bring about a revival of Arab greatness. It called for the unification of the Arab world as one state. Organized on a pan-Arab (''national'') basis, the Ba'th treated existing states as mere ''regions.'' The Ba'th gained a new base of support in 1953 when the Arab Socialist party of Akram al-Hourani, a passionate crusader against ''feudalism'' who had rallied peasants in the region around Hama to his banner, merged with it to form the Arab Renaissance (Ba'th) Socialist party. Other challenges to the old order included the Syrian Nationalist party and a small but vocal Communist movement, not to mention many disaffected army officers, often with partisan connections.

The old order soon broke down. Defeat in Palestine, which gave birth to tales of corruption in the Syrian government, provided a catalyst. Colonel Husni al-Za'im, a would-be Syrian Atatürk, overthrew the parliamentary regime in 1949 with CIA support. Za'im was pro-Hashimite at first, but after a visit to King Faruq, whose flattering reception dazzled him, he joined the Egyptian-Sa'udi alignment. A second coup brought the pro-Hashimite Colonel Sami al-Hinnawi to power, but the prospect of Syria's subordination to Iraq led to a third coup before 1949 was out. The new strongman, Colonel Adib al-Shishakli, consolidated his power in 1951. However, with discontent building up under al-Shishakli's repressive regime, the army intervened again in 1954, this time to restore parliamentary government. Old-guard politicians, including Syria's first president, Shukri al-Quwatli, returned to office, although the military remained the final arbiter. But the relatively free elections later in 1954 brought into the Chamber a large minority of Ba'thists, who, together with other radical deputies, were to become a powerful force in Syrian politics.

RELIGIOUS BALANCE IN LEBANON

Of all the Arab countries, Western-style democracy would find its longest and strongest foothold in Lebanon, although here too its actual working was shaped by local factors. Lebanon's contact with the West over several centuries had left it a semi-Westernized country, and its experience with representative (though hardly democratic) institutions went back to the nineteenth century. Its relatively high per-capita income and literacy rate were two of the common prerequisites for democratic government. The fears of the various Christian and Muslim sects, none of which had a majority of Lebanon's population, of domination by the others also worked in favor of establishing a representative system.

An informal agreement called the National Pact, concluded by Lebanese leaders in 1943, stipulated some of the rules of sectarian balance. The pact provided that Lebanon would remain independent, thus satisfying the Western-oriented Maronite Christians, who, fearing their own submergence by a union with Syria or the Arab world in general, tended to be Lebanese nationalists. But it also provided that Lebanon would maintain an "Arab face" and would not rely on Western protection. According to a pattern that had already evolved, the president, who was the dominant political figure, was always a Maronite Christian, while the prime minister was a Sunni Muslim. The system of representation in the Chamber of Deputies gave Christians six seats for every five going to the Muslims. The constitution even provided for the allocation of civil service positions according to religious quotas.

There were several sources of potential ferment. The six-to-five ratio was based on a 1932 census taken by the French. The higher emigration rate of Christians and the higher birth rate of Muslims were changing the composition of Lebanon's population, but the dominant Christians resisted any new census. The free enterprise system helped to make Lebanon a center for international banking and transit trade. This produced a disproportionately Christian rich class but also a large, heavily Christian middle class. Even the 50 percent of the population engaged in agriculture were perhaps generally better off than most other Middle Eastern peasants. Still, the gap between rich and poor was wide, and there were many destitute (mainly Muslim) peasants in some areas. Some flocked to the outskirts of Beirut in search of employment, often in vain. And many Lebanese, especially the younger ones, disliked the way in which leaders of a few "feudal" families—in traditional Middle Eastern style, despite economic modernization—dominated politics. Growing dissatisfaction with official manipulation of elections and other corruption in the government of President Bishara al-Khuri, who had secured a constitutional amendment exempting himself from the six-year limit on his term of office, caused a temporary alliance of political leaders to form against him in 1952. Following a general strike, al-Khuri stepped down, to be succeeded by Camille Chamoun. But no long-term changes ensued.

THE EGYPTIAN REVOLUTION

Egypt's primary concerns were still to obtain the withdrawal of British forces and the unity of the Nile Valley. The Sidqi-Bevin Agreement of 1946 provided for the evacuation of British troops during peacetime, but its ambiguous language regarding the Sudan led to riots in Egyptian cities and rejection by the Parliament. The British were unwilling to turn the Sudan over to Egypt without Sudanese consent and were in the process of establishing an autonomous government there, which Egyptians saw as a plot to keep the Nile Valley divided. The Sudanese were split on the issue, with the Ashiqqa (Brothers) party supporting union with Egypt and the Ummah (Nation) party asking for independence. In accordance with the 1936 Treaty, British troops withdrew from most of Egypt during the late 1940s, restricting themselves to the Canal Zone. But Egyptian attempts to end this last remnant of the occupation—including bringing the issue to the Security Council in 1947—were unavailing.

The old order was disintegrating. King Faruq, widely admired when he succeeded his autocratic father in 1936, had dissipated his popularity when he submitted to the British diktat in 1942 and as his growing reputation as a degenerate lecher embarrassed the Egyptian people. The Wafd, having consented to serve British imperialism during the war, was losing its claim to represent the Egyptian people. A former Wafdist, Makram Ubayd, published a *Black Book* of damaging revelations about Wafdist leaders in 1943. Nor was the party willing to respond to the needs of a country of great landlords and landless, diseased, and uneducated peasants, of cities burgeoning with unemployed emigrés from the countryside, and with a population that had outgrown Egypt's resources. The splinter parties and the politicians who led non-Wafdist governments from 1944 to 1950 had even less claim to represent the masses or the reformers.

The old regime faced growing challenges. There were sporadic strikes and demonstrations. Attacks on traditional aspects of society appeared in print, notably the modernist Khalid Muhammad Khalid's *From Here We Start,* published in 1950. In it the author blamed traditional religious leaders for the troubles of the Islamic world. Marxist and other radical writers went even further in attacking the status quo.

The Muslim Brethren grew increasingly numerous and influential. Some of them resorted to terror bombings and assassinating Egyptian leaders. When Prime Minister Nuqrashi's government outlawed the Brethren in 1948, he soon fell to one of their assassins. Six weeks later, the movement's leader, Hasan al-Banna, was shot to death, possibly with government complicity. The loss of al-Banna, now replaced by Hasan al-Hudaybi, proved to be a grave setback for the Brethren.

As in the case of Syria, Egypt's defeat in Palestine was the main catalyst for change. Revolutionary cells began to form within the Egyptian army, hitherto a royalist preserve. One of these groups called itself the "Free Officers." Its leader was the intelligent and persuasive Gamal Abd al-Nasir, who had been active in political demonstrations since childhood and who passionately hoped to restore dignity to his country. The son of a minor government employee descended from upper Egyptian peasants of moderate means, Nasir's modest background was like that of many of the Free Officers. While the officer corps had formerly been recruited mainly from Egypt's elite, Nasir and his fellow conspirators were among the first graduates of the military academy after it had been opened up to young men of a broader social background in the late 1930s. Having already long talked among themselves about the need to clean up the country, these officers blamed their government for sending them to Palestine unprepared, with defective weapons that high officials had been bribed to procure. Upon returning to Egypt in defeat, they became a formally organized group in 1949.

Anglo-Egyptian differences helped to finish the old regime. General elections in 1950 brought al-Nahhas back at the head of a new Wafdist government, and negotiations with London resumed. But the British refused to accept Egypt's right to the Sudan or to withdraw without leaving ununiformed British technicians behind to maintain the Suez Canal base and assurances of the right to reoccupy it in case of war. The talks ended in failure in October 1951. A last minute Anglo-American-French-Turkish proposal for a multilateral Allied Middle East Command (the first proposal to establish an eastern counterpart to NATO), with Egyptian participation, was bluntly rejected by Egypt as being simply the substitution of a multilateral occupation for the British one. Instead, the Egyptian Parliament unilaterally proclaimed the abrogation of the 1936 treaty and declared Faruq to be king of Egypt and the Sudan. Egyptian guerrillas, mainly organized by the Muslim Brethren, sporadically attacked the British forces in the Canal Zone, and a boycott of the base by Egyptian workers undermined its usefulness.

In January 1952 British forces attacked the Isma'ilia police station, which was accused of aiding guerrillas. Over fifty policemen were killed, and Egyptians were indignant. A mass demonstration in Cairo turned into a frenzied mob bent on burning the hotels, bars, cinemas, and other symbols of Western presence. Before the day was over, much of the modern sector of Cairo was in ashes. The Wafdist government, which had not dared take action against the mob, made way for a series of short-lived cabinets of the king's choosing.

The Free Officers were preparing to take control. They had come to the attention of the king by defeating his candidate for president of the officers' club and electing General Muhammad Nagib, a popular figure with a good-natured, fatherly image, who had been one of Egypt's few heroes in the Palestine War. General Nagib, though not one of the Free Officers, had been contacted by them and endorsed their objectives. He was finally named the titular leader of the group in order to give it greater standing with a public that had never heard of the thirty-four-year-old Lieutenant-Colonel Nasir. Tipped off that King Faruq was about to arrest them, the Free Officers carried out a quick, almost bloodless coup in the early hours of July 23, 1952. Although they did not declare a republic for almost a year, they forced Faruq to abdicate and to leave Egypt. Pending the formation of a new civilian government, power was placed in the hands of a Revolutionary Command Council (RCC), composed of the leading Free Officers and nominally headed by Nagib, although Nasir pulled the strings from behind the scenes.

A land reform decree of September 1952, the RCC's first major social achievement, chipped away much of the power of the landlord class. Along with other guarantees to peasants, it provided for the confiscation (reimbursed in long-term government bonds) of landholdings in excess of two hundred feddans[2] (with an additional hundred feddans for dependents) and for the sale of small plots to peasants on favorable terms. This merely dented Egypt's large problem of landlessness. The regime's revolutionism seems to have been tempered by its roots in the class of small landowners (of less than fifty acres) that remained dominant on the village level.

The new regime showed its moderation by rapidly settling the dispute with Britain. An agreement in February 1953 accepted the principle of self-determination for the Sudan over a three-year period. Ensuing elections in the Sudan returned a pro-Egyptian majority, but the Sudanese later disappointed the Free Officers when they opted for independence. An agreement on the Suez Base question was formally concluded in 1954, with Britain agreeing on gradual withdrawal, to be completed by June 1956. British forces retained the right to reoccupy the base during a seven-year period in case of an attack by a non-Middle Eastern state on Turkey or any member of the Arab League.

The inclusion of Turkey seemed indirectly to tie Egypt to NATO. Nasir had close ties with U.S. State Department and CIA officials and was regarded as basically pro-American and anti-Communist, although neither he nor most other Arabs were primarily concerned with fears of the USSR. But the Egyptian government,

[2]A feddan is 1.038 acres.

already accused of having conceded too much to Western imperialism, still refused to join any anti-Communist defense organization for the time being, if ever. In any case, the United States, following Secretary of State John Foster Dulles's trip to the region in 1953, had decided that such an alliance should start with the countries of the "Northern tier," such as Turkey and Iran, rather than with the Arab world.

Internally, a new authoritarian order was taking shape under Nasir. Political parties were ordered to clean out corruption, then were dissolved by the RCC early in 1953. To fill the vacuum and to mobilize support for the regime, Nasir established a Liberation Rally, his first try at creating a single party to bolster his regime. The RCC suspended the 1923 Constitution but promised to restore representative, constitutional government by 1956.

Nasir had to overcome challenges to his leadership. By mid-1953, Nagib held the titles of president, prime minister, and chairman of the RCC, while Nasir held lesser offices. Nagib, encouraged by his popularity, wanted to have power concentrated in his own hands. The RCC rejected his request for a veto power and, fearing a return to the old order, opposed his desire to speed up the return to constitutional government. In February 1954, Nagib resigned. Nasir took over as prime minister and chairman of the RCC, but popular opposition, plus a mutiny in the cavalry corps, brought Nagib back. Then, in an adept maneuver that looked like a complete capitulation to Nagib, the RCC announced that it would dissolve itself and permit the restoration of political parties and constitutional government. As Nasir had calculated, those who feared an end to the revolution were united in opposition to Nagib. A strike by the pro-Nasir Transport Workers, demonstrations by the Liberation Rally, and other expressions of opposition to the announcement led to Nasir's return as prime minister in April. Still the strongest popular group in Egypt, the Muslim Brethren had gradually turned against the new leader, whose compromise on the Suez Base issue led one Brother to fire a revolver at Nasir. Suppression of the Brethren ensued, with several thousand arrested and six executed. Following accusations that Nagib was working with the Brethren, the RCC finally deprived him of the already empty title of president in November and put him under house arrest.

ISRAEL: A WESTERN ISLAND?

Israel was in, but not yet of, the Middle East. Immigrants from Europe had built the state. Its culture was European. Some of its indices of modernization paralleled those of Europe. According to UN statistics, in per-capita income, it ranked just below West Germany and the Netherlands but higher than Italy and Austria in the early 1950s. The country was heavily urban and industrialized, but successful reclamation projects were also augmenting the farmland that both Arabs and Jews had long made productive. This progress was achieved despite the flood of destitute Jewish immigrants that roughly doubled the population remaining after the Arab exodus. The Law of the Return, enacted in 1950, guaranteed the right of any Jew to enter Israel and attain citizenship. But in addition to the benefit derived from confiscated Arab property, the influx of foreign public and private assistance had reached a cumulative total of 2 billion dollars by 1955. This included U.S. government aid, United Jewish Appeal contributions, the sale of Israel bonds, and the first installments of West German reparations (according to an agreement reached in 1952) for anti-Jewish atrocities. Besides German payments to the Israeli government, there were also German restitution payments to Jewish survivors. With such financial resources, a highly educated and technically proficient population was able to overcome the obstacles of a largely arid and hiterto underdeveloped country, a rapid influx of immigrants, and hostile neighbors.

Israel became a Western-style parliamentary democracy. Competition flourished among numerous political parties. All were represented in the Knesset (parliament) in proportion to their percentages of the vote in the whole country. The democratic socialist Mapai seemed to be the permanent ruling party, with a plurality in the Knesset that was able to form shifting coalitions with minor parties. Smaller parties included the more leftist and dovish Mapam (from which one faction broke off to form the Ahdut Avodah in 1954), the free enterprise-oriented General Zionists, the rightist and expansionist Herut (a reconstituted Irgun), several religious parties, and a small Communist party.

Israel was not a wholly Western country. One Middle Eastern element was the remnant of the Arab Palestinians who did not flee in 1948. They numbered 160,000 in 1949, and their high birth rate allowed them, despite Jewish immigration, always to exceed 10 percent of Israel's population. These Arabs mostly became Israeli citizens, and despite gross neglect of their needs, sometimes benefited from the country's economic development. But they found themselves in an anomalous position in a state that proclaimed Jewishness as its unifying characteristic and was surrounded by hostile countries whose language, culture, and identity the Arabs shared. Suspected of disloyalty to Israel, they were also subject to special security measures that restricted their movement and placed them under military rule. And a variety of subtle techniques—such as keeping the Arabs dependent on the establishment in obtaining jobs and services—helped to prevent any unified protest movement, despite discrimination in such matters as wages and employment. Much of the Arab population, including some who had taken no part in the 1948 War, found their land confiscated and their villages razed by the government.

A second Orientalizing influence came from the religious parties, which reflected certain similarities between Orthodox Judaism and Islam. Their members in the Knesset were few, but by forming coalitions with them, Mapai gained the majorities necessary to govern. The need to work with such parties made it necessary for a government led mainly by non-observant Jews to make compromises on such issues as enforcing the Sabbath, requiring Kosher food to be served in government cafeterias and military installations, denying official recognition to Conservative or Reform Judaism, and leaving jurisdiction over marriage and divorce to religious courts and religious law. In a remarkable perpetuation of the Islamic pattern, each religious community in Israel has its own law in matters of personal status, and all Jews, however nonobservant, are thus subject to Orthodox jurisdiction.

A third and more effective factor diluting Israel's European character was the arrival of Middle Eastern Jewish immigrants. Eastern Jews had been little involved in the Zionist movement, but the establishment of Israel made them suspect in Arab eyes. Some became victims of bombings and mob attacks, and many perceived open or subtle discrimination by Arab governments that suspected them of having pro-Israeli leanings. Their future was insecure. Also, there is some evidence that Zionist agents pressured Middle Eastern Jews to move to Israel, even to the point of inciting anti-Jewish actions. Many Oriental Jews were very religious and saw the establishment of Israel as a messianic event that called for their "return," and Israel's higher standard of living may have provided another attraction.

The result was the departure of most Jews from Arab countries—and also some from countries like Iran or even India—for Israel. After some initial resistance, the Iraqi and Yemeni governments permitted Jews to leave, and only a handful chose not to participate in the airlifts that followed. Jews from other countries left gradually. Between 1948 and 1954 the more than 370,000 Oriental immigrants slightly outnumbered those from Europe. By 1954 nearly 90 percent of the new immigrants were Easterners, and they were still coming. Their high birth rate was fast making them a majority of Israel's Jewish population.

Aside from sharing a common religion, the Occidental and Oriental Jews were complete aliens to each other. A Jew from Iraq or Libya was culturally more akin to Arabs than to European Jews. His typically dark complexion made him seem indistinguishable from an Arab and sometimes resulted in unofficial racial discrimination. The Eastern and Western Jews tended to live in separate communities, and intermarriage was rare. The Easterners tended to fill the most menial occupations. Relatively few rose to positions in the Cabinet or Knesset or attended universities.

Israeli efforts to help the Middle Eastern Jews integrate into Israeli society brought discouraging results. Some European Israelis expressed their disdain for Middle Eastern culture. Israel's leaders expressed the hope that the country would not turn into "merely another Levantine state." The effort was directed not at merging the two cultures but at assimilating the Oriental, which stirred resentment. Although the Oriental Jews were loyal to Israel (and typically more anti-Arab than anyone else), they did not feel that they had been fully integrated into Israel's society.

THE CONTINUING ARAB-ISRAELI CONFLICT

The expectation of an Arab-Israeli settlement following the armistices in 1949 gradually waned. The Israelis would not permit large numbers of the Arab Palestinian refugees to return. To do so would have diluted the state's Jewish character. At one point Israel officially agreed to accept the return of 100,000 refugees as part of an overall settlement, but it soon backed down under pressure from public opinion, although some offers of compensation were made. At a conference in Lausanne called by the Palestine Conciliation Commission in 1949, Israel and the Arab states accepted the UN partition lines of 1947 as the starting point for negotiations. But Israel later refused to consider any major territorial concessions, arguing that the Arab states' earlier rejection of the partition plan had invalidated it. Even though Ben-Gurion made way for the more conciliatory Prime Minister Moshe Sharett in 1953, the Arab and Israeli positions proved to be basically irreconcilable, partly because Ben-Gurion's supporters still occupied key positions.

Arab countries refused to recognize Israel or to allow it the privileges of other states. Invoking the argument that the armistices had not ended the state of war, Egypt claimed (despite a rebuff by the Security Council in 1951) that it could exclude Israeli shipping through the Suez Canal. On the same logic, it denied Israel access to the Straits of Tiran, which, though in Egyptian territorial waters, constituted the entrance to the Gulf of Aqaba and to the new Israeli port of Eilat. Among other arguments, Arabs pointed out that this town was built on the site of a Palestinian village that Israel occupied after the conclusion of the armistice with Egypt. Arab states boycotted Israeli goods and foreign companies that did business with Israel.

The small demilitarized zones along the armistice lines caused further problems. The Israelis gradually took control of the al-Auja demilitarized zone and established armed settlements there. Israel, despite protests from the UN and Syria, also inched in on the Syrian-Israeli demilitarized zone and expelled the Arab inhabitants, evoking recurrent artillery fire from the overlooking Golan Heights in retaliation. At one point, the United States, which had announced a more even-handed, less pro-Israeli policy with the start of the Eisenhower administration, forced Israel to stop a drainage project in the demilitarized zone by threatening to cut off aid. Israel argued that the UN representatives' almost consistent support for the Arabs was proof of bias and refused to participate in the Syrian-Israeli MAC from 1951 on.

Violence became commonplace. Arab Palestinians could look across the barbed wire to see their homes occupied by Israelis and the fruit being picked from their trees. Despite precautions by both sides, individuals would slip across the frontier, often in attempts to recover possessions. Sometimes they would get killed or they would kill Israelis or commit acts of sabotage, and the Israelis in turn launched "retaliatory" raids. Several such incursions involved indiscriminate massacres of Arab civilians; the bloodiest one, in 1953, resulted in the killing of sixty-six men, women, and children in the West Bank village of Qibiya.

Arab leaders sometimes put their people off with talk about an eventual "second round." Israeli military strength made it impractical for them to take any real action, although they believed that Israel would eventually seek more territory. Indeed, Ben-Gurion secretly spoke of the need for another "round," and his supporters in the ministry of defense continuously tried to provoke such a development even after Sharett became prime minister. Sharett's diary, which was later published, reveals that, from the start, the purpose of the "retaliatory" raids was to force the Arabs into a war they could not win, as well as to encourage a siege mentality among the Israeli people.

A Tripartite Declaration, issued by the United States, Britain, and France in

1950, bolstered the status quo. The declaration stated that the three powers—at a time when there was no other major power to counter them in the area—would not let a resort to force settle the conflict and that they would cooperate in preventing an Arab-Israeli arms race.

CONCLUSIONS

Despite European retreats, the predominance of Europe and the West had not yet ended in 1954. Britain still clung to its privileged position in parts of the Arab world, although it finally agreed in 1954 to withdraw from the Suez Base. The intevention of the old European imperial powers was in some ways replaced by the struggle of the United States and the Soviet Union to add the Middle East to their spheres of influence. So far, the Soviets had been "contained." America's role was one of supporting particular regimes (and sometimes subverting those it did not like), providing economic and military aid, protecting economic interests, seeking military bases and alliances as part of the "containment" policy, and pursuing policies toward sovereign Middle Eastern states that seemed a far cry from old-fashioned colonialism. But the superpowers were joined in the Middle East by a local power of European origin, the Zionist movement transmuted into the State of Israel, whose humiliation of the Arab world and displacement of most Arab Palestinians constituted the clearest proof that the Middle East was still weak and, in many ways, backward.

Calls for reform or revolution were being heard almost everywhere. The old order had survived in places like Iraq. After a brief interlude of radicalism, the Iranian monarch was back in power. In Syria, challenges to old patterns had brought instability. Egypt was in the hands of a junta that was determined to clean out the evils of the old regime, but it was not following a very radical pattern.

Only a few countries were free of the typical ferment. In Yemen and Sa'udi Arabia, who were a generation behind most of the area, traditionalism was barely challenged by Western influence. In Turkey the old order had been replaced a generation earlier, and the revolutionary party was making way for a new phase. And Israel was a Western island, futilely building dikes in an attempt to keep out the Eastern sea.

9
Victories and Setbacks
1955-1973

The first part of 1955 was in some ways a turning point for the Middle East and its relationship with the world. Although the Egyptian Revolution was already two and a half years old, Premier (later President) Gamal Abd al-Nasir had only recently consolidated his leadership. So far, the new regime had brought more continuity than change, particularly in foreign affairs. But with the achievement of a long-sought British commitment in 1954 to withdraw troops from the Suez Canal zone, Egypt was to start a new phase in its foreign policy objectives.

Nasir emerged as more than the leader of Egypt. He came to epitomize the struggle of Arabs and sometimes of non-Westerners generally against the remnants of Western colonialism. Turning Egypt's policy toward pan-Arabism, he gained widespread acclaim from nationalists throughout the Arab world as he defied powerful nations. In response to U.S. and British plans to align Middle Eastern countries on their side in the cold war against the USSR-led bloc, Nasir became a leading proponent of ''positive neutralism'' or ''nonalignment.'' This was a natural reaction in a region whose grievances had long been mainly against Western European (and now increasingly American), not Russian, imperialists. To most Middle Easterners, the cold war appeared to be an intra-Western feud that they should avoid. Moreover, as affronts from members of the anti-Communist bloc continued, one response was to accept support from—which sometimes threatened potentially to become dependence on—the USSR. Such ''new middle class'' leaders as Nasir were also devoted to relatively radical change at home. Traditional monarchies increasingly felt threatened by radical nationalists and depended all the more on ties with the U.S., which their critics deemed "neocolonialist." Only in a non-Arab country like Turkey, where both geography and historic precedent made the USSR appear to be the main threat, was nationalism not largely synonymous with nonalignment. Even in Iran, which had a similar experience with Russian expansionism, underlying nationalist sentiment tended to be directed more immediately against a regime that was widely regarded as a tool of U.S. domination.

The Arab-Israeli conflict began increasingly to occupy center stage. Israel saw itself as a restored ancient Middle Eastern nation, but to the Arabs it appeared to be a European settler state and an instrument of other Westerners against Middle Eastern peoples. Getting renewed support from some Western countries, it sometimes acted in concert with them against Arab nationalism. Continued humiliation at Israeli hands belied the Arabs' ability to cope with the modern world and made their formal independence, once reached, seem like a mirage.

BAGHDAD, BANDUNG, AND GAZA

The first bombshell of 1955 was the announcement in January that Iraq and Turkey were ready to form an alliance, the Baghdad Pact. This was the culmination of efforts from the beginning of the decade to establish a Middle Eastern counterpart to NATO. By the end of the year, Iran, Pakistan, and Great Britain had joined the grouping. The United States responded to the opposition of Arab nationalists and the Israelis, who feared a buildup of Arab armies in the alliance, by avoiding formal membership. Still, Washington proceeded to work closely with the organization and to participate in its committees.

Iraq's membership in the Baghdad Pact accentuated its longstanding rivalry with Egypt, and a struggle ensued between the two countries to line up other Arab states on one side or the other. The Baghdad Pact's leading Arab proponent, Iraqi Prime Minister Nuri al-Sa'id, saw it as a great gain, not only against what he believed to be the danger of communism but also for strengthening Iraq and other potential Arab members against Israel. Nuri could also point out that the pact replaced a bilateral alliance with Britain and allowed that country's air bases to be turned over to Iraq, a gain corresponding to Nasir's success in getting rid of the base in Egypt. But to most of the Arab public, with which the Iraqi leader became more and more out of touch, Nuri again seemed to be showing his true color as a British agent. The Baghdad Pact ultimately proved to be a major step in undermining the Iraqi monarchy.

Although the Egyptian government was anti-Communist and up to then perhaps still a candidate for membership in such an alliance in the long run, it was angry over the Baghdad Pact. Nasir thought that his government had assurances from Nuri that the pact would not be concluded. To him it seemed to undermine the Arab Collective Security Pact of 1950, which still existed only on paper. More than that, Nasir saw the Baghdad Pact as a Western attempt to build up Iraq to replace Egypt as the leading Arab state. A bitter radio propaganda war began in which an already unpopular Iraqi regime was highly vulnerable to attack.

In this conflict between pro-Western Iraq and neutralist Egypt, several Arab countries at first hesitated to take sides. Sa'udi Arabia, because of its old conflict with the Hashimites, and Yemen, because of its conflict with Britain over the Aden colony and protectorate (Southern Yemen), sided with Egypt. For Syria, the pact evoked suspicion of a move toward a Hashimite-led Fertile Crescent, and a pro-pact government soon gave way to alignment with Egypt, with the Ba'thist minority in the Syrian Chamber of Deputies exerting more and more influence. British-subsidized King Husayn of Jordan was naturally inclined to join with his cousin, King Faysal II of Iraq, and a British mission in December brought offers of military aid as part of Jordanian membership in the pact. But the scheme was thwarted as demonstrations and riots indicative of the popular Jordanian mood, particularly among a Palestinian majority that eagerly accepted Cairo Radio's encouragement, threatened to bring his regime down. Soon afterward, King Husayn bettered his own nationalist credentials for a while by suddenly dismissing Sir John Bagot Glubb, whose able command of the Arab Legion had nevertheless put the kingdom's independence in question.

A conference of Afro-Asian leaders at Bandung, Indonesia, in April 1955 gave Nasir's leadership a new thrust. He gained recognition as one of the main Afro-Asian leaders, along with Nehru of India, Sukarno of Indonesia, and Chou en-Lai of China, and became more conscious of belonging to an Afro-Asian world that shared a struggle against Western colonialism. The exclusion of Israel from the conference pointed to gains to be made from working with this wider circle of nations. Although Nasir supported the pro-U.S. positions on some issues at Bandung, the dominant trend among his fellow Afro-Asian leaders in favor of positive neutralism reinforced his own inclination in the same direction.

On February 28, shortly before the Bandung meeting, the conflict with Israel suddenly loomed large for Egypt. The up-to-now generally quiet Israeli-Egyptian armistice line blew up as hit-and-run Israeli forces crossed into the Gaza Strip to destroy the pumphouse that supplied drinking water to Gaza and to kill thirty- eight people. David Ben-Gurion had just returned from his short-lived retirement on a kibbutz to replace Pinhas Lavon as Israel's minister of defense. (He would later become prime minister again.) The Gaza raid signaled a renewed militancy that was designed to provoke another war, already planned for the following year. Even during the previous lull, Israel had continued to violate the demilitarized zone, while Egypt still denied Israeli ships access to the Suez Canal. In late 1954 Israel tested the Canal closure, and one of its ships was confiscated by Egyptian authorities. And an Israeli had recently been killed by an "infiltrator" from the Gaza Strip.

Another event of the previous year was of even greater importance as part of the background of the Gaza raid. In July 1954 Israeli agents appeared in Cairo and Alexandria to firebomb the U.S. Information Service libraries and other U.S. and

British buildings in the expectation that Egypt would be blamed. It was hoped that the consequent disruption of Egyptian relations with the two Western countries would reverse British plans to withdraw from the Canal Zone. But the Israeli agents were apprehended before they could carry out their mission. The hanging of two of them in Cairo on January 27 on seemingly incredible charges provided Israel with one justification for the Gaza raid. The story, however, was confirmed six years later, as responsibility for the unsuccessful "security operation" became a heated issue in Israeli politics, the so-called Lavon affair. More relevant to the Gaza raid was the fact that the "security" failure brought Lavon's fall and put Ben-Gurion in office again, although debate still rages in Israel over whether Lavon or Ben-Gurion's protegés in the Defense Ministry planned the operation.

SOVIET ARMS FOR EGYPT

The Gaza raid was only the beginning of a series of Israeli incursions during 1955–1956. The Egyptian army was so hopelessly weak that Radio Cairo once resorted to reporting a fictitious victory to save face with the public. Nasir proposed that each side pull its troops back one kilometer from the line to avoid incidents, and although the suggestion met Israeli scorn, Egyptian troops moved back unilaterally. But the Egyptian response to the Gaza raid also had a less pacifistic side, as the army began to train Palestinians as *fida'iyin* ("self-sacrificers") to carry out sabotage and terrorist raids deep into Israel. The renewed violence created a climate in which the proposals of an American representative for sharing the waters of the Jordan River, though acceptable to everyone on a technical level, was rejected by Arab governments.

Another Egyptian response was a renewed interest in building up the army. Egypt had hoped to get U.S. arms once the conflict with Britain was settled, but aside from pro-Israeli pressures at home, the United States at this time tended to be irritated with neutralism. This was at the height of the cold war, and many Americans perceived their cause as one of righteousness against the "evils" of communism. Reflecting a common attitude toward those nations that refused to "stand up and be counted," U.S. Secretary of State John Foster Dulles once declared that neutralism was indeed "immoral." While the sale of U.S. arms to neutralist Egypt was not denied outright, the proposed terms of payment were such that Cairo could not accept.

With some reluctance Egypt now approached the USSR, and an arms deal (at first said to be with Czechoslovakia) that stunned many governments in the anti-Communist camp was announced in September. Since Stalin's death in 1953 Moscow had reversed its former ideological rigidity in favor of a new willingness to work with antiimperialist non-Communist ("national bourgeois") regimes in Africa and Asia, such as Nasir's. This support for such regimes, some of which had formerly been condemned as "fascist," carried with it an increasing amount of criticism for Israel. With the arms deal, the USSR seemed to have achieved a major coup by "leapfrogging" over the Baghdad Pact countries to a position of potential influence further south.

For Egypt, too, the arms deal seemed to be a big achievement. No longer would Arab states have to wait meekly for the British, French, and Americans ("the arms monopoly") to mete out weapons. By playing their Russian card, Arab states could hope to make their independence more real, although some of them also possibly feared that they risked falling under Soviet control.

These events gave Nasir a new stature in the Arab world. He was not now perceived, as he had been a year earlier, as one who had unduly compromised with London. As a result of the arms deal and subsequent bold acts, he came to be idolized by increasing numbers of Arabs. Perhaps this was true in other Arab countries more than at home, where he was also seen as the first authentic Egyptian to lead the country since Pharaonic times. Despite his authoritarianism, he gained wide acceptance as a real representative of the Arab masses. Not only did he seem to be sweeping away much in Egypt's society that younger nationalists detested, but the Baghdad Pact had also made him the symbol of opposition to Nuri al-Sa'id and others accused of subservience to colonialism. The acquisition of Soviet arms gave Arabs new hope that the rights of the Palestinians could be restored by the "new Salah al-Din," and some Israelis also began to fear that the Arabs had found their great leader. It was largely in response to acclaim for him in other Arab countries that Nasir began to give more emphasis than ever to the idea that Egypt was part of one Arab nation.

THE HIGH DAM

After showing initial irritation over the arms deal, the U.S. decided to counterbalance the USSR's new position of influence by instituting a dramatic program of its own. The Egyptian government had already decided to seek aid for building a massive High Dam at Aswan, in southern Egypt, to be 365 feet high, and two and one-half miles long. By saving surplus water when the Nile was high, the dam was expected to create an artificial lake in southern Egypt and the northern Sudan. In addition to providing a major source of hydroelectric power, the dam was supposed to enable Egyptians to increase their irrigated land to meet the demands of a rapidly increasing population. In December 1955 the United States, Great Britain, and the World Bank offered to help finance the project, with Washington and London to provide $70 million for the first stage. This was made conditional on a commitment from Cairo to accept certain restraints on its economic policies. For example, the Egyptian government would be unable to obtain other foreign loans without the World Bank's permission. Despite the high priority Egypt gave to this project, it was reluctant to accept such limitations on its independence and consequently delayed its response.

On July 19, 1956, the Egyptian ambassador in Washington nevertheless informed Dulles of his country's acceptance of the offer. But Dulles replied that the United States had changed its mind, offering the excuse that the Egyptian economy was too weak to support the project. Besides insulting the Egyptians, this explanation was unconvincing, since there was no more basis for it than when the offer was made. The real reason was more complicated, involving the opposition of Israel's supporters and of American cotton farmers who feared an increase in Egyptian production as a result of the dam. Some U.S. allies also argued that none of them were getting such a big aid program and that Egypt was thus being rewarded for its neutralism. Although Nasir played down reports that the USSR was willing to help with the dam, U.S. policymakers thought they detected "blackmail" and wanted to call Moscow's bluff. A more immediate reason was one of Egypt's recent actions in keeping with a neutralist policy, namely its recognition of the Communist regime in China in May. This was done partly because that country appeared to be an alternative source of military aid in the event the USSR agreed with the United States, as had been suggested, on a joint arms embargo to the area. But recognition of Beijing was anathema to the United States; although Britain and Israel had already recognized the regime, U.S. officials pointed out that this had occurred before the 1950 "aggression" in Korea.

Nasir heard that Dulles had reneged while he was flying with Nehru to Cairo from Yugoslavia, where they had met with their fellow neutralist, Marshal Tito. To Nasir, Dulles's action seemd like a slap in the face and perhaps an attempt to undermine his government. He did not bide his time for long before responding in a way that would allow him to recoup his prestige.

THE SUEZ CRISIS

Nasir's dramatic response to Dulles's action came on July 26, during the celebration of the fourth anniversary of the overthrow of King Faruq. Evoking wild applause from the crowd and a mixture of joy and apprehension from opponents of Western colonialism in general, Nasir announced that Egypt had nationalized the Suez Canal Company, indeed that Egyptian authorities were taking full control over it at that moment. The Canal Company, a private corporation operating in Egyptian territory and incorporated under Egyptian law but with the shares owned by the British government and by French investors, seemed to be a remnant of European colonialism. The completion of the British withdrawal from the Suez base a month earlier made the company the next logical object of Egypt's antiimperialism. Although the concession was due to expire in 1968 in any case, Nasir had already thought of the possibility of nationalizing the company before that time. The Aswan Dam episode made this an imperative for him.

Nasir now became a bogeyman for much of the West, and the "seizure" of the canal became a rallying cry for some who had already determined to crush him for other reasons. The British and the French were heavily dependent on the waterway, especially for oil shipments, and feared that Egyptian control jeopardized it.

More generally, they saw Nasir as a threat to their remaining colonial and semicolonial arrangements throughout the Middle East and Africa. British Prime Minister Anthony Eden was particularly concerned with destroying the "Egyptian dictator," whom he compared to Hitler. Eden was so obsessed with the appeasement of Hitler at Munich in 1938 that he was unable to deal with the Suez situation rationally. It also seems that Eden's enmity toward Nasir went back to his mistaken belief that the Egyptian leader was the real "culprit" in King Husayn's dismissal of Glubb Pasha and was bolstered by a general tendency to see Cairo Radio's "Voice of the Arabs" as the sole cause of Arab nationalism and anticolonialism.

France had its own reason for wanting to crush Nasir. A revolt had broken out in Algeria in 1954, which increasingly threatened French rule and the position of the dominant European settler minority. Arabs in general sympathized with their Algerian "brothers," and Egypt gave the rebels some aid. But the French convinced themselves that Nasir was the cause of all their trouble and that the road to victory in Algeria went via Cairo. Unlike Britain, the French had little to lose in the Arab East, and from 1954 on, a Paris–Tel Aviv axis emerged. French armaments poured into Israel, which was awaiting the right moment to attack Egypt.

The "Suez Crisis" persisted through the summer and fall of 1956, as Britain, France, and Israel prepared for war against Egypt. As the argument ran, nationalization of the Canal Company was a gross violation of the Constantinople Convention of 1888, which provided that the canal would be open to the ships of all nations. When Egypt and its supporters pointed out that ownership of the Canal Company did not necessarily have anything to do with the right to use the canal, Eden in turn repeatedly scorned such "legal quibbles." Egyptian promises to compensate the stockholders, the major legal requirement for nationalizing foreign-owned property, were ridiculed. In fact, Egypt would not have had any real choice in the matter of compensation, for London, Paris, and Washington had immediately responded to nationalization by freezing Egyptian financial assets, which were more than sufficient to cover the cost of the Canal Company.

Most Westerners assumed that a "backward" country like Egypt could not run the Canal and that this would make Egyptian guarantees for its accessibility to them useless. Britain and France, in effect, attempted to sabotage the waterway by withdrawing all pilots of their nationalities, but they were surprised when the operation ran more efficiently than ever with a drastically reduced personnel. Such a great success was a source of pride to Egypt, although it was in large part due to the inherent ease of operating a sea-level canal, with no locks. Looking for another provocation, Britain and France were also frustrated by Nasir's willingness to allow their ships through the canal and thus to refuse to present a *causi belli* even when they refused to pay.

While the USSR and most of the Afro-Asian states supported Egypt, the United States joined its allies in criticizing the nationalization of the canal. But the United States also opposed the use of force. Dulles and President Eisenhower earned Eden's enmity first by delaying any action. A series of conferences of major maritime nations, held in London, failed to bring about a solution. The First London

Conference, in August, proposed an international board to run the canal, but Egypt adamantly rejected this. A Second London Conference, in September, proposed to set up a Suez Canal Users' Association (SCUA) to operate the waterway from ships positioned at each end. The SCUA was set up, but Eden was angered to discover that Dulles was still opposed to having it "shoot its way through."

SUEZ-SINAI WAR

A series of secret meetings of British, French, and Israeli officials worked out other plans. These called for an Israeli attack on Egypt, with French planes to provide air cover in case Egypt retaliated by trying to bomb Israeli cities. Then, feigning innocence, London and Paris would issue an ultimatum to the two belligerents, demanding that they withdraw ten miles from each side of the canal to protect it from danger and allow an Anglo-French force as a buffer. Israel was not expected to have penetrated that far into Egypt anyway. Since Egypt could not fail to reject such a proposal, British and French forces would then take the "safety" of the canal into their own hands by forcibly occupying it. The three states adamantly denied that any kind of collusion had occurred, but official revelations a decade later removed all doubt.

Events at first went according to plan for the three allies. A series of incidents on the Israeli-Jordanian frontier helped to camouflage Israel's intentions until its forces, commanded by Chief of Staff General Moshe Dayan, struck into the Gaza Strip and the Sinai on October 29 and simultaneously parachuted in to occupy the strategic Mitla Pass in west-central Sinai. Most of the Egyptian forces normally stationed there had been withdrawn to face an expected invasion of the Canal Zone. Although Egyptians fought well in the few cases when they were able to put up resistance, even against overwhelming odds and without air cover, Israel routed them without difficulty. Almost all of Sinai was soon under Israeli control. Egyptian reinforcements were at first sent against the invader but then got orders to return when the Anglo-French ultimatum, presented according to plan, made their presence vital in the Canal Zone. On November 1, Britain and France began bombing Egyptian bases, airports, and other points, but the two powers failed to land their forces at Port Sa'id, at the northern end of the Canal, until November 5. Again Egyptian troops proved helpless, although popular resistance in Port Sa'id slowed the invasion slightly and continued to harass the occupiers.

At the UN the United States joined with the USSR in condemning the invasion. Washington was angry with its allies for having acted behind its back and saw this as a kind of outright aggression that could not be condoned without making its proclaimed principles patently hollow. Soviet hints of retaliation against London and Paris and broadcasts referring to "volunteers" had less impact than did American opposition. While an Anglo-French veto stalled action in the Security Council, a special session of the General Assembly called for a cease-fire and withdrawal of troops. The Suez invasion ground to a halt on November 7, when British and French forces were still only twenty miles south of Port Sa'id. The canal was closed temporarily as a result of damage during the hostilities, particularly by a ship that Egypt purposely sank to delay the invasion. An American offer to provide oil to the two countries at a time of impending scarcity—and financial help to bolster the now-endangered British pound—provided a major inducement for them to quit. The establishment of a UN Emergency Force (UNEF), ultimately to consist of 7,000 men, also facilitated withdrawal, which was complete by the end of the year.

Israel resisted calls for withdrawal and stayed on for a while in the Gaza Strip and at Sharm al-Shaykh, which commands the entrance to the Gulf of Aqaba. This evoked criticism from the United States and a possibility of UN economic sanctions. Finally, with a U.S. endorsement of its right to use the Gulf of Aqaba, Israel ended the occupation in March 1957, and the territorial status quo ante was restored. The UNEF patrolled the armistice line, although its presence was dependent on continued Egyptian permission, as Israel never permitted the force on its side of the line. The UNEF was not designed for fighting, but by separating the two sides it helped to keep the Egyptian-Israeli frontier quiet for a decade. Its units also guarded Sharm al-Shaykh, thus preventing Egypt from closing the Gulf to Israeli ships again. Israel's access to the waterway became its only tangible gain from the invasion, although this demonstration of its military power renewed its self-confidence.

NASIR'S UPSURGE AFTER SUEZ

The victor of Suez was Arab nationalism and its symbol, President Nasir. Britain had been discredited, and its remaining quasi-colonial positions shrank. Even in Jordan, elections in October, the only relatively free ones that the country has ever had, resulted in a nationalist, Nasirite parliament and cabinet, headed by Prime Minister Sulayman Nabulsi. The aftermath of the tripartite attack on Egypt also brought the abrogation of the Anglo-Jordanian Treaty, with Jordan turning to Egypt, Syria, and Sa'udi Arabia to replace the British subsidy. Admittedly, Nasir's army had been crushed, but that did not discredit him with Arab nationalists, for no poor, excolonial country could be expected to stand up against such odds. While, in the past, the British had been able to bring down Egyptian governments, now it was Eden, not Nasir, who fell from power as a result of Suez. Indeed, less than two years would pass before the challenge of Arab nationalism, particularly in Algeria but with the Suez episode in the background, sufficed to bring down the whole Fourth French Republic.

Although the United States saved Egypt from defeat, the American position was not enhanced. Many Arabs gave more credit to the USSR's empty threats against their enemies and to its continuing military and economic aid to nationalist Arab governments. Although Arabs gave Washington credit for opposing aggression in this case, they were not satisfied with other U.S. actions. Arab nationalists pointed out that, while the United States was helping the aggressors recover from the shambles they had brought upon themselves, it continued to freeze Egyptian financial assets. Egypt was not even permitted to obtain polio vaccine from the United States at this time. Trials in Syria that revealed a U.S.–British–Iraqi plot to overthrow the government also helped cancel out the gratefulness that other U.S. policies might have earned.

When Dulles spoke of the new power "vacuum" in the Middle East, Arabs were angered. President Eisenhower announced a plan to help Middle Eastern countries fill this "vacuum" by giving military and economic assistance and even by offering to send troops if needed against the danger of "international Communism." But Arab nationalists interpreted this as a crusade against Arab nationalism and neutralism and as an attempt by the United States to replace Britain as the dominant power in the region. While Turkey and Iran endorsed the Eisenhower Doctrine, as this policy was labeled, even the conservative Arab regimes, except for those of Lebanon and Libya, refused to do so openly.

A bitter conflict ensued between neutralist and pro-Western regimes after Suez. In the face of a growing challenge by nationalists that could be counterbalanced only by U.S. support, King Sa'ud of Sa'udi Arabia was weaned away from his ties with Egypt. Even when the Sa'udi royal family forced the inept, wasteful king to turn over much of his power temporarily to his reputedly pro-Nasir brother, Prince Faysal, in 1958, the resulting budgetary reforms were not matched by lessening opposition to revolutionary forces. Also, King Husayn of Jordan dismissed the Nabulsi government and nipped an army coup in the bud as the U.S. Sixth Fleet made a show of force for him in the eastern Mediterranean. The kingdom's former British subsidy turned out to be replaced by an American, not an Arab, one. This included payments from the CIA that were kept secret for two decades. The threat of Nasirite revolution caused the Sa'udi and Hashimite monarchs to put their old rivalry aside in a new royal solidarity.

The nationalistic government of Syria was the center of much Western and conservative Arab wrath. With some reputedly pro-Soviet figures taking important positions in the government, the Western news media and Western governments exaggerated the imminence of a Communist takeover there. The U.S. was still devoted to replacing this government, and as Turkish troops were mobilized on the Syrian border, it concocted a plan for Jordan and Iraq to invade their neighbor in 1957. But even conservative Arab governments grew nervous about the project. King Sa'ud began to mediate between Turkey and Syria, and the crisis cooled off.

Syrian leaders' fear of communism and their even greater fear of "reactionaries" now began to reinforce their long-standing emotional commitment to "one Arab nation." Various Syrian calls for unity with Egypt culminated in a mission to Cairo in January 1958 that asked for immediate union. President Nasir was skeptical of such an unplanned merger and refused to agree except on his own strict terms. These included the establishment of a unitary rather than a federal state and the abolition of all Syrian political parties, including the Ba'th. The latter, though unsympathetic to Nasir before 1955, had come to see him as fully embodying their own cause. Syrian Ba'thists believed that, even with their party disbanded, they would have a predominant position in any unified Arab state, and so they agreed to Nasir's terms.

After a plebiscite in February, a United Arab Republic (UAR) came into being, with Syria and Egypt transformed into the Northern and Southern regions of the new state. Ecstasy reached a high point among Arab nationalists. Nasir was now and afterward simply "the President" (al-Ra'is) to Arabs everywhere. When he visited Damascus in 1958, the exultant mood seemed to be one of expecting all "artificial" inter-Arab borders, and with them the regimes propped up by "imperialists," to vanish.   While the Yemeni imam sought protection from nationalist criticism by joining with the UAR to form a nominal United Arab States, the Hashimite monarchs of Jordan and Iraq tried to rival Nasir's union by establishing their own loose "Arab Federation," with Nuri as its first prime minister, but few people took this seriously.

The Arab nationalist mood combined with domestic politics to produce a crisis in Lebanon during 1958. Many Arab nationalist Lebanese (i.e., mainly Muslims) went to Damascus to celebrate Nasir's visit and were swept away by emotion. Still, neither they nor Nasir envisaged that Lebanon would give up its separate independence. There was also growing resentment among Muslims against domination by what had been a bare majority of Christians but would by then undoubtedly have been shown to be a minority if a census had been permitted. And many Lebanese were embittered by several of President Camille Chamoun's actions, including his failure to break off diplomatic relations with Britain and France during their attack on Egypt. His endorsement of the Eisenhower Doctrine was another mark against him. In addition, Chamoun manipulated parliamentary elections in 1957 to get his protegés elected, and some of the defeated politicians, Muslim and Christian alike, were now angry. With his own supporters predominating in the Chamber, the Lebanese president was reputed to have plans to push through a constitutional amendment allowing him to be elected for a second term.

The assassination of a pro-Nasir newspaperman in May 1958 brought the crisis to a head. Barricades appeared throughout Lebanon as pro-Chamoun and anti-Chamoun forces fought a desultory civil war. The army, under General Fu'ad Shihab, also a Maronite, stood aside. The conflict was widely presented in much of the outside world in grossly oversimplified terms as one between Christians and Muslims, although even some of the traditional Maronite leaders, including the patriarch of the Maronite Church, aligned themselves with the so-called "Muslim" camp. Some arms were smuggled from the UAR (Syria) to the anti-Chamoun forces, but this was only a minor factor in the struggle.

As the Lebanese crisis heightened, Iraq took center stage on July 14. Part of the army was ordered to move to Jordan to bolster King Husayn, but it was suspected that this was a prelude to intervention in Syria and Lebanon. As units commanded by General Abd al-Karim Qasim and Colonel Abd al-Salim Arif passed close by Baghdad on their way, the awaited opportunity to overthrow the government was taken. This had already been planned in discussions with civilian nationalist leaders. The army quickly took control, while the streets of Baghdad witnessed pent-up fury against a generally hated regime. King Faysal and his uncle, Abd al-Ilah, were shot to death, apparently as the latter tried to resist the soldiers sent to arrest them. The royal family was exterminated. Nuri escaped in a woman's garb but was killed on the spot when the crowd discovered who he was. His body was dragged through the streets and torn apart. With this response to "reaction" and "imperialism," Baghdad soon announced its withdrawal from the "Baghdad Pact," whose name was changed to the Central Treaty Organization (CENTO).

As Arab nationalists celebrated the Iraqi Revolution in the expectation that Baghdad would soon join the UAR, the anti-Communist camp was appalled. Turkey apparently wanted to invade Iraq and to restore the old regime but was restrained by the U.S. British troops flew into Jordan to bolster the king's position. And in response to Chamoun's appeal for help, U.S. marines landed in Lebanon to protect it from an "international Communism" that was almost entirely a product of the imagination as far as that country was concerned. But American forces took no active part in the civil war. Instead, the United States helped to bring about a compromise settlement, with Shihab elected president, and some of the former rebels joining the new cabinet. Little basic change occurred in the Lebanese political system, although the Eisenhower Doctrine was repudiated and relations with Cairo were normalized.

NASIR'S DOMESTIC REFORMS

While Nasir's Egypt led the way against colonialism and Arab disunity, it also adopted revolutionary policies that inspired emulation elsewhere. Economic and social development received increasing attention. Provision of schools, medical care, and potable water for the rural population became high priorities and the country proceeded to make small dents in the miserable conditions that had prevailed for so long. But disease and illiteracy were not easy to wipe out. Even in 1970 only 53 percent of the school age children were enrolled in school, but this represented a considerable achievement in comparison with the 20 percent figure of two decades earlier. Industrialization became another major goal, and projects like a steel mill at Helwan, near Cairo, were built with Soviet assistance. By 1970 industry contributed 38 percent of the GNP, compared with 21 percent in 1950. Land reclamation got attention, with the High Dam, which was completed between 1960 and 1970 with Soviet aid, overshadowing all other efforts. Two successive five-year plans, adopted in 1960, set the unrealistic goal of doubling the GNP by the end of the decade, but economic development proceeded at a respectable rate of about 6 percent a year during the early 1960s. Official attempts to encourage birth control had little effect; the population increased at a rate of over 2.5 percent a year, which meant that much of the economic grain was literally eaten up.

With the effort to increase the "national pie" came attempts to divide it more equally. The mild reforms in the years following the 1952 coup made way for more radical change in the early 1960s. The word *socialism* came increasingly into the official vocabulary, although the only industries nationalized during the 1950s were those owned by enemy nationals during the Suez War. Brussels' intervention in the newly independent Congo (today's Zaire) in 1960 also resulted in the nationalization of Belgian-owned property in Egypt. The Bank of Egypt was nationalized in 1960.

July 1961 saw the promulgation of a whole set of "socialist laws" establishing what was now called "Arab socialism" and a "socialist, cooperative, democratic society." These nationalization measures, together with others that followed in the early 1960s, turned most large businesses into state enterprises, while 51 percent government ownership was imposed on others. The socialist laws also gave employees a share of the profits and representation on boards of directors. Among numerous leveling measures was a highly progressive income tax, which took 90 percent of incomes exceeding ten thousand pounds. Land reform was also extended, with the maximum ownership set at 100 acres in 1961 and reduced to half that amount in 1969. While a shortage of foreign exchange and government control over imports largely kept foreign-produced luxury goods out of the country, subsidies helped enable the poor to buy basic foods.

Still, the extent of leveling can be exaggerated. While dire poverty still prevailed among most of the people, a privileged few flaunted their wealth or else kept much of it out of sight to await what, from their point of view, might be a better day. Even some landowners partly evaded land reform by dividing their estates among members of the family and preserved some of their local influence. New privileged groups emerged, like army officers and technocrats managing state factories, and they resisted leftist pressures to make the revolution more thoroughgoing.

The nationalist and socialist measures undermined the position of some minority groups. Small foreign minorities like the Greeks largely vanished as the members returned to their home countries. With the Arab-Israeli conflict putting their loyalty into question, almost all the Egyptian Jews left Egypt. Several thousand who had not obtained Egyptian nationality were expelled during the Suez War, along with other enemy aliens. Since the minorities, including Copts, were on the whole relatively privileged economically, they sometimes felt that socialism was directed against them. They were generally less antiimperialist and tended not to identify with Arab nationalism and thus were unethusiastic about official policies. Attempts to correct the Muslim majority's underrepresentation in desirable positions also evoked grumbling about alleged discrimination by members of minority groups.

The doctrine and practice of Arab socialism developed pragmatically. For example, the 1961 socialist laws were in large part a response to the problem of carrying out an economic plan when business was under private ownership. But the laws also represented a strong "democratic" bias in the leadership, in the socioeconomic but not the political sense. Communism was rejected, and, in line with methods that varied from benign autocracy to extreme repressiveness, Communists sometimes were given harsh treatment. The Marxist doctrine of class struggle came in for particular criticism from the regime. But individual Marxists were tolerated and given positions in the press and elsewhere after the outlawed Communist party agreed to disband in 1965.

In an attempt to tie the doctrine to the people's previous heritage, Arab socialism was said to be derived from Islam. Nasir sometimes said that all religions teach socialism and cited numerous egalitarian aspects of Islamic teachings and of early Islamic practice to demonstrate his point.

Nasir's revolution contrasted with Atatürk's in that it did not involve an attack on religion. Yet Nasir was a secularist to a large extent. Together with many Arab nationalists, he emphasized an Arab nationalism that incorporated Muslim and Christian Arabs, although some non-Muslims tend to interpret this as a disguised form of Islamic identity. He played down religion in foreign policy, as in failing to support his fellow Muslims in the Cyprus and Indo-Pakistani conflicts. The fundamentalist Muslim Brotherhood was feared perhaps more than any other movement. Members of this group allegedly were caught plotting to kill the president in 1965, and some executions followed. But Nasir showed respect for Islam and justified his policies in accordance with it. His government used religious leaders as a communications channel and prepared sermons for delivery in the mosques. Religion was a required subject in the schools, with each child instructed in his own faith. At the same time the government instituted reforms in the thousand-year-old al-Azhar University, particularly by adding modern subjects to its curriculum. There was no attempt to replace religious law in matters of personal status, and only a few substantive reforms ensued in these matters. But religious courts were abolished in 1956, leaving the regular courts to apply the law of all sects.

The regime of the "Free Officers" set about establishing governmental institutions. When the transition period expired in 1956, a constitution was drawn up and submitted to a plebiscite. Its approval by more than 99 percent of the voters was typical of elections in this and other authoritarian regimes. The election of Nasir, without opposition, by a similar percentage was still another example. A political movement called the National Union, in effect a single political party, also came into existence in 1956, and after a delay caused by the Suez crisis, a National Assembly was elected during the next year from a limited number of approved candidates. The establishment of the UAR in 1958 led to the adoption of a new constitution, with an enlarged National Assembly and National Union. The breakup of the UAR required still another try, and the National Union was replaced by an Arab Socialist Union (ASU) in 1962. A "National Congress of Popular Forces" approved a charter that elucidated the regime's official ideology in the same year, while a new constitution, still deemed provisional, was adopted in 1964.

These institutions were of limited importance. The National Assembly, half of whose members had to be peasants and workers according to the 1964 constitution, acted as an independent legislative body only to a minor extent and usually gave automatic approval to the regime's proposals. There were attempts to breathe some life into the ASU, for example, by excluding "reactionary" elements and by creating an inner category of vanguard members. Its local committees did, in fact, provide a basis for popular participation, but it gained little effectiveness as an organization for mass mobilization and participation on the national level. The leadership was unable to rule through the ASU, and instead, so-called centers of power continued to exist in the society. Notably, the army, whose officers now became a pampered elite, was under the largely independent control of Field Marshal Abd al-Hakim Amir until 1967. Amir, who had the unswerving loyalty of most officers, was also Nasir's close friend and associate, but it was later revealed that the relationship between the two men became tense during the mid 1960s and that the president, fearing an army coup, was powerless to deal with him. Leftists argued that such a weak political order should make way for a more effective ASU, with a clearer ideology, in order to facilitate a real social transformation.

NASIR'S DECLINE

Nasir's position in the Arab world reached its peak in the summer of 1958 and then began to descend. After Iraq's revolution, there was a widespread expectation that it would join the UAR and that other revolutions and an ever larger unity would follow. But subsequent events showed that Arab unity was hard to attain. Qasim was determined to keep power himself, not to turn it over to Nasir, and the ardently pro-Nasir Arif was soon out of favor; at one point he received a death sentence, but this was never carried out. The bitter propaganda war between Iraq and the UAR soon resumed. In order to counter the Nasirites, who were bloodily suppressed when they revolted in Mosul in April 1959, Qasim began to depend on Communist support. Then the Communists' excesses, particularly a massacre in Kirkuk in July 1959, led the government to suppress them too, but no lasting rapprochement with the UAR was possible while Qasim was in power.

As the euphoria of union wore off, Syria proved to be another disillusionment for Nasir. The Nasirite-Ba'thist honeymoon ended when the Ba'thists discovered that they would not be allowed to provide the brains for the new state. Conservative candidates were even allowed to defeat Ba'thists in the Northern Region in the National Assembly elections of 1959. Ba'thist leaders began to resign from the government. In turn, power became increasingly centralized, and Nasir's popularity in Syria was partially eroded, though not destroyed. To some Syrians, the union began to seem more like annexation to Egypt. Then, when the socialist measures were introduced in July 1961, conservative Syrians were embittered, and a group of conservative Syrian army officers staged a coup in September that restored the country's separate independence. Despite an initial impulse to restore Cairo's control, Nasir decided that it would be wiser not to risk an Arab civil war and thus acquiesced in the breakup. But, in order to keep the dream of union alive, Egypt retained the name "UAR" for another decade.

UPS AND DOWNS, 1961–1967

With the breakup of the UAR Egyptians were disillusioned with the other Arabs. Reflecting a temporary tendency to avoid Arab entanglements, Nasir blamed himself for having dealt with "reactionaries," or what he called his former policy of "unity of ranks," and announced a new policy of "unity of purpose"—that is, of working only with other "progressives," of which none at the moment were in control of any Arab government outside Egypt. But other radical regimes soon emerged, beginning with the achievement of Algerian independence in 1962.

In September 1962, Imam Ahmad of Yemen died. He had also turned against Nasir after the adoption of Arab Socialism, and his reputedly more "progressive" son, Badr, succeeded him. It was then that antimonarchical army officers, led by Abdullah al-Sallal, took control and established a republic. Numerous reforms were instituted, ranging from the abolition of slavery to ending the dominance of the *sayyid* ruling group (descendants of the Prophet Muhammad) who had monopolized the bureaucracy. But the *imam* escaped and rallied some Zaydi tribesmen to his side in the rough, mountainous north.

Faced with the threat of counterrevolution, the new regime asked for Egyptian help. With a certain degree of anti-"reaction" crusading zeal, Nasir sent troops to Yemen, while Sa'udi Arabian funds kept the *imam's* opposition alive. As the Egyptians became bogged down in a seemingly interminable conflict in an impossible, unfamiliar terrain, Egypt chose to commit increasingly large numbers of soldiers —70,000 by 1967—in the hope of finally prevailing. The intervention in Yemen at first seemed to be an opportunity to emerge from isolation in the Arab world, but now it was wasting Egyptian energy and funds. It was partly for this reason that the country's economic growth began to slow down. With Egypt sometimes strafing the Sa'udi side in southern Arabia, there seemed to be danger of an all-out Egyptian-Sa'udi war.

The Arab socialist threat helped to bring modest reform to Sa'udi Arabia. With King Sa'ud epitomizing wastefulness and corruption, even some members of his family showed their opposition by moving to revolutionary Cairo. Then the royal family, backed by a *fatwa* (ruling) from high religious authorities, forced Sa'ud to abdicate in favor of his brother Faysal in 1964. Despite his earlier pro-Nasir reputation, King Faysal now became the leading Arab opponent of revolution. His greater ability and his efforts to curb waste made him more effective in this role than his deposed brother. The institution of some social reforms, including the abolition of slavery, blunted Nasir's antireactionary propaganda.

The year 1963 also brought new coups in Syria and Iraq. In each case, Ba'thist-dominated governments were established and, in order to get the stamp of Nasir's approval, proceeded to negotiate an agreement to establish a new UAR. But the agreement soon fell apart as Egypt and the two Ba'thist regimes exchanged diatribes.

Arif, the nominal president of Iraq after the Ba'thist takeover, assumed real control through a coup of his own in November of the same year and entered into close relations with Egypt. Iraq and Egypt even agreed to proceed gradually toward unity, but this too was eventually dropped. In fact, Egypt had no enthusiasm for such a union, particularly in light of the revolt of Kurdish tribesmen in northern Iraq, led by Mulla Mustafa Barzani from 1961 on.

In many ways, the radical regimes that henceforth dominated Syria and Iraq were to parallel Nasir's Egypt. They too were committed to Arab socialism and thus decreed large-scale nationalization measures, although the initial Iraqi enthusiasm for this policy was somewhat toned down by emphasis on "prudence" in the mid-1960s. These were also authoritarian governments brought to power by and continuously dependent on the army. In each case there was some attempt to create a single-party regime, with the Ba'th in Syria and an Arab Socialist Union in Arif's Iraq. The main difference was that the Iraqi and Syrian regimes were long unable to create stability, partly because there was no one with Nasir's stature or charismatic appeal, but also because both countries were deeply divided along sectarian and regional lines. In the case of Iraq, the perennial Kurdish struggle for autonomy undermined national leaders, who were unable to deal with it effectively. A constant danger of coups kept each country from concentrating on basic problems, and repeated purges of army officers drained the defense capability.

INTENSIFICATION OF THE ARAB-ISRAELI CONFLICT IN THE MID-1960s

During this time the Palestine question had not gone away. The number of aggrieved Arab Palestinians continued to grow, while Israel was further consolidated by gradual immigration and by economic development, although by 1966 the country was experiencing increasing unemployment and emigration. The former patterns of Israeli party politics continued, with Mapai (later to form the core of a broader Labor party) the dominant coalition partner in each government. Ben-Gurion retired in 1963 but continued to bedevil his successor, Prime Minister Levi Eshkol, with accusations of weakness and to quarrel over who was responsible in the Lavon affair. He and a few of his cohorts, including Dayan, led their own breakaway party for a while.

From time to time "retaliatory" raids continued to be launched against Jordan and Syria. Because of the presence of the UNEF, the Egyptian frontier remained quiet. But the arms race intensified. Israel obtained weapons from France and other Western countries, while Soviet supplies to Egypt continued. Israel launched a guided missile in 1961, and Egypt offered high salaries to European scientists to help it match the Israeli achievement. Since most of these were West Germans, this led to an Israeli propaganda campaign against "Nazis" in Egypt. The Israeli Secret Service started sending letter bombs to the scientists, and this helped to torpedo Egypt's missile project.

An Israeli project to divert water from the Jordan River to irrigate land in the Negev desert was scheduled for completion in 1964. This provided an issue that brought the Arabs together for a while. Citing Israeli military power and Arab weakness, President Nasir continued to reject calls for the restoration of Palestinian rights by force. Now he hosted a series of Arab summit conferences to deal with the Jordan River problem. As he relaxed his antimonarchical policy for about a year, a show of Arab solidarity ensued. A plan to divert the Jordan's tributaries in Lebanon and Syria was adopted. This was really a tacit agreement to acquiesce in Israel's action by limiting the Arabs' usage to the share that the earlier U.S. proposals had allotted to them. But, since other Arab leaders, such as the Syrians, were involved in formulating this policy, they could not blame Nasir for being so ''soft'' on Israel.

The 1964 summit conference also agreed to establish a Palestine Liberation Organization (PLO). Some Arab leaders, beginning with Qasim, had proposed a Palestinian entity to let the Palestinians liberate their own country. Again leaders such as Nasir seemed to go along with such calls for militancy, but the PLO was really designed to be ineffective. It established a small Palestine Liberation Army (PLA) in the Gaza Strip; however, it was kept under Egyptian supervision. Ahmad Shuqayri, who became the head of the PLO, was known to be inept and capable only of loud talk, which aided Israeli propaganda. But most Arab leaders seemed to be glad to substitute talk for action. Another, more authentic Palestine resistance group, Fatah (a reverse acronym in Arabic for ''Movement for the Liberation of Palestine''), which may have existed informally on a small scale even in the 1950s, also emerged under the leadership of a popular Cairo-educated engineer, Yasir Arafat.

By this time radical Arab governments were recurrently colliding with the anti-Communist West. France was an exception, as the end of the Algerian War permitted it gradually to improve its relationship with the Arab world, although the de facto Franco-Israeli alliance was not repudiated until 1967. Prodded by the United States, West Germany provided arms to Israel from the early 1960s on, and most Arab countries broke diplomatic relations with Bonn in 1965 because of its recognition of the Jewish state. Guerrilla warfare against British rule flared up in Aden, with Egypt aiding the Front for the Liberation of Southern Yemen (FLOSY). Egypt also broke off relations with Britain in 1965 because of its refusal to take action against the white minority government in Rhodesia.

U.S.–Egyptian relations, which had become unusually amicable during the administration of President John F. Kennedy, deteriorated after Lyndon Johnson succeeded to the presidency in 1963. Johnson seemed to detest nationalist leaders like Nasir, and several incidents helped to increase the strain. In 1964 some Egyptian officials organized a demonstration in Cairo of Black African students against U.S. policy in the Congo. The demonstration got out of hand, with the students burning the U.S. Information Library, paradoxically one of the buildings that the Israelis had tried to destroy almost exactly a decade earlier. Although Cairo apologized for this incident, Egyptian policy in Yemen and conflict with pro-American ''reactionaries'' further disrupted relations with the United States. When the Sa'udi and Iranian monarchs proposed an Islamic summit conference in December 1965, Nasir attacked it as an attempt to create a new "reactionary" alliance against "progressive" regimes, and the conservative-revolutionary conflict intensified. With coups, allegedly backed by the CIA in countries like Indonesia and Ghana, Nasir got the impression that Washington was working to destroy radical nationalist regimes throughout the Third World, and in his eyes the cutoff of U.S. wheat sales to Egypt in 1966 confirmed it. For Nasir the establishment of a U.S.-backed rightist dictatorship in Greece in April 1967 seemed to be another warning of things to come elsewhere in the region.

In February 1966 a new faction of the Ba'th took control of Syria. A physician, Nur al-Din Atassi, became president, with General Salah al-Jadid the real strongman. Disproportionately representing the minority Alawi community, a traditionally underprivileged group living in the littoral north of Lebanon, this new breed of Ba'thists was more Marxist than pan-Arabist and espoused a newly militant antiimperialism and anti-Zionism. One of its new approaches was to allow Fatah to carry out commando raids on Israel from Syrian territory, though the raiders usually crossed into Israel via Jordan, whose Palestinian population and long armistice line facilitated such acts. The new Syrian leaders were basically more anti-Nasir than their predecessors, but Cairo entered into a security treaty with Damascus in order to be in a position to restrain it from rash acts.

THE 1967 WAR

The Arab-Israeli conflict exploded again in November 1966 as Israeli forces crossed into the West Bank of Jordan to destroy the village of al-Samu in retaliation for guerrilla raids. Israel received the strongest condemnation ever from the Security Council, with warnings of action if such an attack occurred again. While Arabs considered this and other UN resolutions inadequate responses to aggressive attacks, Israelis branded them one-sided and hypocritical. The Palestinians were in turmoil, and King Husayn, unable to protect them, again seemed endangered by revolution.

The crisis continued into 1967. Israeli leaders repeatedly threatened to invade Syria to topple its government if it did not stop supporting guerrillas. In April, Israeli jets crossed into Syrian airspace to engage in a dogfight that downed several Syrian planes. There were reports of Israeli troops concentrating near the Syrian frontier. Meanwhile, Nasir's Arab critics broadcast statements ridiculing him for posing as a great Arab leader while hiding behind the "skirts" of the UN. It was obvious that the UNEF would make it difficult for Egypt to come to the aid of Syria if the latter was attacked.

With this in mind Egyptian authorities asked the UNEF on May 16 to pull back from some sections of the armistice line. Secretary-General U Thant recognized that the force had no legal right to stay without Egypt's permission but gave President Nasir the choice of having it stay where it was or having it completely withdrawn from Egyptian territory. Nasir chose the latter alternative, and Israel rejected a request to allow the force to move over to its side. As the UNEF units left Sharm al-Shaykh, Egypt announced the closure of the Gulf of Aqaba to Israeli shipping, an act that Tel-Aviv was not expected to tolerate willingly. For Egypt, this seemed to be the removal of the last "fruit of [the 1956] aggression," and Nasir's prestige soared again in the Arab world. But an Israeli armed attack on Egypt appeared increasingly likely.

The Egyptian army went on full alert, and large-scale reinforcements moved into the Sinai. Israel then began to call up its reserves, as a general expectation of war emerged. Prime Minister Eshkol's cabinet was enlarged to include all Israeli parties except the Communists. Even the Herut party of Menachem Begin, then normally regarded as a fringe group by more moderate Israelis, joined the government. On popular demand Dayan became minister of defense, which seemed to be a signal that force would be used.

Some Israeli leaders may have expected an Egyptian attack, although the chief of staff, General Yitzhak Rabin, later admitted that this had been a miscalculation. But while U.S. and Israeli military experts knew that the Egyptian army was hopelessly weak (especially with its best forces tied down in Yemen), much of the Israeli public began to feel threatened with destruction. Correspondingly, some Palestinians experienced a euphoric feeling that the day of their return might be near. This was particularly true after King Husayn flew to Cairo on May 30 to end his feud with President Nasir and to conclude an alliance.

There were threats on all sides. Much of the world's press stressed President Nasir's threat to make any war a total one, in which the destruction of Israel as a state would be the aim. What was often omitted from these reports was his promise not to start a war. In any case, contrary to his former opinion, he seems to have decided that his armed forces were adequate to ward off an Israeli attack or, if not, that Israel would only occupy a little territory and then be pressured by the UN to withdraw. As the major powers warned both sides not to start a war, it was announced that the U.S. and Egyptian vice presidents would visit each other's capitals on June 7, and there was reason to think that a compromise was in the offing. Perhaps, aside from having restored his leadership in the Arab world, Nasir believed that the cards then in his hands would allow him to impose on Israel at least some Arab demands regarding Palestinian refugees and territory it still held in excess of what the UN had allotted twenty years before. But this was the sort of settlement that Israel was not prepared to tolerate.

Instead, Israel saw a chance to end the Arab-Israeli conflict on its own terms and delivered a devastating surprise attack on Egypt on June 5. The Egyptian air force hardly knew what was happening before it was virtually destroyed on the ground. With no air cover, Egyptian troops in the bleak Sinai desert were quickly routed and fell back in disarray. Thousands were captured and then turned loose without shoes or water to try their luck trekking across the burning sand. Jordan and Syria entered the war against Israel, and several other Arab states sent token contributions, but their forces were quickly repelled. In the Security Council, the U.S., despite President Johnson's alleged regret that Israel had started the fighting (others say he provided a "green light"), opposed Soviet demands for a quick cease-fire and withdrawal. Finally, a cease-fire was voted without any mention of withdrawal. Israel, however, went ahead with a campaign against Syria.

On June 11, six days after the battles had started, the cease-fire became effective. Israel now occupied territories more than three times its own size. These included what had up to now been left of Arab Palestine—the West Bank of Jordan (including Arab Jerusalem) and the Gaza Strip—all of Sinai and southwestern Syria (the Golan Heights). A new group of refugees emerged, as roughly 400,000 fled or were expelled from the West Bank and the Gaza Strip, although not to an extent that undid the Palestinian Arab character of these areas. However, during and soon after the fighting, the Golan Heights, including the city of Qunaytra, were nearly cleared of their population of about 140,000. Sunken ships blocked the Suez Canal, and the Israelis occupying its eastern bank refused to allow the Egyptians to reopen it for seven years.

THE AFTERMATH OF THE 1967 WAR

Israeli jubilation was matched by the Arabs' despair. Not only had they been proven inept and weak and found an unbearable situation imposed on them, but the authority of their leaders was also undermined. Admitting his acceptance of full blame for the "setback," Nasir announced his resignation from the presidency. But, aside from an unending affection for their leader, millions of Egyptians united to deprive the Israelis of the joy of having ousted him. Nasir responded to the overwhelming popular plea by agreeing to stay in office until the Arabs' humiliation could be removed. Any real hope for economic growth had to be put aside indefinitely. Several Egyptian generals were tried and punished for negligence. Amir was dismissed and was arrested after being caught plotting a coup. He killed himself soon after. Student demonstrators called for reforms and more severe punishments for the generals, and Nasir supported some of their demands. He announced attempts to strengthen the ASU and brought several university professors into the government.

Zionism now appeared to the world as a uniquely successful movement. Jewish immigration to Israel, even from the United States to a minor extent, began to swell again. With a growth rate of 10 percent a year, an economic boom was on, and the inhabitants of the newly occupied territories provided much of the manual labor. For a short while after the June war most Israelis assumed that peace was imminent, but the "telephone call" from Cairo that Dayan and others said they expected did not come. In any case, Israel had come to be rated as a military power of no mean dimensions.

Israel at first announced that it had no territorial aspirations and that it only wanted to force the Arabs to accept its right to exist in peace. But Arab suspicions were gradually confirmed as Israel began to talk about the necessity of "secure boundaries" and about areas that would not ever be evacuated. Arab Jerusalem was unilaterally annexed, and calls by the Security Council for rescission of this action were to no avail. A call for the return of the new refugees brought compliance in a handful of cases, obstructionism, and the eventual dropping of the issue. Israelis soon started planting settlements in the new territories. Widespread sympathy for Israel throughout the world, much of which believed that the Arabs had provoked the war, was gradually to diminish.

Before long most of the Arab states reluctantly began to acquiesce in the existence of Israel in order to concentrate on getting it to withdraw from newly occupied territories. An Arab summit meeting in Khartum in August 1967, boycotted by militant Syria, agreed to try for a diplomatic solution but also attempted to avoid criticism from hard-liners by proclaiming a policy of "no negotiations, no peace, no recognition." The Khartum meeting also brought an agreement by Nasir to withdraw from Yemen. To many people's surprise, the Yemeni regime survived, though with Sallal replaced by another group of republican leaders. Some former royalists eventually joined the government, which veered in a conservative direction. The rift between "progressives" and "reactionaries" throughout the Arab world narrowed as Egypt was forced to concentrate on the problem of Israel rather than on opposing monarchies. Egypt, Jordan, and Syria became the recipients of subsidies from oil-rich Sa'udi Arabia, Kuwayt, and Libya.

A compromise plan, Security Council Resolution 242, was adopted in November 1967. While calling for an end to belligerency and for mutual recognition, the resolution also rejected "acquisition of territory by war" and reaffirmed the principle of "territorial integrity." It specifically called on Israel to withdraw from "occupied territories," although the failure of the English version, unlike the others, to specify "the" territories soon became the basis for an Israeli argument that withdrawal did not have to be complete. But while interpreting it in different ways, Israel, Egypt, and Jordan (and later Syria) accepted the resolution as the basis for a settlement.

For Arab monarchies Egypt's defeat may have seemed to provide a reprieve from Nasirite radicalism. But the resultant bitterness of Arab nationalism sometimes worked against status quo forces. When Southern Yemen won its independence in December 1967 the Nasir-supported FLOSY lost out, but to a more radical, Marxist group, the National Liberation Front. There was even an abortive coup in Sa'udi Arabia in 1969. The Iraqi government of President Abd al-Rahman Arif, who succeeded after his brother's accidental death in 1966, succumbed to a Ba'thist coup in 1968. The new Iraqi regime, headed by President Ahmad Hasan al-Bakr, adopted a militant, nationalistic stance that for several years often put it at odds with virtually the whole Arab world. Ba'thist Iraq, with which some of the original Syrian leaders of the party aligned themselves, persistently collided with the Ba'thist regime in Syria, where a pragmatic faction of the party, led by another Alawite, Hafiz al-Asad, was brought to power in a military coup in 1970.

In 1969 both the Sudan and Libya experienced military coups led by young, idealistic army officers, Ja'far al-Numayri in the Sudan and Mu'ammar al-Qadhdhafi in Libya. For these men Nasir was still the great Arab hero to be emulated. Among other results of the Libyan coup, the major U.S. air base at Wheelus Field had to be evacuated. The quixotic Qadhdhafi, who tended to see the world in terms of good and evil, began to push for Arab unity. He appeared to others either as a mad fanatic or else as a breath of fresh air, an island of craziness or of naive virtue in an opportunistic world. One of Nasir's close associates described the Libyan leader as "scandalously pure," and Nasir once told him that he reminded him of himself as a youth. And while Numayri ultimately proved to be a conventional, even conservative figure, Qadhdhafi never lost his ardor.

Another result of the 1967 war was Egypt's and Syria's increased dependence on the USSR. A massive Soviet resupply effort restored lost equipment, and Soviet advisers and trainers helped to correct demonstrated deficiencies. Facilities in Egyptian and Syrian ports were opened to the Soviet navy, which became a potential challenge to the U.S. Sixth Fleet in the Mediterranean for the first time. Most Arab states severed diplomatic relations with the United States, which Egypt accused of participating in the June 5 attack. Although Nasir later admitted that this had been a mistake, continuing U.S. support for Israel prevented any improvement of relations with most Arab states. As the United States provided sophisticated weapons and aircraft, including Phantom fighter-bombers, to Israel, the Arab-Israel conflict sometimes came to be viewed as simply a theater of Soviet-American rivalry.

With Arab armies discredited, Palestinians increasingly began to believe that they must depend on themselves to defeat Israel. Fatah increased its commando raids and became the symbol of Arab resistance. After inflicting severe casualties, with the Jordanian army's cooperation, on Israeli raiders at the village of Karamah in 1968, volunteers began to flock to the guerrilla movement. Fatah's new prestige also brought it control over the PLO, now essentially an umbrella for various guerrilla groups. Arafat became the head of the PLO as well as Fatah.

Other guerrilla organizations outdid Fatah in militancy. George Habash, a Palestinian Christian pediatrician and former leader of the (Nasirite) Arab National Movement, now turned to Marxism-Leninism. Habash headed an organization called the Popular Front for the Liberation of Palestine (PFLP), which called for revolution in the Arab world as a prelude to liberating his own country. The PFLP, which later spawned several breakaway groups, became known for its spectacular terrorist activities against Israeli interests throughout the world and particularly for airplane hijacking. Both the outright radical groups like the PFLP and the more widely based Fatah, which unites individuals of diverse political philosophies, called for the defeat of Israel and its transformation into a "secular democratic Palestine" in which Jews and Arabs would live together, a goal that Israelis usually dismissed with derision as being patently insincere.

Various moves to settle the conflict gained no headway. Such were the efforts of the UN representative, Gunnar Jarring of Sweden, as well as Big Two and Big Four meetings. Sporadic battles raged along the cease-fire lines and Israeli shelling destroyed much of the Egyptian cities on the western side of the Suez Canal and forced their people to flee. Hoping to evoke international pressure for a settlement, Egypt began a "War of Attrition" in the form of regular artillery fire across the canal in 1969. Israel, in turn, completed a seemingly invulnerable series of fortifications, known as the Bar-Lev line and eventually escalated the conflict to the level of "deep penetration" raids that reached military and civilian targets near Cairo. Only when Egypt obtained the most up-to-date ground-to-air missiles, manned by Soviet technicians, did the deep penetration raids stop, although the war continued in the canal area for a while.

In July 1970 Egypt and Israel, the latter now led by Prime Minister Golda Meir, accepted a U.S. plan for a temporary cease-fire and increased efforts by Jarring to work out a settlement. This precipitated a massive round of hijackings by the PFLP. King Husayn, in turn, brutally suppressed the resistance movement in his territory. The guerrillas had become a threat to his rule and to the peace-making process.

After "Black September," as the month of their defeat came to be known, the Palestinian guerrillas were barred from Jordan, whose regime became for a while a pariah in the Arab world. With U.S. and Israeli threats of intervention on the king's behalf, Arab talk about helping the guerrillas came to naught, a short-lived Syrian crossing into northern Jordan notwithstanding. There also were unsuccessful attempts by the small, predominantly Maronite Lebanese army to suppress the guerrillas in 1969, but, in the years after "Black September," Lebanon became the main focus of Palestinian resistance.

As Nasir frantically engaged in inter-Arab peace-keeping during the Jordanian-Palestinian crisis of 1970, he suffered a fatal heart attack. Unprecedented mourning, only partly organized by the government, demonstrated that his hold over millions of Egyptians and other Arabs had outlived all his reverses, and the Arab world seemed to have suffered another heavy blow.

One of Nasir's oldest associates, Anwar al-Sadat, who was vice president at the time, automatically succeeded to the presidency. With a reputation as a bumbling protege of Nasir, Sadat was hardly expected to last long. For his potential rivals he seemed to be an ideal choice as an interim chief of state precisely because he was not a real contender. But a series of masterful political tactics soon demonstrated that he had always been underrated. As an early step in consolidating his position (and allegedly foiling a conspiracy against himself), Sadat purged his regime of members of a generally more leftist, pro-Soviet faction led by Vice Premier Ali Sabri, who had been a main proponent of a strong one-party system when he headed the ASU in the mid-1960s. Sadat increasingly gave his own stamp to the regime. With the voices that had pushed with little success for deeper revolutionary transformation now muted, Sadat's regime began to turn to the right and to favor the interests of the emerging privileged groups.

Sadat loosened Egyptian ties with the USSR. Although an Egyptian-Soviet Treaty of Friendship and Cooperation, concluded in 1971, paradoxically appeared to be a further shift from nonalignment to an openly pro-Soviet role, this only camouflaged increasing disenchantment with Moscow. The Russians were seen as overbearing and seemed to be unwilling—especially in the context of an emerging Soviet-American détente in the early 1970s—to provide the kind of weapons required to end the "no war, no peace" situation. In 1972 Sadat suddenly expelled most of the Soviet advisors, not only to end a situation that leading public figures in

Egypt saw as putting their country's independence in question but also in the hope that the United States would now adopt a less pro-Israeli stance and work for an acceptable settlement.

Sadat was bewildered when Washington's policy did not change. Although the Israeli victory had stirred up radical forces and made the Arabs more dependent on the USSR, the United States apparently had begun to see Israel as an invincible instrument to keep the Arab world in line. A powerful Israel seemed to mesh well with the Nixon Doctrine, already announced in 1969, according to which the United States' Asian allies would be armed to act as its regional policemen. Following this approach, a settlement of the Arab-Israeli conflict was less desirable than a continuation of an Israeli-imposed peace.

While not openly rejecting the Nasir era, Sadat turned Egypt gradually away from its revolutionary orientation. Some pro-U.S. figures who had been imprisoned or exiled under Nasir were now given important positions, and some previously sequestered property was returned to its original owners. Harsh attacks on Nasir's policies began to appear openly in print. Sadat showed continuity with his predecessor's policy for a while by agreeing to establish a loose, and eventually meaningless, Federation of Arab Republics with Libya and Syria. But he also began to put emphasis on friendship with and aid from an increasingly rich Sa'udi Arabia, while he and Qadhdhafi began to grow wary of each other. There was an accelerating trend from Arab to Egyptian nationalism. In response to emotional Libyan appeals for a full merger of the two countries, Sadat dragged his feet and eventually put off Qadhdhafi with an agreement in principle to unite, but without any timetable.

After declaring 1971—and then 1972—the "year of decision" in the conflict with Israel Sadat became an international laughing stock when nothing happened. Although he said that his generation of Arabs could not be expected to establish diplomatic relations with Israel, he went to considerable length to express his willingness to make peace, but without results. For example, when Jarring addressed identical notes to Egypt and Israel in 1971 proposing an Israeli withdrawal from all of Sinai in return for a peace agreement, Sadat readily accepted. But Israel angrily ended all dealings with the UN representative.

Israel became more and more famous for derring-do that made the Arabs look hopelessly inept. An Israeli assassination squad entered Beirut in 1973 and was able to kill several PLO officials without getting caught. With more conventional commando raids largely ruled out after the guerrillas' demise in Jordan, small Palestinian groups increasingly resorted to international terrorism to publicize their cause. Thus the world was stunned in 1972 when a group representing a minuscule Palestinian faction called Black September took eleven Israeli athletes hostage during the Olympic Games in Munich in an attempt to force the release of Palestinian prisoners in Israel; a West German rescue attempt ended with the killing of the captives and most of the captors. Each Palestinian action brought massive reprisals in the form of air raids on guerrilla bases and refugee camps in Lebanon. Israeli and Palestinian agents sought out and assassinated each other in Western Europe. To the Arabs Israeli arrogance seemed incomparable when a Libyan civil airliner that accidently veered into the airspace over the Sinai in 1973 was shot down, resulting in over a hundred deaths. Also, the governing Labor party in the upcoming elections, scheduled for October 1973, ran on a platform calling for increased Israeli settlements in the occupied territories. A final Egyptian plea to the Security Council in June met the rebuff of a U.S. veto. Aside from growing diplomatic support from Black African countries and some weakening of Israel's support in Western Europe, the Arab cause seemed hopeless.

IRAN: SEEMING UPSURGE
AND SIMMERING OPPOSITION

The absolute monarchical pattern that emerged in Iran by 1955 was further consolidated during the subsequent two decades. The continuing existence of the 1906 constitution made little difference in practice. The "king of kings and light of the Aryans," Muhammad Riza Shah Pahlavi, ruled entirely through his loyal servants, keeping them tame by playing one against another and encouraging each to outdo the others in corruption so he could use it against them whenever it suited his purposes. The electoral process tolerated only rival supporters of the shah. In 1957 he tried to create a two-party system by fiat, even assigning politicians arbitrarily to the ruling party and the equally pro-shah "opposition." The parliamentary elections of 1960 were so notoriously corrupt that an embarrassed shah decided to hold new ones. Ruthless security forces, including the secret police agency, the State Security and Intelligence Organization, best known by the acronym Savak, ferreted out those of questionable loyalty and subjected them to imprisonment and torture.

In an attempt to preempt a revolution from below (and apparently with the Kennedy administration's nudging), the shah launched his own "White Revolution." In 1963 his program was submitted to a referendum and won the expected 99 percent approval. The key feature of the program was land reform, which, as subsequently enacted, required owners to sell holdings in excess of one village to the government for resale in small plots to cultivators. A later phase provided for further division of estates, although owners were allowed alternatives, such as mechanization and new forms of tenancy. There was a later trend toward large-scale "agribusinesses." The government succeeded in presenting itself as enlightened and progressive in much of the Western world. Indeed, a few peasants, mostly those who already were relatively well off, gained from the land reform, but the overwhelming majority did not.

Iran was closely aligned with the United States. Membership in the Baghdad Pact and endorsement of the Eisenhower Doctrine, as well as the acceptance of over $600 million in U.S. economic and military aid between 1953 and 1967, were matched by hostile Soviet radio propaganda and Soviet support for the exiled leaders of the Tudeh party.

In the early 1960s Iran began to normalize its relationship with the USSR.

This in part represented a delayed response to Moscow's disavowal, following Stalin's death in 1953, of its post–World War II expansionism. Tehran's announcement in 1962 that it would not allow the United States to establish missile bases on its territory provided a signal that began the normalization process. Soviet-Iranian cooperation emerged in certain fields, such as in the USSR's construction of a steel mill in Isfahan in return for Iranian natural gas. The shah later even purchased some military equipment from the USSR. Largely reflecting the worldwide loosening of cold war tensions, this did not involve any real shift from Tehran's pro–U.S. position.

The shah kept aloof from Arab causes. There was always strong anti-Israel sentiment at the popular level, and the regime usually supported the Arabs in UN votes and other superficial ways. But Tehran never considered the Arab-Israeli conflict its concern and recognized Tel-Aviv as early as 1950. The shah's announcement a decade later that he was ready to exchange diplomatic representatives with Israel precipitated a break in Egyptian-Iranian relations that lasted another ten years. Occasional Arab references to the right of their brethen in Khuzistan (adjacent to Iraq) to self-determination, Iran's long-standing claim to Bahrayn (dropped only in 1970), the shah's aspiration to dominate the Persian Gulf (now tellingly renamed the "Arab" Gulf by the countries bordering on the other three sides), and a special fear of the influence of radical Arab regimes with close ties to the USSR propelled Iran into a de facto alliance with Israel. Iranian army officers and Savak got Israeli training, and Iran became Israel's major source of oil. On the other hand, Tehran-Baghdad relations were especially bitter by the early 1970s, with Iran in 1969 renouncing the 1937 treaty that recognized Iraq's title to most of the Shatt al-Arab, the river that forms part of the boundary between the two countries. Iran and Israel provided support for Iraqi Kurdish rebels.

Iran began to assert its hegemony in the Persian Gulf and even to extend its power into the Indian Ocean. The withdrawal of British forces from the Gulf in 1971 and the emergence of several independent Arab amirates provided an important fillip for this Iranian aspiration. Meeting with the shah in 1972, U.S. President Richard Nixon assured him of the availability of unlimited quantities of U.S. conventional armaments. Now the shah's forces, soon bloated by the purchase of massive amounts of such military equipment, could fill the vacuum the British withdrawal created in the Gulf in a way that made Iran a prime example of the kind of regional policemen envisaged in the Nixon Doctrine. Among other actions in keeping with the new role, Iranian forces, in collusion with the departing British, seized three islands belonging to the emerging United Arab Amirates in 1971 and evoked increased resentment in the Arab world. An Iranian expeditionary force managed to suppress a leftist, Southern Yemeni-supported revolt in Oman's Dhufar Province during the mid-1970s. The apprehension of conservative Arab countries, like Sa'udi Arabia (sometimes described as constituting, with Iran, "the twin pillars" of U.S. policy in the Gulf), was numbed by a common concern with combatting revolutionaries and Soviet influence.

The shah's military power was made possible by dramatic growth of oil revenues. This allowed the Plan Organization to carry out a series of economic plans seemingly with unusual success. U.S. economic aid was terminated in 1967, not as a punishment but rather as marking a completed mission. During the decade starting in 1963 Iran registered a real growth rate of more than 10 percent a year, and the annual per-capita income reached $500. Among other indices of economic change, less than half the work force was engaged in agriculture by the early 1970s, but from another point of view this demonstrated the extent to which neglect of agriculture was pushing peasants off the land into fast-growing urban slums. Tehran's population in 1973 was 3.3 million, more than double its size a decade earlier. Technical and managerial weakness notwithstanding, industry was gaining diversity, though not efficiency.

When the shah held a gala celebration in 1971 of the alleged twenty-five hundredth anniversary of the Iranian monarchy, it was in the spirit of an approaching resurgence of greatness going back to the Achaemenids. Others, however, discerned a megalomaniacal and insecure ruler dedicated to his own personal grandeur, piling up weapons like toys at his people's expense. Critics of the regime claimed that the Iranian people gained nothing from the new wealth. While gains indeed went disproportionately to the wealthy and intensified class divisions, improvements were apparently being felt by a wide section of society during this period. However, social advancement did not match the rising per-capita income, and studies that take into account infant mortality, life expectancy, and literacy rates reveal an Iran whose material well-being during the early 1970s was no higher than Egypt's and India's and lower than Turkey's and Syria's.

Most outside observers failed to comprehend the strength of opposition to the regime. The great majority of the people did not identify with it, and its achievements were not popularly perceived as national achievements. Indeed, the shah was widely thought of as a puppet of the United States, although some specialists argue that an initial dependence made way for a more normal alliance during the 1960s. The monarchy's identification with pre-Islamic Iran flew in the face of religious Muslims who traced their spiritual lineage to the early Muslims rather than to the Sasanians.

Much in the tradition of their involvement in opposition to autocracy and foreign domination in 1890 and 1906, the Iranian *ulama* led a serious challenge to the shah's rule in the early 1960s. In 1963 a leading religious scholar (and *marja-i taqlid* of millions), Ayatullah Ruhullah Khumayni, fiercely denounced the government's ties with Israel and the pending proposals, later adopted, to exempt U.S. military advisers from the jurisdiction of Iranian courts. The latter matter was viewed as a shameless servility toward the United States and, in effect, a renewal of the old capitulations. Large-scale riots ensued, with thousands of people shot in the streets, but at the time the revolt proved abortive. Khumayni was arrested and sent into a foreign exile that lasted until 1979.

The regime succeeded in picturing Khumayni's movement as purely reactionary, opposing land reform and woman suffrage. Indeed, many *ulama* had previously opposed the land reform program, partly because of the effects it had on the pious endowments they administered. It is unclear whether Khumayni raised these issues. In any case, far from being an ally of the landlords, he spoke on behalf of the "downtrodden" and against the "dwellers in palaces." In fact, he represented a radical faction within the *ulama*, as shown by his later untraditionalist open rejection of the monarchy in favor of an "Islamic Republic" or even by his teaching of a usually disfavored subject like philosophy.

Older opposition movements such as the National Front and the Communist Tudeh party waned, but new ones arose. Some, like the sociologist Ali Shari'ati, called for a socialist society based on a reinterpreted Islam. (For example, Shari'ati argued that the story of Cain and Abel symbolized the class struggle.) New Marxist groups, including the People's Fida'iyin and the militantly Islamic socialist People's Mujahidin arose among youths in the early 1970s and turned to sporadic guerrilla warfare against the regime. Several attempts to assassinate the shah were foiled. But the regime kept the strong support of the upper class and of the army and police and temporarily won the backing or at least the passive acceptance of parts of the middle class either by providing lucrative jobs or by making opposition look foolhardy.

TURKEY: A SICK MAN AGAIN?

If Iranian fortunes rose in some respects during this period, the earlier Turkish success story turned sour. The Democrat government continued to overspend on development and on the army during the late 1950s; inflation and payment deficits became rampant. But as modern, educated, urban groups became increasingly disenchanted with the government's economic policies and its increasing relaxation in the face of Islamic resurgence, the rural Turkish majority was won over by these policies and also by Democrat support for agriculture and such rural improvements as road building. In a situation of growing polarization of public opinion, Prime Minister Adnan Menderes won the adulation of the less Westernized elements and sometimes even was hailed as a prophet and worker of miracles. If he was the first Turkish leader to have any claim of heading a Western-style democracy, this was being eroded as more and more ardent opposition brought more repression. Amendments in the Press Law, the closing of some newspapers, new rules restricting political campaigns, and arbitrary violations of the tenure of judges and university professors emasculated the constitutional system. Democrat victories registered in successive elections for the Grand National Assembly (GNA) seemed to represent a built-in rural majority, and an increasingly tyrannical one. The army was even ordered to hinder the movement of the revered old national hero and People's Republican party (PRP) leader, Ismet Inönü, during a speaking campaign in 1960.

The actions against Inönü helped bring the crisis to a head. Student demonstrations brought on martial law and the closing of the universities. Then the War College cadets marched in protest. On May 27, 1960, the army stepped in, and a thirty-eight-man junta, the National Unity Committee, headed by General Cemal

Gürsal, took power. A "High Court of Justice," established to try 601 officials of the previous government, found most of them guilty of violating the constitution and other charges. Twelve people, including Menderes, were subsequently executed.

The Turkish army's brutality was matched by an unusual inclination to return to its barracks. The failure of two attempted coups in 1962 by army officers favoring continued military rule showed that this was not the dominant trend. A Constituent Assembly wrote a new constitution, which set up a system of checks and balances, including a bicameral GNA (National Assembly and Senate) and restraints on legislative power protected by a Constitutional Court. This was intended to limit the tyranny of the democratically elected majority in the future. The constitution was approved in a national referendum in 1961, although the mere 60 percent majority it received seemed to be a warning that much of the Turkish nation remained loyal to the now-proscribed Democrat party. It is possible that the junta's determination to go ahead with Menderes's execution was bolstered by a realization that his popularity would otherwise eventually bring him back to power. But with the army continuing to serve as the watchdog, the Second Turkish Republic restored the electoral, constitutional process.

A Turkish age of trouble lingered on. With the general elections of October 1961 giving the PRP the largest number of seats in the GNA, Inönü headed a new government based on a shifting coalition of parties, which at first oddly included the new Justice party. The latter, which was supported heavily by rural voters (except in the most conservative regions in the east, where minor parties flourished) was known to be essentially the successor to the Democrats. In 1965 the Justice party got an absolute majority in the GNA, and its leader, Suleyman Demirel, became prime minister. By 1969 a tendency of the parties to splinter made him again dependent on a shaky coalition.

By this time Turkey was rife with conflict. Militant groups grew on both the extreme right and the extreme left, and also among the Kurdish minority. Urban guerrillas engaged in terrorism, and the government seemed unable to cope with them or with the deeper social and economic problems coming from burgeoning cities and landless peasantry in some areas. In 1971 the army intervened again in a "coup by communiqué" that led to a government of technocrats headed by a former PRP member, Nihat Erim. Martial law and other restrictions on civil liberties were imposed. But weak coalition governments soon emerged again, with a new polarization of the conservative Justice party and the PRP. The latter was now led by the journalist Bülent Ecevit, and it began to assume the role of a left-of-center, social democratic party favoring labor unions and land reform. It then seemed to be reduced to a permanent minority position.

Turkish foreign policy gradually shifted away from its total identification with the U.S.–led camp. The waning of the cold war and the Soviet Union's renunciation of its post–World War II demands facilitated a degree of normalization of relations with that country, as demonstrated by growing trade and official visits. The alliance with the United States lost some of its former centrality as other issues evoked anti–U.S. sentiment. The problem of Cyprus, with its roughly 18 percent Turkish population living amid a Greek majority, gained attention during the late 1950s, with Turkey resisting any plan for *Enosis* ("union") of Cyprus and Greece. The island gained independence from Great Britain in 1960 under a compromise formula forbidding *Enosis* and with cumbersome procedures designed to protect the Turks from unlimited majority rule, but the scheme soon proved unworkable. The possibility of Turkish military intervention in Cyprus evoked a harsh, threatening letter from President Johnson in 1964. This caused much bitterness in Turkey toward the United States. U.S. attempts during the early 1970s to have Turkey ban the growth of opium brought additional resentment. No one could take Turkey's allegiance for granted any more, although its continuing alignment with the United States still had a solid base in public opinion. No major party favored withdrawing from NATO or adopting nonalignment.

A BRIGHT SPOT: OIL

While large countries such as Turkey and Egypt continued to endure poverty, oil provided unprecedented riches for those bordering on the Persian Gulf. An industrial world that had become increasingly dependent on oil slowly was growing aware of an approaching "energy crisis" by the 1970s. Sa'udi Arabia alone was believed to have one-fourth of the world's oil reserves, and its good-will was coming to be recognized as essential in order to prevent a severe shortage in the future. The effective use of oil as a political weapon in the Arab-Israeli conflict began to seem more feasible than before, although most oil-importing nations were still not ready to worry much about such a possibility.

Oil had long been a bonanza for some Middle Eastern countries. A small underpopulated state like Kuwayt now had a per-capita income exceeding that of any Western country and combined a nearly absolute monarchy (a freely elected parliament notwithstanding) and a traditional social structure with an enviable modern welfare state. The impact of oil revenues on countries like Iraq and Sa'udi Arabia already was significant, though still far from Kuwayt's fairy-tale version. Sa'udi Arabia's annual oil revenue reached $5 billion in 1973, but fewer than 11,000 pupils—including only 700 girls—were enrolled in secondary school. In terms of the literacy rate, average life expectancy, and the like, it was one of the world's most underprivileged countries.

From the late 1950s on, oil exporters were subject to unfavorable trends. A few large Western companies controlled the industry. The world was experiencing an "oil glut," and the bargaining power of producer governments was nearly nil. With Iran's experience during the early 1950s in mind, even radical regimes were long frightened from considering nationalization. The companies were able at will to lower the "posted prices" on which payments were based. Such a reduction in 1960 evoked the formation of an Organization of Petroleum Exporting Countries (OPEC) for collective bargaining, but for another decade only a few minor gains were registered.

Then a convergence of several factors brought the first breakthrough in the early 1970s. The closing of the Suez Canal as a result of the Israeli occupation of Sinai cost the world billions of dollars in extra shipping costs. This also made North African oil particularly attractive to Europe. By now, both Algeria and, even more, Libya were important producers, although their resources were minor in comparison with those of the Persian Gulf countries. The temporary accidental disruption of the pipeline crossing Syria in 1970, at a time of increased demand for oil in Europe, gave the North African countries extra leverage. And this was soon after the militantly nationalistic regime of Qadhdhafi came to power. With Libya holding out for higher prices and using nationalization as a threat, the companies succumbed. In 1971 negotiations in Tehran between OPEC and the oil companies brought a general increase of $.33 in the posted price. Subsequent increases raised the posted price of oil, which was (depending on the variety) $1.80 in 1970, to $2.59 by early 1973. Revised arrangements also began to give producer countries greater control. The Libyan government took over some of the operations in 1971, and Baghdad nationalized the Iraq Petroleum Company in 1972. The consortium of Western companies set up in 1954 turned over full control of the industry to the Iranian government in 1973 in return for a privileged position as contractor and buyer. Other countries began to get "participation" agreements, whereby they obtained partial, but gradually increasing, ownership of the oil operations.

CONCLUSIONS

From 1955 on, Middle Eastern peoples confronted the remnants of Western colonial rule and undertook serious efforts to modernize. Phrases like "positive neutralism," "nonalignment," "Arab socialism," "five-year plan," and "Palestine resistance" epitomized the continuing domestic and international struggle. By the early 1970s, the last outposts of formal colonialism were gone, but weakness perpetuated more subtle kinds. The wealth that a few countries now received from oil was matched by the seemingly insurmountable economic problems of more populous countries. There was little indication of progress in developing viable political orders, and internal and intraregional conflict held back the area. Even Turkey, one Middle Eastern country that had previously seemed to find its way, suffered severe economic and political maladies.

The Arabs' encounter with Israel more than ever exposed their weakness. The occupation of additional territory and displacement of more people intensified bitterness not only against Zionism but also against those Western nations that, in a crunch, seemed to the Arabs always to demonstrate a double standard against them. The conflict seemed interminable as Arabs refused to accept the unbearable terms of their seemingly invincible foe. With the breakup of Pakistan and its defeat by India in 1971 fitting into the same pattern, failure seemed to beset the whole Islamic world.

10

The Crossing and After

1973-1982

On October 6, 1973, Egyptian and Syrian artillery interrupted the calmness of "no war, no peace" in the Arab-Israeli confrontation. Few imagined that the Arabs would dare fight what experience had shown to be an unbeatable enemy. Even the Israelis and the CIA failed until nearly the last minute to take obvious Syrian and Egyptian war preparations seriously. The offensive came at an unlikely time, during the Muslims' holy month of Ramadan and took the name "Operation Badr," after the historic victory of the early Muslims over their Meccan persecutors. This was also the holiest day of the Jewish calendar, Yom Kippur ("The Day of Atonement").

The Egyptians had skillfully planned for a time when the light of the moon and the water currents in the Suez Canal would be optimal for an offensive. Egyptian commandos had already slipped over to the other side to close off the pipes through which burning napalm was supposed to pour into the water if an army ever tried to cross. After the artillery cleared the way, Egyptian troops began to cross the canal in rubber boats and then over the pontoon bridges that were quickly put into place. High pressure water hoses washed away the mountains of sand that the Israelis had piled up as a further barrier, and the Bar-Lev line began to crumble. Simultaneously, the Syrian army moved into the Golan Heights.

An already surprised world was incredulous when it discovered that the Egyptian and Syrian armies had not been immediately crushed. Early victories reported by the Israelis were often taken at face value but turned out to be just as fictitious as Arab accounts had been in 1967. Using Soviet-made antitank and antiaircraft weapons, the Syrians temporarily retook most of the Golan Heights, while Egyptian forces recovered a strip of territory all along the eastern side of the canal. The Arabs themselves were amazed to see that they had achieved more in a short time than they had ever thought possible. Their main purpose had been to stir the world from its apathy in order to stimulate movement toward a diplomatic settlement of the conflict, and success in occupying small beachheads was deemed sufficient for this. The Egyptians eventually pushed further in an attempt to take the strategic mountain passes. It is sometimes argued that only an initial lack of confidence prevented them from moving on successfully to this objective while the initial momentum of surprise made it possible. Indeed, some Israeli leaders panicked as the Arabs seemed momentarily to pose a threat to their existence. According to one Israeli account, a weeping Moshe Dayan proposed that his country surrender.

WHOSE VICTORY?

If the October War destroyed the assumption of Israeli invincibility, it hardly brought an Arab military victory. After mobilizing their reserves, the Israelis at first concentrated on driving the Syrian army back to the former cease-fire line. Then they pushed on to occupy a further salient that ended less than twenty miles from Damascus, now in range of Israeli artillery fire. For a while, the prospect of an occupation of the Syrian capital seemed real, although it is likely that long-range dangers of holding such areas, with their hostile populations, would in any case have induced the Israelis to steer clear of this. But the Syrians avoided a disorderly rout and managed to hold a defensive line. A still viable Syrian army, aided by contingents from such countries as Morocco, Iraq, and Jordan, was able to keep fighting as the enemy began to concentrate on its southern front.

The tide of battle also turned in the Suez Canal area as a massive airlift of weapons from the United States restored the capability of the Israeli army. The USSR resupplied the Egyptians and Syrians. With a great tank battle raging in the Sinai that had been surpassed few times, even during World War II, the Israelis found a gap in the Egyptian center, between the Second Army in the north and the Third Army in the south. Before their enemy realized what was happening, a few Israeli tanks slipped through and crossed to the western side of the Suez Canal. Wreaking havoc on Egypt's antiaircraft defense from the rear, the force began to grow as more troops and heavy weapons crossed over. The Security Council ordered a cease-fire on October 22, but the Israelis kept up their offensive for several more days. After the United States rejected a Soviet suggestion that the two powers send in a joint force to stop the fighting, the seeming prospect of a unilateral Soviet intervention on Egypt's side was checkmated when U.S. armed forces throughout the world went on alert. The Israeli-occupied area on the western bank, which now extended all the way to the Gulf of Suez, covered more square miles than did the

Egyptian-held parts of Sinai. Egypt's First Army, defending the capital, was depleted, and the road to Cairo seemed to offer a relatively easy challenge to the Israelis. The Egyptian Third Army was nearly surrounded, and supplies were cut off.

While the Israelis had again won militarily, the October War was an Arab victory in some ways. At least the Arabs felt that they had regained their honor, for no one now disputed that they too could fight. Egypt's success completed the process whereby Sadat became not just Nasir's interim successor but a leader in his own right. The possibility of a greater victory for the Arabs in the future was no longer far-fetched to anybody, and they even tended to forget about the ultimate outcome of the October War. Sadat later pointed out that he had missiles aimed at enemy cities. While this may have helped deter the Israelis from further advances, the actual use of such missiles would have also brought retaliation and unbearable losses for Egypt. But, aside from the fact that it forced diplomatic overtures for peace, the "Crossing" appeared as a great historic turning point to the ebullient Arabs and to the increasingly pessimistic Israelis. The "Crossing" came to refer to not just one amphibious operation, but also symbolically came to convey the idea that Arabs had, or were about to, catch up with the modern world. To others, though, the "Crossing" was from Nasir's era to Sadat's; from the perspective of many Arabs, the latter seemed paradoxically to become one of capitulation to forces so long defied.

The Israelis began to feel that everything was suddenly going wrong. Over 2,500 Israelis were killed in the 1973 war, far fewer than the number of Arab losses but too many for the country's small population to take without severe trauma. The period between 1967 and 1973 seemed like a dream that turned into a nightmare. The Israelis were still determined, and a post-1973 military buildup gave them a new edge. But they now seemed less sure that they could survive in the long run. It became well known, though not fully admitted officially, that they had developed nuclear weapons, which could be used in a dire situation. But it was assumed that some Arab states would also get these weapons, making their use suicidal for each side. Tel-Aviv's dependence on the United States became more obvious during the 1973 war. U.S. aid, mainly military, soon regularly surpassed $2 billion a year, and Israelis knew that this could be used as leverage, especially if their intransigence seemed to threaten the oil supply.

While strong support for Israel continued in some Western countries, it increasingly took on the role of an international pariah. Even West European countries were now so wary of antagonizing the Arabs—and also genuinely critical of Israeli policies—that only the rightist dictatorship in Portugal, soon overthrown, allowed U.S. planes resupplying Israel to use its airspace. Virtually all Black African governments that had not already done so broke off relations with Israel in the aftermath of the 1973 war. In part, this was in response to the importance of Arab oil and the large amounts of Arab economic aid made possible by higher oil prices, but it was also a result of an increasing tendency to see Israel as a European settler state, a Middle Eastern version of South Africa. Growing Israeli–South African cooperation was widely presented as evidence of a basic affinity of the two societies. Reflecting the new voting strength of non-Western countries, the General Assembly officially declared Zionism to be a form of racism in 1975, evoking bitter rejection by the United States and a few other Western governments. It often seemed likely that Israel would be excluded from the General Assembly, but United States opposition kept this from happening.

Economic woes ate away at Israeli morale. The inflation rate crept upward, exceeding 130 percent in 1980, as real wages and the standard of living began to decline. The military consumed over a third of the GNP. Increases in crime pointed to a weakening of the social structure. Public opinion polls showed that large portions of the population favored a more authoritarian type of government. The possibility of vastly increased immigration from the USSR provided a bright spot for a while. But continuing Soviet restrictions and a growing tendency for Jewish emigrants to settle elsewhere brought disappointment. In fact, Israel began to experience a net loss of emigrants over immigrants. Israeli morale sometimes soared temporarily, as in July 1976, when an airborne force succeeded in rescuing hostages held by a small Palestinian guerrilla group in faraway Uganda, but this could not last.

Israeli politics were subject to increasing strains. The Arab minority grew to over 15 percent of the population and more and more identified with Palestinian nationalism. They may have formed a slight majority in Galilee by 1980. Reflecting resentment against attempts to "Judaize" the area by confiscating their land, Israeli Arabs increasingly voted for the small Communist party. Within the Jewish community, blame for being caught napping in 1973 became another divisive factor, although a commission appointed to study the situation relieved the Israeli leaders of onus. In any case, popular dissatisfaction led Prime Minister Meir and Defense Minister Dayan to resign. Meir's successor as prime minister, Yitzhak Rabin, also had to resign when it was revealed that he had an illegal foreign bank account and other scandals began to surface. The old idealism seemed to be waning, although it was sometimes argued that this merely reflected the continued existence of high standards.

A new political party, the Democratic Movement for Change, based its campaign in the 1977 elections on the need for reform in various areas, and its relative success (but only this one time) in taking votes from other parties pointed to widespread dissatisfaction. Even more so did the emergence of the hawkish right-wing Likud, the successor to a series of parties whose origin went back to Herut and the terrorist Irgun, as the largest political bloc. The old Irgun leader, Menachem Begin, became prime minister. Support for the Likud by the Oriental Jews (by now a majority of the population but with average per-capita incomes less than half as high as those of European background) was a major factor in its success. The Orientals expressed their discontent with the Labor government, but they continued—though somewhat less so after another election four years later—to suffer from their usual underrepresentation in the Cabinet and Knesset. Also, the conservative economic policies of the Begin government seemed to bear heavily on the poor, largely Oriental Jews. It could be argued that a new government, the first that had not been dominated by the Labor party, meant either that the system was getting an infusion of badly needed new blood or that this was an indication of deep-seated decay.

MOVES TOWARD ARAB-ISRAELI PEACE

A series of steps toward peace emerged from the October War. Although the United States gave unprecedented help to Israel during the war, it also realized that an overwhelming Israeli victory would in the long run not serve anybody's purposes. Fearing Soviet involvement, the United States pressured the Israelis to allow supplies to reach Egypt's beleagured Third Army via a regular corridor. Secretary of State Henry Kissinger flew from capital to capital trying to work out agreements on troop disengagement. In January 1974 an Egyptian-Israeli agreement provided for an Israeli withdrawal to a line several miles east of the Suez Canal, with limited force zones and a new United Nations Emergency Force in between. A similar agreement between Israel and Syria, also concluded through Kissinger's shuttle method, brought an Israeli withdrawal from its newly occupied salient and from another narrow slice of territory, including the city of Qunaytra. The Israelis, however, utterly obliterated that city just before returning it. In another round of shuttle diplomacy, Kissinger arranged for a further minor Israeli withdrawal on the Sinai front in 1975.

Sadat began to calculate that he had much to gain by strengthening ties with the United States, which would be able to pressure Israel into a settlement. Egypt became the leading recipient of U.S. economic aid, which soon exceeded $1 billion a year. An "opening" to the U.S. and other capitalist countries was also expected to draw massive private investment, although an uncertain political situation and a cumbersome bureaucracy helped to prevent this from occurring. Correspondingly, relations with the USSR deteriorated, and the supply of weapons dried up. With Moscow refusing to reschedule the payments on Cairo's $5 billion debt, Sadat unilaterally renounced the Treaty of Friendship and Cooperation. As a result he forfeited any opportunity to get Soviet weapons again, and the United States was also unwilling to provide much military aid to a frontline Arab state in the conflict with Israel. The Egyptian military capacity kept deteriorating while the USSR built the Syrian and Iraqi armies to new levels. However, the United States would begin a massive arms supply to Egypt after the latter made peace with Israel in 1979.

A Geneva Conference, jointly chaired by the United States and the USSR, opened briefly in December 1973 to move toward a comprehensive Arab-Israeli settlement. But the Conference never reconvened, partly because Israel, Egypt, and the United States preferred to keep the USSR out of the picture. The question of the PLO's role became the big roadblock.

The dominant elements in the PLO now expressed their willingness to establish a Palestinian authority in the West Bank and the Gaza Strip. Except for small "rejectionist" groups like the PFLP (supported by Libya and Iraq), Palestinian leaders relegated their goal of a unified, nonsectarian Palestine to a distant "dream." The PLO continued to object to Security Council Resolution 242's failure to call for a Palestinian state. No Palestinian organization officially committed itself in advance to peace with Israel, but there were indications that such a stance would be considered as part of a settlement.

In 1974 an Arab summit conference in Rabat, Morocco, unanimously proclaimed the PLO to be the "sole legitimate representative" of the Palestinian people. Jordan no longer claimed to represent the West Bank, at least not openly. But Israel, backed by the United States, adamantly refused to negotiate with the PLO on the ground that the latter is a "terrorist" organization, which negates its "right to exist." In any case Israel rejected the idea of establishing a Palestinian state. For some Israelis, including Prime Minister Begin, the West Bank ("Judea and Samaria," as they call it) is an integral part of the ancient—and thus the modern—Jewish homeland and cannot be given up. Some other Israelis would be willing to return part of the area (whose annexation would endanger Israel's Jewish character in the long run) to Jordan, but not to a separate Palestinian state.

CONFLICT WITHIN
THE ARAB WORLD

The unprecedented Arab unity of October 1973 soon gave way to new levels of inter-Arab conflict. The 1975 Egyptian-Israeli disengagement agreement embittered some Arabs, particularly Syria and the Palestinians, for Egypt seemed to be deserting its allies in order to recover what it could of its own territories. Rivalry between the two Ba'thist regimes in Damascus and Baghdad also intensified. By contrast, Iraq and non-Arab Iran underwent a rapprochement in 1975. Baghdad accepted Iranian sovereignty over part of the Shatt al-Arab in return for an end to Tehran's help for the troublesome Kurdish rebellion. This revolt, the renewal of which the United States and Iran had promoted in 1974 in order to weaken militant Iraq, immediately collapsed. With Qadhdhafi aspiring to inherit Nasir's mantle as an Arab leader and resenting Sadat's conciliatory attitude toward Israel and coolness toward Arab nationalism, Libya strengthened its ties with the USSR, and a bitter antagonism began to color relations between Egypt and Libya. Mutual subversion became rife, and Sadat launched an indecisive air attack on Libyan forces in 1977.

Lebanon became a maelstrom of local and inter-Arab conflict. Right-wing Maronite Lebanese resented the growing Palestinian presence in the country and blamed it for Israeli attacks. Other Lebanese, mainly Muslims, aspired to end the domination of the Christian minority and also identified with the Palestinian cause. Two largely Muslim "belts of misery"—the southern, eastern, and northern parts of the country and a crescent of slums around Beirut enlarged by flights of Shi'ites from Israeli raids in the south—formed around the prosperous, largely Christian sections. Beginning in 1975 civil war pitted rightist Maronites against a "leftist" coalition of Palestinians and mainly, though not entirely, Muslim Lebanese and left almost 100,000 dead. Syrian troops intervened during the next year, not to impose defeat on the rightists, as might have been assumed, but rather to act as mediators. In fact, the Syrians saved the rightists from defeat and allowed them to brutally overwhelm some armed Palestinian refugee camps. With Sa'udi pressure to end the crisis, Syrian troops soon became the core of an Arab League peace-keeping force, and in effect Damascus's hegemony over the country was accepted. The rightists continued to control part of the country, and Israel refused to permit the Arab force to enter the south, where the war between Maronite rightists and Palestinians continued. Reacting to guerrilla raids, Israel occupied much of the area in 1978. In response to international pressures, the invaders withdrew in favor of a UN peace-keeping force but also left a buffer zone controlled by close rightist allies. Lebanon continued to witness chaos periodically, with Syrian forces sometimes clashing with rightists and with even greater violence among various leftist and Palestinian factions and among rival rightist groups. Also, Israeli incursions into the south continued from time to time.

AN EGYPTIAN-ISRAELI PEACE

In the Arab-Israeli arena, the new administration of U.S. President Jimmy Carter in 1977 seemed ready for a comprehensive settlement involving some kind of Palestinian "homeland." In October, Washington and Moscow accordingly agreed to reconvene the Geneva Conference. But Sadat was unhappy about the prospect of Soviet involvement. He also was eager to assure himself a central role in negotiations and wanted a quick settlement that would allow him to concentrate on Egypt's severe economic problems and to consolidate his alliance with the United States. In November, he consequently initiated a new kind of "electric shock" diplomacy by announcing his willingness to visit Israel. Responding to the invitation that immediately followed, he flew there to speak before the Knesset. With most of the Arab world fearing a sell-out, an anti-Sadat "Steadfastness Front" (Syria, Libya, Algeria, South Yemen, and the PLO but not still ultra-militant and anti-Syrian Iraq) was unable to foil his plans, and oil-rich monarchies seemed for a while tacitly to accept the new tactic by continuing their aid.

A meeting of Sadat, Begin, and Carter at Camp David, Maryland, in September 1978 managed to work out a framework for a peace treaty that would gradually return all of Sinai to Egypt in return for fully amicable relations between the two longtime foes. Israel also committed itself to negotiate with Egypt, Jordan, and local Palestinian leaders (not the PLO) with regard to establishing autonomy and an end to the military government (though not the military presence) in the West Bank and Gaza Strip. The agreement committed Israel then to try to move toward a settlement of the final status of these areas within another five-year period. The nature of the settlement—whether they would be annexed to Israel, become an independent Palestinian state, or whatever—was not specified in advance.

Most Arab governments believed that a separate peace between Egypt and Israel could leave the latter in a position to offer a settlement on its own terms as the only alternative to the status quo. In response to the Camp David agreements the Steadfastness Front announced its intention to bring Sadat down, and a summit meeting of all other Arab League members condemned his policy and agreed to impose sanctions if he concluded a peace treaty. Even conservative oil-rich regimes, like that of Sa'udi Arabia, on which Egypt was heavily dependent for economic aid, started to show their anger. Or perhaps the ongoing revolution in Iran made them fear that they too would be vulnerable if they supported policies that went against the nationalist and Islamic grain. In what some observers saw as potentially counterbalancing the loss of Egypt to the anti-Israel camp, Iraq and Syria began to patch up their old differences and to talk about a future merger, but the rapprochement soon made way for greater antagonism than ever between the regimes in Damascus and Baghdad.

Some Israelis foresaw that relinquishing the Sinai would be a prelude to pressures for withdrawal from the other occupied areas and feared a piecemeal achievement of Arab objectives. They argued that Israel was being induced to give up tangible benefits—the Sinai's strategic depth and its oil (hereafter available only at market prices), as well as removing settlements and air bases at great expense—in return for friendly relations with Egypt that might be illusory or might simply evaporate in the future.

After repeated setbacks, intensive diplomatic efforts succeeded in finalizing an Egyptian-Israeli peace treaty and a framework for the future settlement of the status of the West Bank and Gaza Strip in March 1979, basically along the lines agreed on at Camp David. A decision of other Arab states to suspend Egypt's membership in the Arab League (whose headquarters were moved to Tunis) and to sever economic and diplomatic relations with Cairo initiated a new phase of inter-Arab animosity. New levels of U.S. military and economic aid to both Egypt and Israel emerged, and Sadat was accused by his enemies of trying to replace Iran as a U.S. policeman in a tacit alliance with Israel.

For a while, Sadat's new approach seemed to evoke widespread popular backing in Egypt, based on a resurgence of local (as opposed to pan-Arab) nationalism and also on the hope that peace would bring prosperity. Still, growing resentment against an alleged new role as a U.S. surrogate and against the separate peace, particularly as the promise of prosperity failed to bear fruit, began to strengthen militantly anti-Sadat forces, especially those with an Islamic and, to a lesser extent, a leftist cast.

With both local Palestinian leaders and the Jordanian government refusing to participate, subsequent Egyptian-Israeli negotiations on establishing autonomy for the West Bank and Gaza Strip provided little to vindicate Sadat's approach in the Arab world. The Israelis argued that they had never accepted the principle of autonomy for the area, but only for its "inhabitants." Israeli proposals called for an administrative council that would have no legislative or judicial authority. Arab East Jerusalem, excluded from the Israeli definition of the West Bank, was to be denied representation on such a council. Israel refused to consider ending its now-accelerated policy of establishing Jewish settlements, including some on land that continued to be expropriated from Arab owners. Nor would it allow any autonomous authority the right to control water resources—already being drained away from Palestinian villages by the deep wells that only the new settlers were permitted to drill—or to control public land. Any possibility of independence, even at the end of the transition period, was utterly rejected as the Israeli government insisted that it had a historic and God-given right to the territories and that they were vital to its security.

Palestinians spoke with contempt of proposals that made South African bantustans seem appealing in comparison. Backed by growing world opinion that blamed Israeli intransigence (even in Israel to some extent), Cairo also considered such proposals unworthy of consideration. Tensions recurrently flared up in the occupied Palestinian territories, as Israeli troops sometimes fired on student demonstrators and sent local officials into exile or even razed the homes of those accused of supporting "terrorists"—indeed, both Palestinians and Israelis became victims of the others' terrorist attacks. Egypt sometimes temporarily broke off the autonomy talks to protest against Israeli policies, as in the case of Israel's formal declaration in 1980 that the whole of Jerusalem was the Israeli capital. The failure of an expected Labor party victory to materialize in the 1981 Israeli elections ended the only hope for a breakthrough in the negotiations, although no major group in Israel appeared willing to accept complete withdrawal from the occupied territories or the establishment of a Palestinian state. On a bilateral level the Egyptian-Israeli peace process continued, with an exchange of ambassadors coming on schedule, and the withdrawal from Sinai was finalized in 1982. At least for the foreseeable future, Egypt was outside the circle of Israel's enemies, who thus could offer no credible military challenge. But the Israeli desire for truly friendly relations with Egypt—as in the development of trade, tourism, and joint economic projects—could not so easily be achieved by fiat.

REVOLUTION IN WORLD ECONOMICS

In 1973 the Arabs supplemented their new military leverage with economic leverage. In order to induce the world to pressure Israel during and after the October War, Arab oil exporters announced that they would reduce production in stages until the occupation of Arab territories was ended. Only those countries adopting stands favorable to the Arab position were to be exempt from the consequences of this action. A total boycott was declared against the United States because of its aid to Israel. It is unclear to what extent the producers really carried out such actions. In any case, there were "leaks," and the boycott and cutback were ended early in 1974, without the final objective being achieved, but real or imagined fuel shortages in many countries made them take the Arabs seriously. Utterly dependent on Middle

Eastern oil, Japan and Western European countries fell in line with demands that they proclaim their support for a complete Israeli withdrawal.

A by-product of the use of the oil weapon was a sudden jump in prices that made the increases of the early 1970s seem small in comparison. For a while shortages produced by the cutback caused oil to be auctioned off at as much as $20 a barrel. From now on, OPEC was able to dictate prices without having to negotiate with the companies. Oil that had sold for $2.59 a barrel in early 1973 sold for $11.65 a year later. Price hikes continued from time to time but were minimized by the resistance of some Arab monarchies, particularly Sa'udi Arabia, whose small population and high level of production evoked less need for increases than was true of countries like Iran or Algeria. Also, fearing adverse economic consequences for the non-Communist world (and despite the danger of further alienating more nationalistic elements), the Sa'udi regime was in a position to increase production and thus undermine price increases set by other OPEC members.

The price per barrel was scheduled to reach $14.55 in 1979 (cheaper than five years earlier if inflation is considered), when revolution in Iran—until then second only to Sa'udi Arabia in oil exports—and resultant cuts in production generated a new series of price explosions. By the end of 1980 the cost per barrel ranged from $32 to $41, as inexorable economic forces seemed for a while to make collective price-setting almost redundant. However, as Sa'udi Arabia increased its production and as high prices helped bring decreasing demand, the ensuing short-run glut forced some prices down. OPEC settled on a common price of $34 a barrel for its "benchmark" grade late in 1981. Still, decreasing sales tempted some countries to sell for less, and some experts questioned whether OPEC could survive even after a decision in 1982 to decrease production further. Sa'udi Arabia, which previously seemed to have control of the situation, appeared to be unable to reduce its production much more without endangering its ability to meet its financial commitments. Others pointed out that further political upheavals—for which decreasing revenues might provide a catalyst—could bounce prices to new heights.

With the jump in oil prices, a torrent of riches poured into the producer states. There were calculations that Middle Eastern monetary reserves would reach fantastic proportions, and there was talk in the West about kings and amirs virtually buying out the world. These fears turned out to be exaggerated, as most of the "petrodollars" returned to industrialized countries—particularly to multinational corporations—in payment for consumer and capital goods and services and for arms. Some leading oil exporters—like Iran, which received $23 billion for oil in 1977—at times faced financial deficits. Despite revenues that exceeded $100 billion in 1980, even Sa'udi Arabia's reserves, largely deposited in Western banks, proved much more manageable than had been expected.

Still, the ironic phenomenon of rich underdeveloped countries emerged on a big scale. By 1975 the per capita GNPs of Kuwayt and the United Arab Amirates, the world's highest, reached the $11,000 range. Sa'udi Arabia's per capita GNP was still only about $3,000 at that time, but it also exceeded that of all Western countries by the end of the decade.

Other Middle Eastern states remained poor. Admittedly, a country like Egypt had an annual per capita GNP (about $300) that was double that of a truly poor nation like India and almost triple that of Bangladesh. The Middle East (unless areas on the periphery, like Afghanistan or Somalia are included) did not have such extremely poor countries. Turkey had a per capita GNP of $860 in 1975, while Syria's and Jordan's reached $660 and $460 respectively. Still, except for the oil producers, Israel with a per capita GNP of nearly $3,600 (almost as high as Great Britain's), was the only country in the Middle East to have surpassed relatively poor European countries like Italy, Ireland, and the USSR. For millions of unemployed or underemployed of rural origin in the slums of Turkish or Egyptian cities, largely the result of being pushed out by the utter hopelessness of life in their overpopulated native villages—Cairo's population approached 10 million by the late 1970s—figures on national per capita GNPs are meaningless. With a 30 percent inflation rate, Egypt's minimum monthly wage rose from $29 to $36 in 1981; university graduates entered guaranteed, often redundant jobs for $64 a month (up from $43). Continued rapid population growth—reaching 42 million in 1980 and projected to grow to 74 million in twenty more years—left little room for optimism. The oil exporters provided a new source of aid, along with jobs and remittances, but even billions of dollars could not undo the poverty of so many.

The rich realized that money alone would not solve their own problems. The benefits could last only if used to finance the difficult and uncertain process of economic development. Materials, machinery, expertise, and often most of the labor force were imported for building infrastructures—roads, airports, harbors, and such—and for developing industries. Sa'udi Arabia adopted a $142 billion Five-Year Plan in 1975 and a second such plan, expected to cost $285 billion, in 1980. Some people envisaged countries like Sa'udi Arabia and Iran as industrial nations during the twenty-first century; in the mid-1970s, Muhammad Riza Shah Pahlavi predicted that Iran would be one of the greatest powers in the world in another generation.

Success was not assured, as industrialization was not simply a matter of building. Skills and modern habits were hard to come by. Even literacy, still limited to a minority of the adult population in most countries, could not be bought in the short run, although billions of dollars were being invested in schools and universities. A country recently having only a few literate people, Sa'udi Arabia had 1.5 million pupils enrolled in school in 1980.

WEAK POLITICAL ORDERS

Even less did money buy viable political orders. Some absolute monarchies gained a new lease on life as a result of the new wealth, but perhaps only for a short time. In Sa'udi Arabia, for example, economic opportunities turned many heads away from political opposition, which in any case was restrained by the firm clutch of a gigantic royal family, whose perhaps three thousand princes filled many key positions. But the continuation of the past legitimacy of a basically medieval regime was unlikely in a society being so rapidly exposed to modern developments like urbanization and literacy. More people become politically relevant under such circumstances and modern structures allowing for participation—either on a competitive basis or in a single-party system—seemed to be a prerequisite to effectiveness and stability. Signs soon appeared that the new wealth indeed was undermining the regime. A modern educated group—the so-called "new middle class"—grew and demanded opportunities of a professional and a political nature, and pious Muslims reacted against rampant materialism, inequality, and corruption. To many, the Sa'udi regime no longer remained a true Islamic government, despite its revivalist origins and its continuing enforcement of the *shari'ah*. According to critics of the royal family, all the strict Islamic rules enforced on the ordinary people were violated within palace walls. In keeping with the quasi-democratic ideals of early Islam, the idea was taking hold that both kingship and extremes of economic inequality are un-Islamic.

In the absence of a consensus based on strong liberal democratic traditions and of appropriate socioeconomic conditions, Western-style representative systems scarcely seemed to offer a real alternative. Those in Turkey and Lebanon had succumbed to chaos and military intervention (domestic or external) by 1980. The continuing vitality of elective, parliamentary procedures in Israel, a society established by immigrants from Europe, was an exception that confirmed the rule. Aside from the fact that the majority of Palestinians were refugees, Israel could not claim to be a democracy while retaining control over the Arab-inhabited Gaza Strip and West Bank short of becoming a binational state, which was hardly thinkable to many Israelis. As for Iran, the aftermath of the revolution provided some signs of a new synthesis of populist Islam and Western-originated democracy, and the new regime showed strength based on institutional procedures and widespread legitimacy that were absent in other countries. But the limits of free political competition grew narrow, while violent opposition evoked repression.

The Middle East has had little more success in attempts to establish viable radical authoritarian regimes based on single parties that involved the masses in a controlled way and provided new legitimate structures. Southern Yemen, whose Marxist ideology and Leninist-inspired Yemen Socialist party (previously the National Liberation Front) emerged from one of the few popular revolutions in the area, may have provided us with the only exception so far. Regimes established by military coups, on the other hand, have had trouble transmuting themselves into anything more than shaky dictatorships resting on force. Charismatic leadership sometimes has provided a temporary basis for legitimacy, as in Nasir's case, but transferring this to permanent institutions has proved more difficult.

The Ba'thist regimes of Iraq and Syria were cases in point, although both showed some signs of having become true single-party regimes. (In each case, the Ba'th was united with some minor parties in a "National Front.") It is notable that a nonmilitary party leader, Saddam Husayn, emerged as the dominant personality in the post-1968 Iraqi regime and finally assumed the presidency in 1979. He ruled through a party with an organization of devoted cadres that reached all facets of the society, including the army. At long last, the first parliamentary elections since the 1958 coup were held in 1980; they allowed a limited choice but at least provided a start with the kind of symbolic act that helps to legitimatize real single-party regimes. Among the regime's successes in truly transforming the society was a compulsory literacy program in the late 1970s that made major strides against illiteracy among the under-forty-five age group. But continued repressiveness, including the execution of several of the new president's associates in 1979 on charges of plotting a coup and reports of hundreds of other executions in later months, pointed to underlying instability. Separatism that still simmered among the Kurdish minority and a revived Islamic fundamentalism that flourished particularly among the Shi'ite majority left a militantly secular socialist regime whose leaders and following seemed largely limited to the Arab Sunni minority. Indeed, the leadership to a large extent was a personalistic clique hailing from one place, the town of Tikrit. Despite continuing revolutionary rhetoric, increasingly pragmatic policies made way for the emergence of a privileged technocratic class in both Iraq and Syria.

The Ba'thist regime in Syria shared the remarkable longevity and superficial stability of its Iraqi rival. The former's weaknesses were, however, more obvious. Corruption was on the upsurge, and widespread opposition of religious fundamentalists and others to the Alawite-dominated regime evoked increasing repression. The Muslim Brethren—membership in which became a capital offense—led a series of uprisings from 1979 on, starting with an attack on the largely Alawite military academy in Aleppo that led to hundreds of deaths of people connected with the regime and to the execution of many of its opponents. The year 1982 saw a full-scale fundamentalist Sunni revolt in Hama that the army was able to suppress only by destroying much of the city and by killing thousands of people. Rival regional centers and sectarian diversity (despite a large Sunni majority) had always made Syria a difficult country to govern. President Asad was heavily dependent on the military, particularly on the mainly Alawite special forces headed by his allegedly corrupt brother.

Sadat's Egypt seemed to regress from the limited political development in Nasir's time. For a while Sadat permitted more freedom of expression than formerly existed, especially for rightists, and competitive—though apparently rigged— elections were conducted, but within limits that barred comparison with a true parliamentary system. Sadat began by allowing three "platforms" within the Arab Socialist Union (ASU)—including small leftist and rightist "opposition" groups—to criticize his own majority faction. The three groups were permitted to act as separate political parties from 1976 on, and they were later joined by others, including a New Wafd. But, following violent riots in January 1977, directed heavily against the growing symbols of economic privilege and sparked by proposals for removing subsidies on basic foodstuffs, a decree, backed by 99.4 percent of the voters in a plebiscite, made strikes and demonstrations punishable by hard labor. In 1978 the New

Wafd decided to disband and the leftist National Progressive party temporarily suspended its "mass political activities" after Sadat obtained a 98.27 percent affirmative vote in a referendum proposing that pro-Soviet and prerevolutionary parties be banned. He later announced the formal abolition of the ASU in favor of a National Democratic party, presumably always to be guaranteed an overwhelming majority of the vote, while some minor parties continued on the periphery. With the number of millionaries and even the extent of corruption allegedly exceeding the level under King Faruq, Sadat did not seem to be following either the Western democratic or the revolutionary, mobilizational road to political development. The regime had become essentially a personal autocracy backed by the military and the police, as well as by affluent classes glad to be rid of Nasirite radicalism.

"Fundamentalist" Islamic organizations gained strength, particularly among Egyptian youths. University student bodies came under their control. Ultramilitant groups like the Society for Repentance and Retreat—which believed in the need for its members to retreat into the desert from a degenerate society as a prelude to establishing a just, egalitarian Islamic order—sporadically warred with the regime, while the more moderate Muslim Brethren were long officially tolerated. The regime's resort to more repressive measures in 1981, followed by the assassination of Sadat, will be dealt with later.

ISLAMIC RESURGENCE:
THE ZEALOT APPROACH

The 1970s saw increasing signs of Islam's vitality as a political force. In the first place, it was an expanding faith, largely because of the Muslims' continuing high birth rate at a time when modernization was increasing life expectancy. By 1980 the Muslims of the world numbered about 800 million. As a case in point, the Soviet census of 1979 showed that the Muslim peoples of the USSR increased 25 percent (to 43 million) in a decade, five times the rate of non-Muslims. Some population projections gave the USSR a Muslim majority in less than a century. Among "untouchables" in India, a movement was underway in the early 1980s to escape from their age-old degradation by embracing Islam. Conversion to Islam was continuing in Africa and—now often in less heterodox forms than before—among some black Americans.

Seemingly reversing the earlier trend toward secularization, Middle Eastern Muslims increasingly asserted their Islamic identity. Many women in various countries who had looked on their mothers' or grandmothers' clothing as antiquated began to return to wearing scarves and long dresses.

Governments began to show new concern with shoring up their Islamic credentials. Qadhdhafi's regime in Libya supplemented its pan-Arabism with pan-Islamic—but in some ways unorthodox—tendencies from the start and also, along with Pakistan, restored some Islamic rules. Moves in Egypt to reinstate the death penalty for apostasy from Islam were rejected, and a new law in 1977 even imposed a few limitations on polygamy and easy divorce for men. But respect for religious sentiment was demonstrated by such actions as limiting the sale of alcoholic drinks and a constitutional amendment declaring the *shari'ah* the main source of Egyptian law. In fact, conservative regimes such as Sadat's encouraged the new trend as a weapon against leftists only to have it come back against them in a radical, populist, egalitarian form. The "fundamentalist" movement remained diverse, with some elements committed to the socioeconomic status quo and supported by wealthy businessmen and the Sa'udi regime.

Numerous reasons for the seeming religious upsurge were suggested. Some pointed out that this was a worldwide phenomenon and, in a local context, extended to groups like Copts too. Correspondingly, there were occasional violent incidents that pointed to a growing tension in Muslim-Coptic relations. Indeed, while Muslims and Christians sometimes continued to be united under an Arab nationalist banner, they faced enemies like Israeli Jews and Lebanese Maronites who defined themselves in a sectarian way that may have encouraged emulation in their own camp. The conflict with Israel, notably the issue of Jerusalem, was especially conducive to being seen in religious terms.

In some ways there was nothing new in this visibility of religion. Intersectarian identities always were fragile, and the masses had been most effectively moved by appeals to religion. The return to religion involved many dangers, including the alienation of secularists and balkanization along sectarian lines, but also promised to be more effective than secular nationalism precisely because it did not cut across the grain of deep-seated feelings. The Egyptian army's replacement of uninspiring secular slogans with "God is great" is said to have been a factor—although presumably a minor one—in the successful crossing of the Suez Canal in 1973. And while traditional values had a special appeal to people whose lives were disrupted by rapid change, the influx of millions of villagers into urban slums—and also the spread of literacy and of the mass media's impact—helped to politicize strata of the population for whom secularism always had been alien. Perhaps the secular elements of society were getting more numerous in the period of "Islamic resurgence," but the nonsecular masses were becoming more salient and politically relevant. They also were reacting against increasing non-Islamic influences via television and the cinema as well as the physical presence of large numbers of Westerners and the existence of secular (including Marxist) movements and regimes.

Both successes and failures may have encouraged a religious upsurge. Defeat by Israel in 1967 left some Arabs with the feeling that there was nowhere else to turn and sometimes that God would not have deserted them if they had been more faithful. Some governments, like Nasir's, began to mute their secularism. Then, with the failure of secular movements to solve the area's problems and, after Nasir's death, the absence of another charismatic figure of comparable stature, religious fervor waited to fill the vacuum. Finally, the military and economic successes starting in 1973 were taken as renewed proof of God's favor. This was a reversal of the centuries-old situation in which the course of history demoralized Muslims by flying in the face of what they thought it should be. Still, the perception of continuing imperialist control and increased corruption, tyranny, and social injustice turned heads to radical movements, and those who posed their calls for revolutionary change in Islamic terms possessed an enormous advantage.

IRAN'S ISLAMIC REVOLUTION

Iran provided special circumstances that enabled the Zealot approach to find a remarkable manifestation. For the first time in the modern Middle East, a national government succumbed to a mass revolution, one that was unique in the modern non-Western world in not being based on a Western ideology. Despite its traditionalist garb, Iran's upheaval showed some signs of portending the only truly revolutionary change the area had known.

Iran's undreamt-of riches after the oil price increases of 1973 evoked unprecedented grandioseness on the part of the shah's regime. Suddenly money was available to increase the allotment for the recently adopted Five-Year Plan from $36 billion to $69 billion. By 1978 the average annual per capita GNP exceeded $2,000. Funds for the military especially burgeoned, as the armed forces grew to nearly half a million men. Military purchases from the United States alone amounted to over $20 billion in six years.

Paradoxically, these riches provided a catalyst that hastened the royalist regime's undoing. Military spending by a regime the populace had never identified with only bred resentment, as did the influx of over 100,000 Westerners as technicians and advisers. Waste and corruption abounded. The country's infrastructure could not handle the flood of imports, and backlogs in ports brought shortages and delays in massive projects. Shortages of funds forced cutbacks in the wild spending in 1975. By contrast, relatively little was being spent on social development, with the literacy rate not surpassing 50 percent and with Tehran, its population swollen to over 5 million, lacking such amenities as a sewer system. Neglect of agriculture increased the need to import food. Most of all, overspending spawned uncontrollable inflation that reached 50 percent a year. The rich gained, but the plight of the majority actually worsened.

The opposition grew more active and ultimately encompassed the vast majority of the population. The government admitted to holding a few thousand political prisoners; the opposition put the figure at 100,000. According to one interpretation, short-lived liberalization in response to the Carter administration's emphasis on human rights whetted Iranian appetites for more freedom, while the regime quickly returned to former practices in the apparent belief that Washington was not seriously concerned with applying this ideal to Iran.

Again, the Iranian *ulama* provided the opposition with its most potent leadership. The regime could hardly prevent people from going to the mosque, which thus provided a vital and unsurpassed communication network. When mullas[1] retold the

---

[1]Mullas are ordinary *ulama*, as opposed to *mujtahids* (those qualified to exercise *ijtihad*). Top *mujtahids* are given the unique Shi'ite title of Ayatullah, literally sign (*ayat*) of God (*Allah*). The word *ayat* also refers to verses in the Qur'an.

stories of Umayyad despotism and of the battle of Karbala, it was as though they were speaking in a well-understood code about their own time. For the masses, the inveterate opposition of Ayatullah Ruhullah Khumayni, now exiled at the mosque college at Ali's grave in Najaf (Iraq), remained the most powerful influence. Diverse antishah leaders made their way to Najaf, and tape cassettes of Khumayni's sermons eluded the censors to be bootlegged in Iranian bazaars and to keep alive the call for revolution.

Riots broke out in Qum in January 1978, after the Iranian press published libelous accusations against Ayatullah Khumayni, and soon spread over the whole country. The popular anger intensified as the army shot into the crowds, which produced a claim (undoubtedly exaggerated) that there were 60,000 martyrs. A general strike brought oil production to a virtual halt and, with it, an end to the regime's economic prop.

A military government, headed by a loyal general, tried to restore order with martial law. Announced reforms, like forbidding members of the royal family from engaging in business activities, which had provided lucrative opportunities for corruption, were to no avail. Neither was an attempt to name scapegoats, as in the arrest of Amir Abbas Hoveida, longtime prime minister and key figure in the shah's inner circle. Instead, the number of demonstrators against the regime—often crying "Death to the shah!"—swelled to several million.

By the beginning of 1979 the shah's position had deteriorated so far that he left the country ("on vacation") in a last-ditch attempt to stave off full-scale revolution. Shahpour Bakhtiyar, the only leader of the National Front now willing to play such a role, took the helm as prime minister. He instituted several changes, ranging from the abolition of Savak to banning the sale of oil to Israel and South Africa, but failed to appease the opposition. Most Iranians were satisfied with nothing less than the return of Khumayni, whose last months in exile were spent in France. He was no longer welcomed by an Iraqi regime anxious to preserve its rapprochement with the shah and fearful of an Islamic revolution that might not be limited to Iran. In France, Khumayni had freer access to other enemies of the Pahlavis and the advantages of coverage by the world's news media. For a while, Iranian airports were closed to keep him from returning.

The old regime finally disintegrated as Imam[2] Khumayni (to use his now-current title) flew to Iran in February 1979 amidst the rapturous response of millions. With common soldiers joining the crowds and whole army units attacking forces still loyal to the monarchy (and top commanders declaring the army's neutrality), Bakhtiyar fled to rally counterrevolutionary forces abroad. The *imam* was able to designate Mahdi Bazargan, a French-educated engineer and leader of the moderate, liberal antishah Freedom Front, as the new prime minister in a prudent prelude to a later acceleration of the revolution.

---

[2]Despite possible messianic overtones, this does not mean that he was considered to be one of the Twelve *imams*.

Paralleling the moderate formal government were local committees and a Revolutionary Council, mostly representing the more militant ulama-dominated Islamic Republican Party. Revolutionary Guards supplemented—and countered likely counterrevolutionary tendencies in—the largely shattered armed forces. Revolutionary tribunals carried out hasty trials that brought the executions up to an estimated total of at least a thousand within the next eighteen months. Included were many members of the old elite who had not fled as well as lesser individuals found guilty of torture and other crimes.

A militantly religious political system emerged. A plebiscite replaced the monarchy in favor of an "Islamic Republic." A new constitution approved by 98.2 per cent of the voters (in each case, large numbers of people boycotted the election) established a governmental structure—with a president, prime minister, and Consultative Assembly—that in many ways did not depart from modern Western patterns.

Other provisions of the constitution provided an Islamic—and specifically, a Twelver—character to the government. A Council of Guardians, with members chosen for six-year terms, partly by the Consultative Assembly, and not limited to the *ulama*, was given authority to determine whether proposed laws were contrary to Islam. (However, the very concept of law made by people was a deviation from traditionalism.) Another provision was unique, reflecting Khumayni's radical version of the Twelver doctrine of the role of the *ulama*—that is, his call for the guardianship of the *faqih* ("jurist," *fiqh* specialist)—during the absence of the Twelfth Imam. Thus the office of *faqih* was created, with Khumayni designated to this position for life. He was to be replaced on his death only if another generally accepted candidate emerged; otherwise his function would be filled by a collective Leadership Council. The *faqih* (or Leadership Council) was to stand above the rest of the governmental system in that he had authority to appoint half the members of the Council of Guardians and all the top judicial personnel, to dismiss the president in certain situations, to declare war, and to command the armed forces.

This essentially institutionalized the de facto charismatic authority already possessed by the imam. Seemingly uncorruptable and content to live the simplest life, devoid of all luxuries, he exercised such influence sporadically and with seeming reluctance as he chided those in charge for their weakness or for failing to revolutionize the society fast enough.

A reinstituted Islamic order reversed much westernization and secularization. The execution of adulterers and prostitutes reemerged, as did a strict ban on alcoholic beverages. Women were told to dress "modestly," evoking protests from Westernized middle-class circles. Women working for the government were later ordered to wear Islamic dress, but this did not have to be the long, enveloping black chador; a headscarf sufficed for many, and even those who wore the chador did not usually cover their faces. Women were not relegated to the traditional seclusion, for chador-clad women could be seen demonstrating and even carrying guns. But such actions as the suspension of the 1975 law modifying the unequal status of men in matters of marriage and divorce seemed to many to represent a backward step for women. Universities were closed as the new regime implemented its "cultural revolution."

Even those Western observers who were sympathetic with the Iranian Revolution found cause for concern. Many of its excesses could be dismissed as nearly inevitable aspects of revolutionary turmoil and foreign invasion, even as being mild in comparison with what had happened in other such situations. But the populist regime in some ways seemed to inherit the repressive methods of the shah's dictatorship; what had been known as Savak was revived under a new name and employed many of the same people. Although non-Muslim minorities were guaranteed the right to practice their religion and even given representation in the Consultative Assembly in proportion to their numbers, many were naturally unhappy with the theocratic nature of the regime. Some individuals were suspected of working with Westen powers and suffered accordingly. The Baha'i minority, the legitimacy of whose religion was always rejected by the ulama, was dismissed as a mere political group and denied the rights of other religious minorities. There were allegations that the Baha'is were facing outright persecution.

A militantly nonaligned stance reversed the shah's foreign policies. Military cooperation with the United States and the existence of electronic surveillance bases on the Soviet border were ended. With Tehran's withdrawal from CENTO, the organization finally disappeared. More importantly, the new regime renounced Iran's role as a "surrogate" of the United States in the Persian Gulf region. In economic matters, Iran was no longer inclined to restore oil production to levels desired by importers, levels that would deplete its own reserves too rapidly. Preferential sales to the oil consortium were ended. The mood was one of defying both superpowers, but suspicion was directed especially against the United States, independence from whose intervention seemed inseparable from ending the royalist order.

Revolutionary Iran combined an emphasis on pan-Islamic solidarity with rhetoric about supporting the "dispossessed" throughout the world. Iran severed relations with South Africa and Israel. Arafat was received with great emotion in Tehran, and Khumayni announced support for the Palestinian cause. The former Israeli mission in Tehran was turned over to the PLO, and Israel began to fear that Iranian troops would eventually be encamped with the Arabs on its eastern frontier.

The Islamic Republic's radicalism, with its widespread popular appeal transcending Iran's borders, found itself at odds with other types of regimes. The subversive call went out to all Muslims (Khumayni always played down sectarian differences) but appealed especially to Shi'ites. Khumayni's appeal among Iraq's Shi'ite majority terrified the Baghdad regime. Shi'ites in Bahrayn (a majority there too) and in Sa'udi Arabia's Eastern Province—and also Sunnis in the Sudan, Gaza, and elsewhere—frightened their governments by demonstrating in favor of the Iranian Revolution. Sadat's Egypt, where the dying exshah found his last refuge, became another avid enemy of the new regime and the source of CIA-supported radio broadcasts calling for its overthrow.

With the end of the monarchy, divisions began to appear among the makers of the revolution. Imam Khumayni seemed to retain the overwhelming loyalty of the poor classes (the "dispossessed"). But secularist liberals and generally the upper middle class often deemed the Islamic Republic worse than the shah's regime. Having failed to understand the significance of the politicized masses and their radical clerical leadership (thinking Khumayni was just a symbol), middle-class opponents of the shah now complained that the Revolution had been "stolen" from them. Marxist groups, which Khumayni sometimes strongly condemned, also posed a future threat to the Islamic direction of the Revolution. Although the Tudeh party and the "Majority Section" of the People's Fida'iyin continued to back Khumayni, some other Marxist groups, but mainly the non-Marxist People's Mujahidin, clashed with the Revolutionary Guards. Also, the radical aspects of the new regime were not to the liking of many *ulama*, and none of the other leading *mujtahids* really supported Khumayni. Supporters of the much less revolutionary Ayatullah Shari'at-Madari, the leading *marja-i taqlid* of Azarbayjan and some other areas, clashed with the followers of the *imam* at times, and Shari'at-Madari was kept under house arrest. The long-standing separatist sentiment of ethnic minorities, such as Turkomans and Khuzistani Arabs, came into the open. Most of all, the Kurds were in rebellion (with Iraq and Iran said to be subverting those in each other's territory), and violent attempts to suppress them ensued.

With an explosion of competitive politics, diverse centers of power emerged among those who worked under the umbrella of the Islamic Republic with the *imam's* blessing. Such for a while was Abu al-Hasan Bani-Sadr, a relatively pragmatic, French-educated economist who advocated a combination of Islam and socialism and won the first presidential election. On the other hand, the Islamic Republican party got overwhelming control of the Consultative Assembly and gradually won out in a growingly bitter conflict with Bani-Sadr, who was impeached and then dismissed from office by the *imam* in June 1981.

Attempts to overthrow the government were periodically uncovered. A large-scale plot, involving parts of the military and calling for bombing the *imam's* residence, was aborted in July 1980. A cacophony of counterrevolutionary groups emerged among exiled members of the old elite. Despite a plea from Khumayni to remain at home as a thinker and writer, Bani-Sadr fled to France with Mas'ud Rajavi, leader of the People's Mujahidin, to add another voice in opposition to the *imam*. A subsequent terror campaign by the Mujahidin decimated the leadership of the Islamic Republican party, killing seventy four leaders of the party in one explosion, but was unable to unseat it. Instead, the opposition appeared to be largely crushed by an accelerated reign of terror—though still on a small scale compared with that of the French Revolution—that brought the number of executions since the Revolution to at least the four thousand mark by 1982. But it remained questionable whether the Islamic Republican party, itself loosely organized, could maintain the continuity of the system after the death of Khumayni, now an ailing octogenarian.

Generally described as opposing modernization, the Islamic Revolutionaries obviously condemned much of what the royalist regime had meant by that term, especially Westernization and secularization. They also rejected excessive urbanization, concentration on prestigious industrial projects, and the like. But their emphasis on economic equality and the goal of improving conditions of life was in line with more sophisticated concepts of modernization. They seemed to favor the development of agriculture and small-scale industries, improvements in medical care, emphasis on vocational education and teacher-training, the extension of literacy, rural electrification, and other programs that arguably represent much of the essence of real modernization. There was no opposition to modern technology.

Many of the steps—and the rhetoric—of this Revolution might have been labeled *socialist* had current Islamic radicals been inclined to use such Western terminology. Banks and insurance companies were nationalized, as were many industries. Wages for most workers were dramatically increased, while high salaries were reduced. Workers' councils took charge of factories. Peasants began to take over large landholdings, with some local committees declaring that all land belongs to God, although the final shape of the official land reform seemed unclear.

This latter issue was one of several divisive ones within the Islamic Republican party. A conservative wing aligned with the traditional businessmen of the bazaar opposed many of Khumayni's egalitarian ideas and sought to gain control after his death.

Despite this division, support for the "dispossessed" colored all the regime's pronouncements, and indeed the backing of the overwhelming majority of the poor provided the main hindrance to those who wanted to overthrow it. But whatever the intent, the Revolution, consequent international crises, and the disruption that followed created large-scale unemployment amid continuing high rates of inflation, and this, at least in the short run, caused much suffering, as has been true of other revolutions.

U.S.—IRANIAN CRISIS

A new crisis in relations with the United States from November 1979 on provided severe dangers but also accelerated the revolution. When the exshah, now dying of cancer, left his most recent refuge in Mexico for medical treatment in the United States, many Iranians believed that a plot was underway to restore him to power, as in 1953. Militant students took control of the U.S. embassy in Tehran (the "den of spies," as they called it) and held the American diplomatic and consular personnel hostage, demanding the exshah's return for trial and the restoration of the billions of dollars he was accused of embezzling. Declaring the United States to be the "Great Satan," Imam Khumayni endorsed the students' action and ultimately left the matter for the Consultative Assembly, then still not elected. While pragmatists wanted to accept some compromise formula, many members of the Islamic Republican party demanded that the hostages be tried as spies. After decades of intervention in their affairs, few Iranians were impressed by talk about international law.

The students failed to achieve their declared objectives, although they succeeded in making fearful governments (Sadat's being one exception) withdraw their welcome to the ex-monarch. But the students became another important center of power in Iran and helped to fuel the radicalization of the Revolution. One of the first results of the embassy takeover—and perhaps its real motivation—was the resignation of the moderate Bazargan government, which helped propel the Revolution to another stage. The resultant outside threats served to unify the country behind the new regime.

Such a blatant violation of diplomatic immunity threatened dangerous international repercussions. The International Court of Justice demanded release of the hostages, and the Security Council condemned Iran's action. The United States also imposed economic sanctions on Iran, which included freezing about $12 billion of its assets and ending all trade. Western European countries and Japan also reluctantly agreed to a boycott, though with many loopholes.

U.S. policy vacillated from conciliatory positions to threats of force. An airborne rescue attempt in April 1980 turned into a fiasco in the Dasht-i Kavir desert. For Khumayni's supporters throughout the Islamic world the "miraculous" effects of "God's radar" had thwarted the world's greatest power. The United States later agreed in principle to accept a four-point formula (a promise of noninterference, unfreezing of assets, cancellation of legal claims relating to the hostages, and the return of the exshah's wealth) proposed by the *imam* and adopted by the Consultative Assembly. The prisoners were finally freed in January 1981 in return for the immediate release of about a fourth of Iran's frozen assets, with the rest set aside to repay loans and to cover legal claims (to be arbitrated). Only a vague, and seemingly unmeaningful, U.S. commitment to facilitate the return of the ex-royal family's wealth was obtained.

Dramatic shows of popular solidarity with Iran throughout the Islamic world, as well as sparks of Islamic revolution in some countries, helped to restrain the U.S. In the midst of the hostage crisis in November 1979, the Islamic year 1400 began, and with it the well-organized armed takeover of the Great Mosque, seat of the Ka'bah, in Mecca by rebels, one of whom had added "al-Mahdi" to his name. Uprisings may have been planned in other parts of the kingdom. Sa'udi troops were able to capture and kill the rebels, but only after two weeks had passed and with many soldiers killed or wounded. The choice of such a holy place as the site of rebellion helped to discredit the rebels, but not entirely, and stories are told of young men passionately awaiting an opportunity to join them. The widespread notion that the Sa'udi monarchy was popular and secure in power came to be disputed more than ever before, and all the conservative (and secular radical) regimes felt increasingly threatened by the new revolutionary theocratic wave. When Khumayni expressed his suspicion that Washington was behind the Meccan revolt (the Western press was then inaccurately reporting it as an act of Iranian Shi'ites), there were fierce anti-U.S. riots and demonstrations in many countries. The U.S. embassy in Pakistan was set aflame by angry crowds.

RENEWED SUPERPOWER INVOLVEMENT

While the Iranian crisis was in full swing in December 1979, a crisis in Afghanistan provided a new strand to complicate the international relations of the region. Soviet troops entered the country in full force—their number a few months later was put at 85,000—supposedly on the invitation of the year-old Communist government, which incongruously was immediately replaced by another Afghan Communist faction. There were diverse interpretations of the Soviet action. Some saw it as a basically defensive move, considering that the faction the Soviets overthrew was the more extreme one and that its antireligious fervor threatened to bring about its overthrow by militantly Islamic rebels. As this view sometimes goes, the Soviets were threatened not only by a potentially hostile regime in Afghanistan but also by the possibility that this would infect the growing numbers of Soviet Muslims, ethnically related to those in Afghanistan.

Others, however, saw a new Soviet aggressiveness, with the invasion of Afghanistan being a step (perhaps via an eventually disintegrating Iran) into the Persian Gulf and Indian Ocean area. Note was made of Soviet facilities and bases in Ethiopia and South Yemen and of large numbers of Soviet troops in Transcaucasia, near the Iranian border. Some observers pointed to a possible motive of depriving the U.S. and its allies of oil. A CIA report that projected an end to the Soviets' self-sufficiency in that vital resource within the next few years also colored the reaction to Soviet moves, although later U.S. government studies increasingly showed this to be fallacious.

Whatever the USSR's motive, it suddenly found itself widely condemned in the Islamic world. Even as Iran was preoccupied with its conflict with the U.S.— and while the new crisis in Soviet-American relations led the USSR to veto sanctions against Iran in the Security Council—it too condemned the invasion of Afghanistan and gave some aid to the Afghan rebels. Sadat's Egypt became the rebels' major source of weapons and training, and perhaps 2 million Afghans took refuge in Pakistan (and others in Iran). Washington seemingly was also restrained from taking vindictive actions against Iran, which might have played into Soviet hands. Only a few Middle Eastern countries, like South Yemen and Syria, whose renewed ties with the USSR were evidenced by increased arms shipments and a treaty of cooperation, generally failed to condemn the Soviet action.

The United States began increasingly to shore up its muscles in the Indian Ocean region. South Yemen's close relationship with the USSR and its clash with North Yemen early in 1979 had already brought U.S. military aid to the latter and official expressions of a new willingness to be involved in the region. Now the Iranian pillar of U.S. policy was gone, and regimes of other vital oil producers were left impotent in the face of new dangers, if largely internal ones. Then the passions aroused by the hostage crisis, together with the Soviet move into Afghanistan, helped overcome America's post-Vietnam War reluctance to become militarily involved. A large-scale U.S. naval buildup occurred in the Indian Ocean, and agreements were negotiated for base facilities in Somalia, Kenya, Oman, and Egypt, while joint maneuvers of the U.S. and Egyptian air forces ensued from bases near Cairo. Washington also accelerated its plans to develop a Rapid Deployment Force of 225,000 expected to cost $75 billion, especially designed for large-scale operations in the Middle East by the mid-1980s. The Carter Doctrine of 1980 defined any outside attempt to control the Persian Gulf as "an assault on the vital interests" of the U.S. that, if necessary, would be countered by the use of "military force."

WAR BETWEEN IRAQ AND IRAN

The immediate threat to stability, however, came from within the region as Iraq launched a major armed attack on Iran in September 1980. The messianic appeal of the Islamic Revolution to millions on the Iraqi side of the border provided a main reason for the conflict. Soon after the revolution in Iran the two regimes began to clash militarily and to subvert each other, with some Iranian leaders calling for revolt against Iraq's "infidel" regime and Iraq backing Arab separatists in Iran. Iraq also expelled thousands of Shi'ites, especially those of Iranian origin, across the border, and hundreds were executed, including the Shi'ite religious leader Ayatullah Muhammad Baqir al-Sadr. Iranian counterrevolutionaries such as General Ghulam Oveissi gathered in Iraq to join in action against the Islamic Republic. Formerly isolated within the region by its doctrinaire radicalism, the Iraqi regime increasingly forged a de facto alliance with the monarchies against the threat of Islamic revolution.

Iraq also saw what looked like a unique opportunity to replace the shah's Iran as the dominant power in the Persian Gulf and even to become the leader of the Arab world. Egypt, which previously overshadowed Iraq, was now conveniently excluded from the inter-Arab arena by virtue of its peace treaty with Israel. The Iraqi army grew to 280,000 men, seemingly unchallenged in the Gulf region now that the Iranian military had fallen apart through desertions, absence of trained officers, and the unavailability of spare parts and proper maintenance. Since the drop in Iran's oil production, Iraq had replaced it as the second largest exporter, gaining immense financial capacity. With Iraq having discarded its image as a Soviet client since 1978 and with the hostage crisis continuing, there was no likelihood that the United States would actively oppose an attack on Iran. In fact, Iranians generally believed, though apparently erroneously, that the United States masterminded the attack.

The goals of overthrowing Iran's Islamic Republic before its contagion could overwhelm Arab regimes and of establishing Iraqi primacy in the region overshadowed specific, announced objectives. The latter included the restoration of Iraqi sovereignty over the Shatt al-Arab to the Iranian shore, that is, a reversal of the humiliating concession to the shah in 1975; Iraqi control over a disputed border area; the return of three islands occupied by Iranian forces in 1971 to "Arab sovereignty" (presumably to the United Arab Emirates); and autonomy for Iran's Kurdish and Arab regions.

The Iraqis succeeded in occupying some Iranian territory. Perhaps 2 million Iranians were turned into refugees. But military experts were stunned by the fierce resistance of Revolutionary Guards with little training and by military units without effective overall command that turned the expected quick Iraqi victory into a long war. Nothing could have been better calculated to unite Iranians, including opponents of the regime who saw the homeland threatened. For weeks the Iranian city of Khurramshahr defied repeated Iraqi announcements that it had fallen, and some pockets of resistance held out in what was renamed Khuninshahr ("the City of Blood"). The other cities of Khuzistan came under attack but refused to give way and provided a continuing series of "miracles" for the revitalized Islamic regime. Even Iran's air force, with its few remaining pilots and without spare parts, managed to control the skies for a while at the beginning of the war. Bombings devastated important economic targets on each side, reducing oil exports by both to a small fraction of their former levels.

The Iraqi regime found the Iranian Kurdish rebels to be allies but failed to gain the expected backing of Khuzistan's Arabs. Meanwhile, appeals from Iran—including taped broadcasts by the "martyred" Ayatullah Baqir al-Sadr—provided a potential threat to Baghdad. In fact, a populist regime in Iran was able to survive great hardships as financial reserves vanished, but a financially solvent Iraqi government feared that discontent would get out of hand if its people were asked to sacrifice much. Also, President Husayn dared not launch offensives that would risk heavy casualties on his side for fear that his people would turn on him.

As for the Iranians, fervent believers in their revolution provided "human waves" willing to sacrifice themselves. By the latter part of 1981, they seemed clearly to be winning; March of the following year saw them inflict major losses on the Iraqis and push them back several miles. Confident of victory and contemplating an eventual citizen "Army of Twenty Million" men and women, revolutionary Iran refused to consider the kind of compromise peace that the regime in Baghdad now desperately wanted. Horrified by the Islamic Republic's military momentum and by its calls for exporting the revolution, supporters of the status quo saw an allegedly Iranian-backed abortive coup in Bahrayn in 1981 as an omen of things to come in the Gulf region.

There were some signs of renewed vigor of existing regimes. Many former proponents of revolution seem to have been dismayed by the example of turmoil in Iran. Jolted by the Meccan revolt of 1979, the Sa'udi regime took steps to combat corruption and to spread the increasing oil revenues more widely than before. Opposition may have dwindled. But none of these regimes could afford to be confident about their future.

The war had an important impact on Iranian politics. As commander-in-chief, President Bani-Sadr found his political position somewhat strengthened, but only temporarily. The conduct of the war provided issues to fuel the conflict between him and his Islamic Republican party opponents. Perhaps being on the front gave him less access to the *imam* and thus contributed to his downfall. And with the army engaged in battle, it was difficult for army officers to plot a coup. The war also brought home the need to end the country's isolation and particularly to have its assets unfrozen. It thus provided a major incentive to resolve the hostage issue. In the struggle for survival, the regime even put aside its anti-Zionism long enough to buy weapons from Israel.

The Iraqi-Iranian War threatened to spread. The Arab monarchies gave more or less open diplomatic and financial support to Iraq, and Jordan's port of Aqaba became a back-door supply route. Some Jordanian "volunteers" joined Iraqi forces in 1982. U.S. radar aircraft (AWACs) were flown to Sa'udi Arabia to guard against an enlarged war. But Iraqi attempts to evoke Arab solidarity by portraying the conflict as one between Arabs and Persians had little success on the popular level. Many Arabs saw Khumayni as an Islamic rather than merely as an Iranian or even a Shi'ite leader, although his enemies did have some success in reviving anti-Shi'ite feelings. Revolutionary-minded Arabs also tended to blame the Iraqi regime for having attacked the "wrong enemy"—in fact, a new ally against Israel—and some regimes favored Iran for largely opportunistic reasons.

As an example of the latter, Syria's renewed enmity toward Iraq and Jordan pulled it into the Iranian camp. Syrian forces massed on the Jordanian border in late 1980, perhaps partly to prevent Jordanian troops from entering the war against Iran but also in an attempt to induce King Husayn to stop aiding Muslim Brother guerrillas in Syria and to restrain him and other Arab leaders from reneging (as rumor had them about to do) on the 1974 Rabat declaration that the PLO is the sole representative of the Palestinians. Libya, whose rapprochement with Syria was symbolized by an unpromising announcement in 1980 of plans to unite, strongly favored Iran, as seemingly did Algeria and South Yemen in less obvious ways. Many Palestinians looked with hope to the Iranian Revolution, although they often favored leftist forces like the Mujahidin over the Islamic regime. Later news of Iran's dealings with Israel brought some further disillusionment. But the start of the war found the PLO in a difficult predicament. Arafat's attempts to mediate between the two countries evoked resentment from each, and their internecine war was an obvious blow to the Palestinian cause. The Iraqi-Iranian conflict gave a new dimension to the Lebanese civil war, as pro-Iraqi and pro-Iranian factions sometimes battled against each other. Sadat ridiculed his opponents for being in such disarray, but he offered military protection in case revolution threatened the Sa'udi regime and even sold weapons to Iraq. There were unconfirmed reports of a few Egyptians fighting on the Iraqi side in the war.

STRATEGIC CONSENSUS?

With the beginning of President Ronald Reagan's administration in 1981, Washington stepped up its campaign against the alleged Soviet threat to the Middle East. Proclaiming the goal of a "strategic consensus," the new administration in effect called on all Middle Eastern governments—Arab and Israeli alike—to give priority to the common danger that should, in its view, reduce every other issue to relative insignificance.

At least for a while, Washington relegated settlement of the Palestine problem to the back burner. Israel came more openly than ever before to be proclaimed a great strategic asset for the United States in the region, and a vague U.S.–Israeli agreement on "strategic cooperation" actually was concluded even at a time when some of the initial enthusiasm had worn off. The new administration promised not to criticize Israel. Some leading spokesmen for the administration proclaimed that heretofore-condemned Israeli acts, like building settlements in the occupied territories and carrying out raids into Lebanon, were not illegal. Statements by conservative Arab leaders that they considered Israel a greater threat than the USSR seemed to be met with disbelief by an administration whose anti-Soviet campaign was reminiscent of the priority given to forming alliances in the Middle East during the 1950s.

Such states as Libya and Syria were pictured by Washington essentially as extensions of the USSR in a region whose internal dynamics were played down. Libya, with which Egypt and the Sudan were engaged in mutual subversion, became singled out as the greatest *bête noire*, with the Reagan administration apparently giving high priority to the overthrow of the Qadhdhafi regime, which turned out to be a frustratingly elusive goal.

Washington stepped up its commitments to other Middle Eastern states. Pakistan—bordering on Soviet-occupied Afghanistan and, in return for large amounts of petrodollars, a potentially important military protector of the Sa'udi regime against revolution—gained $3.2 billion in economic and military aid from the United States, while Egypt got increased military credits. Besides increasing ties with the other Arab monarchies in the Persian Gulf region by forming a Gulf Consultative Council, Sa'udi Arabia apparently hoped to be able to depend on military support from any of several conservative regimes against any internal threat. President Reagan also issued assurances that the United States would not allow the Sa'udi monarchy to be overthrown, although it was not clear whether he was committing the United States to send troops in such a case. The United States concluded an $8.5 billion agreement to sell arms, including AWACS, to Sa'udi Arabia, creating a controversy that dominated American politics for a while. The proposed sale barely failed to be rejected by Congress in the face of pressures from the White House and bitter Israeli opposition that greatly annoyed the administration.

The reality of intraregional and intrastate dynamics had already begun to threaten "strategic consensus" in other ways. Conflict in Lebanon seemed about to get out of hand during 1981 as rightists built a road connecting the main area under their control with their supporters in the town of Zahlah, in eastern Lebanon, a move that threatened to upset the status quo in their favor. In subsequent clashes between Syrian forces and the Lebanese rightists, Israeli warplanes intervened to shoot down Syrian helicopters. Syria, in turn, installed surface-to-air missiles in Lebanon, allegedly contrary to earlier understandings and threatening Israeli supremacy in the skies. Despite initial anti-Syrian statements, the United States assumed a mediatory role in trying to end the crisis as the president's special envoy, Philip Habib, flew from capital to capital. Under U.S. pressure, Israeli promises to destroy the missiles were not fulfilled, meaning that Syria, so far, had won this round of mutual bluff.

Other Israeli actions that demonstrated continuing priority for the conflict with the Arabs and threatened to undermine the prospects for "strategic consensus" created anger in Washington. The world was startled in June 1981 by news that Israel—using U.S.-supplied planes—had destroyed Iraq's nuclear reactor, which had been nearly completed with French assistance. With strong U.S. support, the Security Council denounced the raid, and the United States delayed, though only temporarily, the shipment of fighter planes to Israel. In July, before the shock of the raid on Iraq was over, Israel accelerated its conflict with recently strengthened Palestinian forces in southern Lebanon in an apparent attempt finally to crush them. An artillery war between Israel and the PLO raged for days, and Israel escalated it by carrying out an air raid on Beirut, again with U.S.-supplied weapons, that killed about three hundred people. Again, Washington condemned the Israeli action and delayed shipments of warplanes a bit longer. The United States, dealing with the PLO via Sa'udi Arabia, also helped to arrange a cease-fire. Israel's annexation of the Golan Heights in December brought it renewed condemnation and led Washington to suspend the agreement on "strategic cooperation" only eighteen days after its conclusion.

Finally, growing resentment in Egypt against Sadat's policies threatened to bring down a main pillar of U.S. policy in the region. In September 1981 the Egyptian president ordered the arrest of 1,536 people, including former cabinet ministers and other prominent individuals. Accused of "religious fanaticism," they actually were a diverse group, only some of whom were religious zealots. Accusing the USSR of conspiring with his opponents, Sadat expelled the Soviet ambassador and the last remaining Soviet technicians.

Then on October 6, during the military parade celebrating the anniversary of the Crossing, participants in the parade gunned down Sadat as he watched from the reviewing stand. The assassins allegedly were associated with an organization called "al-Jihad" and hoped to spark a revolution on the Iranian model but failed in that objective, at least for now. The First World, particularly U.S. audience that Sadat had played to joined in bereavement unprecedented for any foreign leader; the majority of his own people surprised many outsiders by showing little grief.

Sadat's vice president and handpicked successor, Husni Mubarak, a former air force commander, quickly took over the presidency with the usual ritualistic 98.5 percent vote of approval. The same regime thus continued under a new head, although subtle differences soon began to emerge. Mubarak showed some signs of greater sensitivity to the gap between rich and poor and took action against certain symbols of conspicuous wealth that Sadat had been associated with. He also tried to seem less accommodating than Sadat in dealing with Israel, although he was careful not to endanger the final stage of withdrawal from Sinai, which—despite growing Israeli reluctance—was completed on schedule in April of 1982. Many observers expected Egypt now to gravitate back into the Arab camp while not repudiating the peace treaty with Israel and to find ready acceptance by the conservative regimes in particular.

Few observers felt confident that the Egyptian regime would last. However, the open rebellion of militant Muslims that occurred in various parts of Egypt immediately after Sadat's death was suppressed. Many of the people Sadat had arrested were released, and some were invited to the palace and interviewed on television. The regime won the backing of some of Sadat's moderate opponents.

TURKEY: CONTINUING TROUBLES

Though in some ways aloof from its neighbors' affairs, Turkey shared in many of their troubles. The People's Republican party leader, Bülent Ecevit, became premier after the October 1973 elections, but this was made possible only by an incongruous, shaky coalition with the Islamic fundamentalist National Salvation party that epitomized the beginning of increased political instability. But the premier's prestige soared as he dealt forcibly with a new phase of the Cyprus problem during the following summer. When pro-Enosis army officers took control of Cyprus with the connivance of the rightist Greek military dictatorship, Turkey invaded the largely Greek-populated island and occupied the northern 40 percent of it. Ecevit soon resigned in the belief that new elections would follow and give his party a majority, but Justice party leader Suleyman Demirel surprised him by mustering enough support to form his own government.

The invasion of Cyprus was a great boost for Turkish national pride. Reminiscent of the 1920s, 200,000 Greek refugees were the product of Turkish victories. Both this situation and conflicting claims to the mineral resources of the Aegean aggravated tensions between Turkey and Greece.

With the invasion of Cyprus, a new U.S.–Turkish rift emerged. Citing the use of U.S.–supplied weapons in the operation, the U.S. Congress banned future American arms shipments to Turkey. Turkey in turn closed important U.S. intelligence bases near the Soviet border. Ankara also improved its ties with Moscow, and the two governments signed a nonaggression pact in 1978. Still, the Turks refrained from carrying out threats to withdraw from NATO or otherwise to loosen ties with the U.S.–led bloc. With the ongoing revolution in Iran making it more conscious of Turkey's importance, Congress lifted the arms embargo in 1978, allowing the U.S. bases to be reopened.

Turkey's internal problems seemed to snowball as it faced higher oil prices. Also, the economic slowdown in Western Europe in the mid 1970s resulted in the layoffs of thousands of "guest workers," whose remittances were a major source of foreign exchange for Turkey. Inflation increased to a rate of 118 percent a year by 1980, and balance-of-payments problems brought recurrent devaluation of the Turkish lira. Foreign debt exceeded $15 billion by 1980, while industries operating at 55 percent of capacity resulted in an unemployment rate of 20 percent. Slum population grew at a rate of 6 percent a year, and the per capita GNP seemingly declined during the late 1970s.

As extreme factions grew on both left and right, riots and terrorism tore the country apart. Calculations in 1980 put the number of deaths at about three thousand during the previous two years. The toll reached two hundred a month by the first half of 1980. Whole towns temporarily established their independence, and nighttime control of large sections of the big cities fell into the hands of urban guerrillas. This sometimes took on a religious dimension; the leftists came disproportionately from the roughly 8 percent Shi'ite minority in eastern Anatolia, while the rightists were largely Sunnis. Martial law prevailed in much of the country after December 1978, and international human rights groups began to report "widespread and systematic torture." Weak coalition cabinets—Ecevit formed a new government in 1978 but made way for Demirel after the next year's elections—were unable to deal with the problem effectively.

During 1980 the generals issued several warnings to the political parties to unite to solve the country's problems. Finally, in September of the same year the army engineered another coup, and a junta headed by General Kenan Evren took control. Martial law extended to the whole country, and thousands of people, including members of the Grand National Assembly and the top civilian leaders, were arrested at least temporarily. Ruthless measures by the military regime caused the number of political killings to plunge. At least in the short run, the country experienced an economic upturn as production and exports increased and as the rate of inflation fell. The military was expected, as in 1960, eventually to restore the democratic system under a new constitution, one that would abolish the proportional representation that encouraged political parties to proliferate, minimize the checks and balances that hindered elected majorities, and perhaps establish a strong presidency modeled after that of the Fifth French Republic. But it was hard to see how either a temporary dictatorship or a tampering with governmental organization could solve the country's deep-seated economic and social problems.

CONCLUSIONS

From 1973 on, the Middle East began to assume a shape that few could previously have foreseen. The gap between Arabs and Israelis—and perhaps more broadly between the Middle East and the West—showed signs of closing. For some the military Crossing of the Suez Canal and the increased oil prices symbolized a beginning of the swing of the pendulum of history back to the East. The Iranian Revolution and the overall upsurge of Islamic identity gave evidence of a new militancy against Western political, economic, and cultural supremacy. Corresponding to elation on the Eastern side, some Westerners began to open dusty copies of Spengler's *The Decline of the West* or even to issue exaggerated pronouncements about an Islamic East that, figuratively speaking, was prevailing in a second Battle of Tours.

In truth, the Middle East was an underdeveloped area still struggling to bridge the gap between itself and a West that for centuries had undergone accelerated modernization. It was still the Middle East that found itself subjected to varying kinds of Western domination, not vice versa. The fact that the whole Arab world was still unable to defeat the minuscule state of Israel and that even within that country a minority of Western origin remained dominant best demonstrated the continuing civilizational gap. The advantages of oil wealth accrued mainly to a few countries, not including most of the ones with large populations. Even those who became rich could not buy modernity overnight, and a tragic possibility loomed that all the money would be squandered sometime in the twenty first century, before the area achieved a modern technological level. The quest of Middle Eastern nations for viable political orders promised to be even more arduous than that for economic development, and internal and interstate conflict threatened to destroy everything. Furthermore, a fundamental indicator of how far the Middle East had to go was that what military successes it had achieved was with weapons imported from Western countries like the United States and the USSR. An even deeper measure may be the relative meagerness of recent Middle Eastern productivity in cultural and scientific fields. Reflecting its Western origins, Israel alone surpassed the whole Arab world in scientific publication by more than a two-to-one ratio.

Despite all this, predictions that the Middle East, after about three centuries in the shadows, would resume the central place in the world that it occupied during most of human history did not sound nearly as far-fetched in 1982 as they might have a decade before. More realistically, the area could hope for a kind of equality that recent centuries denied it. If, as some said, a modern global civilization had long replaced those of East and West alike in many spheres, each still preserved much of its own distinctiveness. More than ever before, the recent upsurge of the Zealot approach to resisting both political and cultural domination belied the notion that the modernization of the world, once achieved, would necessarily amount to its Westernization. Still, the immediate future seemed likely to bring more setbacks for Middle Eastern peoples.

Bibliographical Essay

Selected Works in English

A listing of even the major works in the field would fill hundreds of pages. For such a relatively complete bibliography, the reader is referred to Claude Cahen, *Jean Sauvaget's Introduction to the History of the Muslim East: A Bibliographical Guide* (Berkeley: University of California Press, 1965) and, although their organization is cumbersome, to J. D. Pearson, *Index Islamicus, 1906–1955* (London: Mansell, 1958) and subsequent five-year supplements. Since 1977 this has been continued in the form of a periodical, *The Quarterly Index Islamicus*. Also see Peter M. Rossi and Wayne E. White (eds.), *Articles in the Middle East, 1947–1971* (Ann Arbor, Mich.: Pierian Press, 1980). Other suggestions may be found in Reeva Simon, *The Modern Middle East: A Guide to Research Tools in the Social Sciences* (Boulder, Colo.: Westview, 1976). Leonard Binder (ed.), *The Study of the Middle East* (New York: John Wiley, 1976) provides in-depth analyses of scholarship in various disciplines, including history. *The Middle East Studies Association Bulletin* (Tucson, Ariz.) provides course syllabi, bibliographies, and other useful materials.

For attacks on conventional scholarship, see Edward Said, *Orientalism* (New York: Pantheon, 1978) and *Review of Middle East Studies* (London).

The most useful journals include *The International Journal of Middle East Studies* (New York) and *The Middle East Journal* (Washington). Other journals include *Arab Studies Quarterly* (Detroit); *Bulletin of the School of Oriental and Afri-*

can Studies (London); *Iranian Studies* (Los Angeles); *Journal of Palestine Studies* (Beirut); *Journal of the American Oriental Society* (Baltimore); *Journal of South Asian and Middle Eastern Studies* (Villanova, Penn.), *Middle Eastern Studies* (London); and *Muslim World* (Hartford, Conn.).

GEOGRAPHY AND WORLD HISTORICAL PERSPECTIVE

General geographical works include Peter Beaumont et al., *The Middle East: A Geographical Study* (New York: John Wiley, 1976) and W. B. Fisher, *The Middle East,* 7th ed. (New York: Barnes & Noble, 1979).

For the Middle East in world historical perspective, see William McNeill, *The Rise of the West* (Chicago: University of Chicago Press, 1963). Though often leaving much room for debate, invaluable insight may be gained from Arnold Toynbee's works, notably *A Study of History,* 12 vols. (New York: Oxford University Press, 1933–1961), also available under the same title in a two-volume abridgement by D. C. Somerville (New York: Oxford University Press, 1947–1957). Many of Toynbee's themes may be found in narrative form in his *Mankind and Mother Earth* (New York: Oxford University Press, 1976). Also see International Commission for a History of the Scientific and Cultural Development of Mankind, *History of Mankind,* 6 vols. (New York: Harper & Row, 1963–1966).

THE PRE-ISLAMIC BACKGROUND

All of the early civilizations have their own bodies of literature. See, for example, A. Leo Oppenheim, *Ancient Mesopotamia* (Chicago: University of Chicago Press, 1964) and John A. Wilson, *The Burden of Egypt* (Chicago: University of Chicago Press, 1951). Broader surveys include Jean Bottero et al., *The Near East: The Earliest Civilizations* (New York: Delacorte Press, 1967) and Jacquetta Hawkes, *The First Great Civilizations* (New York: Random House, 1973). For an overall account of the history of the area to c. 500 B.C., see Sabatino Moscati, *the Face of the Ancient Orient* (London: Routledge & Kegan Paul, 1960). For a later period, see W. W. Tarn and G. T. Griffith, *Hellenistic Civilization,* 3rd ed. (Cleveland: World Publishing Co., 1961). On the period from Alexander the Great to the conversion of Constantine, I recommend F. E. Peters, *The Harvest of Hellenism,* 2nd ed. (New York: Simon & Schuster, 1970). The reader may want to continue with A. A. Vasiliev, *History of the Byzantine Empire, 324–1453,* 2nd ed. (Madison: University of Wisconsin Press, 1952). On ancient (and early Islamic) Iran, see Richard Frye, *Heritage of Persia* (New York: Collins Publishers, 1963). Also see R. Ghirshman,

Iran (Baltimore: Penguin, 1978). An especially interesting facet of Middle Eastern history is covered in Richard Bulliet, *The Camel and the Wheel* (Cambridge: Harvard University Press, 1976). For a revealing archaeological study of ancient and Islamic Mesopotamia see Robert Adams, *Land Behind Baghdad* (Chicago: University of Chicago Press, 1966).

Covering ancient to modern times is Salo Baron (ed.), *A Social and Religious History of the Jews,* 17 vols., 2nd ed. (New York: Columbia University Press, 1952–1980).

Philip Hitti, *History of Syria Including Palestine and Lebanon* (New York: Macmillan, 1951) is an interesting account of ancient and Islamic eras.

The ancient Arabs are covered in many books on Islamic history and Arabic literature (see below). Philip Hitti, *History of the Arabs,* 9th ed. (New York: St. Martin's Press, 1967) is a detailed account that bridges ancient and medieval periods and is still unsurpassed in many ways. Also see G. Levi della Vida, "Pre-Islamic Arabia," in Nabih Faris (ed.), *Heritage of the Arabs* (Princeton, N.J.: Princeton University Press, 1944). De Lacy O'Leary, *Arabia before Muhammad* (New York: Dutton, 1927) is still valuable.

ISLAMIC HISTORY: GENERAL WORKS

As for general treatments of Islamic history, P. M. Holt et al., *The Cambridge History of Islam,* 2 vols. (Cambridge: Cambridge University Press, 1970) is indispensable, though not definitive. Marshall Hodgson, *The Venture of Islam*, 3 vols. (Chicago: University of Chicago Press, 1974) is a monumental, inspiring work. For a shorter but—to the beginner—detailed and dull survey, see Carl Brockelmann, *History of the Islamic Peoples* (New York: Capricorn Books, 1960). Another excellent work is Bertold Spuler. *The Muslim World: A Historical Survey,* 3 vols. trans. by F. R. C. Bagley (Leiden: Brill, 1960–1969). J. Stewart-Robinson (ed.), *The Traditional Near East* (Englewood Cliffs, N.J.: Prentice-Hall, 1966) contains some good essays on pre-nineteenth-century history.

For maps, see Harry Hazard, *Atlas of the Middle East* (Princeton, N.J.: Princeton University Press, 1954) or Roelof Roolvink, *Historical Atlas of Muslim Peoples* (Cambridge: Harvard University Press, 1957). For rulers and dates, see Clifford Bosworth, *The Islamic Dynasties: A Chronological and Genealogical Handbook* (Chicago: Aldine, 1967). A variety of useful materials may be found in Jere Bacharach, *A Near East Studies Handbook,* 2nd ed. (Seattle: University of Washington Press, 1977).

A new edition of the *Encyclopaedia of Islam* (Leiden: Brill, 1954 –) is in progress. The first four volumes have been published. The old edition (Leiden: Brill, 1913–1934) is thus still useful.

FROM MUHAMMAD TO THE
MONGOLS AND MAMLUKS

The following works deal mainly with this period: Gustav von Grunebaum, *Classical Islam: A History, 600–1250* (Chicago: Aldine, 1970); Bernard Lewis, *The Arabs in History* (New York: Harper & Row, 1966); J. J. Saunders, *A History of Medieval Islam* (London: Routledge & Kegan Paul, 1965); and Joseph Schacht and C. E. Bosworth (eds.), *The Legacy of Islam,* 2nd ed. (Oxford: Clarendon Press, 1974). For interesting sketches, see Philip Hitti's *Makers of Arab History* (New York: Harper & Row, 1968) and *Capital Cities of Arab Islam* (Minneapolis: University of Minnesota Press, 1973).

For socioeconomic matters, see E. Ashtor, *A Social and Economic History of the Near East in the Middle Ages* (Berkeley: University of California Press, 1976); M. A. Cook (ed.), *Studies in the Economic History of the Middle East from the Rise of Islam to the Present* (London: Oxford University Press, 1970); and Maurice Lombard, *The Golden Age of Islam,* trans. by Joan Spencer (New York: American Elsevier, 1975). Also see S. D. Goiten, *A Mediterranean Society: The Jewish Communities of the Arab World as Portrayed in the Documents of the Cairo Geniza,* 3 vols. (Berkeley: University of California Press, 1967–1978).

On the Prophet's life, the beginner may want to consult W. Montgomery Watt, *Muhammad: Statesman and Prophet* (London: Oxford University Press, 1961). The same author has written two more detailed studies: *Muhammad at Mecca* (Oxford: Clarendon Press, 1953) and *Muhammad at Medina* (Oxford: Clarendon Press, 1956). Also see Maxime Rodinson, *Muhammad* (New York: Pantheon, 1980). Tor Andre, *Mohammed: The Man and His Faith* (New York: Harper & Row, 1960) is a short analysis. The medieval Ibn Hisham's *Life of the Prophet* is also available in English translation: Alfred Guillaume (trans.), *The Life of Muhammad* (Lahore: Oxford University Press, 1955). Also see Nabia Abbot, *Aisha, the Beloved of the Mohammed,* reprint (New York: Arno Press, 1977).

The "Wars of Apostasy" are covered in Elias Shoufani, *Al-Riddah and the Muslim Conquest of Arabia* (Toronto: Toronto University Press, 1973). For the details of the subsequent conquests, see Philip Hitti's translation of al-Baladhuri's *Book of the Conquest of Countries,* published under the title of *The Origins of the Islamic State,* reprint (Beirut: Khayats, 1966). The standard account of the Umayyads is J. Wellhausen, *The Arab Kingdom and Its Fall,* reprint (Beirut: Khayats, 1966). Also see H. A. R. Gibb, *The Arab Conquests in Central Asia* (London: Royal Asiatic Society, 1923).

Sir John Bagot Glubb, former British commander of Jordan's Arab Legion, has written some interesting popular accounts of Islamic history. These include *Empire of the Arabs* (Englewood Cliffs: Prentice-Hall, 1965); *The Great Arab Conquests* (Englewood Cliffs: Prentice-Hall, 1964); and *The Lost Centuries: From the Muslim Empire to the Renaissance of Europe, 1145–1453* (Englewood Cliffs: Prentice-Hall, 1967).

For a synthesis of material from medieval chronicles, readable but with some old-fashioned ethnocentrism, see Sir William Muir, *The Caliphate,* reprint (Beirut: Khayats, 1963). For a debatable interpretation, see Henri Pirenne, *Mohammad and Charlamagne* (London: Allen & Unwin, 1965). A Soviet view of the Islamic world to the ninth century may be found in E. A. Belyaev, *Arabs, Islam and the Arab Caliphate* (New York: Praeger, 1969). Also see Kamal Salibi, *Syria under Islam: Vol. 1, Empire on Trial, 636–1097* (Delmar, N. Y.: Caravan Books, 1977).

M. A. Shaban is the author of three controversial revisionist studies: *Islamic History,* A.D. *600–750 (*A.H.*132): A New Interpretation* (Cambridge: University Press, 1971); *Islamic History: A New Interpretation,* A.D. *750–1055 (*A.H *132–448)* (Cambridge: University Press, 1976); and *The Abbasid Revolution* (Cambridge: University Press, 1970).

Recent works on the Abbasids include Jacob Lassner, *The Shaping of Abbasid Rule* (Princeton, N.J.: Princeton University Press, 1980) and Muhammad Ahsan, *Social Life under the Abbasids* (London: Longman, 1979). Some examples of older books include N. Abbot, *Two Queens of Baghdad* (Chicago: University of Chicago Press, 1946); Harold Bowen, *The Life and Times of 'Ali b. 'Isa, the Good Vizier* (Cambridge: University Press, 1928); Guy Le Strange, *Baghdad During the Abbasid Caliphate* (Oxford: Clarendon Press, 1924); and Guy Le Strange, *Lands of the Eastern Caliphate,* 2nd ed. (New York: Barnes & Noble, 1966).

Works on regional dynastics include Hafizullah Kabir, *The Buwayhid Dynasty of Baghdad* (Calcutta: Iran Society, 1964); C. E. Bosworth, *The Ghaznavids* (Edinburgh: Edinburgh University Press, 1963); Marshall Hodgson, *The Order of the Assassins* (The Hague: Mouton, 1955); Bernard Lewis, *The Assassins* (Cambridge: University Press, 1940); and De Lacy O'Leary, *A Short History of the Fatimid Khalifate* (New York: Dutton, 1928).

On Anatolia, see Claude Cahen, *Pre-Ottoman Turkey* (New York: Taplinger, 1968) and Speros Vryonis, Jr., *The Decline of Medieval Hellenism in Asia Minor and the Process of Islamization from the Eleventh through the Fifteenth Century* (Berkeley: University of California Press, 1971).

For a thorough recent work on the Crusades that also deals with related aspects of the area, see Kenneth Setton (ed.), *A History of the Crusades,* 4 vols. (Madison: University of Wisconsin Press, 1969). Also see Andrew Ehrenkreutz, *Saladin* (Albany: State University of New York Press, 1972) and Stephen Humphreys, *From Saladin to the Mongols* (Albany: State University of New York Press, 1977).

On the Mongols, see Bertold Spuler, *History of the Mongols: Based on Eastern and Western Accounts of the Thirteenth and Fourteenth Centuries* (Berkeley: University of California Press, 1972) and John Saunders, *The History of the Mongol Conquest* (New York: Barnes & Noble, 1971). An excellent study that puts the Mongols in the perspective of other Central Eurasian peoples is René Grousset, *The Empire of the Steppes* (New Brunswick, N.J.: Rutgers University Press, 1970).

An old-fashioned chronology of the Mamluk and earlier periods may be found in Stanley Lane-Poole, *A History of Egypt in the Middle Ages,* 4th ed. (London: Methuen and Company, 1925). For a similar work, see Sir William Muir, *The Mameluke or Slave Dynasty of Egypt,* reprint (New York: AMS Press, 1973).

A leading student of the Mamluks is David Ayalon, author of *Studies on the Mamluks of Egypt (1250–1517)* (London: Variorum Reprints, 1977) and *Gunpower and Firearms in the Mamluk Kingdom,* 2nd ed. (London: Cass, 1978). For an unusually penetrating study of urban society in Mamluk Syria, see Ira Lapidus, *Muslim Cities in the Later Middle Ages* (Cambridge: Harvard University Press, 1967). An account of the greatest catastrophe of the period may be found in Michael Dols, *The Black Death in the Middle East* (Princeton, N.J.: Princeton University Press, 1977).

IRAN: GENERAL STUDIES

Some major works on Iran bridge the ancient and Islamic periods. J. A. Boyle (ed.), *The Cambridge History of Iran,* 8 vols. (Cambridge: at the University Press, 1968–) is of special value, although only vols. 1, 3, and 5 have appeared so far. Sir Percy Sykes, *A History of Persia,* 3rd ed., 2 vols. (London: Macmillan, 1951) is still useful. Other important books include Donald Wilber, *Iran: Past and Present,* 9th ed. (Princeton, N.J.: Princeton University Press, 1981) and Ann Lambton, *Landlord and Peasant in Persia* (London: Oxford University Press, 1953). Yahya Armajani, *Iran* (Englewood Cliffs: Prentice-Hall, 1972) is a short survey.

ISLAM: RELIGION
AND INSTITUTIONS

General books on Islam include H. A. R. Gibb, *Mohammedanism* (New York: Oxford University Press, 1963) and Alfred Guillaume, *Islam,* 2nd ed. (Baltimore: Penguin, 1956). For works by Muslims, see Abd al-Rahman Azzam, *The Eternal Message of Muhammad* (New York: Devin-Adair, 1964) and—on an advanced level—Fazlur Rahman, *Islam,* 2nd ed. (Chicago: University of Chicago Press, 1979). Anthologies of primary materials, with introductory comments, include Arthur Jeffrey (ed.), *Islam: Muhammad and His Religion* (Indianapolis: Bobbs-Merrill, 1958) and John Alden Williams (ed.), *Islam* (New York: Washington Square Press, 1963).

There are numerous English translations of the Qur'an. One of the best is Arthur J. Arberry, *The Koran Interpreted* (New York: Macmillan, 1955). An example of one by a Muslim is Abdullah Yusuf Ali, *The Holy Qur-an: Text, Translation and Commentary,* 2 vols. (New York: Hafner, n.d.).

On another important aspect of Islam, see Arthur Arberry, *Sufism* (New York: Macmillan, 1951) or Reynold Nicholson, *The Mystics of Islam* (London: Routledge & Kegan Paul, 1966).

On the origins of sectarianism, see Husayn Jabri, *Origins and Early Development of Shi'a Islam* (London: Longman, 1979) and Muhammad Husayn Tabataba'i, *Shi'ite Islam,* trans. and annotated by Seyyed Hossein Nasr (Albany: State University of New York Press, 1979). Bernard Lewis, *The Origins of Ismailism* (Cambridge: University Press, 1940) is still essential.

The best works on jurisprudence include Joseph Schacht, *An Introduction to Islamic Law* (London: Oxford University Press, 1964); N. J. Coulson, *A History of Islamic Law* (Edinburgh: Edinburgh University Press, 1964); Majid Khadduri and Herbert Liebesny (eds.), *Law in the Middle East* (Washington: Middle East Institute, 1955); and A. A. A. Fyzee, *Outlines of Muhammadan Law,* 3rd ed. (London: Oxford University Press, 1964). Modern developments are covered in J. N. D. Anderson, *Islamic Law in the Modern World* (New York: New York University Press, 1959); Sir Norman Anderson, *Law Reform in the Muslim World* (Atlantic Highlands, N.J.: Humanities Press, 1976); and Herbert Liebesny, *The Law of the Near and Middle East: Readings, Cases, and Materials* (Albany: State University of New York Press, 1975).

Another highly recommended book is Ignaz Goldziher, *Introduction to Islamic Theology and Law,* trans. by Andras and Ruth Hamori (Princeton, N.J., Princeton University Press, 1981).

On political institutions, see Sir Thomas Arnold, *The Caliphate,* 2nd ed. (New York: Barnes & Noble, 1965). An important political phenomenon is analyzed in Patricia Crone, *Slaves on Horses: The Elaboration of Islamic Polity* (Cambridge: Cambridge University Press, 1980). Works on political theory include Erwin Rosenthal, *Political Thought in Medieval Islam* (Cambridge: Cambridge University Press, 1962) and W. Montgomery Watt, *Islamic Political Thought* (Edinburgh: Edinburgh University Press, 1968). On the *dhimmis,* see A. S. Tritton, *The Caliphs and Their Non-Muslim Subjects,* 2nd ed. (London: Cass, 1970).

More comprehensive studies of institutions include Maurice Gaudefroy-Demombynes, *Muslim Institutions* (London: Allen & Unwin, 1950); Reuben Levy, *The Social Structure of Islam* (Cambridge: Cambridge University Press, 1965); Gustave von Grunebaum, *Medieval Islam,* 2nd ed. (Chicago: University of Chicago Press, 1953). For later developments, see Nikki Keddie (ed.), *Sufis, Scholars, and Saints: Muslim Religious Institutions since 1500* (Berkeley: University of California Press, 1972).

The notion that Islam has been detrimental to economic progress is countered in Maxime Rodinson, *Islam and Capitalism* (Austin: University of Texas Press, 1978). Also see John Esposito (ed.), *Islam and Development* (Syracuse, N.Y.: Syracuse University Press, 1980).

For a journalistic account of the seemingly renewed Islamic sentiment of the 1970s, see G. H. Jansen, *Militant Islam* (New York: Harper & Row, 1979). Several scholarly papers on this subject may be found in Alexander S. Cudsi and Ali E. Hillal Dessouki (eds.), *Islam and Power* (Baltimore: Johns Hopkins University Press, 1981).

ISLAMIC CIVILIZATION

A good place to start on Islamic civilization would be one of several anthologies of translations. These include Arthur Arberry (ed.), *Aspects of Islamic Civilization as Depicted in the Original Texts* (Ann Arbor: University of Michigan Press, 1967); Bernard Lewis (ed.), *Islam from the Prophet Muhammad to the Capture of Constantinople,* 2 vols. (New York: Walker & Walker, 1974); and John Williams (ed.), *Themes of Islamic Civilization* (Berkeley: University of California Press, 1971). Also see Gustav von Grunebaum, *Medieval Islam,* 2nd ed. (Chicago: University of Chicago Press, 1953) and D. M. Dunlop, *Arab Civilization to* A.D. *1500* (New York: Praeger, 1971). Good introductory essays may be found in R. M. Savory, (ed.), *Introduction to Islamic Civilization* (Cambridge: Cambridge University Press, 1976).

Of the many works on art and architecture, recommended general studies include K. A. C. Cresswell, *A Short Account of Early Muslim Architecture* (Baltimore: Penguin, 1958); Oleg Graber, *The Formation of Islamic Art* (New Haven: Yale University Press, 1971); Ernst Kühnel, *Islamic Art and Architecture* (Ithaca, N.Y.: Cornell University Press, 1966); and David Rice, *Islamic Art* (New York: Praeger, 1965).

On philosophy and theology, a good place to start would be W. Montgomery Watt, *Islamic Philosophy and Theology* (Chicago: Aldine, 1962). For a more thorough account, see Majid Fakhry, *History of Islamic Philosophy* (New York: Columbia University Press, 1970). A major portion of F. E. Peters, *Allah's Commonwealth: A History of Islam in the Near East, 600–1000* A.D. (New York: Simon and Schuster, 1973) deals with philosophy and theology. Good translations of Islamic (and Christian and Jewish) philosophers can be found in Ralph Lerner and Muhsin Mahdi (eds.), *Medieval Political Philosophy* (New York: Free Press, 1963). For a useful handbook, see Eugene Myers, *Arabic Thought and the Western World in the Golden Age* (New York: Ungar, 1964). For the life of an important theologian, see W. Montgomery Watt, *Muslim Intellectual: A Study of Al-Ghazzali* (Chicago: Aldine, 1963).

As for Ibn Khaldun, most readers would benefit from starting with Charles Issawi (ed.), *An Arab Philosophy of History* (London: John Murray, 1950). For a complete translation, see Ibn Khaldun, *The Muqaddimah,* 3 vols., trans. by Franz Rosenthal, 2nd ed. (Princeton, N.J.: Princeton University Press, 1967).

LITERATURE

For literature, I suggest an anthology, such as Najib Ullah, *Islamic Literature: An Introductory History with Selections* (New York: Washington Square Press, 1963). James Kritzeck is the editor of two excellent volumes: *Anthology of Islamic Literature from the Rise of Islam to Modern Times* (New York: Mentor, 1964) and *Mod-*

ern Islamic Literature, From 1800 to the Present (New York: Holt, Rinehart & Winston, 1970).

Recommended studies of Arabic literature include Reynold Nicholson, *A Literary History of the Arabs* (Cambridge: Cambridge University Press, 1907); H. A. R. Gibb, *Arabic Literature: An Introduction,* 2nd ed. (Oxford: Clarendon Press, 1963); I. Goldziher, *A Short History of Classical Arabic Literature* (Hildesheim: Georg Olms, 1966); and Ilse Lichtenstadter, *Introduction to Classical Arabic Literature* (New York: Schocken Books, 1976).

For a time-tested, thorough work on Persian Literature, see E. G. Browne, *A Literary History of Persia.* 4 vols., reprint (Cambridge: Cambridge University Press, 1956–1959). Shorter studies include Arthur Arberry, *Classical Persian Literature* (London: Allen & Unwin, 1958) and Reuben Levy, *An Introduction to Persian Literature* (New York: Columbia University Press, 1969).

On the Turks, see E. J. W. Gibbs's monumental work, *A History of Ottoman Poetry,* 6 vols. (London: Luzac, 1900–1909).

THE OTTOMAN EMPIRE
TO MODERN TIMES

Stanford J. Shaw, *History of the Ottoman Empire and Modern Turkey: Volume I: Empire of the Gazis: The Rise and Decline of the Ottoman Empire, 1280–1808* (Cambridge: Cambridge University Press, 1976) is a long-awaited basic work, although it did not live up to high expectations. A Victorian-style work, Edward S. Creasy, *History of the Ottoman Turks,* reprint (Beirut: Khayats, 1961) is not entirely superseded. For the early period an excellent work is Halil Inalcik, *The Ottoman Empire: The Classical Age, 1300–1600* (New York: Praeger, 1973). For a first-rate short analysis, see Norman Itzkowitz, *Ottoman Empire and Islamic Tradition* (New York: Knopf, 1972). Also see Bernard Lewis, *Istanbul and the Civilization of the Ottoman Empire* (Norman: University of Oklahoma Press, 1973). Expansion in Europe is covered in Carl Max Kortepeter, *Ottoman Imperialism During the Reformation* (New York: New York University Press, 1972).

Paul Wittek, *The Rise of the Ottoman Empire* (London: Royal Asiatic Society, 1938) is an important study of the earliest period. On Ottoman institutions, see Albert Lyber, *The Government of the Ottoman Empire in the Time of Suleiman the Magnificent* (Cambridge: Harvard University Press, 1913) and H. A. R. Gibb and Harold Bowen, *Islamic Society and the West: A Study of the Impact of Western Civilization, Volume One* [others were never published]. *Islamic Society in the Eighteenth Century,* 2 parts (London: Oxford University Press, 1950). However, some aspects of both books, particularly their distinction between the "religious" and "governing" institutions, are subject to criticism. John Saunders (ed.), *The Muslim World on the Eve of Europe's Expansion* (Englewood Cliffs, N.J.: Prentice-Hall, 1966) contains enlightening short readings on various Islamic states in the sixteenth century. On the whole Mediterranean world in the sixteenth century, see Fernand Braudel, *The Mediterranean and the Mediterranean World in the Age of Philip II,* 2 vols. (New York: Harper & Row, 1972).

On opposite corners of the empire, see L. S. Stavrianos, *The Balkans since 1453* (New York: Holt, Rinehart & Winston, 1958) and P. M. Holt, *Egypt and the Fertile Crescent, 1516–1922* (London: Longmans, 1966).

THE SAFAVIDS AND IRAN TO THE LATE EIGHTEENTH CENTURY

By comparison, the Ottomans' contemporaries in Iran suffer a dearth of treatment, although Roger Savory has filled an important gap with his *Iran under the Safavids* (Cambridge: Cambridge University Press, 1980). Savory is also the author of numerous specialized articles on Safavid institutions (see *Index Islamicus* for lists of these). Another important work on Safavid society and institutions is V. Minorsky, *Tadhkirat al-Mulūk: A Manual of Safavid Administration* (London: Luzac and Co., 1943). The relevant chapters in *The Cambridge History of Islam,* written by Savory and Ann Lambton, are also recommended.

Other specialized studies include Eskandar Beg Monshi, *The History of Shah 'Abbas the Great,* 2 vols., trans. by Roger Savory (Boulder, Colo.: Westview, 1979) and John Perry, *Karim Khan Zand: A History of Iran,* 1747–1779 (Chicago: University of Chicago Press, 1979).

THE MODERN MIDDLE EAST: GENERAL

The "modern" Middle East is often thought of as starting in 1774, 1798, or some such date when the impact of modernity gained momentum. Still, it may be relevant to mention Thomas Naff and Roger Owen (eds.), *Studies in the Eighteenth Century Islamic History* (Carbondale: Southern Illinois University Press, 1977). For the next century, an excellent collection of specialized studies may be found in William Polk and Richard Chambers (eds.), *Beginnings of Modernization in the Middle East* (Chicago: University of Chicago Press, 1968). For a more general anthology, see Richard Nolte (ed.), *The Modern Middle East* (New York: Atherton, 1963).

There is no fully satisfactory general survey of the modern Middle East. William Yale, *The Near East: A Modern History,* 2nd ed. (Ann Arbor: University of Michigan Press, 1968) deals mainly with diplomatic history. Good surveys of several countries may be found in Joseph Malone, *The Arab Lands of Western Asia* (Englewood Cliffs, N.J.: Prentice-Hall, 1973).

For an important leftist interpretation, see Samir Amin, *The Arab Nation,* trans. by Michael Pallis, 2nd ed. (London: Zed Press, 1978).

Works on economic history include Charles Issawi (ed.), *The Economic History of the Middle East, 1800–1914* (Chicago: University of Chicago Press, 1966) and Z. Y. Hershlag, *Introduction to the Modern Economic History of the Middle East,* 2nd ed. (Leiden: Brill, 1980).

The most essential work on diplomatic history is J. C. Hurewitz (ed.), *The Middle East and North Africa in World Politics,* 2 vols. (New Haven: Yale University Press, 1975, 1977). A second important work is M. S. Anderson, *The Eastern Question, 1774–1923* (New York: St. Martin's Press, 1966).

The following works focus on the international relations of the World War I period: Brinton Busch, *Britain, India, and the Arabs, 1914–1921* (Berkeley: University of California Press, 1971); Elie Kedourie, *England and the Middle East, 1914–1921* (London: Bowes & Bowes, 1956); Harry Howard, *The Partition of Turkey* (Norman: University of Oklahoma Press, 1931); Harry Howard, *The King-Crane Commission* (Beirut: Khayats, 1963); Jukka Nevakivi, *Britain, France, and the Arab Middle East, 1914–1920* (London: Athlone Press, 1969); and Howard Sachar, *The Emergence of the Middle East, 1914–1924* (New York: Knopf, 1969).

Later decades are covered by Arnold Toynbee, *The Islamic World Since the Peace Settlement* (London: Oxford University Press, 1927); Elizabeth Monroe, *Britain's Moment in the Middle East, 1914–1956,* 2nd ed., (Baltimore: Johns Hopkins University Press, 1981); Lukaz Hirshowitz, *The Third Reich in the Arab East* (Toronto: University of Toronto Press, 1966); George Kirk, *The Middle East in the War, 1939–1945* (London: Oxford University Press, 1952); George Kirk, *The Middle East, 1945–1950* (London: Oxford University Press, 1954); and Howard Sachar, *Europe Leaves the Middle East, 1936–1954* (New York: Knopf, 1972).

As for surveys of the area's recent international relations, see Tareq Ismael et al., *The Middle East in World Politics* (Syracuse, N.Y.: Syracuse University Press, 1974) and George Lenczowski, *The Middle East in World Affairs,* 4th ed. (Ithaca, N.Y.: Cornell University Press, 1980).

Relations with the superpowers are covered in J. C. Hurewitz (ed.), *Soviet-American Rivalry in the Middle East* (New York: Praeger, 1969).

On the United States role, see Faiz Abu-Jaber, *American-Arab Relations from Wilson to Nixon* (Washington: University Press of America, 1979); John Badeau, *The American Approach to the Arab World* (New York: Harper & Row, 1968); Thomas Bryson, *American Diplomatic Relations with the Middle East, 1784–1975* (Metuchen, N.J.: Scarecrow, 1977); George Lenczowski (ed.), *United States Interests in the Middle East* (Washington: American Enterprise Institute, 1968); William Polk, *The Arab World,* 4th ed. (Cambridge: Harvard University Press, 1980), which also traces Arab history from ancient times; and Robert Stookey, *America and the Arab States* (New York: John Wiley, 1975). For first-hand revelations about

CIA activities, see Wilbur Eveland, *Ropes of Sand* (New York: W. W. Norton & Co., 1980).

As for the other superpower, see Robert Friedman, *Soviet Policy toward the Middle East since 1970,* 2nd ed. (New York: Praeger, 1978); Walter Laqueur, *The Soviet Union and the Middle East* (New York: Macmillan, 1959); George Lenczowski, *Soviet Advances in the Middle East* (Washington: American Enterprise Institute, 1971); and Alvin Rubinstein, *Red Star on the Nile* (Princeton: Princeton University Press, 1976). For a different point of view, see Fred Halliday, *Soviet Policy in the Arc of Crisis* (Washington: Institute for Policy Studies, 1981).

For a thorough study, see Joe Stork, *Middle East Oil and the Energy Crisis* (New York: Monthly Review Press, 1975). Leonard Mosely, *Power Play: Oil in the Middle East* (Baltimore: Penguin, 1975) is a readable popular account. Charles Issawi, *Oil, the Middle East and the World* (New York: Library Press, 1972) is an excellent short analysis. More recent books, which deal with the problem of oil on a worldwide basis, include Raymond Vernon (ed.), *The Oil Crisis* (New York: W. W. Norton & Co, 1976) and Peter Odell, *Oil and World Power,* 5th ed. (Baltimore: Penguin, 1979).

As for analyses of Middle Eastern politics, see Manfred Halpern's profound and still relevant *The Politics of Social Change in the Middle East and North Africa* (Princeton, N.J.: Princeton University Press, 1963) and James Bill and Carl Leiden, *Politics in the Middle East* (Boston: Little, Brown, 1979). For a more limited area, see Michael Hudson's excellent *Arab Politics: The Search for Legitimacy* (New Haven: Yale University Press, 1977). A still-useful concise introduction may be found in Dankwart Rustow, *Middle Eastern Political Systems* (Englewood Cliffs, N.J.: Prentice-Hall, 1971). Studies focusing on ruling classes include George Lenczowski (ed.), *Political Elites in the Middle East* (Washington, D.C.: American Enterprise Institute, 1976) and Frank Tachau (ed.), *Political Elites and Political Development in the Middle East* (Cambridge: Schenkman, 1975). Also see Fuad Ajami, *The Arab Predicament* (Cambridge: Cambridge University Press, 1981).

Some of the recent country-by-country surveys of Middle Eastern politics include Don Peretz, *The Middle East Today,* 3rd ed. (New York: Holt, Rinehart & Winston, 1978) and Bernard Reich and David Long (eds.), *The Government and Politics of the Middle East and North Africa* (Boulder, Colo.: Westview, 1980). Also see Bruce Borthwick, *Comparative Politics of the Middle East* (Englewood Cliffs, N.J.: Prentice-Hall, 1980).

General surveys include Michael Adams (ed.), *The Middle East: A Handbook* (New York: Praeger, 1971) and Peter Mansfield (ed.) *The Middle East: A Political and Economic Survey,* 5th ed. (New York: Oxford University Press, 1980). A basic reference work is *The Middle East and North Africa, 1981–1982,* 28th ed. (London: Europa Publications, 1980). Another valuable, regularly updated work is *U.S. Policy, Israel, Oil and the Arabs,* 5th ed. (Washington: Congressional Quarterly, 1981).

Chronologies of events may be found in Menahem Mansoor, *Political and*

Diplomatic History of the Arab World, 1900–1967: A Chronological Study, 7 vols. (Washington, D.C.: Microfilm Editions, 1972); the eighth volume is *A Biographical Dictionary* (1974). Also see the Chronology in each issue of *The Middle East Journal.*

MODERN INTELLECTUAL DEVELOPMENTS

The impact of Western ideas on Middle Eastern thought is dealt with in books listed on various countries. For a penetrating short analysis of overall trends, see Bernard Lewis, *The Middle East and the West* (Bloomington: Indiana University Press, 1963). An essential work is Albert Hourani, *Arabic Thought in the Liberal Age, 1798–1939* (London: Oxford University Press, 1962). Excellent but more restricted studies include Ibrahim Abu-Lughod, *The Arab Rediscovery of Europe* (Princeton: Princeton University Press, 1963) and Hisham Sharabi, *Arab Intellectuals and the West: The Formative Years, 1875–1914* (Baltimore: Johns Hopkins University Press, 1970). Other works dealing with diverse ideas are Majid Khadduri, *Political Trends in the Arab World: The Role of Ideas and Ideals in Practice* (Baltimore: Johns Hopkins University Press, 1970) and Leonard Binder, *The Ideological Revolution in the Middle East* (New York: John Wiley, 1962). Translations of important writings may be found in Kemal Karpat (ed.), *Political and Social Thought in the Contemporary Middle East,* 2nd ed. (New York: Praeger, 1982).

Books dealing with the impact of modernity on Islam include H. A. R. Gibb, *Modern Trends in Islam* (Chicago: University of Chicago Press, 1945); Wilfred Cantwell Smith, *Islam in Modern History* (New York: Mentor, 1957); and Gustave von Grunebaum, *Modern Islam: The Search for Cultural Identity* (Berkeley: University of California Press, 1962).

On Afghani, see Nikki Keddie, *Sayyid Jamal ad-Din "al-Afghani": A Political Biography* (Berkeley: University of California Press, 1972); Nikki Keddie, *An Islamic Response to Imperialism: Political and Religious Writings of Sayyid Jamal al-Din "al-Afghani"* (Berkeley: University of California Press, 1962); and E. Kedourie, *Afghani and 'Abduh* (London: Cass, 1966).

Works specifically dealing with Turkish and Iranian nationalisms are listed elsewhere. Analyses of various nationalisms may be found in William Haddad and William Ochsenwald (eds.), *Nationalism in a Non-National State: The Dissolution of the Ottoman Empire* (Columbus: Ohio State University Press, 1977).

Despite some shortcomings, George Antonius' readable *The Arab Awakening,* reprint (New York: Capricorn Books, 1965), first published in 1938, is still a good place to start on the rise of Arab nationalism. For a book that corrects Antonius on some points, see Zeine Zeine, *The Emergence of Arab Nationalism,* 3rd ed. (Delmar, N.Y.: Caravan Books, 1973). Other research is presented in C. Ernest Dawn, *From Ottomanism to Arabism* (Urbana: University of Illinois Press, 1973).

Also see Sylvia Haim (ed.), *Arab Nationalism, An Anthology* (Berkeley: University of California Press, 1962).

SOCIETY AND CULTURE

The major works on Middle Eastern society and culture include Gabriel Baer, *Population and Society in the Arab East* (New York: Praeger, 1964); Morroe Berger, *The Arab World Today* (New York: Doubleday, 1962); Carleton Coon, *Caravan: The Story of the Middle East*, 2nd ed. (New York: Holt, Rinehart & Winston, 1958); Dale F. Eickelman, *The Middle East: An Anthropological Approach* (Englewood Cliffs, N.J.: Prentice-Hall, 1981); John Gulick, *The Middle East: An Anthropological Perspective* (Pacific Palisades, Calif: Goodyear, 1976); and Raphael Patai, *Society, Culture and Change in the Middle East*, 3rd ed. (Philadelphia: University of Pennsylvania Press, 1969).

For anthologies of specialized papers, see Sydney Fisher (ed.), *Social Forces in the Middle East* (Ithaca, N.Y.: Cornell University Press, 1955); Abdulla Lutfiyya and Charles Churchill (eds.), *Readings in Arab Middle Eastern Societies and Cultures* (The Hague: Mouton, 1970); and Louise Sweet (ed.), *Peoples and Cultures of the Middle East*, 2 vols. (New York: Natural History Press, 1970).

On urban life, see L. C. Brown (ed.), *From Madina to Metropolis* (Princeton, N.J.: Darwin Press, 1976); V. F. Costello, *Urbanism in the Middle East* (New York: Cambridge University Press, 1977); and Ira Lapidus (ed.), *Middle Eastern Cities* (Berkeley: University of California Press, 1969). For one of the few area-wide studies of rural life, see Richard Antoun and Iliya Harik (eds.), *Rural Politics and Social Change* (Bloomington: Indiana University Press, 1972).

Studies of Middle Eastern women have mushroomed in recent years. One of the best examples is Lois Beck and Nikki Keddie (eds.), *Women in the Muslim World* (Cambridge: Harvard University Press, 1978). For further titles, see Ayad Al-Qazzaz, *Women in the Middle East and North Africa: An Annotated Bibliography* (Austin: University of Texas Press, 1977).

On interconfessional conflicts, see Suad Joseph and Barbara Pillsbury (eds.), *Muslim-Christian Conflicts* (Boulder, Colo.: Westview, 1979).

An invaluable encyclopedia of ethnic groups is Richard Weekes (ed.), *Muslim Peoples: A World Enthnographic Survey* (Westport, Conn.: Greenwood Press, 1978).

MODERN TURKEY

On the late Ottoman Empire and the Turkish Republic, see Stanford J. Shaw and Ezel Kural Shaw, *History of the Ottoman Empire and Modern Turkey, Vol. II: The Rise of Modern Turkey, 1808–1975* (Cambridge: Cambridge University Press, 1977). A shorter account is Geoffrey Lewis, *Modern Turkey*, 3rd ed. (New York: Praeger, 1965). Two essential works on the impact of the West are Bernard Lewis,

The Emergence of Modern Turkey, 2nd ed. (London: Oxford University Press, 1968) and Niyazi Berkes, *The Development of Secularism in Turkey* (Montreal: McGill University Press, 1964). Also see Charles Issawi (ed.), *The Economic History of Turkey, 1800–1914* (Berkeley: University of California Press, 1980). Works on selected periods include Roderic Davison, *Reform in the Ottoman Empire, 1856–1876* (Princeton: Princeton University Press, 1963); Serif Mardin, *The Genesis of Young Ottoman Thought* (Princeton, N.J.: Princeton University Press, 1962); and Ernest Ramsaur, *The Young Turks* (Princeton, N.J.: Princeton University Press, 1957).

On nationalism, see D. Kushner, *The Rise of Turkish Nationalism, 1876–1908* (London: Cass, 1977). For the thought of an influential nationalist, see Ziya Gökalp, *Turkish Nationalism and Western Civilization* (New York: Columbia University Press, 1959) and Uriel Heyd, *Foundations of Turkish Nationalism: The Life and Teachings of Ziya Gökalp* (London: Luzac, 1950).

The most readable and comprehensive biography of Kemal Atatürk is Lord Kinross, *Atatürk* (London: Weidenfeld and Nicolson, 1964). Great insight may be gained from the first-hand accounts of Halide Edib Adivar, including *Memoirs of Halide Edib* (New York: Century, 1926) and *The Turkish Ordeal* (New York: Century, 1928).

On later decades, see the writings of Kemal Karpat, including *Turkey's Politics* (Princeton: Princeton University Press, 1959) and *Social Change and Politics in Turkey* (Leiden: Brill, 1973). Other important studies include Frederick Frey, *The Turkish Political Elite* (Cambridge: MIT Press, 1965); C. H. Dodd, *Politics and Government in Turkey* (Berkeley: University of California Press, 1969); Feroz Ahmad, *The Turkish Experience in Democracy, 1950–1975* (Boulder, Colo.: Westview, 1977); and Z. Y. Hershlag, *Turkey: The Challenge of Growth* (Leiden: Brill, 1968). Richard Robinson, *The First Turkish Republic* (Cambridge: Harvard University Press, 1963) is an excellent general treatment of the period from Atatürk to 1960.

MODERN IRAN

Despite some antinationalist bias, Peter Avery's *Modern Iran* (New York: Praeger, 1965) is the logical place to start on this topic, particularly for the nineteenth century. See also John Upton, *The History of Modern Iran* (Cambridge: Harvard University Press, 1960) and L. P. Elwell-Sutton, *Modern Iran* (London: Routledge & Kegan Paul, 1976).

If you want to go beyond political matters, see Charles Issawi (ed.), *The Economic History of Iran, 1800–1914* (Chicago: University of Chicago Press, 1971); continue with Julian Bharier, *Economic Development in Iran, 1900–1970* (London: Oxford University Press, 1971). Richard Cottam's important analysis in *Nationalism in Iran,* 2nd ed. (Pittsburgh: University of Pittsburgh Press, 1979) extends over most of the modern period. On relations with the rest of the world, see Rouhollah Ramazani, *The Foreign Policy of Iran: A Developing Nation in World Affairs,*

1500–1941 (Charlottesville: University Press of Virginia, 1966). For an analysis in relation to recent events, see Nikki Keddie, *Roots of Revolution: An Interpretive History of Modern Iran* (New Haven: Yale University Press, 1981).

Specifically for the pre-1914 period, Hamid Algar's *Religion and State in Iran, 1785–1906* (Berkeley: University of California Press, 1969) is an indispensable analysis of an aspect of Iranian society neglected by many writers. Nikki Keddie's work in the same area is also important; see her *Religion and Rebellion in Iran* (London: Cass, 1966) and her *Modern Iran: Religion, Politics and Society* (London: Cass, 1979). For more succinct treatments, see Keddie's and Algar's essays in the former's *Saints, Sufis, and Scholars* (cited above under "Islam: Religion and Institutions"). More specialized works include Hamid Algar's *Malkum Khan* (Berkeley: University of California Press, 1973) and two older books: Morgan Shuster, *The Strangling of Persia* (New York: Century, 1912) and E. G. Browne, *The Persian Revolution of 1905–1909* (Cambridge: University Press, 1910).

On a later period, see Hossein Amirsadeghi (ed.), *Twentieth Century Iran* (New York: Holmes & Meier, 1977). For generally flattering portrayals of the Pahlavi dynasty, see George Lenczowski (ed.), *Iran Under the Pahlavis* (Stanford, Calif.: Hoover Institution Press, 1978). The following works deal mainly with the inter-War period: Amin Banani, *The Modernization of Iran, 1921–1941* (Stanford, Calif.: Stanford University Press, 1961); George Lenczowski, *Russia and the West in Iran, 1918–1948* (Ithaca, N.Y.: Cornell University Press, 1949); and Donald Wilber, *Riza Shah Pahlavi* (Hicksville, N.Y.: Exposition Press, 1975).

On the recent period, see James Bill, *The Politics of Iran* (Columbus, Ohio: Chas. E. Merrill, 1972); Leonard Binder, *Iran: Political Development in a Changing Society* (Berkeley: University of California Press, 1962); Robert Graham, *Iran: The Illusion of Power,* 2nd ed. (London: Croom Helm, 1980); Fred Halliday, *Iran: Dictatorship and Development,* 2nd ed. (Baltimore: Penguin, 1979); Rouhollah K. Ramazani, *Iran's Foreign Policy, 1941–1973* (Charlottesville: University Press of Virginia, 1975); Amin Saikal, *The Rise and Fall of the Shah* (Princeton, N.J.: Princeton University Press, 1980; and Marvin Zonis, *The Iranian Political Elite* (Chicago: University of Chicago Press, 1971). Also see Ahmad Jabbari and Robert Olson (eds.), *Iran: Essays on a Revolution in the Making* (Lexington, Ky.: Mazda Publishers, 1981).

The role of the *ulama* in politics is covered in Shahrough Akhavi, *Religion and Politics in Contemporary Iran* (Albany: State University of New York Press, 1980) and Michael Fischer, *Iran: From Religious Dispute to Revolution* (Cambridge: Harvard University Press, 1980).

MODERN IRAQ

See two books by Stephen Longrigg: *Four Centuries of Modern Iraq* (Oxford: Clarendon Press, 1925) and *Iraq, 1900–1950* (New York: Oxford University Press, 1953). The most general twentieth-century political histories have been written by

Majid Khadduri: *Independent Iraq: A Study in Iraqi Politics from 1932 to 1958* (New York: Oxford University Press, 1961); *Republican Iraq: A Study in Iraqi Politics since 1968* (New York: Oxford University Press, 1969); and *Socialist Iraq: A Study in Iraqi Politics Since 1968* (Washington: Middle East Institute, 1978). Other important studies include Hanna Batatu, *The Old Social Classes and the Revolutionary Movements of Iraq* (Princeton, N.J.: Princeton University Press, 1978); Edith Penrose and E. F. Penrose, *Iraq: International Relations and National Development* (Boulder, Colo.: Westview, 1978); and Abbas Kelidar (ed.), *The Integration of Modern Iraq* (New York: St. Martin's, 1979).

THE ARABIAN PENINSULA

H. St. John Philby wrote numerous books on Sa'udi Arabia; see especially *Sa'udi Arabia* (London: Benn, 1955). Other works include Willard Beling (ed.), *King Faisal and the Modernization of Saudi Arabia* (Boulder, Colo.: Westview, 1980); Gerald de Gaury, *Faisal, King of Saudi Arabia* (New York: Praeger, 1966); Christine Moss Helms, *The Cohesion of Saudi Arabia* (Baltimore: Johns Hopkins University Press, 1980); David Howarth, *The Desert King* (New York: McGraw-Hill, 1964); Helen Lackner, *A House Built on Sand* (London: Ithaca Press, 1978); Emile Nakhleh, *The United States and Saudi Arabia* (Washington: American Enterprise Institute, 1975); William Quandt, *Saudi Arabia in the 1980s* (Washington: Brookings, 1981); John Shaw and David Long, *Saudi Arabian Modernization* (New York: Praeger, 1982); Gary Troeller, *The Birth of Saudi Arabia* (London: Cass, 1976); and R. Bailey Winder, *Saudi Arabia in the Nineteenth Century* (London: Macmillan, 1965).

On the two Yemens, see Manfred Wenner, *Modern Yemen, 1918–1966* (Baltimore: Johns Hopkins University Press, 1967); Robert Stookey, *Yemen: The Politics of the Yemen Arab Republic* (Boulder, Colo.: Westview, 1978); Harold Ingrams, *The Yemen: Imams, Rulers and Revolutions* (London: John Murray, 1963); Eric Macro, *Yemen and the Western World Since 1571* (New York: Praeger, 1968); and Tom Little, *South Arabia* (London: Pall Mall Press, 1968).

On various Arabian states, see Derek Hopwood (ed.), *The Arabian Peninsula: Society and Politics* (Totowa, N.J.: Rowan and Littlefield, 1972). Fred Halliday, *Arabia without Sultans* (New York: Vintage, 1974) provides a leftist perspective. Numerous thorough studies are to be found in Alvin Cottrell (ed.), *The Persian Gulf States: A General Survey* (Baltimore: Johns Hopkins University Press, 1980).

Specifically on Eastern Arabia, see Mohammed Abdullah, *The United Arab Emirates: A Modern History* (New York: Barnes & Noble, 1978); John Duke Anthony, *Arab States of the Lower Gulf* (Washington, D.C.: Middle East Institute, 1975); John Brinton Busch, *Britain and the Persian Gulf, 1894–1914* (Berkeley: University of California Press, 1967); J. B. Kelly, *Britain and the Persian Gulf, 1795–1880* (London: Oxford University Press, 1968); Robert Landon, *Oman in the*

Late Nineteenth Century and After (Princeton: Princeton University Press, 1967); David Long, *The Persian Gulf: An Introduction to Its People, Politics, and Economics,* 2nd ed. (Boulder, Colo.: Westview, 1978); and Wendell Phillips, *Oman: A History* (Mystic, Conn.: Verry, 1972).

MODERN EGYPT

A general, if spotty, account is P. J. Vatikiotis, *The History of Egypt from Muhammad Ali to Sadat,* 2nd ed. (Baltimore: Johns Hopkins University Press, 1980). For a competent synthesis, see Sir John C. B. Richmond, *Egypt, 1798–1952* (New York: Columbia University Press, 1977). Tom Little, *Modern Egypt* (New York: Praeger, 1967) deals mainly with the twentieth century. Also see John Marlowe, *A History of Modern Egypt and Anglo-Egyptian Relations, 1800–1956,* 2nd ed. (Hamden, Conn.: Archon Books, 1965) and Robert Collins and Robert Tignor, *Egypt and the Sudan* (Englewood Cliffs, N.J.: Prentice-Hall, 1967).

For an important collection of scholarly papers on Egyptian society throughout the modern period, see P. M. Holt (ed.), *Political and Social Change in Modern Egypt* (London: Oxford University Press, 1968). On social history, Gabriel Baer, *Studies in the Social History of Modern Egypt* (Chicago: University of Chicago Press, 1969) is indispensable.

Books on modern Egyptian intellectual developments include Nadav Safran, *Egypt in Search of Political Community: An Analysis of the Intellectual and Political Evolution of Egypt, 1804–1952* (Cambridge: Harvard University Press, 1961). Also see Charles Adams, *Islam and Modernism in Egypt* (New York: Russel, 1968); Jamal Ahmad, *The Intellectual Origins of Egyptian Nationalism* (London: Oxford University Press, 1960); and Malcolm Kerr, *Islamic Reform: The Political and Legal Theories of Muḥammad 'Abduh and Rashīd Riḍā (Berkeley: University of California Press, 1961).*

An important study that challenges some older notions is Peter Gran, *Islamic Roots of Capitalism: Egypt, 1760–1840* (Austin: University of Texas Press, 1979). On the same period, see Huseyn Efendi, *Ottoman Egypt in the Age of the French Revolution,* trans. by Stanford J. Shaw (Cambridge: Harvard University Press, 1964) and Christopher Herold, *Bonaparte in Egypt* (New York: Harper & Row, 1962). Interesting first-hand accounts may be found in Christopher Lloyd (ed.), *The Nile Campaign* (New York: Barnes & Noble, 1973).

Although it is superficial, you may be advised to use Henry Dodwell, *The Founder of Modern Egypt: A Study of Muhammad 'Alī* (Cambridge: University Press, 1931). A more profound study (and less specialized than one might infer from the title) is Helen Rivlin, *The Agricultural Policy of Muhammad 'Ali in Egypt* (Cambridge: Harvard University Press, 1961).

Works dealing with the development of imperial interests include John Marlowe, *World Ditch: The Making of the Suez Canal* (New York: Macmillan,

1964) and David Landes, *Bankers and Pashas: International Finance and Economic Imperialism in Egypt* (Cambridge: Harvard University Press, 1958).

British-occupied Egypt is dealt with in Peter Mansfield, *The British in Egypt* (New York: Holt, Rinehart & Winston, 1971); Afaf Lutfi al-Sayyid Marsot, *Egypt and Cromer* (London: John Murray, 1968); and Robert Tignor, *Modernization and British Colonial Rule in Egypt, 1882–1914* (Princeton, N.J.: Princeton University Press, 1966). For the attitudes of Lord Cromer, see his *Modern Egypt,* 2 vols. (New York: Macmillan, 1908).

A massive (and, to the beginner, perhaps formidable) study concentrating on the pre-1952 period is Jacques Berque, *Egypt: Imperialism and Revolution* (New York: Praeger, 1967). On the anti-British struggle, see Mahmud Zayid, *Egypt's Struggle for Independence* (Beirut: Khayats, 1965). On the politics of the inter-War period, see Afaf Lutfi al-Sayyid Marsot, *Egypt's Liberal Experiment, 1922–1936* (Berkeley: University of California Press, 1977) and Marius Deeb, *Party Politics in Egypt: The Wafd and Its Rivals, 1919–1939* (London: Ithaca Press, 1979). The Muslim Brethren are dealt with in the context of broader aspects of Egyptian history in Christina Harris, *Nationalism and Revolution in Egypt* (The Hague: Mouton, 1964). For a more thorough study, see Richard Mitchell, *The Society of the Muslim Brethren* (London: Oxford University Press, 1969).

For an analytical study of Nasir's Egypt, see R. Hrair Dekmejian, *Egypt Under Nasir: A Study in Political Development* (Albany: State University of New York Press, 1971) and, from an Egyptian leftist's point of view, Anouar Abdel-Malek, *Egypt: Military Society* (New York: Random House, 1968). Peter Mansfield, *Nasser's Egypt,* 2nd ed. (Baltimore: Penguin, 1969) is a good survey. Also see Mahmud Hussein, *Class Conflict in Egypt: 1945–1970* (New York: Monthly Review Press, 1973). Biographies of Nasir include Anthony Nutting, *Nasser* (New York: Dutton, 1972) and Robert Stephens, *Nasser: A Political Biography* (New York: Simon & Schuster, 1971). On economic aspects, see Charles Issawi, *Egypt in Revolution: An Economic Analysis* (New York: Oxford University Press, 1961) and Robert Mabro, *The Egyptian Economy, 1952–1972* (London: Oxford University Press, 1974). Nasir's foreign policy is covered by Charles Cremeans, *The Arabs and the World: Nasser's Arab Nationalist Policy* (New York: Praeger, 1963); Malcolm Kerr, *The Arab Cold War: Gamal 'Abd al-Nasir and His Rivals, 1958–1970,* 3rd ed. (London: Oxford University Press, 1971); and A. I. Dawisha, *Egypt in the Arab World, 1952–1970: The Elements of a Dynamic Foreign Policy* (New York: Halsted Press, 1977).

The Suez Crisis of 1956 is the subject of a special body of writing. See Erskine Childers, *The Road to Suez* (London: Macgibbon & Key, 1962); Kennett Love, *Suez: The Twice-Fought War* (New York: McGraw-Hill, 1969); Hugh Thomas, *Suez* (New York: Harper and Row, 1966); Anthony Nutting, *No End of a Lesson* (New York: C. N. Potter, 1967); and Donald Neff, *Warriors at Suez* (New York: Simon & Schuster, 1981).

Mohamed Hassanein Heikal, an Egyptian journalist closely associated with

Nasir, has written several books that provide important insight. These include *The Cairo Documents* (New York: Doubleday, 1973); *The Road to Ramadan* (New York: Ballantine Books, 1975); and *The Sphinx and the Commissar: The Rise and Fall of Soviet Influence in the Middle East* (New York: Harper & Row, 1979).

Perhaps oddly, Sadat's regime has not inspired much scholarly writing. For a short analysis, see R. Michael Burrell and Abbas Kelidar, *Egypt: The Dilemma of a Nation, 1970–1977* (Beverly Hills: Sage Publications, 1977). Also see John Waterbury, *Egypt: Burdens of the Past, Options for the Future* (Bloomington: Indiana University Press, 1978). Raymond William Baker deals to some extent with the Sadat period in his *Egypt's Uncertain Revolution Under Nasser and Sadat* (Cambridge: Harvard University Press, 1978). Finally, see Anwar al-Sadat, *In Search of Identity: An Autobiography* (New York: Harper and Row, 1978).

For an important study of the social foundations of the post-1952 regime, see Leonard Binder, *In a Moment of Enthusiasm: Political Power and the Second Stratum in Egypt* (Chicago: University of Chicago Press, 1978).

ZIONISM, PALESTINE, ISRAEL, AND THE ARAB-ISRAELI CONFLICT

For a detalied, sympathetic account of Zionism, see Walter Laqueur, *A History of Zionism* (New York: Schocken Books, 1976). Highly laudatory articles may be found in Raphael Patai (ed.), *Encyclopedia of Zionism and Israel,* 2 vols. (New York: Herzl Press, 1971). A short, less sympathetic account is Alan Taylor, *Prelude to Israel* (New York: Philosophical Library, 1959). Strongly anti-Zionist cases are presented in Abdelwahab Elmessiri, *The Land of Promise* (New Brunswick: North American, 1977) and Alfred Lilienthal, *The Zionist Connection* (New York: Dodd, Mead, 1978).

Works on Israeli politics and society include Amos Elon, *The Israelis: Founders and Sons* (New York: Holt, Rinehart & Winston, 1971); Leonard Fein, *Israel: Politics and People* (Boston: Little, Brown, 1968); Don Peretz, *The Government and Politics of Israel* (Boulder, Colo.: Westview, 1979); Howard Sachar, *A History of Israel from the Rise of Zionism to Our Time* (New York: Knopf, 1976); Nadav Safran, *Israel: Embattled Ally* (Cambridge: Harvard University Press, 1978); Michael Seltzer, *The Aryanization of the Jewish State* (New York: Black Star, 1968); and Sammy Smooha, *Israel: Pluralism and Conflict* (Berkeley: University of California Press, 1978).

For contrasting pictures of the Arab minority in Israel, see Sabri Jiryas, *The Arabs in Israel,* 2nd. ed. (New York: Monthly Review Press, 1976) and Jacob Landau, *The Arabs in Israel* (London: Oxford University Press, 1969). A recent scholarly study is Ian Lusitick, *Arabs in the Jewish State* (Austin: University of Texas Press, 1979).

Broader studies of the Arab Palestinians include Ibrahim Abu-Lughod (ed.), *The Transformation of Palestine* (Evanston, Ill.: Northwestern University Press,

1971); John Cooley, *Green March, Black September* (London: Cass, 1973); Ann Lesch, *Arab Politics in Palestine, 1917–1939* (Ithaca, N.Y.: Cornell University Press, 1979); Joel Migdall et al., *Palestinian Politics and Society* (Princeton, N.J.: Princeton University Press, 1979); Emile Nakhleh, *The West Bank and Gaza* (Washington, D.C.: American Enterprise Institute, 1979); Khalil Nakhleh and Elia Zureik, *The Sociology of the Palestinians* (New York: St. Martin's, 1980); Yehoshua Porath, *The Emergence of the Palestinian National Movement, 1918–1929* (London: Cass, 1973); Yehoshua Porath, *The Palestinian Arab National Movement, 1929–1939* (London: Cass, 1978); William Quant et al., *The Politics of Palestinian Nationalism* (Berkeley: University of California Press, 1973) and Richard Ward et al., *The Palestinian State* (Port Washington, N.Y.: Kennikat Press, 1977).

For a thorough work (especially on the period from 1947 to 1967) see Fred Khouri, *The Arab-Israeli Dilemma,* 2nd ed. (Syracuse: Syracuse University Press, 1966). Fuller treatment of earlier periods may be found in J. C. Hurewitz, *The Struggle for Palestine,* reprint (New York: Schocken Books, 1976); William Polk et al, *Backdrop to Tragedy* (Boston: Beacon Press, 1957) and Christopher Sykes, *Crossroads to Israel* (New York: Collins Publishers, 1965). Also see Walid Khalidi (ed.), *From Haven to Conquest: Readings in Zionism and the Palestine Problem until 1948* (Beirut: Institute for Palestine Studies, 1971).

Other works include Ibrahim Abu-Lughod (ed.), *The Arab-Israeli Confrontation of June 1967* (Evanston, Ill.: Northwestern University Press, 1970); Aharon Cohen, *Israel and the Arab World* (Boston: Beacon Press, 1976); Theodore Draper, *Israel and World Politics: Roots of the Third Arab-Israeli War* (New York: Viking Press, 1968); Isaiah Freedman, *The Question of Palestine, 1914–1918* (New York: Schocken Books, 1973); Frank Gervasi, *The Case for Israel* (New York: Viking Press, 1967); Dan Kurzman, *Genesis 1948* (New York: New American Library, 1970); Robert John and Sami Hadawi, *The Palestine Diary,* 2 vols. (New York: New World Press, 1970); David Hirst, *The Gun and the Olive Branch* (New York: Harcourt Brace Jovanovich, 1977); Malcolm Kerr (ed.), *The Elusive Peace in the Middle East* (Albany: State University of New York Press, 1975); Walter Laqueur, *Confrontation* (New York: Bantam, 1974); Neville Mandel, *The Arabs and Zionism before World War I* (Berkeley: University of California Press, 1976); Don Peretz, *Israel and the Palestine Arabs* (Washington, D.C.: Middle East Institute, 1950); William Quandt, *Decade of Decision: American Policy Toward the Arab-Israeli Conflict, 1967–1976* (Berkeley: University of California Press, 1977); Maxime Rodinson, *Israel and the Arabs* (New York: Pantheon Books, 1968); Maxime Rodinson, *Israel: A Colonial Settler State?* (New York: Monad Press, 1973); Nadav Safran, *From War to War: The Arab-Israeli Confrontation, 1948–1967* (New York: Pegasus, 1969); Edward Said, *The Question of Palestine* (New York: Times Books, 1979); Hisham Sharabi, *Palestine and Israel: The Lethal Dilemma* (New York: Pegasus, 1969); Edward Sheehan, *The Arabs, Israel and Kissinger* (New York: Reader's Digest Press, 1976); Ernest Stock, *Israel on the Road to Sinai, 1949–1956* (Ithaca, N.Y.: Cornell University Press, 1967); and Alan Taylor and Richard Tetlie (eds.), *Palestine: A Search for Truth* (Washington, D.C.: Public Affairs Press, 1970).

Many Israelis have published memoirs or autobiographies. These range from Chaim Weizmann, *Trial and Error* (New York: Harper & Row, 1949) to Yitzhak Rabin, *The Rabin Memoirs* (Boston: Little, Brown, 1979). Revelations unfavorable to Israel may be found in Livia Rokach, *Israel's "Sacred Terrorism": A Study of Moshe Sharett, A Personal Diary* (Detroit: Arab-American University Graduates, 1980).

MODERN SYRIA, LEBANON, AND JORDAN

A useful survey is Tabitha Petran, *Syria* (New York: Praeger, 1972). A heavier work, imbued with an Arab nationalist point of view, is A. L. Tibawi, *A Modern History of Syria, Including Lebanon and Palestine* (New York: St. Martin's Press, 1969). Also see Albert Hourani, *Syria and Lebanon: A Political Essay* (New York: Oxford University Press, 1946). Earlier developments are analyzed in Hourani's "The Fertile Crescent in the Eighteenth Century," in his *A Vision of History* (Beirut: Khayats, 1968); Herbert Bodman, *Political Factions in Aleppo, 1760–1826* (Chapel Hill: University of North Carolina Press, 1963); and Moshe Ma'oz, *Ottoman Reform in Syria and Palestine, 1840–1861* (Oxford: Clarendon Press, 1968). Also see Iliya Harik, *Politics and Change in a Traditional Society: Lebanon, 1711–1845* (Princeton, N.J.: Princeton University Press, 1968).

Works on specific periods in the twentieth century include Zeine Zeine, *The Struggle for Arab Independence,* 2nd ed. (Delmar: Caravan Books, 1977); Patrick Seale, *The Struggle for Syria: A Study of Post-War Politics, 1945–1958* (New York: Oxford University Press, 1965); Gordon Torrey, *Syrian Politics and the Military, 1945–1958* (Columbus: Ohio State University Press, 1964); Itamar Rabinovitch, *Syria Under the Ba'th, 1963–1966* (New York: Halsted Press, 1966); and Nikolaos van Dam, *The Struggle for Power in Syria: Sectarianism and Tribalism in Politics, 1961–1978* (New York: St. Martin's Press, 1979). See also Kemal Abu Jaber, *The Arab Ba'th Socialist Party* (Syracuse, N.Y.: Syracuse University Press, 1966) and John Devlin, *The Ba'th Party* (Stanford, Calif.: Hoover Institution Press, 1976).

Much has been written on Lebanon. For a useful survey, see Kemal Salibi, *The Modern History of Lebanon* (New York: Praeger, 1965). Studies emphasizing twentieth-century politics include Leonard Binder (ed.), *Politics in Lebanon* (New York: John Wiley, 1966) and Michael Hudson, *The Precarious Republic* (New York: Random House, 1968).

A spate of books has begun to appear on the civil war of the 1970s. See Marius Deeb, *The Lebanese Civil War* (New York: Praeger, 1980); Edward Haley and Lewis Snider (eds.), *Lebanon in Crisis* (Syracuse, N.Y.: Syracuse University Press, 1979); and Kemal Salibi, *Crossroads to Civil War: Lebanon, 1958–1976* (Delmar, N.Y.: Caravan Books, 1976).

Books on Jordan include Aqil Hyder Abidi, *Jordan, A Political Study, 1948–1957* (New York: Praeger, 1971) and P. J. Vatikiotis, *Politics and the Military in Jordan* (New York: Praeger, 1971). For first-hand accounts, see *Memoirs of King Abdullah of Transjordan* (New York: Philosophical Library, 1950); King Abdullah's *My Memoirs Completed* (New York: Longman, 1978); King Husayn, *Uneasy Lies the Head* (New York: B. Geis Associates, 1962); and John Bagot Glubb, *A Soldier with the Arabs* (New York: Harper & Row, 1957).

UPDATING

Such a newspaper as the *New York Times* (with its accompanying index) is useful. But other types of publications provide more depth and diverse outlooks. See, for example, *Afro-Asian Affairs* (London); *Middle East International* (London); *The Middle East* (London); *Middle East Economic Digest* (London); *American-Arab Affairs* (Washington); *Middle East Monitor* (Totowa, N.J.); *MERIP Reports* (Washington); and *New Outlook* (Tel-Aviv). Useful articles often are found in such general publications as *Current History* (Philadelphia); *Foreign Affairs* (New York); *Foreign Policy* (New York); and *World Today* (London). More useful than *Index Islamicus* (cited earlier) on current events are the *Social Science Index* (New York), *Humanities Index* (New York), and *The Middle East: Abstracts and Index* (Pittsburgh).

OTHER TEXTBOOKS

Some other textbooks are available on this subject. All have their weak and strong points. See Yahya Armajani, *The Middle East—Past and Present* (Englewood Cliffs, N.J.: Prentice-Hall, 1970); Sydney Nettleton Fisher, *The Middle East: A History*, 3rd ed. (New York: Knopf, 1978); or Arthur Goldschmidt, Jr., *A Concise History of the Middle East* (Boulder, Colo.: Westview, 1979).

Index

A

Abbas the Great, Shah, 112, 117, 123
Abbas Hilmi, Khedive, 155, 170
Abbas Mirza, 161, 162
Abbasids, 55–56, 60–62, 69–72, 75–76, 97, 109
Abd al-Aziz, Sultan, 144, 147, 153
Abd al-Hamid II, 147, 149, 150, 158
Abd al-Ilah, Prince, 220, 222, 239, 261
Abd al-Malik (Caliph), 52, 54
Abduh, Muhammad, 154, 194, 213
Abdullah (Amir, King), 159, 186, 197, 220, 234
Abdullah (son of Zubayr), 52
Abu al-Abbas, 56
Abu Bakr, 37, 39, 43–44, 50
Abu Sulfyan, 42, 43
Abu Muslim, 55–56, 65
Abu Salama, 65
Abu Talib, 36, 39
Achaemenids, 16, 277
Adah, 66
Aden, 227, 239, 267 (*see also* Southern Yemen)
Adnani, Arabs [*see* Northern (Adnani) Arabs]

Adrianople (Edirne), Treaty of, 140
Al-*
Al-Afghani, Jamal al-Din, 151, 153, 163, 194
Aflaq, Michel, 240
Afshars, 128–129
Aghlabids, 70, 74
Ahali group, 217
Al-Ahd, 158, 171
Ahmad ibn-Hanbal, 86
Ahmad, Imam, 238, 260, 265
Anglo-Iranian Oil Company, (AIOC), 163, 235–237
A'ishah, 41, 43, 49
Akhbaris, 159
Akkadian language, 10, 12
Alamut, 76
Alawites, 200, 268, 271, 294
Alexander the Great, 18–19
Alexandretta, 199, 200–201
Alexandria, 19, 20, 25, 152
Ali (son-in-law of Muhammed), 37, 39, 44, 48–50
Ali Bey, 127
Alids, 55 (*see also* Shi'ites)

*The Arabic definite article (al-) at the beginning of an entry does not affect its alphabetical order.